King's Gambit

King's Gambit

A SON, A FATHER,
AND THE
WORLD'S MOST DANGEROUS GAME

Paul Hoffman

HYPERION

New York

Excerpts from IF I RAN THE CIRCUS by Dr. Seuss,
TM & copyright © by Dr. Seuss Enterprises, L.P. 1956,
renewed 1984. Used by permission of Random House
Children's Books, a division of Random House, Inc.

Library of Congress Cataloging-in-Publication Data

Hoffman, Paul
    King's gambit : a son, a father, and the world's most
dangerous game / Paul Hoffman. — 1st ed.
        p. cm.
    ISBN: 978-1-4013-0097-5
    1. Chess—Anecdotes.   2. Chess players.   3. Chess—
Psychological aspects.   4. Hoffman, Paul, 1956–   5.
Fathers and sons—United States.   I. Title.
    GV1449.H55 2007
    794.1—dc22   2007013024

Hyperion books are available for promotions,
premiums, or corporate training. For details contact
Michael Rentas, Proprietary Markets, Hyperion,
77 West 66th Street, 12th floor, New York,
New York 10023, or call 212-456-0133.

Design by Guenet Abraham

FIRST EDITION
10   9   8   7   6   5   4   3   2   1

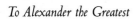

To Alexander the Greatest

CONTENTS

ACKNOWLEDGMENTS

I was restless while writing this book and had difficulty working at home. I wrote mostly in coffee shops, restaurants, and bars that let me linger with my laptop for hours and plied me with caffeine, steamed juicy pork buns, and red wine.* I want to thank all of these establishments—particularly Bread Alone in Woodstock, New York, which sacrificed its choice window table for *King's Gambit*. Not only did I complete the book in these places, I also made new friends, at a time in my life when this was particularly important.

I'm grateful to Matt Freedman, whom I've known since college, for his warm encouragement throughout this project and to Peter Matson, Will Schwalbe, and especially Alice Truax, for their editorial suggestions.

Many thanks, too, to Pascal Charbonneau and Jennifer Shahade for their help and friendship. I also want to acknowledge the other chess players—particularly Garry Kasparov, Irina Krush, Joel Lautier, Bruce Pandolfini, and Nigel Short—who opened their minds to me. I want to

---

* Greg Infanti, the bartender who was on duty during my most productive late-night writing marathons, was unaware of the old Russian proverb "Chess and wine are born brothers." There are many stories about the drinking habits of the Russian players who have dominated chess for more than half a century. Efim Bogoljubow (1899–1952) was a chubby, bombastic drunkard known for his delusional thinking that he was invincible: "When I play White, I win because I have the first move. When I play Black, I win because I'm Bogoljubow!" He reportedly knew only one word of English and, to the delight of his fellow players, had a chance to use it at the great international tournament at Nottingham in 1936. When a waiter in the hotel asked him for his room number, Bogoljubow replied, "Beer." Bogoljubow died of a heart attack in 1952 after giving an exhibition in which he played several opponents simultaneously (*Grandmasters of Chess*, Harold Schonberg, 1972: J. B. Lippincott, p. 162).

thank my mother for not shying away from revisiting difficult events in our shared past; sadly, she did not live to see this book published. Finally, I want to thank all my opponents over the years, good sports and bad, for many exciting encounters at the chessboard.

King's Gambit

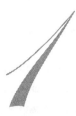

THE INSANITY DEFENSE

"All I want to do, ever, is play chess."
—BOBBY FISCHER

"No chess grandmaster is normal; they only differ in
the extent of their madness."
—VICTOR KORCHNOI

AFTER MY PARENTS SEPARATED IN 1968, WHEN I WAS TWELVE,
I lived a kind of double life. Until I went to college, I usually spent weekdays with my mother in Westport, Connecticut, a quiet, Cheeveresque
suburb an hour's train ride from New York City, and weekends with my
father in Manhattan's Greenwich Village. My classmates in Westport
were jealous of my regular trips to the city. Their dads were doctors and
lawyers and advertising executives who came home every evening for dinner. My father was a James Joyce devotee who wrote celebrity profiles under female pseudonyms for movie magazines and never ate a single meal
in his apartment. He was also a poker player, a billiards and Ping-Pong
hustler, a three-card monte shill, and an erudite part-time literature

professor at the New School for Social Research, whose specialty was what he proudly called "the grotesque and perverse" in twentieth-century American and Anglo-Irish fiction. He ate breakfast, lunch, and dinner in the Village Den, Joe's Dinette, the White Horse and Cedar Taverns, and other watering holes that were central to bohemian culture in the late 1960s, and he took me along. A few of my dad's friends smoked dope in front of their children and swapped wives. My high school buddies in Connecticut who didn't know me well imagined that I was rocking out at the Bottom Line and getting high at poetry readings, but in truth I never saw a single band, did drugs, or heard Patti Smith speak verse. Instead I spent my weekends playing chess.

Although I had learned how to move the pieces when I was five, I only became fully immersed in the game when my parents' marriage was falling apart: chess offered a tidy black-and-white sanctuary from the turmoil in the rest of my life. The Village was a chess mecca, with its many chess cafés and clubs, and my father lived only a ten-minute walk from its epicenter, Washington Square Park. My dad accompanied me to these places and, when he wasn't watching me play, passed the time reading novels and preparing his New School lectures. In the southwest corner of the park stood nineteen stone chess tables; these were occupied by all breeds of chess addict, from complete beginners who set their queen up on the wrong square to world-class players eager to demonstrate their command of double-rook endings and the Nimzo-Indian Defense. In those days the park didn't have a curfew, and people played chess at all hours. Cops on horseback gathered near the tables, and on slow nights, when they weren't breaking up couples having sex or escorting acid freaks to St. Vincent's Hospital, they'd look down from their high mounts and critique the moves on the boards—a time-honored tradition in chess known as *kibitzing*. When it was cold or raining, the park habitués retreated to three smoky chess parlors on Thompson and Sullivan, where they rented boards for pennies an hour to continue their games.

One autumn evening in the early 1970s, my dad and I ended up in the chess shop owned by Nicholas Rossolimo, a Russian émigré who had been the champion of France in 1948 and had gone on in the 1950s to compete successfully in the United States. Rossolimo was a grandmaster—an exalted ranking in chess that is exceeded only by the title of world champion.

There were just ninety grandmasters in 1970, one-third of whom lived in the Soviet Union. Being a grandmaster in America was rare enough, but even within this exclusive club Rossolimo had the special distinction of being immortalized in the chess literature for the "Rossolimo Variation," a particular sequence of moves characterized by an early light-squared bishop sortie by White.

Very few grandmasters are able to earn a living on the tournament circuit, though, and by 1970, when Rossolimo turned sixty, his championship days were long behind him. He drove a yellow cab, gave the occasional chess lesson, and babysat the woodpushers in his small chess salon. Rossolimo was also an old-school romantic whose pursuit of beauty at the chessboard sometimes blinded him to the impending brutality of his opponent's provocations. He was like the dreamy architecture student who sprains his ankle in a huge pothole in the sidewalk because his gaze is fixed on the gargoyles and cornices above.

On the evening of our visit, my father and I were greeted by the smell of garlic. Rossolimo was steaming a large pot of mussels on a hot plate balanced atop a wooden chessboard. My father and I stepped over a broken bottle in the entranceway and took our places at another board. Rossolimo was happy to see us—we were the only people there. He motioned to our board with an expansive gesture and urged us to play. My father declined, explaining that I was too good. Rossolimo laughed.

We watched him uncork a bottle of white, pour three glasses, and place one in front of each of us. I was fourteen or fifteen, and no one had ever offered me this much wine before. Had he failed to notice, I wondered, that I was conspicuously underage? Perhaps serving liquor to minors was a European custom. My father, who avoided alcohol because it aggravated his stomach ulcers, pretended to drink. Rossolimo gulped down half of his glass. I raised mine, clinked it against my father's, and sampled it cautiously. I announced that the wine was great. My father looked uneasy, but I knew he wouldn't spoil our bonding moment with the grandmaster by objecting to my drinking.

Rossolimo told my father that I was a fine boy and he proposed playing me a game. My dad was afraid he was going to charge us, but Rossolimo waived his customary fee and told us we were his friends and drinking companions. He turned off the hot plate and scooped the mussels into a wooden salad bowl. They were shriveled and overcooked but he didn't seem to notice.

I raised my glass to Rossolimo's and offered a toast to the generosity of our host and the quality of the wine. My father watched helplessly as I took another sip. In fact, it tasted terrible, and I considered dumping a little out of my glass under the chess table so that it would look as if I'd consumed more than a tablespoon.

Rossolimo told me to take White and challenged me to show how good I was. After two moves apiece I found that we had stumbled into the precise position in which I could employ the Rossolimo Variation against *him*. Charmed by my youthful cheekiness in making him face his own patented weapon, the grandmaster complimented me on copying the best.

As is typical in many lines of the Rossolimo Variation, I exchanged the light-squared bishop for a knight in a way that forced him to double his pawns, creating a structural weakness in which one of his foot soldiers blocked a comrade. Doubled pawns are not necessarily a great hindrance; if, however, the combat continues for many moves to the stage known as the endgame, in which most of the pieces have been exchanged, the immobility of the rear pawn can prove decisive—it's like being a pawn down. Rossolimo didn't seem perturbed. Mostly, he seemed to be moving reflexively as he entertained my father with a long boozy rant about Sartre and Nabokov. I was antsy because all of his chattering was making it hard to concentrate. I thought for a while whenever it was my turn to move—five minutes here, ten minutes there—but he always rattled me by responding instantly. Did he not need to think because he had seen this all before and had an ingenious grandmasterly plan to turn the game in his favor? Or was he truly being careless and was the endgame, in which the doubled pawns would put him at an increasing disadvantage, sneaking up on him? The latter proved to be the case.

When Rossolimo finally paused in his monologue about literature to look at the board, he immediately saw that he had a losing position: because of his formal, Soviet-style chess schooling, he knew the fine points of this kind of endgame infinitely better than I did. Rather than face the ignominy of a protracted defeat, he abruptly picked up his king and dropped it, crown first, into the bowl of garlicky broth. Mussel juice splattered across the table. Then he pushed the chess pieces into a heap in the center of the board before I had a chance to enjoy the final position. Glancing at his watch, he stood up, berated us for staying past the closing time, and ushered us out the door.

I was certainly pleased that I had defeated a chess legend, but I wasn't impudent about it. I don't think I even said a word to my dad. I knew that heavy drinking had impaired Rossolimo's play. I had never been close to drunk myself; indeed I had never taken more than the few sips of wine that I'd had that evening. But I had understood how disorienting alcohol could be from movies like *Dumbo*, in which the little elephant goes on a long hallucinatory bender, and *Who's Afraid of Virginia Woolf?*, a favorite of my mother's because it made her marriage seem comparatively happy.

Even though I knew that Rossolimo had effectively defeated himself, my father made sure that I knew: he informed me that Rossolimo had consumed five bottles of wine during the course of the evening. I argued that that was impossible, that he'd have been lying on the floor, that he'd had only two. My dad claimed that I had been too engrossed in the chessboard to notice what was happening. I found it unsettling that the game, which had started promisingly as a pleasant encounter over drinks, had degenerated into Rossolimo's kicking us out and my father's diminishing my victory.*

IN THE 1755 *DICTIONARY OF THE ENGLISH LANGUAGE,* SAMUEL JOHNSON defined chess as "a nice and abstruse game, in which two sets of puppets are moved in opposition to each other." Had I known the words *abstruse* and *opposition* when I was small, I would have agreed with Johnson's naïve definition.[1] But as I plunged further into the New York chess scene as a teenager and encountered the likes of Rossolimo, I understood that the game was not an innocent recreation but rather a unique amalgam of art, science, and blood sport. I learned that passionate eruptions were common at the chessboard and hardly confined to alcoholic veterans. One of the mysteries of this ancient game is how mere puppets moving in oppo-

---

* In 1975, Rossolimo's body was found at the bottom of a flight of stairs in his Greenwich Village apartment building. He had apparently been drinking, lost his footing, and fatally banged his head.

sition to each other have the capacity to stir up bizarre behavior in champions and amateurs alike.

DEFEAT IN CHESS IS ALWAYS PAINFUL. ROSSOLIMO WAS A SAINT COMPARED TO other wounded losers. William the Conqueror reportedly smashed a chessboard over the Prince of France. Pascal Charbonneau, the champion of Canada and my closest friend in the chess world, told me how a childhood contemporary broke all the furniture in a hotel room at a tournament and retired from chess.[2] The Spanish writer Fernando Arrabal once signaled his resignation with a theatricality that surpassed Rossolimo's. He grabbed his king, climbed up on the chess table, extended his arm horizontally, and dropped the king so that it bombed the board.[3]

When I was a spectator in 2003 at the annual chess tournament at the Foxwoods Casino, where 630 players were battling for a prize fund of $93,500, I was nearly struck by a chess clock that an irate loser hurled in my direction. I'm sure I wasn't the intended target, but I had to duck, and the clock smashed into the wall behind my head and broke into pieces.

When a player gets violent, his wrath is often directed not at spectators or his opponent but at himself. One contemporary Russian grandmaster has been known to pick up the pointiest chess piece, usually the bishop or a knight with a particularly jagged mane, and stab his own head until it bleeds. Then he rushes out of the tournament hall only to return for the next round as if nothing untoward has happened. At one event, this grandmaster was among the tournament leaders who were playing on an elevated stage. When he lost a key game, he bloodied his face and then, in an extreme masochistic flourish, dove off the three-foot-high stage, belly-flopping onto the hard floor.

Such behavior is exceptional, but even stable personalities have trouble accepting defeat. Garry Kasparov, the thirteenth world champion, frequently storms off like a bull, shoving aside spectators who are in his path. Pascal can be withdrawn and sullen for hours. When I lose, I repeatedly remind myself that chess is only a game. Yet even that reminder doesn't stop me from replaying in my head not only the moves of the game where I went astray, but also all the other things in my life that have gone wrong.

Chess is apparently as hard on the body as it is on the mind. Researchers at Temple University found that a chess master expends as much energy at the board as a football player or a boxer and that blood pressure and breathing rates rise considerably during a game. "Chess is very unhealthy," explained Nigel Short, the top British player of the twentieth century, when I visited him in the Athens apartment he shares with his Greek wife. Short was speaking from more than three decades of experience. During his world title bout with Kasparov in 1993, Short ate normally yet lost ten pounds—7.5 percent of his body weight—in just the first three games. "What could be more unnatural," Short said, "than sitting still for four or five hours while your heart is racing sometimes at 140 beats per minute? There's no outlet for all the stress. You can't punch the guy, kick a ball, or run laps." Illness during games is not uncommon. Even Kasparov himself, arguably the best player in the history of chess, has broken out with fever blisters in the heat of battle.

Most of the world's top players have strenuous exercise routines to balance their sedentary chess playing. Bobby Fischer worked out regularly long before it was fashionable, and Kasparov pumped iron, swam, and rowed as part of his chess training. "Your body has to be in top condition," Fischer said. "Your chess deteriorates as your body does. You can't separate mind from body."

YOU DO NOT HAVE TO BE LOSING TO SUCCUMB TO THE TENSION OF THE game. The pursuit of victory can also disturb your equilibrium. In March 2005, Pascal Charbonneau was playing a game in France against Petar Drenchev of Bulgaria. For more than a year the twenty-year-old Canadian champion had been in a slump, starting off strongly in tournaments and then faltering whenever he was close to earning the title of grandmaster. This game, he hoped, would be different. Pascal had White, which meant that he had the advantage of moving first. As he and Drenchev shook hands—the ritual that begins all chess encounters—and sat down at the board, Pascal sized up the twenty-seven-year-old Bulgarian. "I recall thinking," he told me later, "he's a sly little man. I'd better watch it."

The beginning of a chess game is an elaborate dance, with each player contriving to steer the game into a situation that's more familiar to him than to his opponent. White grabs Black's arms and says, "Let's tango!"

Black pulls away and says, "No, how about a waltz?"

"Too slow," White says. "What about the foxtrot?"

"Too old," counters Black. "I've forgotten the moves. How about something modern—like crunk?" Finally one of the players imposes his will on the other.

Pascal is known on the chess circuit as a wild, fast dancer, but against Drenchev he initially feigned interest in a slow waltz, the so-called Closed Sicilian, because he wanted to avoid the Bulgarian's favorite Najdorf Sicilian. But on his fourth move the Canadian champion picked up the pace and started to transform the closed game into a wide-open frenetic mutual king hunt called the Dragon Sicilian—a not unwelcome development for Drenchev, who also liked the Dragon. (The opening is called the Sicilian because Black's first move was originally favored by players on the island of Sicily, and it is a Dragon Sicilian because the chess masters who chose the name apparently convinced themselves, maybe after a few cocktails, that the Black pawn formation, which certainly had the potential to scorch the enemy, had the shape of a fabulous serpent as well.)

World-class players generally follow certain standard sequences of opening moves—like the Rossolimo Variation—until one of them forgets what has been previously played or purposefully varies with an intended improvement. In this encounter the two combatants quickly deviated from established play, although the position they reached had themes familiar to anyone who knew the Dragon. White responded with the so-called Yugoslav Attack and was pursuing Black's monarch on the kingside, bombarding him with pawns and pieces, and Black was counterattacking on the queenside. The Black side of the Dragon is not for the timid; because Black moves second, he is often one tempo behind in the race for the king. To mix things up, Black sometimes employs a double-edged maneuver called an exchange sacrifice—giving up a rook for a knight. The rook is generally a much stronger piece than the knight, but Black initiates the trade in order to strip White's king of a protective wall of pawns. Black is going for broke when he willingly parts with the powerful rook. He accepts a weaker army in return for an acceleration of his attack. If he doesn't quickly checkmate White's king, or restore the material balance by capturing a couple of loose pawns, the rook's absence will eventually defeat him.

Pascal spent eight minutes on his fourteenth move trying to make sense of what would happen if Drenchev offered the exchange sacrifice. Caissa, the muse of chess, was kind that day, and the Canadian had an inspiration seconds into his long think. He saw that he could respond with an unexpected sacrifice—or "sac" in chess lingo—of his own. He could boldly refuse to execute the offered rook, thereby giving up his own knight and effectively pardoning the rook for capturing it, and simply press ahead with his own all-out assault on Drenchev's king. Pascal concluded that his attack would be so fast that he'd succeed in checkmating Drenchev long before his opponent could profit from the extra knight. To ignore the gift rook was a deliciously devilish idea, but there was an unfortunate problem: it was all fantasy unless the Bulgarian actually decided to sac the exchange. Pascal made a bishop move typical of the Dragon in the hope of enticing the sac, and then he sat back quietly, calmly, drawing on whatever acting ability he had to conceal his enthusiasm and deviousness. Two moves and less than half a minute later, Drenchev fell into the trap and grabbed the knight.

When Pascal refrained from immediately making the "obvious" rook capture, Drenchev looked uncomfortable. The Bulgarian knew from the hesitation that something was up. Pascal in fact was checking his analysis one last time before electing to spare the rook, and the longer he thought—albeit this happened in seconds, not minutes—the more Drenchev squirmed.

For Pascal's part, he could not fully enjoy the success of his swindle because he was feeling increasingly queasy. "I had eaten a ton for breakfast," he told me later. "I was completely stuffed." He said that he hadn't gotten much sleep because his girlfriend kept him up late playing Internet poker. And then he pointedly added: "My position in the game was much too exciting."

As Pascal studied the chessboard, he became so nauseated that he had to stop thinking and just proceed as planned. He got up from the table. He knew he couldn't make it to the restroom, so he rushed out a side door of the tournament hall and, with no one watching, vomited in the grass. Then he headed to the washroom, cleaned his face, and returned to the game. Fortunately his analysis was airtight. Drenchev also saw that checkmate was inevitable and testily resigned after only five more moves. The hour-long, twenty-two-move encounter was an exquisite miniature in a competition in which the games typically lasted four hours and at least forty moves. Drenchev dismissed the loss as a cheap trick and insisted he would have had the better position if he'd played differently at certain junctures. Pascal replayed the game on a chessboard in his mind. He tried the Bulgarian's suggested improvements and saw immediately that they would have failed, but he kept the refutations to himself. "He was angry," Pascal told me. "I didn't want to antagonize him further."

IN CHESS IT IS HARD TO HIDE FROM DEFEAT. WHEN YOUR CROQUET BALL mysteriously veers to one side, you can always look for pebbles in the grass. When his aces beat your kings, you can always blame the cards. But when your bishop is deflected, you cannot search for imperfections in the playing surface or lament the roll of the dice. Of course, there is a small element of luck in chess: I was lucky that Rossolimo was inebriated. I am fortunate if my opponent adopts the one opening I happened to cram the day before. But most players consider chess the consummate game of skill and therefore, rightly or wrongly, associate success at it with overall intelligence. That's why losses are so hard. No good player ever readily admits to himself that he was defeated because of his opponent's brilliance.

That may be why there is an enormous amount of rationalization among chess players. The loss of a chess game has been so often attributed to illness that more than one master has joked that he's never defeated a healthy opponent.[4] After an unwelcome defeat, the loser may blurt out an explanation—"I was too tired," "The tournament hall was too hot," "Camelovich's cough was distracting"—but if he is sane, he knows in his heart that this is just an excuse. Nothing can belie the annoying reality that even a truly clever tactical strike, to which there is no adequate response, could not have been launched if the loser had played differently at an earlier point. (Pascal's mating attack, for instance, would not have succeeded if Drenchev had restrained his rook from capturing Pascal's knight.) This knowledge is foremost in the loser's mind. He cannot rest until he discovers where he went awry. To this end, he goes over the game repeatedly, on the board or in his head, mulling over lost opportunities. Chess players live in an alternative world of what might have been.

There's also no way to disown the damage that you and your opponent deliberately do to each other. You cannot apologize when your bishop skewers his queen, and he offers no excuses when his pieces descend on your king. And when you announce "Checkmate!" any effort to sound soft and sweet goes unnoticed. He still detects malice and smugness in your voice—and most of the time it's not his imagination. Chess is a zero-sum game.

And yet I don't know of any pastime that is more addictive. Because chess is so hard on the ego and stressful on the body, it is surprising that players, particularly those who lose disproportionately, don't simply abandon it. A few of them do, but many more try to make up for their losses by immersing themselves further in its intricacies and lore—hoping, ultimately, to conquer the game. At various points in history, clerics of different faiths have banned chess because they believed it to be so consuming that men who took it up might neglect spiritual and family life. (The pope, cardinals, and bishops defied the prohibition by playing secretly among themselves.) More recently, Afghanistan under the Taliban and Iran under Ayatollah Khomeini outlawed chess for much the same reason.[5]

MANY PLAYERS CLAIM TO HAVE BEEN SEDUCED BY THE INHERENT BEAUTY of the game, and chess masters sometimes describe themselves as artists. They regard the chessboard as a painter views a blank canvas or a sculptor a lump of clay. Chess may be esoteric—you need to have extensive experience with it to appreciate it fully—but that doesn't make it any less of an art.[6] There is mesmerizing splendor to a well-played game, and the aesthetic satisfaction is different depending upon the style of the player. For example, the games of Anatoly Karpov, Kasparov's archrival and predecessor as world champion, have a certain classic elegance. Karpov's graceful coordination of pieces and pawns is as pleasing to the eye as is the formal geometry of the Parthenon. Pascal's victory over Drenchev has a wittier, more contemporary form of beauty. Kasparov's games, in which he so decisively overpowers his opponents, have the terrifying appeal of a tornado or a tidal wave.

In practice the possibilities in chess are boundless, although theoretically it is a mathematically finite activity—there are, for example, 988 million positions that can be reached after four moves for White and four for Black. In any given position one move is undoubtedly best, although in most positions we as a species lack the mental resources (as well as, for the moment, the computer resources) to determine that move. If we knew with certainty the best move, there'd be no point in playing. The game would be as silly and mindless as tick-tack-toe.

Without being able to calculate the best move, you develop plans and strategies and play accordingly. That's the fun of the game. Every grandmaster agrees, for example, that it's important to control the central squares, but how to achieve this is a matter of long debate. Some players think it's best to immediately occupy the central squares with pawns. Others hold back the pawns and bring bishops and knights to bear on those squares. The intellectual joy of chess is that you can have a considered opinion about which plan is best and stand behind that opinion by trying the plan in actual games.

Chess also endures: the moves of a good game from a top-level tournament are recorded for posterity and examined by future generations of players. Of all board and card games, only chess has this kind of immortality. Instructional bridge books often show hands played by famous champions, but the culture of bridge does not require all students of the game to know these particular hands. But every devoted chess player has studied the games of the 1972 World Championship, in which Bobby Fischer defeated Boris Spassky. And every conscientious chess student has played move by move through the nineteenth-century attacking masterpieces known as the Immortal Game and the Evergreen Game, whose very names capture their transcendent nature. The creation of lasting beauty makes those who have mastered the sixty-four squares believe that chess is more than a game. When a grandmaster plays a game, he is doing much more than engaging in a cerebral battle with a human opponent. He is contributing to the evolution of chess technique.

And yet aesthetic considerations alone cannot explain why men and women become obsessed with chess. The thrill of competition, the euphoria of victory, is what really keeps players returning to the board. Its warlike struggle awakens the minds and bodies of people who may be anesthetized to other aspects of their worlds. "Chess is like life," Spassky once proclaimed. Fischer was more extreme: "Chess *is* life."

Perhaps unsurprisingly, chess has traditionally been a male domain. Only 3 percent of U.S. tournament competitors are female. A study described in the *Journal of Personality and Individual Differences,* which engendered much snickering in the popular press, found that the testosterone levels of male masters (and 99 percent of all U.S. masters are male) rose in anticipation of playing a game and shot up again as they mated their opponents. The researchers measured depressed testosterone levels in men who were on the receiving end of a mating attack. I'm sure I'm not the only player who was disquieted by these findings. I delved further into the scientific literature and was relieved to learn that researchers also expected testosterone spikes in male medical students waiting in line at a graduation ceremony to receive their MD degrees, CEOs calling their brokers to cash in stock options, and home run hitters rounding third base. It seems that those of us who are endowed with XY chromosomes are simple creatures. Anything that gives us pleasure and confirms our mastery of the world elevates our testosterone.

ALTHOUGH CHESS IS REGARDED AS A GAME OF GREAT INTELLIGENCE, AT THE same time it is often associated with insanity and obsession. Every chess club, it seems, has at least one resident who left his wife or job to play the game all day. The only two Americans to reach the pinnacle of chess, Paul Morphy and Bobby Fischer, suffered from paranoia. Morphy withdrew from tournament chess at the peak of his career, in 1859, and spent the next two decades worrying that relatives and friends wanted to kill him. Fischer, whose mother was Jewish,[7] believed there was a worldwide Jewish conspiracy to destroy him, and he praised 9/11 because of the number of Jews who were killed in the World Trade Center. He reportedly had the fillings in his teeth removed because he feared that they were capable of receiving radio messages beamed by his enemies.

In addition, an entire body of literature, psychoanalytic and fictional, from Ernest Jones's "The Problem of Paul Morphy" to Stefan Zweig's *Chess Story*[8] and Vladimir Nabokov's *The Defense,*[9] depicts the game as an incubator for psychopathology. Of the fictional works, Nabokov's 1930 novel is the most well-known portrayal of the chess player as madman. Nabokov's story reached a wide audience in 2001 with the release of the film *The Luzhin Defense,* starring John Turturro as Luzhin and Emily Watson as his fiancée. Luzhin's chess teacher, Valentinov, is thoroughly evil. He is the most important figure in the young player's life, but leaves his protégé when he thinks Luzhin doesn't have what it takes to become world champion. Years later, when Luzhin is playing against the Italian maestro Turati for the World Championship, Valentinov appears in the tournament hall to rattle his former pupil's concentration and sabotage his chances. Luzhin has a breakdown at the board and abandons the game in the middle, but in his delirium sees how he can finish Turati off with an improbable rook move. Luzhin's doctor tells his fiancée that he must never be allowed to resume the game or play any chess whatsoever. Valentinov then kidnaps Luzhin so that he can complete the game with Turati, but Luzhin escapes. He decides to make one final move in what he sees as the chess game of life, exiting the world by leaping from a high-story window.[10]

The movie engendered much fretting in the chess press. "Chess players once again have to come to terms with chess being depicted on screen as the mental equivalent of a dangerous drug," *British Chess Magazine* opined. And yet the magazine decried the "alarming number" of real-life players who had killed themselves by jumping from windows or bridges: the Estonian grandmaster Lembit Oll, in 1999; the Latvian international master Alvis Vitolins, in 1997; the Armenian international master Karen Grigorian, in 1989; and the Russian international master Georgy Ilivitsky, that same year.

The first player to kill himself in this unusual manner was the German master Curt von Bardeleben, who had been on the receiving end of one of the most famous mating attacks in chess history, orchestrated by world champion Wilhelm Steinitz at Hastings in 1895. Von Bardeleben was so sickened by the position of his exposed king that he disappeared from the tournament hall before Steinitz had a chance to finish him off with a beautiful checkmate in ten forced moves. Von Bardeleben's suicide in 1924 undoubtedly influenced Nabokov, who—in the kind of coincidence that befell his fictional characters—rented an apartment from one of von Bardeleben's relatives, a one-legged general "solely occupied in working out his family tree."

Self-defenestration is now engrained in the mythology of chess. The latest fatality, in June 2006, was Oxford-bound Jessie Gilbert, a nineteen-year-old talent on the English women's chess team whose father faced charges of sexually abusing her and other young women. During a tournament in Pardubice, Czech Republic, Gilbert plunged from the eighth-floor window of her hotel room.[11] (In December 2006, a jury acquitted Gilbert's father of all charges.)

In a remarkable essay called "The Jump," in the magazine *New in Chess,* Dutch grandmaster Genna Sosonko was forthright about the extent of psychosis and suicide in modern chess. "In no other type of sport," he wrote,

> does one encounter such a large number of peculiar people, engrossed in themselves and living in their own world.... Any chess game contains a wide range of emotions, with joys and vexations, great and small. This accompanies any type of creativity. But whereas in painting or literature, for example, it is possible to cross out, rewrite or change, in chess a movement of the fingers, communicated by the mind, is final: often it can be repaired only by sweeping the wooden pieces off the board. Or you can castigate yourself, by hitting your head against a wall, or by rolling around on the floor, as one modern grandmaster does after losing a game.

Sosonko observed that it is the rare game in which a player steadily accumulates advantages and turns them into a full point. "But even in this case," he wrote, "a player who is honest with himself knows what he was afraid of at a certain moment, what he was hoping for, and how he flinched after miscalculating in a variation." More commonly a grandmaster game is a seesaw battle, proceeding often along the following lines: "slightly worse, clearly worse, a mistake by the opponent, joy, winning chances, time trouble, missed opportunities, draw." The mood swings rattle a player's "inner mental core...which can lead to difficult, far-reaching consequences, especially if this core is shaky or diseased." Were people with "shaky unstable psyches" especially attracted to the game, Sosonko wondered, or was the game itself—what Nabokov called this "complex, delightful and useless art"—inherently destabilizing? In Luzhin's case, the mental fatigue of tournament play may ultimately have broken him, but it was a childhood undermined by a harsh, disapproving, adulterous father and a withdrawn, suicidal mother that set the stage.

Sosonko noted that two of the jumpers, Alvis Vitolins and Karen Grigorian, were much better at speed chess than they were at long tournament games. "The time allotted for play allows one to sink into thought, generating doubts and uncertainty. And for them—with their sharp falls in mood and excitable nervous system—this served only as a stimulus for mistakes and oversights. Blitz [chess], however, demands instant reactions; psychology and self-reproach retreat into the background, and there remains only that which is obvious in them—great natural talent."

Many chess professionals wish that Sosonko, and even Nabokov, had kept their thoughts about chess insanity to themselves. They fear that "The Jump" and *The Defense* harm the game by contributing to the stereotype of chess masters as eccentrics and social misfits. Most grandmasters, they argue, are just regular guys like Vladimir Kramnik, Kasparov's successor as world champion, who is considered normal, bland, and unexceptional in every way except his chess (and even his chess seems a bit dull, with some pundits claiming that he beat Kasparov by boring him to death), and Boris Spassky, who went to the opera and the finest restaurants in Reykjavík between games during the 1972 championship while Bobby Fischer was closeted alone in his hotel room, huddled over a chessboard.

Nigel Short is one of the few grandmasters who, like Sosonko, has publicly acknowledged the extent of the insanity in their profession. In a review of *The Luzhin Defense,* called "Chess Can Seriously Damage Your Health," Short wrote that he found the movie all too real:

> The intermittently institutionalized Mexican champion Carlos Torre once described the strains of top-level chess as "maddening." The ten time British champion, Dr. Jonathan Penrose (who is, fortunately, far from batty), collapsed during an Olympiad. And only a fortnight ago Vladimir Bagirov dropped dead, practically at the board.

Short also could not resist commenting on the otherworldliness of his fellow players. The review continued:

So awkward, clumsy, poorly dressed and inarticulate is our dear Luzhin that it is a wonder that any woman should find him attractive, and yet a romance of sorts, and even a marriage, eventually occur. . . . I cannot help being reminded, wicked though that may be, of one or two of my colleagues, who against all odds somehow enter into matrimony. Literally being unable to knot a tie or tie a shoelace is apparently no impediment to conjoining with the fairer sex.

I believe that madness is rampant in championship chess, particularly in the tier of players just below the top. After all, to reach the pinnacle of chess requires a certain psychological stability. The world's top grandmasters are successful in part because they are able to recover from devastating losses.[12] Every player, even Garry Kasparov, collapses in the odd game, but he has the inner strength to pull himself together and not let defeat unduly interfere with his subsequent concentration and performance. A lack of confidence can stop players who are close to the summit from making the final ascent. They may devote even more time to the game than the champions (and therefore be more isolated from the rest of the world) because they think that an extra fifteenth hour of study a day will get them to the summit. On the other hand, if their self-worth depends solely on their chess results, they may not recover if they stumble and lose a random game.

But is the pastime bad for the players, or are certain players bad for the pastime? Former British champion Bill Hartston once observed, "Chess doesn't drive people mad. It keeps mad people sane." Morphy and Fischer's behavior became truly bizarre only after they retired from the game. Their fate should not stop anyone from playing chess any more than Van Gogh's hacking off his ear should deter people from becoming painters or Mark McGwire's alleged steroid use should discourage children from playing baseball.

Certainly, those who avoid chess are depriving themselves of something sublime. Siegbert Tarrasch, a nineteenth-century champion, famously put it this way: "I have always a slight feeling of pity for the man who has no knowledge of chess, just as I would pity the man who has remained ignorant of love. Chess, like love, like music, has the power to make men happy." Or, as Short said, "The most important thing for anyone close to me to understand is how much enjoyment I get from playing chess and not ever to think of it as some little game to make money at."

THE CHESS WORLD IS LIKE A HIERARCHICAL MEDIEVAL KINGDOM, WHERE TITLES and rank are all-important: as the British grandmaster Raymond Keene observed, when three chess players pass through a swinging door, they do so in descending order of rating. I'm not a professional chess player. I'm not even a master. I'm an amateur—affectionately if derisively known as a woodpusher—but for an amateur I'm not bad. Of the eighty thousand members of the United States Chess Federation, my numerical rating of 1915, based on my tournament results, puts me in the top 95 percent of all U.S. competitors. I am what's called a Class A player—the classes begin at J, which corresponds to a rating between 0 and 200—and after one particularly good tournament I was fortunate to have my rating cross the 2000 threshold into the Expert category.[13]

A rating of 2200 makes you a master. The title international master, or IM, is granted by FIDE (pronounced fee-day), the French acronym for Fédération Internationale des Échecs, the international chess federation, and usually corresponds to a comparable rating of 2400 and a certain level of performance, called a *norm,* in three international tournaments. A grandmaster, or GM, generally has a rating above 2500 and has achieved three higher norms. There are just over one thousand grandmasters in the world. When Pascal Charbonneau and I became friends during the summer of 2004, he was rated 2474 and had the title international master and two-thirds of the norms required for the grandmaster title. Bobby Fischer, at his peak, was rated 2785. Garry Kasparov achieved the highest rating ever, 2851, in July 1999. God is said to be rated 3000.

This means that I'm like the guy at the karaoke club who everyone says has a good voice because professional musicians never visit. If you gathered five hundred random people off the street and organized a chess competition, I'd be victorious unless I was extremely unlucky and a serious player on a rare break from his chess studies happened to be walking down the avenue. And yet the difference between my command of the game as an A player and Kasparov's, or even Pascal's, is almost unfathomable. They can work magic on the chessboard while I'm still struggling to hold the wand, let alone wave it to make rabbits appear.

I BECAME DISILLUSIONED WITH CHESS IN HIGH SCHOOL AND STOPPED PLAYING altogether for two decades after college. But then in the year 2000, when I was forty-three, I experienced a series of personal and professional crises that were as bewildering and unnerving as my parents' separation had been three decades before. The crises strained my own marriage (after unsustainable rallies, Ann and I eventually split up, as I was writing this book) and precipitated a career change. But they also brought me unexpectedly back to chess.

After ten good years in the magazine business, first as the editor in chief of the science monthly *Discover* and then in various executive positions at the Walt Disney Company, I moved to Chicago in the summer of 1997 to become the publisher of Encyclopaedia Britannica. My charge was to reinvent the esteemed if crusty 229-year-old publication that was faltering in the Internet age. I was hired by Britannica's rumpled new owner, Jacqui Safra, a reputed gazillionaire in his fifties whose family, it was jokingly said, had invented banking during the Ottoman Empire. My interview with Safra was disconcertingly short. He looked over my résumé and asked only two questions. "You say you like mathematics," he said. "Then tell me, what is thirteen times thirteen?" Of course I immediately answered 169. "You say you like chess," he continued. "Well, what's the shortest possible mate?" Two moves, I said without hesitation, and I proceeded to describe the so-called Fool's Mate.[14] The answers to these simple questions won me the complex job of managing hundreds of academics around the world who were revising and updating the forty-four million words in Britannica.

When I moved to Chicago with Ann, a children's book author, we both thought that Britannica might be the ideal job for me. I had spent my editing career making scientific ideas hip and accessible without robbing them of nuance and subtlety. I could now do that at Britannica with a much wider range of academic subjects. I am a bookworm at heart, and I enjoyed reading the entries in older editions of Britannica, in which Trotsky wrote about Lenin, and Houdini detailed the history of magic. I also liked to imagine the conversations between the world-famous authors and their anonymous schoolmarmish editors. Albert Einstein once wrote the entry on physics ("Professor Einstein, let me review when it is appropriate to use the pluperfect tense"), and Stephen Hawking also contributed to Britannica ("Splitting atoms may be possible, Dr. Hawking, but not splitting infinitives").

The Britannica offices were as fusty as the see-through Indian paper on which the old editions were printed, and the company clearly needed a new editorial and business model. Internet users of Britannica expected current information, and the entries were conspicuously out of date; revisions had lagged because the company no longer enjoyed a strong revenue stream from the door-to-door salesmen who had convinced families that their children's ticket to success was a thirty-two-volume set of encyclopedias. Before Safra arrived with his checkbook, one editor might spend hours updating an obscure entry in mathematics while embarrassing howlers in a widely read entry on telecommunications ("Cable television is an experiment," I think it said) remained uncorrected.

Unfortunately, although Safra resembled the ideal boss—an absentee owner who paid me much more than my *Discover* salary—he did not leave me alone to supervise the staff and set a new direction. From locations in New York, Chicago, Paris, Switzerland, and the Napa Valley, he reversed my big decisions and micromanaged my small ones. Like the president's press secretary, I sometimes had to put a rosy spin on directives that I didn't agree with.

The job had its amusing moments, and Safra himself, who was Woody Allen's chief financial backer before their relationship ended in society-page litigation, was not uninteresting. He had small parts in three movies (under the pseudonym J. E. Beaucaire, the name of a character in a Bob Hope film). Safra was quirkily paternalistic: before letting me get into a cab alone, he'd eyeball the driver to size up whether he looked like the sort who'd crash the car or otherwise do me harm. And then Safra would call me later to make sure that I had reached my destination unscathed.

(Personal security was an issue in his family: his uncle Edmond famously died when a male nurse set fire to Edmond's home in Monaco.) And yet, despite Jacqui Safra's concern for me, I found him largely unavailable. Sometimes Safra established specific dates for us to get together but didn't reveal where we were going to meet. At the last moment I might end up walking a few blocks to see him in a Chicago hotel or racing to O'Hare to fly all the way to Switzerland to join him for breakfast. Once I was summoned to Paris on short notice, where Safra then left a terse message at the front desk of my five-star hotel announcing that pressing business prevented our meeting. I was subsequently awakened in my gold-gilded hotel room at 2:30 A.M. by the phone. It was Safra calling from somewhere nearby. For more than an hour, we reviewed the state of Britannica. The next day, without ever meeting him in person, I returned, utterly exhausted, to Chicago.

Another time he scheduled a two-day retreat at his Napa vineyard (whose mansion was used in the soap opera *Falcon Crest*) with me and a man who ran many of his businesses; we were supposed to spend the weekend brainstorming about the role of the encyclopedia in the digital age. Again Safra did not show up, but he also did not cancel the chef he'd hired for the weekend. Instead of exploring Napa's epicurean restaurants, we were largely confined to the mansion, like newlyweds on a romantic getaway, eating truffle omelets and kumquat mousse.

My visits to Britannica's operations in Eastern Europe, London, Tokyo, and Rio de Janeiro were the best part of the job. I spent vodka-infused evenings in Budapest and Poznan, Poland, working with academics who were translating the encyclopedia into Hungarian and Polish. But, in the fall of 1998, I cut back on business travel because Ann, to our delight, was pregnant. The job in Chicago became increasingly grim, and I cloistered myself in my Michigan Avenue office, stymied in my attempts to make decisions.

That winter I became very sick for the first time in my life. On a frigid Chicago night, I ended up in the emergency room at Northwestern Hospital with a 104.5 degree fever and a hacking cough, waiting to see a doctor as a triage team tried to save the frostbitten toes of a California businessman who'd been walking around outside in sandals in sub-zero temperatures. The chief doctor sent me home at 3:00 A.M. with antibiotics and codeine cough syrup. I quarantined myself in one room of our apartment for two weeks while Ann, who was in her second trimester, slipped food and *The New York Times* around the door.

One morning I woke up to discover that half of my right hand, including my pinkie and ring finger, was numb and tingling. During the night, I had pinched the ulnar nerve in my elbow (the nerve is relatively unprotected and is responsible for the funny-bone sensation when you whack your elbow). Normally the discomfort would have caused me to straighten my arm in my sleep before the nerve was damaged, but I was apparently too disoriented by my fever to react. People who pass out in a drunken stupor with their arm bent often pinch their ulnar nerve. Hence the condition has been called Saturday Night Syndrome or Drunken Man's Elbow.

First I was given steroids for a few weeks to shrink the inflamed nerve, but I could only take so many of them before my immune system would be weakened and my whole body would puff up. The doctor switched me to megadoses of ibuprofen. Although I had taken ibuprofen many times in my life without side effects, this time I had a severe allergic reaction—my right cheek and particularly the right side of my upper lip blew up as if I had taken a hard punch. I also got hives on my chest and a half-dollar–size welt on my forearm. To top it off, I was nauseated. The doctor took me off the ibuprofen, and when my face recovered after more steroids, I tried another anti-inflammatory drug for my elbow called Relafen. Again my face inflated, a large welt appeared on my bicep, and I vomited. The last drug he tried was Naproxen, and I had the same adverse reaction. He discontinued all medications and I entered the medical Twilight Zone.

Every few weeks, my lip and cheek ballooned for no apparent reason. First I'd become slightly queasy, usually at about 4:00 A.M., and my cheek would feel taut. I'd take a super antihistamine and, if I was fortunate, it would arrest the tautness. But if my cheek began to bulge and my lip tingled, I'd take a strong dose of steroids. If that didn't work, I'd race, EpiPen in hand, to the hospital so that the swelling could be monitored to make sure that it didn't extend to my throat or escalate into anaphylactic shock. I was warned to always stay within a few miles of an emergency room and not to fly.

A leading allergist at Northwestern took an interest in my condition because another patient of hers, a district attorney, had the same peculiar swellings, and it was inconvenient, to say the least, if his face blew up while addressing the jury. She pricked my skin with a standard panel of likely allergens—grasses, elm, oak, ragweed, cockroaches, dust mites, mold, mouse dander, and rat scat—and found that I tolerated everything. The diagnosis: *idiopathic angioedema*. At first I was relieved: if my condition had a name, maybe medical science had a cure. I soon learned, though, that *idiopathic* meant "of unknown cause." I didn't need a doctor to tell me that I had swollen skin (*angioedema*) of undetermined origin.

So now I had a deadened hand, a bloated face, unsightly hives, frequent nausea, and a chronic cough. I also developed cough-induced asthma, which meant that the mildest cold went straight to my chest, and I needed a steroid inhaler to breathe normally. I began to feel as though I were losing my mind. It wasn't simply that I felt so terrible; it was that the doctors had no idea what was responsible, which made *me* feel somehow responsible. In my darker moments, I thought that perhaps I should look for a hospice while I still had the mental faculties to judge the quality of care.

At work I stopped venturing out of my office for lunch, because I was afraid someone would corral me in the elevator and demand to know why he couldn't proceed with employing new people that I had given him permission to hire a month before. One of the benefits of my job was the private bathroom that came with my corner office. It was a good place to hide—and check on my hives.

It was during these lunch hours, barricaded in my office, that I began surfing the Web and discovered the Internet Chess Club, or ICC, where people with pseudonyms like Monster Pawn and Nerd Man played speed chess against each other online. At first I had trouble rapidly manipulating the mouse with my numb right hand, but soon I learned. I immediately rediscovered the game's magic. Not only did ICC offer an hour or two of welcome escape from my problems, but I could see myself improving from one day to the next. My chess victories were evidence, I told myself, that my mental faculties were not, in fact, deteriorating. I could call off the hospice search.

My early morning jog along Lake Michigan took me past a congregation of granite chess tables where people were always playing. I had gone by these tables dozens of times without pausing or slowing down. But a week after I discovered ICC, I stopped to watch. An elderly Russian challenged me, and after swindling him out of a rook—I had forgotten how fun it was to set a trap and snare someone—I was hooked again.

Ann gave birth to Alexander on May 20, 1999. Her timing was perfect: she went into labor two-thirds of the way through a marathon session of the *Godfather* trilogy, before we had to watch the disappointing finale. Alex, on the other hand, was three weeks late, and a big baby. His hands were so large that the pediatrician said that either he'd be a piano player or run the Teamsters. The arrival of this nine-pound-two-ounce squirmy little guy was an incredible bright spot in our lives: I called him ProSobee, after the only kind of formula he could digest, and Alexander the Greatest.

Unfortunately, everything else in our lives continued to be very difficult. Ann contracted childbirth fever, from an infection acquired during delivery, which killed women in the age before antibiotics. We returned to the hospital. I was scared. Ann had gone into convulsions and her lips had turned white. Fortunately the doctors were able to reduce her fever, but she then had an allergic reaction to the antibiotics they administered intravenously.

My job was now completely untenable: the fickleness of Britannica seemed unimportant compared to raising a child and recovering my health. I could no longer face meeting with my staff. I didn't want to contradict myself one more time and pretend that all the company's changes in direction were savvy. On the other hand, it was hardly a propitious moment to look for a new job: I had a tiny baby, a wife who was just regaining her strength, and a mysterious health condition that made my face look as if I'd been pummeled. Ann thought that I should just quit and become a full-time writer: my biography of the eccentric peripatetic mathematician Paul Erdös, called *The Man Who Loved Only Numbers*, had been published the year before and reached the number two spot on England's best-seller list, sandwiched between a pair of racy reminiscences of Princess Diana. Ann's idea was appealing, but I had reservations about breaking my contract with Britannica and derailing my career as a publishing executive. I hoped that one day Safra would wake up and see the wisdom of leaving me alone to rescue his company. I also wondered if his seemingly haphazard actions might be part of an arcane business strategy that somehow eluded me.

To Ann's chagrin, I started entering the occasional chess tournament in Chicago. She was bothered by the stories of how chess had absorbed me in my youth, and it was a game whose appeal she did not understand. I needed to play chess to engage my mind, which was otherwise atrophying at Britannica. I wanted to see how long it would take me to recover my college playing strength, and of course I wanted to surpass it. I knew that my brain cells were too ossified for me to become a champion. I did not expect to earn a certain title or win a specific tournament. I just wanted to play a really great game against a formidable adversary. A tournament game can take five hours, and unless you are constantly vigilant, you can throw away a winning position that you've painstakingly built up over the afternoon with a single ill-considered move.

Most intellectual and professional pursuits—academics; my career in publishing, writing, and television; other games that I have taken up—have come easily to me. I was the valedictorian of Staples High School in Westport, a summa cum laude graduate of Harvard College, and the editor in chief of a national magazine at the age of thirty. I performed mathematical paper-folding tricks on *David Letterman,* and spent an entire hour on *Oprah* talking not about my dysfunctional childhood but about the future of consumer technology. (To give Oprah and her millions of viewers a glimpse of this future, I strapped her into a virtual hang glider while she claimed I was ogling her butt.) Chess—and Britannica—were the chief exceptions to this success; the finer points of the game eluded me in a way that nothing else had. I had learned the rules of chess as a youngster but wasn't able to master the game. If I couldn't make Britannica work, I was now determined to conquer chess.

IN LATE SPRING OF 2000, AROUND ALEX'S FIRST BIRTHDAY, I FINALLY ESCAPED from Britannica and moved my family halfway across the country to Woodstock, New York, into a two-centuries-old converted barn. *The Man Who Loved Only Numbers* had been published in fourteen languages, and I had a contract to write another book, *Wings of Madness,* the story of Alberto Santos-Dumont, a flamboyant Brazilian inventor who piloted a flimsy flying machine around the Eiffel Tower in 1901, two years before Kitty Hawk. A fringe benefit of my research in early aviation—and the consulting work I was now doing for magazines and Internet companies—was that it took me almost weekly to New York City, where I had greater access to the chess world.

I visited my old haunts around Washington Square Park and played in tournaments at the renowned Marshall Chess Club. I also picked up assignments to write about chess from *The New Yorker, Smithsonian, The New York Times*, and *The Wall Street Journal*, which helped to justify my increased involvement in the game. Very few journalists covered chess in the mainstream press; my articles received attention, and I became the master of ceremonies for a few high-profile chess events in New York City and the color commentator on ESPN2 for seventeen tense hours of live chess between Kasparov and a computer. I even had the opportunity to face Kasparov in a game, and later I helped him prepare a speech—on achieving one's full potential in life—that he delivered to a group of Swiss bankers.

As I waded back into chess, I strove to separate my own chess playing from the overall insanity of the pastime. I tried to ignore my opponents' behavior and react solely to their moves on the board. In other words, I tried to play pure chess. Like so many goals I've had regarding the sixty-four squares, this one also proved to be elusive.

EARLY IN MY RETURN TO CHESS, I WENT BACK TO HARVARD TO PLAY IN A FOUR-round tournament, on a wintry weekend when the Charles River that runs past the campus was freezing over. I had not spent a night at Harvard in two and a half decades. The college arranged for me to sleep in a guesthouse among the freshmen dormitories in Harvard Yard. I was delighted with the accommodations because it was actually the first time I had stayed in the Yard. In my college days, the historic dormitories housed all but a few freshmen, and I was one of those who didn't make it. Consigned by the university to an off-campus apartment building, where a dean's secretary had been murdered, I missed out on the excitement, camaraderie, and freshman bonding of the Yard.

So often in my life I've felt on the sidelines—even at times when, by any external measure, I wasn't. But I was actually marginalized my freshman year, and it was mostly my own doing. I had outsmarted myself when Harvard inquired about my roommate preferences. Asked on a form for the time I went to bed, I was supposed to check one of three boxes: early, average, or late. Now, I had been a poor sleeper most of my life. If I didn't get eight hours, I'd wake up with a headache or mild nausea. As for falling asleep, it usually took me a while, with all the events of the day swimming in my head, and so I needed to allow for an extra hour to wind down. To get sufficient rest and make it to high school on time, I had to go to bed at 8:45 P.M. Most of my friends needed much less sleep, and I had an exaggerated idea of late-night college life.

I hoped to go to bed at Harvard at 11:00 P.M., but I thought "early" on the form meant midnight, "average" meant 2:00 A.M., and "late," 4:00 A.M. So I drew a thick line through all the boxes and, in a panic that my 11:00 P.M. plan was too ambitious, wrote 8:00 P.M. in the margin.

The dean's office unfortunately did its job too well and paired me with two other oddballs who presumably also returned the forms with marginalia and who often hit the sack by 8:00 P.M. One was a Zoroastrian (causing me to consult an encyclopedia even before my classes began) and a brilliant budding physicist who, while still in high school, was reportedly part of a team of researchers who discovered a new subatomic particle. My other roommate hailed from the South, and I arrived at Harvard on my first day to find a Confederate flag in the common room, which doubled as his bedroom. I think I was the embodiment of everything he found distasteful, an Eastern liberal intellectual atheist from modern-day Sodom, New York City. He had the annoying habit of taping index cards with words he was learning in German One to the bathroom mirror. He would close all the window shades in our fourth-floor suite before he would change so much as his shirt, never mind his pants. Once I woke up in the middle of the night and was distressed to find him standing by my bed in his pajamas, looking at me. The few times I brought a girl back to our suite, both of my roommates were either as giddy as Teletubbies or absurdly formal, as if the Queen of England were visiting. If I wanted sane company my freshman year, I should have spent more time at the Harvard Chess Club.

My return to the campus years later did not go well. I was hoping that the four-round Harvard Open, which anyone could enter, would be my breakthrough as an adult player. I wanted to defy the general view that tournament chess was primarily a young man's game and perform better than I had in school. I wanted to execute brilliant maneuvers in front of the current members of the Harvard chess team, who had not been born when I played for the same team. In the first round, I faced an older master, John Curdo, once the strongest player in New England. Although he was ranked substantially higher in the chess world than me, I hoped to win because he was past his prime, and I convinced myself that if we got into a tactical melee, my middle-aged mind could calculate variations faster than his seventy-year-old mind. But I soon got an inferior position because I fell for an opening trap that every self-respecting player except me seemed to know. For the remainder of the game Curdo tortured me and proved me wrong by outcalculating me.

In the second game, I played a newly minted Harvard graduate and achieved a decent setup only to throw it away when I couldn't find a constructive continuation. Then I reflexively checked his king three times, which gave me some fleeting emotional satisfaction, but unfortunately didn't bring me any closer to cornering his king and in fact just drove it to a safer place on the board while misplacing my own pieces that had participated in the feeble assault. (There is a dismissive saying in chess, "*Patzer* sees a check, *patzer* gives a check." *Patzer*, from the German *verpatzen*, "to mess things up," is a pejorative term for a clueless player. It is correct to check, or attack, the enemy king when it has nowhere to move to; the king is then in checkmate and the game is over. But if the king can flee, as my opponent's could, the check may not accomplish anything or even make things worse.) Now all my adversary's pieces were on better squares than mine, and over the next wearisome forty-two moves, he ground me down, won a key pawn, and forced me to give up a rook. All I had left were two pawns and my king versus his rook and king. I saw that I could not stop him from picking off my pawns. With no remaining army to protect my poor monarch, I knew he would be able to use his rook to drive my king to the edge of the board and snare it. I resigned rather than give him the pleasure of actually mating me.

In the third round, I squared off against a twenty-something jabberer who had the same pathetic score of 0–2 (zero wins and two losses) as me. I played unusually passively and he eventually won a pawn. In the fifth hour, I introduced complications in an endgame that he should have won. We were both exhausted. He went astray in the thicket of possibilities and the game petered out into a sterile ending in which each of our respective armies was so depleted that neither of us had sufficient firepower to checkmate the other. We agreed to a draw.

In the fourth and final round, I faced a doughy boy who looked even younger than his thirteen years and who, like me, was at the bottom of the tournament ladder. I was in a foul mood to begin with and his behavior made it worse. He blitzed out all his moves and left the board whenever it wasn't his turn. I thought he was making an arrogant show of trying to beat me without thinking about the moves. I played the opening carelessly, overlooked an opportunity for a clear advantage, and instead blundered away a pawn. As the child took advantage of my error and eagerly captured my pawn, he let out a loud, snotty snort. I thought he was lampooning my lame play. On the fourteenth move, he shifted his queen so that it opposed mine, forcing what he thought would be the exchange of ladies, which would bring him closer to realizing his pawn advantage. He smiled, got up from the table, and skipped around the room. I saw no alternative than to comply with his plan. But after I made my move, I realized that I had overlooked a killer continuation that would have won his queen (not simply swapped his queen for mine) and subsequently the game. I was angry at myself for missing it. Once you make a move in tournament chess, it is absolutely forbidden to retract it. But the child was still away from the table, frolicking with his friends, so he didn't know that I had moved. I glanced at the players at the neighboring boards, and when I saw that they were so engrossed in their own games that they would not witness what I was doing, I reached out, took back my move, and assayed the winning continuation instead. Ignorant of my infraction, the boy returned to the board and saw that I had won his queen. He gasped, resigned the game, and left abruptly.

When he gasped, I felt terrible, and my humanity returned. What the fuck had I done? It was obvious to me then that I had read too much into his behavior. He probably intended no disrespect by his quick and distracted play but just wanted to get the miserable tournament over with and go home. I also realized that he had a cold and what I'd interpreted as a snort of derision was simply an effort to clear his clogged nose. Two acne-pocked members of the Harvard chess team came over and congratulated me on my false victory. I was disgusted with myself. I had let myself become so unhinged by a board game that I had cheated a child. It was my only ethical lapse ever at chess, a game that had once symbolized for me a pure refuge from the vicissitudes and pettiness of everyday life. It made me question whether I could ever play inspired chess and remain a whole person. Here, sadly, I had managed to do neither.

The Harvard experience made me very contemplative. For me, chess was clearly unfinished business: I needed to explore the complex personal issues—psychological, philosophical, and familial—that the game raised. I needed to understand why this noble activity brought out the monster as well as the artist in those who played it. My immersion in the game was largely a psychological odyssey, a mission of self-discovery.

I wanted to know what it was like to compete at the top and whether the demands on the psyche were as great as they appeared. I wanted to get a sense of how the minds of champions worked and whether their minds differed from mine. I wanted to witness how chess professionals handled the emotional highs and lows of victory and defeat. I wanted to talk to others who were as excited and bewitched by the game as I was. I wanted to figure out why chess was so addictive. I wanted to understand why there weren't more women playing and become acquainted with some of the few who had managed to penetrate this testosterone-charged domain. I needed to know if I could play chess without compromising my humanity.

Insanity, I should add, may be something to avoid in life, but it certainly is not incompatible with strong chess. From December 1883 to March 1884, the Cambridge University chess team collaborated in a game played by mail against the Bedlam Insane Asylum. The mental patients won, reportedly on the Black side of the Sicilian Defense, in a brisk twenty-five moves.

FATHERS AND SONS

"The apple never falls far from the tree."
—*a proverb in forty-two European languages*

"Luzhin walked through all three rooms, looking for
a place to hide the pocket chess set. Everywhere was
insecure. The most unexpected places were invaded in
the mornings by the snout of that rapacious vacuum
cleaner."
—VLADIMIR NABOKOV,
The Defense

MY FATHER LOVED GAMES, AND WORDS, AND PLAYING GAMES
with words. He was famous among my childhood friends as an affable
raconteur and prankster. He tried, for instance, to convince them that he
owned the local oil company. Whenever a truck with "Hoffman Fuel"
emblazoned on its side barreled past the school bus stop in Westport,
he'd smile and shout at the driver, "How's business?" At election time,
he'd stand up in a Volkswagen convertible parked by a supermarket, wave
to shoppers, and ask for their votes. Sometimes he built an audience by
delivering an impromptu stump speech. He also liked to entertain my
friends with nonsense verse—"Of all the fishes in the seas/ my favorite is
the bass/ who climbs up on the seaweed trees/ and slides down on . . . his

hands and knees"—and captivate them with intriguing tales of the Russian Revolution, the Spanish Civil War, and other political upheavals that he believed had been just. The kids at the bus stop would recite political songs that he'd taught them: "A tisket, a tasket/ Put Hitler in a basket/ Defeat that meanie Mussolini/ And his henchman Franco." When we were a bit older, he told us wild stories about his unconventional life, like the time a pornographer made a movie in his Greenwich Village apartment.

Before my parents' divorce, my father's words literally filled our house: an errant cigarette butt once set fire to his office because there were so many papers and manuscripts scattered about. There were also piles of files devoted to the celebrities whose peccadilloes and misdeeds he enthusiastically wrote about for national magazines. At the peak of my dad's article-writing business, he employed two ladies part-time to read dozens of newspapers from around the country, clip any juicy gossip—about the actress who swam nude in the White House pool, or the CEO who was in rehab—and file the items so that he could crib from them later in his own lurid pieces.

Puns were his forte. He called a story about the Fondas' drinking problems "Absinthe Makes the Fondas Grow Heartier." He also put his mind for wordplay to good use as a writer of radio jingles for advertisers and captions for *New Yorker*–style cartoons. He once asked an artist to sketch a person at a cocktail party speaking to J. Edgar Hoover and titled the picture "Have you booked any good reds lately?"

My dad favored simple, direct prose, and he was such a facile stylist that a leading women's magazine once hired him to write an entire issue, with each saucy story appearing under a different pseudonym. When he edited *Pageant* magazine in the mid-1960s, he put racy and provocative titles on the cover that tapped into people's unarticulated fears and desires. As a kid I was titillated by these cover lines and derived naughty pleasure from reading the accompanying articles:

DOCTORS PHOTOGRAPH BEDROOM BEHAVIOR!
How Their Findings Can Help You . . .

OPEN LETTER TO NEGROES:
Why We Whites Really Fear You

CHASTE . . . MISUNDERSTOOD . . . RESTLESS:
THE AMERICAN NUN
   A special report on her unspoken problems

HOW FEMALE TEACHERS WARP OUR BOYS

THE MEN WHO STEAL CHILDREN'S PETS—
   for profit & slaughter

THE 'QUEER' ONES:
   Why one man in six can never respond to a woman

A MINISTER'S OWN STORY:
   "WITH LSD I SAW GOD"

EVERY NIGHT OVER 60,000,000 AMERICANS BREAK THE LAW
IN BED—
   Do you?[1]

It wasn't just that the titles were arresting and hyperbolic; the articles themselves pushed the boundaries of formerly taboo discourse in supermarket magazines. Today such cover lines are commonplace, and we are numb to them, but in the 1960s they drove hundreds of thousands of newsstand sales.

My father was as comfortable with high literary culture as he was with pop culture. He spent his days in the world of tawdry magazines and his evenings at the New School lecturing on Thomas Pynchon and demystifying trilingual puns in *Lolita* and obscure historical references in *The Waste Land*. One summer he made a pilgrimage to Europe to visit Yeats's and Joyce's childhood haunts. He had a near photographic memory for literature and would recite long passages verbatim from Djuna Barnes, Henry Miller, and Nathanael West. He could even tell you the physical location of a passage he was reciting ("a quarter of the way down page 119"). An Evelyn Wood speed-reader, he often consumed two or three novels a day. He particularly liked the writers whose work—often banned in its day as obscene—explored homosexuality, sadomasochism, and erotica in general.

MY FATHER'S RELATIONSHIP WITH ME WAS SO COVERTLY COMPETITIVE THAT it took me half my life to become a writer. When I was young, my father applied his rapacious black pen to any writing of mine—a letter, a school essay—that he could get his hands on. No sentence I wrote went untouched. No matter how sensible any particular editorial correction of his might be, the cumulative effect of his marking up one page with two or three dozen changes was to leave me feeling unmoored and resentful. He did this throughout my school years, and I always hated how he clinically dissected every sentence; wasn't there a single phrase worth saying something nice about—or at least leaving unmolested? Hadn't I expressed one interesting thought that wasn't in need of revision? I couldn't help but feel that he was trying to score points and parade his verbal intelligence.

My father's persistence in correcting me was very debilitating but at least it led to a good result: I learned how to write. My prose had been stiff and convoluted, as if I thought that inaccessible meaning signaled a deep, sphinxian intelligence on the part of the author. My father disabused me of the notion that good writing required long words, long sentences, and a thicket of relative clauses nestled within other relative clauses. He taught me that complex ideas were best expressed in unadorned language in which the words themselves did not distract or overpower the message.

During his lifetime I was nevertheless intimidated by his command of literature—we couldn't even discuss a book like *Charlotte's Web* when I was a kid without his offering some brilliant insight into the pig's motivation—and I avoided the humanities in school. I was an avid reader of nonfiction but skipped *The Catcher in the Rye*, and most other novels, until I was an adult. In grade school I gravitated toward the sciences and mathematics, subjects about which he knew little. In fourth grade, I wanted to be an animal behaviorist; I liked reading Konrad Lorenz and the stories of the orphaned ducks that latched onto him as their mother and waddled after him. Although watching animals was emotionally satisfying, it wasn't intellectually challenging. By the time I left high school, I wanted to be a physicist and had grandiose notions of determining the fate of the universe. When I graduated from college, I thought about going back to school for a doctorate in philosophy of science.

Now I regret that my father didn't live long enough—he died in 1982, when I was twenty-six—to see me manage to turn what he'd taught me into a profession. By the end of his life, I had already been an editor at *Scientific American* and was the author of a monthly column of mathematical brain teasers for another science magazine, so he was at least aware of the first step I took on my journey from man of science to man of letters.

But it was in 1987, when I became the editor in chief of *Discover*—after Time Inc. had lost tens of millions of dollars on the magazine—that I really put my father's skills to use. After all, it was second nature for me to call an article about a new fetal-imaging technology "Womb with a View," rather than a sober title that would have attracted only the most committed readers. Combining low and high culture in my approach to science journalism, I brought a pop sensibility to *Discover*'s covers, while at the same time augmenting the actual scientific content of its articles. The circulation soared to over a million. *Discover* won awards and finally turned a profit, and I acquired somewhat of a reputation in the magazine industry as an editorial boy wonder.

Even though my dad had been oddly competitive with me, as an adolescent I preferred the weekends with him to the weekdays with my mom. At the time I believed that she didn't love me because she seemed to dismiss me so readily. When I suggested grilling hamburgers for dinner at one of the barbecue pits at the beach a few miles from our home, she refused on the grounds that rain might ruin our cookout. But the sky was clear, I said. It could change, she countered. I guess it theoretically could, I said, but the day is beautiful and in the unlikely event of rain we can always return home and cook the meat on the stove. Too much trouble, she said, although she wasn't busy and was in fact planning to labor over our meal. When I shared my acceptance letter from Harvard with my mother, she said nervously, "That's a real school. It's a lot of work." She had similar reactions when I got into Yale and Princeton—I was at the top of my high school class, and she was acting as if I should go to a junior college. When I was finishing my senior year at Harvard and *Scientific American* offered me a job, she said, "That's a real magazine," as if she expected me to work as a hot dog vendor. And in 1988, when I won a National Magazine Award for a profile I'd written for *The Atlantic Monthly* of the mathematician Paul Erdös, my mother responded, "I didn't know the article was that good." If my father's problem was taking me too seriously, my mother's was not taking me seriously enough.

MY PARENTS HAD CONFLICTING ACCOUNTS ABOUT THEIR FIRST DAYS TOgether. My father said it was love at first sight when he met my mother in a used bookstore in the West Village, where she worked part-time. He said he sent her up a ladder, on the pretense of wanting an out-of-reach novel, so that he could get a better view of her legs. She claimed that they got involved only after they started sharing an apartment as a matter of convenience because neither of them had enough money to live alone. She said the sex wasn't very good and that my father was so ambivalent about their relationship that he proposed they visit the Central Park Zoo and get married only if a certain Asian civet called a binturong happened to make eye contact with them.

The female binturong is known to biologists for the unusual anatomical feature of a false penis. Leave it to the perverse streak in my dad to stake the future of his relationship with my mother on a freak of nature. He may have expected the binturong to be asleep because the animal is nocturnal and they were going to the zoo during the day. This particular binturong was having a restless time, though, and looked them right in the eye.

Regardless of how my parents met, they were a sharp-looking couple, judging from photos I have of them from the mid 1950s, before I was born: they are blowing smoke rings as they lounge happily against the arch in Washington Square Park. My mother was a model for *Vogue* then—the editor in chief had stopped her on the street when she was sixteen—and my dad resembled a handsome Diego Rivera. (In time he'd look more like Rodney Dangerfield, so much so that strangers would mistake him for the comedian and ask for his autograph, and he'd convincingly play along.) Early in my parents' marriage he put on at least seventy pounds and started chain smoking. My mother mocked his weight and said that he should hire himself out as a mold for bathtubs. He certainly did not take care of himself, and over the years I'd run into friends of his who hadn't seen him for a while and they would marvel that he was still alive.

I never saw my mother and father argue. She'd yell at him a lot but he wouldn't respond. Then she'd scream at me instead because I'd fight back. My father did have a subversive way of provoking her: within her hearing, he'd tell me stories about an intolerably bitchy llama named Leopold (my father loved gender-bending) that bore a remarkable resemblance to my mom. These stories drove her nuts because he denied that the llama was my mother, and she worried that he was turning me against her.

I have a brother, Tony, two years my junior, who always retreated to his room as soon as my mother started hollering. At the time I thought I had a raw deal because he was off doing whatever he wanted while my parents fought through me. Now I realize that Tony must have grown up feeling neglected because, for better or worse, I was the center of attention.

IT WAS MY DAD WHO INTRODUCED ME TO CHESS. WHEN I WAS FIVE YEARS OLD, I fell in a pile of old leaves in the woods and was stung by a swarm of yellow jackets. To keep my mind off the pain, he got me a chess set. And so, from my very first moments with chess, I welcomed the game as a distraction. (It was far more narcotic than Candy Land, which I'd played enthusiastically at the age of three with a kindly psychologist named Mrs. Perrutz; my parents believed that it was never too early to start therapy.)

The rook, my father said, begins the game immobilized in the very corner of the board but makes its power felt in the middle game and endgame when the board is less cluttered. The rook glides horizontally or vertically across any number of squares. The bishop moves diagonally, he told me. While the rook has the potential to visit every square on the board, the bishop can occupy only half of them. If the bishop starts on a light-colored square, it is confined to light squares for the remainder of the game. Likewise for the dark-squared bishop. (The fact that the light- and dark-squared bishops can never occupy the same squares prompted Boris Spassky to say of his ex-wife: "We were like bishops of opposite color.") The queen is the strongest piece; she has the power of the rook and bishop combined because she can move like either of them. The knight is the only chessman that can jump over the others, and its gait is the hardest for beginners to fathom. When the knight moves, it traces the letter L (an L in any physical orientation), by moving one square laterally and two squares perpendicularly. The pawn is a slowpoke. It advances only one square at a time except when it first moves and has the option of getting a head start in the world by venturing forward two squares.

Chessmen are not allowed to violate the laws of physics, so no two pieces are permitted to occupy the same square at the same time. You can move to a square possessed by your adversary by capturing the occupying piece—Oh yeah!—and replacing it with one of your own. Pawns are the only chessmen that capture in an unusual manner. The other chessmen can capture an adversary on any square to which they can move. The pawn can't do that; it is prohibited from taking a piece on the square directly in front of it. Instead the pawn can capture an enemy on either of the squares diagonally in front of it. (Some commentators have suggested that this is because real soldiers would have thrust their swords at an angle.) But the pawn, so plodding and restrictive in its movements, is also a dreamer. If the lowly foot soldier can inch its way clear across the board to the opponent's home rank—and that usually happens only late in the game, if it happens at all—it can morph into a queen or any other piece. As a child, I liked how all the pieces moved, but I was particularly pleased with the pawn's ability to assume a totally new identity.

THE VERY FACT THAT MY DAD HAD TO TEACH ME HOW THE PIECES MOVED did not bode well for my prospects of becoming a champion. The giants of the game, if we trust their memoirs, are rarely taught the rules of chess but assimilate them on their own by watching others play. José Raúl Capablanca, the post–World War I champion from Cuba who was more famous than Fischer in his time, learned the moves at the age of four by observing his father, a Spanish cavalry captain, play a fellow officer. "Without disturbing the silence that prevailed," Capablanca recalled,

> I took a position at the table where I could view the proceedings comfortably. My boyish curiosity soon grew to wonder, and very shortly, after observing how my father was moving those peculiarly shaped figures from square to square of the board, I felt a sudden fascination for the game. The impression came upon me that this curious game must have a military significance, judging from the interest the two soldiers manifested. I then began to concentrate my mind on discovering how

the pieces moved; and at the conclusion of the first game I felt sure that I had learned the rules for the movement of chessmen.

The men continued to play for the next two days. On the third day, "there occurred an incident which launched me upon my chess career," Capablanca wrote.

> As I looked on, my father, a very poor beginner, moved a knight from a white square to another white square.[2] His opponent, apparently, not a better player, did not notice it. My father won and I proceeded to call him a cheat and to laugh. After a little wrangle, during which I was nearly put out of the room, I showed my father what he had done. He asked me how and what I knew about chess. I answered that I could beat him; he said that that was impossible, considering that I could not even set the pieces correctly. We tried . . . and I won. That was my beginning.

Kasparov, not to be outdone by his great predecessor, began his own autobiography, *Child of Change*, with a story of unexpected childhood genius. "My parents used to like solving the chess problems that were published in our local Baku [Azerbaijan] newspaper, *Vyshka*," Kasparov wrote. "At the time, I did not play chess, although I was always close by, studiously following each move of the pieces on the board. Once, to my parents' utter amazement, I suggested how to solve a problem. My father said, 'Well, since he knows how the game ends, he ought to be shown how it begins,' and with that he began explaining the rules to me."

Karpov, in his memoir *Karpov on Karpov*, said he learned the rules at the age of four while sitting on his father's lap and watching him play friends, although he confessed, in a rare show of modesty for a world champion, that he needed to ask his dad to explain the concepts of castling and capturing *en passant*.[3] But even at four, Karpov began to understand the essence of the game and showed himself to be a master psychologist at reading other players' emotions:

> I felt the harmony of the game, the way in which the pawns and pieces move about. Their invisible cohesion, hitherto incomprehensible to me, became perfectly real. Sometimes, though, the impression of harmony vanished. I still didn't understand why this was so, but I sensed that something was not quite right. From the tension in Father's knees,

on which I was sitting, or from the withdrawal of his hands embrac-
ing me, I realized that he too had seen something wrong and didn't
like his position.

David Short started the biography of his son, *Nigel Short: Chess Prodigy*,
with the words "Nigel's first exposure to chess may not have been as dramatic as that of the infant Capablanca, but his family still remembers it
vividly." He then told the story:

> I suppose I was a better player than Capablanca senior—at least it
> took Nigel a couple of weeks before he started denting my ego.... We
> think Nigel was six when he sat intently on the arm of a chair and
> watched me explain the moves to his elder brother, Martin, two years
> his senior.... After half an hour or so I was ready to pack the game
> away, but Nigel pleaded to play. "You're too young," I told him. "I'll
> teach you when you're a bit older." Mother's intervention prevailed and
> a rather bored father had to reset the pieces. The boredom vanished al-
> most immediately. Hardly anything needed to be repeated. Nigel had
> picked up an amazing amount.[4]

I MAY NOT HAVE HAD A PROPER CHAMPION'S BEGINNING, BUT EVEN IN MY
swollen, stung condition, I took to the game. Nothing on the chessboard
seemed to be left to chance or luck. Although I made many foolish
moves and hardly knew what I was doing, I realized that the chessmen
were under my command. The appearance of the pieces and board appealed to me. The beauty of chess was its very starkness: six kinds of
pieces, all elementary in design, interacting on an unadorned board.[5]
The pieces cried out for me to make sense of them, but in their austerity
offered little help. I promised myself that I would learn to coordinate
them and discover their secrets. I stopped short, however, of painting a
chessboard on the ceiling of my bedroom, as had the young Bobby Fischer.

In the two weeks it took my body to purge itself of yellow jacket tox-
ins, my dad and I played dozens of times. A year later he would start losing to me. (Aha! At last I was like the young Kasparov—"It became
difficult to drag me away from the game, and a year later I was already
beating my father.") Throughout elementary school in Westport, I played

chess during my free periods but not as often as I wished, because few of my classmates knew the rules. I cannot recall losing, and the lack of opponents made me turn to other games. I played gin and 500-card rummy with my dad, and on weekends we had spirited Scrabble contests. He was proud of my obvious talent at games but needed me to believe that he, too, was a natural. I remember him confounding me at Scrabble with words like *ai* (a three-toed sloth), *ko* (twelfth-century Chinese porcelain), and *oe* (a violent whirlwind off the Faroe Islands) and acting as if they were part of his normal vocabulary.

In fourth grade I discovered my first chess book on my father's shelves. I cannot exaggerate my excitement at learning that games between topflight players were recorded in special notation, preserving them forever. I was astounded that the book analyzed games played more than one hundred years ago and that, after all that time, chess authorities did not always agree on which player stood better in certain thorny positions.[6] There was something very satisfying about setting up the disputed positions on my own chessboard and reaching my own conclusions about how, say, Lionel Kieseritzky could have repelled Adolf Anderssen's mating attack in London in 1851. Moreover, I was tickled that I could record the moves of my own games with the same notation the grandmasters used. I learned what was called English descriptive notation; P-K4, for example, means the pawn in front of the king moves to the fourth rank. Today players use algebraic notation, in which each square is uniquely defined by a letter and a number. The files or columns are labeled a to h, and the rows 1 to 8. In algebraic notation, the move P-K4 would be rendered e4, or more expansively e2-e4, indicating that the pawn in the second row in the e-column moves to the fourth row.

This gave me the idea of inventing a cryptic chess notation of my own so that I could play the game long-distance with my closest childhood buddy, who now lived in Cape Cod. (Chess had barely figured in our friendship when we were together, but we liked the challenge of figuring out how we could play remotely.) I assigned a male first name to each of the sixty-four squares and a last name, too. Then I'd place a collect call from "Michael Mastin" to my friend. He'd decline the call—sparing my family the phone charge—and he'd know that I had moved the piece on the Michael square to the Mastin square. Later I'd get a collect call from, say, "Damian Touby," and then I'd know that he had responded by shifting the piece on the Damian square to the Touby square. This stratagem required our parents—and anyone else who answered the phone—to decline the calls and remember the names. It worked beautifully for a couple of weeks, until an AT&T auditor found it suspicious that fifty collect calls had been declined between the same two phone numbers.

From that first chess book I learned that there were favored sequences of opening moves with names like the Max Lange Attack, King's Gambit, Bird's Opening, Albin Counter Gambit, Modern Benoni, and Fried Liver Attack. Before I knew enough about chess to have an opinion of the merit of each opening, I studied the ones whose names I liked. I hated the taste of fried liver, but I thought it was a swell name for an attack, and so it was the first opening I deliberately played.

I DISCOVERED THE CONTEMPORARY TOURNAMENT SCENE FOUR YEARS LATER, at the age of thirteen, when I was taking the train to Manhattan to see my father. On my seat someone had left a copy of *Chess Life & Review*, the magazine published by the United States Chess Federation. At the end of the magazine, which is still published today under the name *Chess Life*, was a list of upcoming tournaments. I was delighted to see that an event for beginners was scheduled that weekend at the now-defunct Hotel McAlpin near Penn Station in Manhattan. I implored my father to take me. I won four games, drew two, and lost none, a performance that netted me a prize of $25 worth of chess books.

On subsequent weekends I continued to enter open tournaments[7] at the McAlpin, the Hotel Roosevelt near Grand Central Station, and the Skyline Motor Inn located in what was then the rough neighborhood known as Hell's Kitchen. I bought dozens of chess books, subscribed to two British chess journals, and purchased back issues of the leading Soviet chess periodical and, to help me follow them, a booklet called *A Chess Player's Guide to Russian*.

I confess, though, that I couldn't make it through most of what I acquired. For a player of my level, chess books were a struggle to read because I usually couldn't follow the analysis in my head and had to set up each position on a board. I read what I could and skimmed the rest. I had this fanciful idea that I would become a stronger player just by owning the right books and magazines, and I hoped that someday I would have enough talent and motivation to go back and read them all. I did study in detail a couple of openings for White and for Black, and I committed key move sequences to memory. I also solved composed chess problems—White to mate in three or Black to win material in two—and honed my tactical skills in late-night blitz games in Washington Square Park. My tournament rating advanced, in a period of three years, from Class E to Class B.

THE DEFINING MOMENT OF MY TEENAGE CHESS PLAYING WAS A MEMORABLE slugfest with the Danish grandmaster Bent Larsen, one of the top ten players in the world, at a simultaneous exhibition in New Haven. In a so-called simul, a grandmaster plays numerous games at once against all comers. This form of competition, in which rank amateurs can take on a champ, makes chess unique among sports; it's not as if youthful basketball players can shoot hoops with Shaquille O'Neal or neophyte golfers can join Tiger Woods on the fairway.

In a simul, the grandmaster charges from board to board, barely pausing at each one to make a move, and he continues circumnavigating the room until all the games are over. During the first few trips around, the grandmaster takes the measure of his opponents. Usually, most of the players are noticeably unpracticed, and he doesn't think about those games because he knows he can mechanically finish them. A few players, however, may put up a tremendous defense or launch a crafty attack. The grandmaster commits those games to memory so that, as he travels around the room, he can mull them over and come up with a good plan. By analyzing the difficult positions in his head while he mindlessly plays out the easy ones, he is able to continue making moves at a fast pace, thereby maintaining the illusion of total control.

The simultaneous exhibition generally taxes the grandmaster's feet more than his mind. Few players will draw a game against him, let alone beat him. But there is more than one way for the amateur to emerge feeling victorious. All he need do, although even this is not easy to pull off, is to make a move that forces the grandmaster to stop and think. It is at that rare moment, when the grandmaster pauses to study a position, that the amateur is admitted to the brotherhood of chess players. But it can also be a dangerous moment, for it is often the point of no return. Carried away by his small triumph, the amateur may decide that he has within himself the stuff of champions. No matter how slow his subsequent progress at chess may be—indeed, even if there's no progress at all—he will never be free of the gnawing thought that he, too, could be a grandmaster if only he applied himself.

Sometimes the amateur succeeds. Joel Lautier, the 2005 French champion, showed me a photograph of himself at the age of ten playing Mikhail Tal in a simul in a Paris Metro station. The photo records that Tal, the eighth world champion and legendary tactician, whose dizzying but not always theoretically sound combinations defeated the world's best players, not only paused but went so far as to pull up a chair and sit down opposite young Lautier. Tal won the game, but Lautier went on to become, at the age of fifteen, the youngest world junior champion ever.

Only the most jaded youngster can fail to be inspired by the experience of facing a chess legend in a simul.[8] Thirteen-year-old Mikhail Botvinnik participated in an exhibition given by former world champion Emanuel Lasker in Moscow in 1924. Because Lasker was playing many opponents it took him a while to make his way around the room back to any given board, even though he moved quickly in each game. Most of the participants undoubtedly appreciated the delay because it gave them time to think. Botvinnik, on the other hand, was bored by the slow pace and simply abandoned the game completely "after 15 moves because it was already time for a schoolboy to be asleep." Fortunately the dulling effect of this encounter did not cause the Russian teen to renounce chess altogether: the following year he entered a simul in Leningrad and defeated the reigning world champion, José Capablanca. Botvinnik went on to become world champion himself for thirteen years between 1948 and 1963.

Most grandmasters take the White pieces in every game in a simultaneous exhibition. Bent Larsen, I had heard, was an exception, generously playing Black in half the battles. A month before the exhibition, I decided to study every published game of Larsen's I could find in which he played Black. I figured that if I had White against Larsen, I might be able to direct the game, by virtue of having the advantage of the first move, into positions that he had previously reached and, consequently, for which I was well prepared. It never occurred to me that he, too, would be ready for any position he had reached before and allowed to be reached again. That month I studied dozens of his games, to the exclusion of most everything else. My mother was somewhat alarmed by how I raced through my schoolwork and wolfed down dinner so that I could return to the chessboard in my bedroom. My father was proud of my determination and at the same time envious of my ability to be so single-minded.

My obsession with the game was fortunately confined to the board itself. Unlike Nabokov's morose Luzhin, I did not fantasize "that with a Knight's move of this lime tree . . . one could take that telegraph pole." And, unlike my childhood hero Fischer, I did not plan to use any money I might win in tournaments in order to hire the "best architect" and have him build me a house in the shape of a chess piece. "Yeah, that's for me," Fischer said. "Class. Spiral staircases, parapets, everything. I want to live the rest of my life in a house built exactly like a rook."

On the day of Larsen's exhibition, my father drove me to New Haven. I sat down at a board behind the White pieces, joining forty-nine other fanatics who had each put up $7.50 to take on the Dane. Aside from a "Thank you" in response to someone's warm welcome, Larsen said very little as he walked briskly around the room and made his first move on each board. For him we were all one faceless enemy.

In his first seven trips around—350 moves in all—no one had succeeded in forcing him to break stride. I was pleased, however, by the way my game was progressing. As I recall, Larsen and I duplicated move for move a From's Gambit that he had played against a little-known Swedish master. The Swede had played passively and was ferociously vanquished. His trouble, I believed, began with his ninth move, which put him on the defensive, from which he never recovered. I had come up with an improvement that I planned to unveil if Larsen made the same eighth move. And there was no reason he wouldn't, because it had served him so well before.

I had difficulty looking at the board as Larsen came around to make his eighth move. His hand shot out, grabbed a pawn, picked it up, moved it forward one square, and set it firmly down, his fingers lingering for a fraction of a second as they screwed the pawn into the board. Sure enough, he was following my plan. I would punish him, the robotic fool, for lazily making moves he had made before! I confidently studied the position, confirming for the umpteenth time the soundness of my plan. Then, as I extended my hand to make the move I had carefully prepared, something terrible happened. My fingers went numb. I feared that my hand was no longer under my control and that, in spite of the clear image of the correct move in my mind, my fingers might rebel and select some other move that would brand me as an imbecile.

Even world-class players have been known to suffer psycho-physiological paralysis. At the 1970 Chess Olympiad in Siegen, Germany, the top Romanian, Florin Gheorghiu, lost control of his fingers against, of all players, Bent Larsen. Gheorghiu had a winning position and, according to the tournament book,

> Eye witnesses present at the closing stages of this amazing encounter reported that Gheorghiu reached out his right hand to administer the lethal blow, Knight to Bishop Six, but at this precise moment the said hand was seized with a convulsive tremble which rendered the Romanian Grandmaster incapable of transferring the piece to the required square. In the act of summoning up sufficient reserves of will-power to overcome this unfortunate and paralytic state of affairs, Gheorghiu overstepped the time limit.

Luckily, I fared better than Gheorghiu. I reached out and made the move I intended and waited for Larsen to return. He arrived and, just as I hoped, he paused. He studied the position for what seemed like ages and then looked up at me, smiling. "That's a better move," Larsen said, "but no matter." The smile disappeared and his voice became grim. "I shall crush you anyway, like I crushed him." And he proceeded to do just that.

Larsen's aggressive outburst and victory did not tamp my enjoyment of our encounter. OK, I felt a bit foolish that I thought my opening improvement would defeat him, but I was delighted that he had taken me seriously and spoken to me and not the others. My father praised my performance, instead of misbehaving as he had when I defeated Rossolimo. I was now completely hooked.

There were one- and two-month stretches in which, from the moment I came home from school to the time I went to bed, I'd crouch over the board, reviewing popular sequences of opening moves and searching for little-known ideas that I could spring on unwary opponents. But it was one thing to go over openings in the quiet of my own bedroom, and quite another thing to use them against flesh-and-blood opponents who savored winning as much as I did and who were equally compulsive in their pregame preparation. Besides, I was ahead of myself in my studious approach to chess. I would undoubtedly have improved faster if I had played more and studied less. Memorizing the latest grandmaster suggestion for the tenth move in a sharp line of the Sicilian Dragon only helps if you already possess the skills to punish your opponent if he deviates from established theory on the ninth move or the eighth move or even earlier. Something similar had happened in my game with Larsen. Not that he deviated—I was actually the one who purposely varied from his earlier game. But my move, though a clear improvement, didn't give me enough of an advantage to put him away. Larsen still understood the resulting middle game much better than I did and effortlessly outmaneuvered me.

CHESS WAS APPARENTLY FIRST PLAYED IN INDIA AS EARLY AS THE FIFTH CENtury and eventually made its way through Persia and the Arab world to the West. One legend has it that the game was invented as a substitute for war to placate a mother who had lost two sons on opposite sides of a battle. To be sure, the game has always been a favorite of military leaders, particularly in Europe. Napoleon was a fanatical player, as was Trotsky when he led the Red Army. Charles XII, the early eighteenth-century Swedish military genius, liked to march his king across the chessboard rather than adopt the general practice of tucking it safely in the corner behind a wall of pawns. Voltaire denounced this strategy as a reckless one that needlessly exposed the king to attack, and Frederick the Great, while retreating on the battlefield, wrote in his journal, "I am like the chess king of Charles XII, always marching."

The board itself is essentially the same today as it was in ancient India. Early boards had sixty-four squares arranged in an eight-by-eight array.

The squares were initially all the same color. The adoption by the four-teenth century of the now-familiar two-tone board, with alternating light and dark squares, did not affect how the game was played but merely made it easier to follow diagonal routes. There have always been six kinds of chessmen, although their names and physical representations varied from one culture to another and changed over time. In India, where the game was called *chaturanga*, Sanskrit for "four parts," the pieces were modeled after the four elements of the military. There were foot soldiers, cavalry, chariots, and elephants, which corresponded later in Western chess to pawns, knights, bishops, and rooks.

The rules of the game have undergone remarkably few changes, but what modifications were made can be seen as loosely reflecting the social currents of their times. In early versions of chess, the capture of the king marked the conclusion of the game. When European royalty started playing, there was a subtle change in how the game ended. The chess king became immune to actual capture; the game was called off just shy of that when the king was under direct attack and had no square to move to that was not controlled by the enemy. One can imagine how this end—checkmate—might be more palatable to real kings who were terrified of falling into enemy hands. The word *checkmate* comes from the Persian *shah mat*, "the king is defeated," or, more cruelly, "the king is dead."

The most substantial change in the game occurred in the late fifteenth or early sixteenth century. Originally, all the chess pieces were male, and a piece known as the king's counselor stood by his majesty's side. In me-dieval chess the counselor was even weaker than the king; it, too, could move just one square, but only in a diagonal direction. The counselor would keep the king company but was too limp to defend his master. Nor did the counselor become more powerful when, for reasons lost to history, the piece underwent a sex change in about the year 1000 and be-came a queen.

In the early Renaissance, when the ranks of chess players included willful women like Lucrezia Borgia, Queen Isabella of Spain, and Catherine de Médicis, the chess queen exploded in power. The timing may be coincidental. (There is no smoking gun, like an eyewitness ac-count of Isabella threatening to behead a courtier unless her husband, King Ferdinand, made the chess queen an Amazon.) In any event, the transformed piece became by far the strongest one in the game. She could shift in one bold move from the home court of her king to the heart of enemy territory on the far side of the board. In other words, one moment the chess queen was the wife standing by her man, and the next a lioness out for the kill. No matter what the queen did, however, her hapless husband usually stayed home.

Isabella and Catherine de Médicis were apparently both strong players, and they were said to exhibit particular skill in their handling of the queen. With the piece's ability to engage the enemy from afar, the pace of the game picked up considerably—as did the pace of life itself during this period. Some of the Old Guard had trouble adapting to the new form of the game, which they scoffingly called "mad chess" or "chess with the mad queen."

Still, until the 1880s and the introduction of chess clocks, there was generally no limit on how long a player might think, and the successful competitor had to have *Sitzfleisch* ("sitting flesh") as well as brains. Several games in the first international tournament, in London in 1851, lasted twelve hours, and one dragged on for twenty. One player spent two and a half hours on a single move. The Germans had a word for this, *todsitzen*, which means to sit until your opponent dies. Howard Staunton, the English champion who organized the tournament, disapproved: "When a player, upon system, consumes hours over moves when minutes might suffice, and depends, not upon outmaneuvering but outsitting his antagonist, patience ceases to be a virtue and one cannot help expressing deep regret that there is not some legal or moral force which might be brought to bear upon the offender."

In 1852, various solutions were proposed in Staunton's magazine, *The Chess Player's Chronicle*. One contributor suggested that players be fined a guinea each time they spent more than twenty minutes on a move. Another proposed that "each player have a three hours' sand-glass at his elbow, and a friend on each side to turn it. While the player is thinking, the sand must be allowed to run; while his opponent is thinking his glass will be laid horizontally on the table and the running suspended."

None of these suggestions were implemented in an 1858 match between Paul Morphy and Louis Paulsen, a German émigré who grew tobacco and ran a distillery in Dubuque, Iowa. The longest Morphy spent on any one move was twelve minutes, and that was when he offered his queen to Paulsen in return for a colossal attack. Morphy was annoyed when Paulsen spent seventy-five minutes deciding whether or not to capture the queen, and he swore to a bystander that he would defeat Paulsen in every future game they played. He was true to his word. Legend has it that in another encounter, Morphy and Paulsen sat at the board for eleven hours without saying anything or making a move. Finally, Morphy lost patience, looked up, and stared at Paulsen. "Oh," said Paulsen, "is it my move?"[9]

The timing device that eventually became standard in every tournament is made up of two clocks, one for each player. When it is your turn to move, your clock is running. After you make a move, you immediately press a button that shuts off your clock and starts the opponent's. Each clock face has a tiny red flag whose staff is attached to a pivot mounted just to the left of twelve o'clock. Normally the flag hangs vertically, but when the minute hand approaches the hour, it catches the flag and starts pushing it into the horizontal position. When the minute hand reaches the precise hour, it disengages the flag, which swings back abruptly to the dangling, vertical position. The clocks are set before the game so that the time expires when the minute hand reaches the hour. The function of the flag is to eliminate arguments about when the time is over; the time is over when the flag falls.

Today flagless digital clocks have largely replaced the clocks of my youth. They show the time to a hundredth of a second and flash 00:00 when the time has elapsed. In blitz chess, each side typically has five minutes for the whole game. In rapid chess, twenty-five minutes. In classical tournament chess, an average of two and a half to three minutes a move. There is often more than one time control in classical chess. For instance, in the 2006 World Chess Cup, each player had ninety minutes for the first thirty moves and then was granted an additional hour for all the remaining moves. According to tournament rules, there is no difference between a loss on time and a defeat by checkmate.

All chess players know the tyranny of time. Many celebrated games have involved one player making the last move of the time control with only hundredths of a second to spare. Emanuel Lasker, who was world champion for an unprecedented twenty-seven years, from 1894 to 1921, reportedly never wore a watch.

I myself am a horrible blitz player. Even though I am serious about chess, I've played too few chess games in my life, compared to other people of my rating, for the moves to have become second nature. In blitz I think too much and lose when the flag falls like a little guillotine. Or else I blunder grotesquely when I'm in a frenzy to beat the clock. Like Lasker, I never wear a watch.

A systematic way of identifying the world's best chess player was a late development in the history of the game. The accolade *world champion* was apparently used for the first time in 1886, when Wilhelm Steinitz, from Austria-Hungary, and Johanne Zukertort, a Riga-born linguist who spoke Arabic, Turkish, and Sanskrit, agreed to play a match in New York for that title. Steinitz was a diminutive man (he barely cleared five feet) who rejected the reckless attacking chess that was common in his day. He disposed of Zukertort with a cautious, methodical, scientific style that he described as the "accumulation of small advantages." After Steinitz, there were four world champions—Emanuel Lasker, José Capablanca, Alexander Alekhine, and Max Euwe—who haggled over the terms of matches in back-room negotiations. Until the World Championship was organized by FIDE, in 1948, world title bouts were private affairs, with the reigning champion often imperiously refusing to put his title on the line unless the prospective challenger came up with enough cash and satisfactory terms and conditions.

FIDE was founded in 1924 at the first international chess team competition, which was held at the Hotel Majestic in Paris and staged concurrently with the Paris Olympic Games. The federation's effectiveness was initially undermined by the absence of the one chess superpower, the Soviet Union. It did not join FIDE until 1947, following a year of chaos when world champion Alekhine died and there was no process in place to determine his successor. FIDE, whose motto was *Gens una sumas*, Latin for "We are one people," brought welcome standardization to the process of choosing a champion by establishing a three-year cycle. The cycle began with a series of zonal tournaments in designated geographical regions, or zones, around the world. The United States was a zone, for example, and the U.S. Championship was a zonal tournament. The winners of the zonals came together for an interzonal championship, with the eight highest scorers advancing to a Candidates Tournament. The Candidates was either a round-robin event or a series of knockout matches that produced a challenger to the chess throne. The challenger and the world champion then played a gruelingly long match, typically twenty-four games. If the champion retained his title, the three-year cycle began anew. If he lost, he had the right to a rematch a year later.

This system worked pretty well until 1993, when world champion Garry Kasparov and challenger Nigel Short bolted from FIDE because they felt they were not being sufficiently consulted about the details of their forthcoming match. The two men set up their own organization, the Professional Chess Association, to run the match and continue the century-old tradition of lengthy World Championship bouts with each game played at a classical time control. FIDE went ahead without Kasparov and Short and staged its own World Championship—a series of short knockout matches played at a controversial faster time control. Even though the PCA eventually disbanded, the existence of two rival World Championships continued for thirteen years, confusing chess fans and corporate sponsors who wanted to know who the true king was and who was just the pretender.[10]

The competing titles were finally unified in October 2006. FIDE is now one of the largest umbrella sports organizations in the world, representing 159 national chess federations and more than five million registered players. And yet the international chess scene is far from harmonious—the unification match almost went down the toilet, as it were, over allegations that one of the players had cheated when he was in the privy.

The insanity in chess extends all the way to the reputation of the game's ruling czar, Kirsan Ilyumzhinov, a businessman who has been the president of FIDE since 1995. Ilyumzhinov has another job: he is the authoritarian Buddhist president of Kalmykia, a desolate, poverty-stricken semiautonomous Russian republic on the northwest coast of the Caspian Sea. Ilyumzhinov has been accused of human rights violations, money laundering, drug and caviar smuggling, and letting his countrymen suffer while he drained the republic's coffers to promote his personal passion. He is notorious for such odd proclamations as: "In my country there is only one man who plays politics, and that is me. The other men have to work, the women have to bear children, and the children have to play chess."

Ilyumzhinov is friends with many of the world's most brutal dictators, and he has turned to them, rather than Fortune 500 companies who are afraid of his unsavory reputation, to fund chess. He was close to Saddam Hussein, whom he said deserved the Nobel Peace Prize—so close, in fact, that he was apparently the last foreign leader to see Hussein's son Uday before the United States invaded Iraq on March 20, 2003. Ilyumzhinov cajoled Hussein into funding and hosting the 1996 world title bout between Anatoly Karpov and the American prodigy Gata Kamsky, but the match never took place there, because the U.S. State Department refused to let Kamsky travel to Baghdad. Ilyumzhinov suggested Tehran as another venue for a title match, but Washington vetoed that as well.

In 2004, Ilyumzhinov was true to character in selecting inhospitable locations for both the women's and overall World Championships. The women's event was scheduled for late May in Adzharia, a rebellious region of Georgia whose feisty leader, Aslan Abashidze, was blowing up bridges to isolate his territory from the rest of Georgia. Although the region was on the brink of civil war, FIDE insisted that Adzharia was a safe place for chess, but jittery players recalled the 1999 World Junior Championship in Yerevan, Armenia, where a coup broke out during the games and the tournament organizers tried to conceal the uprising by attributing the gunfire to a holiday celebration. When Abashidze himself, who had guaranteed the chess queens of the world $700,000 in prizes, abdicated to Moscow two weeks before the championship, Ilyumzhinov scrambled to move the event to Elista, the capital of Kalmykia. The FIDE World Championship took place a month later in Libya, funded by $1.5 million of Muammar Gadhafi's personal assets.

Grandmasters joke that they may have to go to North Korea to play in a World Championship. Wealthy despots who can spend their country's money on the game without answering to anyone are an endangered species in the twenty-first century. Chess players, who by their very nature are always thinking one move ahead, are understandably worried that Ilyumzhinov is running out of friends who can fund their magnificent obsession.

WHEN I ENTERED MY FIRST RATED TOURNAMENT, IN 1970, MY FATHER WAS the editor of *Lithopinion,* a handsome graphic arts and public affairs quarterly that the lithographers union published in order to show off the beauty of this form of printing. My father worked directly for the president of Local One, Amalgamated Lithographers of America, who lived up to my stereotype of a union boss. When the guy took my dad and me to lunch, around the corner from their offices at Thirteenth Street and Fifth Avenue, he would pay from a rolled-up wad of $50 bills and never ask for change. If we dined at a steak place and the check came to $36.53, the waiter would keep $13.47. If we ate in a coffee shop and the bill came to $13.27, the waitress won the lottery—she'd go home with $36.73. My father was embarrassed when I told his boss that he should tip less and give my dad a raise.

I was always more direct than my father. As a child I usually said whatever I was thinking. I remember a couple who visited our home when I was three or four. They did not sit on the couch together but sat as far apart as the furniture in our living room allowed. "What's the matter?" I asked. "Is your marriage in trouble?" There was self-conscious laughter— my intuition was correct. In time, of course, I learned to stifle observations that might unnecessarily hurt people. Now, as I watch my young son Alex struggle to understand what thoughts he should keep to himself—"That woman is really fat, Dad"—I am nostalgic for the time in early childhood when I spoke freely and said whatever was on my mind.

For the Winter 1970 issue of *Lithopinion,* my father wrote an article called "Chess: Once the Game of Kings, Now the King of Games" about the passions that chess inspires. He didn't tell me he was writing the piece. I learned about it by accident one afternoon in Washington Square Park when an artist with a large sketch pad sought my permission to draw me at the chessboard and publish the picture. I asked him where the illustration was going to appear and he said *Lithopinion.* I didn't know if my father planned to conceal the article from me forever or intended to surprise me with my picture in the magazine. In any event, I made sure that I read the article when it came out.

The piece began by recounting a joke:

> Wherever chess nuts gather (and that's almost anyplace, except Red China where the game is banned because it represents "Western decadence"), international grandmasters (the world's best players), *patzers* . . . , woodpushers (mediocre players) and kibitzers (non-playing compulsive advice givers) swear the following dialogue actually once took place:

> CHESS PLAYER NO. 1: "My wife threatened to leave me if I don't give up chess."
> CHESS PLAYER NO. 2: "That's terrible."
> CHESS PLAYER NO. 1: "Yes, I shall miss her dreadfully."

> Yet, if you listen to the words of poet William Butler Yeats, it may be true that the game of kings (or the king of games) also binds lovers together—at least in an attempt to slow time's steady erosion: "They know there was nothing that could save them,/ And so played chess as they had any night/ For years . . ."[11]
> Whether it triggers apartness or engenders togetherness, chess is an obsession for many of the 15 million Americans (conservative estimate) who play it more or less regularly. . . . Edward Lasker, an American chess luminary, recalled that when Harry Nelson Pillsbury toured Europe in 1902 giving blindfold exhibitions daily he came to his (Lasker's) hometown: "The men in charge of arrangements had permitted me to take a board, but my mother forbade me to go out in the evening to play chess. Little do mothers know what an all-consuming fire the passion for chess can be. After brooding all day over the tragedy into which my mother was about to turn my life by preventing me from playing with the famous chess star, I ran away from home!"
> The question, of course, is what is there about this "game in which thirty-two bits of ivory, horn, wood, metal, or (in stalags) sawdust stuck together with shoe polish are pushed on sixty-four alternately colored squares" (George Steiner's description) that makes children leave home, men leave their wives and women leave their senses.[12]

I was pleased with my picture in *Lithopinion,* and I found my dad's prose catchy and engaging but also glibly contrived. The opening joke was amusing, but I was bothered by the fact that I had never heard *anyone* in the chess world swear that the dialogue had actually taken place.[13]

When I reread the article in college, seven years later, I debated in my mind the journalistic ethics of what he had done. I wondered why he couldn't just tell the joke without embellishing the context. The way he wrote it, any knowledgeable reader who thought about his words would know his rendition couldn't literally be true. Did he really expect chess fans to believe that "wherever chess nuts gather" they swear by the dialogue? Or was he so enraptured by the punning phrase "wherever chess nuts gather" that he didn't care if it was true or not? Or was he, from the very start of the article, trying to clue the discerning reader in to the fact that he was playing a game, much like the game he was writing about? Or was I the one with the problem because I was unnecessarily deconstructing and ruining a perfectly enjoyable article? To be fair, the joke my father told was completely harmless and—so what if the context was false?—it accurately captured the addictive nature of chess.

I now think that my focusing on the innocuous chess-nut story was a way of avoiding my discomfort with the rest of the article. My father had written all about me. On the one hand, that made me proud. On the other hand, he never asked me if I was comfortable being his subject, or whether he could share our private conversations with the world. He never said he was interviewing or profiling me, and his descriptions were not altogether flattering. He recounted, for instance, how I chatted up an opponent during an important game. I was fourteen and my adversary was a girl a year or two older whose rating was 1069. I did not yet have a rating. It was the final round, and I had a minus score of three wins and four losses. I needed a win to break even, and she needed a win to receive a trophy for being the top scoring girl in the tournament.

> The game lasted a long time, almost three hours. Having finished their own matches, the other players crowded around these two. I sat over on the side, trying not to be a chess father, and pretended to read a book. Occasionally, the ranks of the kibitzers would part for a few seconds and I'd see my son's face, calm and smiling, as he chatted with the girl. She was pretty, true, but he was usually so serious during a chess game. I couldn't understand it.
>
> The girl's father joined me. He was a teacher and he made a stab at

correcting student papers. Suddenly he jumped up, walked over to the game, studied the position on the board, and then came back.

"Your boy's in trouble," he said. "She's got his queen."

A few minutes later he got up again, looked again, came back again. "I don't know," he said, "he's got his rooks doubled."

Back to the table, then back to me. "I think she's got him."

I looked at my watch and realized we'd be lucky to make the last train back to Connecticut. There was so much chattering at the table—I could hear his voice—that surely he wouldn't object if I reminded him it was getting late.

I went over and said, "We don't have much time . . ." when he cut me off with a "Please don't bother me now."

Uncharacteristic. Puzzling. But I guessed the pressure was getting to him.

Report from the girl's father: "I think she's in time trouble."

Further report: "I know she's in time trouble."

Final report: "She has just two minutes to make fifteen moves."

A voice cried out—not Paul's, not hers—"It's a mate!"

The kibitzers moved off and I saw Paul shaking hands with the girl. She left and I took my son aside.

"What happened?" I asked.

"I won," he replied. "I checkmated her just as the little flag fell indicating her time was up."

I have always been particularly irritated by this last quote. I would never have said "little flag"—that's a writer's prissy touch. I was very familiar with the flag, and so was he. I would have said just "flag." Once again, his description of the game, even if he occasionally fabricated my words, got across the larger emotional truth of how tense chess could be; but it also demonstrated how wrapped up in my own playing he was, and how energetically he lived through me. The article concluded:

In the cab to the train station he apologized for snapping at me during the game. "When you said the word 'time,' " he explained, "I was afraid you'd remind her she was in time trouble. That's why I kept talking to her—to keep her mind off the clock. I don't feel this was wrong because I think some of the boys there were kind of trying to help her. So I kidded with her and made the most complicated moves I could—there

towards the end—so she'd really have time problems. But I beat her before the clock did anyway."

"You seemed so calm," I said.

"Calm above maybe, but I was shaking under the table."

He looked out of the window for a while and then said softly,
"This is the greatest moment in my life."

This final quote was the most upsetting part of the article for me.
Not simply because it was untrue but because it felt like such a serious
thing for him to lie about—the greatest moment of my life!—for the
sake of achieving a pat, writerly conclusion. I had to wonder whether
there was anything about me he'd leave intact.

THE PANDOLFINI VARIATION

"The 'great game' of chess is primarily psychological,
a conflict between one trained intelligence and another,
and not a mere collection of small mathematical
theorems."
—G. H. HARDY,
A Mathematician's Apology

WHEN I TRAVELED TO NEW YORK CITY FOR WORK AFTER I
left Britannica, I looked up Bruce Pandolfini, a friend of my father's from
the Village who was now famous, as chess players go, for his televised
chess commentary and because Ben Kingsley portrayed him in the 1993
movie *Searching for Bobby Fischer.* Pandolfini was the only person I knew in
the chess world—he was a bridge to my chess past—and I didn't know
him all that well. We hadn't seen each other for a couple of decades. He
and my father had been colleagues at the New School. They met in 1973
when my dad, unbeknownst to me, audited his chess course. My father
had helped him with his writing, and in return Pandolfini, who is eight
years older than I, had given me half a dozen chess lessons.

Many strong chess players struggle just to pay the rent, but Pandolfini has managed to make $250,000 a year from the game. A Fortune 500 company once hired him, at $7,500 an hour, to sit with its top executives and share with them the mind-set of a chess master, in the hope that they could apply it to their corporate strategy. Pandolfini has written two dozen chess books, which have sold more than a million copies. He charges $200 an hour for private lessons in New York City and has started them as late as 1 A.M., even though most of his students are under the age of ten. He teaches not just any kids, but those who already display a gift for the game, and he will drop his fee if the parents of a particularly talented child are not well off. "I want to work with the smartest kids," he told me. "I won't let a smart one get away." After we reestablished contact, I accepted an assignment from *The New Yorker* to write a profile of him.

In December 2000, I joined Pandolfini and his current students at the National Grade School Championship in Orlando. I was curious to see how kiddie chess had changed since my days of playing, in the early 1970s. I knew from watching *Searching for Bobby Fischer* that the atmosphere at scholastic tournaments was now even more intense, with parents prohibited from observing their children's games as my dad had. But *Searching for Bobby Fischer* was a Hollywood movie, so I didn't know how much of it to trust.

As the first round of the championship began, the tournament director ordered the parents out of the playing hall—a hotel ballroom—and the doors were sealed with police caution tape. Inside, 1,442 kids sat at long tables. Over the weekend, they would play six rounds of tournament chess against kids in their own grade—a schedule so tight that no one had time to go to Disney World. The clocks were started, and the room was quiet except for lots of nervous coughing and the occasional sound of a chess piece being aggressively slammed on the board. If a kid needed to go to the bathroom—and some had to go every few minutes—he was allowed to exit through a side door but was told not to speak to his parents, lest one of them blurt out how he could checkmate in two moves. The pushiest parents crowded around the door and, when it opened, craned their necks for a glimpse of their son or daughter (only 10 percent of the players were girls). Did their son's dour expression mean that he was being mated? Or was he frowning so that he wouldn't

give away the trap he was about to spring? Down the hall from the tournament, dozens of rosy-cheeked young girls were competing in a beauty
pageant; their parents were markedly calmer.

PANDOLFINI'S METHOD AT THE ANNUAL SCHOLASTIC TOURNAMENT IS AL-
ways the same. During the rounds, he relaxes in his hotel room because
he, like the parents, is not allowed in the playing hall, and if he appears
outside it, he is accosted by strangers who want to know how to turn
their child into a world champion. But, as the rounds finish, he races from
one student's hotel room to another, rapidly analyzing their games—
finding something the kid did right even in the most one-sided loss—and
psyching the kid up for the next round. His students were among the
tournament veterans.

Adam Weser, a nine-year-old from Long Island and one of Pandolfini's
students, had been a co-champion at the National Elementary Chess
Championship held in Phoenix in May 2000. This time, he was hoping to
be the sole champion out of 199 fourth-graders. His father, Matthew; his
mother, Bonnie; and her parents, Naomi and Seymour, had flown to
Florida from New York with Adam.

In the first round, Adam came from behind to eke out a victory. Afterward, Pandolfini, who had coached Adam for two years, joined the
family in their hotel room to replay the game. Adam is by nature a coun-
terpuncher: he enjoys defending, being pushed to the brink of defeat and
then bouncing back when his opponent has overreached. It is nerve-
racking to watch, and Adam's parents never know whether he is about to
lose or rebound to victory, but his approach reminded Pandolfini of his
own style when he played tournament chess, in the 1960s.

"Adam shouldn't have to live on the edge," Matthew told Pandolfini.

"He has so much talent," Bonnie added. "He should just be able to
crush the other kids."

Pandolfini ignored their remarks as he examined Adam's score sheet and
replayed the moves. "How are you going to survive this?" Pandolfini asked,
shaking his head at the terrible position Adam had got himself into.

"I'm the best! I'm the best!" Adam shouted in response, thrusting his
fist into the air and jumping on one of the beds.

"If you're so good," his father said, "why do you have to play moves like this? You should have moved here." Matthew reached over and demonstrated.

"Great!" Bonnie said. "My husband thinks he's Bobby Fischer. I love my husband. But please, Bruce, put him in his place."

"Adam, you're giving him more material," Pandolfini said. "What's this, Bargain Day at Macy's? How did you get out of this?"

"My opponent touched a piece he didn't mean to move," Adam said, "and I made him move it."

"You've always been good at enforcing the touch-move rule and, for that matter, every other rule," Pandolfini said.

"Then look what happened," Adam said, demonstrating how he had mopped up the opponent's pawns. "I moved my rook here! Look at the move. I love it!"

"You're a human vacuum cleaner," Pandolfini said approvingly. "But, next time, take command from the beginning and you'll play even better."

"He certainly can't play any worse," Matthew said.

Pandolfini looked at his watch again. "The round's about to start," he said. "Go out there, Adam, and take command." He patted Adam on the back.

Adam beat his opponents decisively in the next three rounds; he didn't need much psyching up. Then, in the fifth round, he lost a bruising back-and-forth battle, after his opponent surprised him on the first move with the rare Englund Gambit, an immediate sacrifice of the king pawn. "Adam cried for half an hour and I couldn't console him," Bonnie said. "He kept screaming, 'They're going to take my championship away!'"

During the sixth and final round in Orlando, Adam's parents and grandparents were camped outside the playing hall, praying that he'd forge a comeback and win. Bonnie read a book called *The Panic-Proof Parent*, and Matthew paced like a caged tiger.

"I don't understand why you put Adam through this," Bonnie's mother said. "I wouldn't do this to my children. And look at your husband—he won't stop walking or biting his fingernails."

"If I didn't let Adam play," Bonnie said, "he'd be a lot more upset."

This time, Adam's opponent once again surprised him on the very first move—pushing his queen-knight pawn forward two squares, the unusual Orangutan Opening—but Adam remained calm and built up a winning position. At last, he gamboled out of the hall, his arms raised in victory.

"What's this?" Pandolfini said, reviewing Adam's score sheet. "You had the chutzpah to put four exclamation points after one of your own moves?"

Yes," Adam said. "It's a brilliant move. Besides, writing all the exclamation points shook up my opponent."

He ran off, punching the air. At times like these, he has talked about playing chess until he can beat Bobby Fischer. "I wish I could fly," Adam once wrote in a school assignment, "so that I could play chess with God."

IN 1972, PANDOLFINI BECAME THE FIRST SUCCESSFUL FULL-TIME CHESS teacher in the country after his analysis of the Fischer-Spassky match on public television made him a star. *Searching for Bobby Fischer,* adapted from Fred Waitzkin's acclaimed book about his son Josh, one of Pandolfini's top students, was a further advertisement for Pandolfini and chess itself. The movie has an uplifting ending: Josh wins the big tournament, preserves his own humanity (through the very Hollywood but unrealistic device of offering his chief rival a draw in a position in which Josh knows he can beat him), and leads—like Spassky—a happy, robust, balanced life, squeezing in fishing trips with his dad between tournaments. Adam Weser, for one, was so taken with the movie that he demanded chess lessons with Pandolfini. Ben Kingsley portrayed Pandolfini as a stern, enigmatic taskmaster with an Irish brogue who was scarred by a devastating chess loss years before—a character out of a Beckett play. By the time, just before shooting, Kingsley met the real Pandolfini, who is of Italian-Jewish heritage, the actor had fallen in love with the Irish accent.

The real Pandolfini is neither stern nor aloof, although he did abandon tournament chess three decades ago after playing a game in which he missed a simple win. He has an easygoing warmth to which kids respond. At the end of most lessons, he rewards his students with a Beanie Baby. He is not without his own peculiarities; the parents of his students often have difficulty reaching him, because he doesn't answer his home phone or cell phone, and sometimes he doesn't respond to their messages for days. They do not know if he is married or not, and they have never seen his apartment. All they know is that his regular visit to teach chess is often the high point of their child's week.

Pandolfini did not start playing chess until he was thirteen—unlike most of his students, who have already entered, if not won, scholastic tournaments by that age. In his early childhood, in Borough Park, Brooklyn, he was preoccupied with baseball and basketball. "It was easy to be hooked on baseball after the first game I watched, at Ebbets Field in 1954, when I was six," Pandolfini said. "That day, I saw Willie Mays hit a home run and Jackie Robinson steal a base."

Pandolfini's father, a WPA-era realist painter, played chess socially at clubs and coffeehouses but did not teach his son the game, because he thought it was a deadbeat activity. At one point, his father had managed the Marshall Chess Club, on West Tenth Street in the Village, and seen too many people spend their days and nights slumped over chessboards without becoming good players. Pandolfini took up the game on his own, in 1961, when he stumbled upon the chess books in the stacks of the Brooklyn Public Library.

"I was fascinated by the books, all the little diagrams of chessboards, the cryptic notation in which the games were recorded, and the anecdotes about world chess champions and their challengers," Pandolfini recalled. "I loved the players' names—Efim Bogoljubow, Saviely Tartakower, José Raúl Capablanca." And, like me, Pandolfini loved the names of openings: Anti-Meran, Grob, Semi-Slav Botvinnik Variation. "There was something like thirty chess books in the library," he said. "I wanted to check out one or two, but I couldn't make up my mind, so I took them all out and skipped school for a month to read them."

During the summer of 1962, Pandolfini began taking the subway from Borough Park to the Village, where he played speed chess at the stone tables in Washington Square Park. "I couldn't always get a game, because the people there often wanted to play for a quarter, and twenty-five cents meant a lot to me then," Pandolfini said. In his youth—and mine—the faces at the tables were white and American. Today they are also black and Eastern European—and gambling $20 on a five-minute game is not the only way they make money. The enterprising ones show up at dawn, fend off junkies to stake out a table, and then charge tourists

$3 a game for the privilege of playing them. Many of the hustlers talk incessantly during the game, providing an aggressive, expletive-ridden commentary ("You think you can fuck with my queen?," "Retreat, bitch, or I'll take you," "Bend! Resign now and spare yourself the humiliation!") that is designed to rattle their mark and entertain passersby. Before the filming of *Searching for Bobby Fischer*, Pandolfini took Laurence Fishburne to the park and taught him how to pass as a chess con.

Pandolfini entered his first tournament, at the Marshall, in 1963, just before his fifteenth birthday. The club still has the musty aroma of a men's smoking club, and over the years it has had an A-list clientele. "It wasn't surprising to see famous people at the Marshall," said Pandolfini. "Celebrities have always been drawn to chess. Today it may be rock and film stars—Sting, Madonna, Will Smith—who like the game." In the eighteenth century it was *philosophes* and politicians—Voltaire, Rousseau, Robespierre, Diderot, Benjamin Franklin, Napoleon—playing chess at the Café de la Régence in Paris. In the 1940s scientists gravitated to chess. "I've seen the moves of games played at Los Alamos by Edward Teller, Robert Oppenheimer, Richard Feynman, and Leo Szilard," Pandolfini said. "Einstein's son was also a chess player." In the 1950s and '60s it was artists and photographers who came to the Marshall. "I remember watching a handsome, well-mannered gentleman play," Pandolfini recalled. "It was Marcel Duchamp. Another time Alfred Eisenstadt came in and snapped my picture with a Brownie camera. John Cage hung out at the Marshall." These artists were drawn to chess players, who seemed more mysterious and weirder than themselves and yet were also in search of artistic truth—not on a canvas but on a chessboard.

In that first tournament at the Marshall, which lasted ten weeks, Pandolfini got off to a poor start and lost four games in a row. Then he drew a game and rallied to win his last five—the final one against a nationally ranked expert. His debut earned him an official rating of 1732 from the USCF; that meant that at fifteen he was considered a better player than about 80 percent of all tournament competitors.

Pandolfini's success encouraged him to study the game more diligently. At a used-book store in the Village, he found a two-volume set, in Russian, containing five hundred games played by Mikhail Botvinnik, the sixth world champion and the father of modern Soviet chess. Pandolfini studied the games for a year. Then he resolved to play sixty games from the 1941 Absolute Championship of the Soviet Union in his head, move for move, without sight of the board or pieces. "It was very hard," he said. "But I forced myself to do it. If I lost a position in my mind, which was quite common at first, I started again from the first move. To remember the moves, I would create a storyline that tied all the logic of the game together. I would impart a reason to a player for doing a move without being sure it was the player's actual reason. You need a good memory for blindfold chess. But that's certainly not it alone. I picture the board. I feel things. I feel connecting points. I say a lot of things to myself. I find relationships between the board and the pieces, the way certain squares naturally tie into typical maneuvers. And then it becomes part of you. You develop an intuitive sense of how to handle similar positions and your moves flow naturally."

That experience—mastering blindfold chess as a sixteen-year-old—became the core of his future instructional method. Today he teaches by narrative, forming a story out of every game or position. He rarely lets his students touch the pieces when they analyze. He often goes one step further and gingerly sweeps the pieces from the board, urging his students to form a mental picture of the position and discover its secrets unencumbered by the physical manifestation of the pieces. (In a crude parody of Pandolfini's approach, in the movie an impatient Ben Kingsley knocks the pieces clear across the room and commands young Waitzkin to solve a nettlesome problem in his head.)

Pandolfini was an undergraduate at the Brooklyn campus of Long Island University when the USCF bestowed on him the title of chess master, putting him in the top 1 percent of tournament players. "I remember the game that clinched it," Pandolfini said. "I played the Caro-Kann Defense against Lawrence Day, a Canadian international master. I was on the verge of defeat, but then Day ran out of gas. I was thrilled. I wondered how far I could go. Did I have what it takes to become world champion? I thought I was the only lunatic who wondered about such things, but then I found that all my chess buddies fantasized about being world champion. But we gave up these illusions when we saw Fischer play. He was the real thing."

In 1970, Pandolfini dropped out of graduate school—he was studying chemistry at the University of Arizona—to play in the National Open

Championship in Reno, Nevada. "Needless to say, my parents weren't happy," he said. "My father knew how hard it was to make a living at chess, and my good Jewish mother wanted me to become a doctor or a lawyer. I had ended up studying to be a chemist because chemistry was the only A I got my first semester in college. But my heart wasn't in it."

At the National Open, he reached the last round tied for second place, only half a point behind the leader, grandmaster Larry Evans, a former United States champion and consigliere of Bobby Fischer's. In the final, Pandolfini played Evans on Board One. If he pulled off an upset victory, he would tie for first place. They each had two hours to make their first fifty moves, but the game quickly became so thorny—Pandolfini, in what's now called the Grand Prix Attack, sacrificed his king-bishop pawn to open lines for an early assault on Evans's king—that both players consumed considerable time working through the maze of possibilities. Toward the end, they each had only one minute for twenty moves.[1] Dozens of spectators closed in around them, standing on chairs to get a better view.

"I kept glancing at the clock, watching the seconds tick away," Pandolfini said. "I had a winning game. In fact, I had four different ways to win. I saw this beautiful combination. Just as I reached out to make it, Evans offered me a draw, which wasn't fair, because I was thinking." The rules require that he offer a draw only when it's his turn to move. "I don't think he was trying to bend the rules," Pandolfini said, "but who knows? I think he was just nervous and afraid of losing. Anyway, I declined the offer. But my mind blanked. By accident, I still played one of the four winning moves. But it was the least good of the four." And Pandolfini didn't follow it up correctly: he went for a mate that wasn't there. "I managed by a miracle to pull off a perpetual check"—the continued checking of the king with no mate—Pandolfini said, "and draw the game."[2]

Pandolfini tied with five other people for third place. "My prize was fifty dollars," he said, "and I lost that at the blackjack tables that happened to be in my way as I walked back to my hotel room. 'Why am I doing this?' I asked myself. Here I had dropped out of school, driven hundreds of miles, and poured my heart into the game and gotten so little—neither money nor satisfaction."

Afterward, Pandolfini went to Berkeley to visit a chess-playing buddy from the Marshall and found himself confronted with the same question. "We were playing speed chess at two or three in the morning," Pandolfini said. "I won the first two games, but I didn't deserve to. In other words, he was clearly outplaying me, and I won through cheap tricks and gross blunders on his part. He was getting angrier and angrier. In the third game, he was outplaying me again, and once more he let his advantage slip. I began to feel terrible. Then I lost on time. He looked at me and said, 'Justice triumphs.' And I thought, Justice triumphs? He wasn't just making a statement. He really meant it—that he was the Just and I was the Unjust. It became very philosophical for me. I started to question whether I thought the same. Was I there just to beat him? Is that what it's all about? Blind self-expression? I didn't want to confront my own aggressive impulses. After that I gave up competitive chess."

Also in the back of his mind was the suicide in Central Park of an acquaintance whom he had defeated eight times in tournament play. "I read in the paper that he had hanged himself because he had been drafted into the Vietnam War," Pandolfini told me. "My friends joked that it was because I had beaten him too many times. His death affected me profoundly. Could my life, I wondered, come to nothing in the same way?"[3]

Pandolfini went back to New York and, with no marketable skills, had a series of odd jobs over the next couple of years. He worked at Gimbels as a salesman but was fired for truancy and violating the dress code. He got a job at the post office on the graveyard shift. "I can understand why they shoot each other," he said, "boxing mail at three in the morning."

Pandolfini ended up working at the Strand bookstore. "The Strand was great because I loved books," he said. "But I certainly missed competitive chess, the thrill of coming up with a strong, unexpected move." One day after work in 1972, Pandolfini ran into Shelby Lyman, an old friend and fellow master from the Marshall.

"Guess what?" Lyman said. "We're going to cover the Fischer-Spassky match on PBS—live coverage five hours a day." An Albany studio of New York's Channel 13 would produce the show.

A few days later, Pandolfini got a call from Lyman's producer, Mike Chase, asking if he wanted to appear as a backup chess analyst on the program. Chase couldn't afford to pay Pandolfini or put him up in a hotel, but he offered to reimburse him for his train fare to and from Manhattan.

"I immediately agreed," Pandolfini said. "I don't know what came over me. I had to quit the job I liked at the Strand. It was three hours each way to Albany, and I had to make the trip every other day. I didn't anticipate that the job would turn into anything. I did it because I loved Bobby Fischer."

At the Marshall a decade earlier, Pandolfini had seen the young Fischer rummage through a moldy index-card file of nineteenth-century games—King's Gambits and Evans Gambits, swashbuckling, incautious games for the player with the White pieces. "Fischer resurrected these very gambits to win the 1963–1964 United States Championship," Pandolfini said. "I was a wall boy there, at the Henry Hudson Hotel, moving the pieces on giant demonstration boards so that chess fans in the back of the playing hall could follow the games. Now I wanted to be a part of history and watch him topple the Soviet champion."

By 1972, Fischer's playing style had matured. He had put the sketchy nineteenth-century gambits back in the file box. His games were now the work of someone who strove to be in complete control. He won an unprecedented twenty consecutive games against the world's elite. "While Fischer has always been an extremely *aggressive* player, all-out for the win," Timothy Hanke wrote in *American Chess Journal*,

> his style is classical in the sense that he strives for clarity in the position. He will not usually take tactical risks, preferring to play rationally and coldbloodedly; his games are not known for irrational or speculative Tal-like eruptions. It can be illuminating to read Tal's notes to Fischer's games, in which Tal mentions various tactical avenues that Fischer might have taken but avoided in the interest of clarity and simplicity.

Outwardly Fischer was a gentleman at the chessboard, but his extraordinary inner drive enervated his opponents. Boris Spassky felt bombarded by a psychic force field at Siegen 1970, in the last game that they played before their world-title bout:

> We were in the fifth hour. He was lost, ruined, not a chance! I knew it, he knew it. But he sat there—almost an hour!—calculating, calculating, calculating! Inside, he was screaming. He was pale, like a dead man, but this force was going through him like millions of volts. I could feel

it smashing and smashing at me across the board. Well, it had an effect, I can tell you that. Five or ten minutes—all right. But an hour! In the end, *I* was the one screaming inside. When you play Bobby, it is not a question if you win or lose. It is a question if you survive.

Fischer's adversaries knew that he derived unwholesome pleasure from ravishing them. "I like to see 'em squirm," he famously said. When Fischer was alone in a hotel room, psyching himself up for a tournament game, people in the hall would hear him shout comic-book words—*Slam! Bam! Zowie!*—as he banged pieces down on the board.

The 1972 World Championship was a classic Cold War battle. Fischer, who was twenty-nine, threatened to pull out, because he didn't like the playing conditions, and Henry Kissinger urged him to stay and fight on behalf of his country. The accompanying television show was a huge success, setting a record for PBS and attracting millions of viewers who did not know how to play chess. Pandolfini's role in the coverage was minimal—Lyman did most of the talking—but he stood out because he had a shaggy, reddish blond, shoulder-length Afro. "I was a real hippie at a time when that was starting not to be so cool anymore," Pandolfini said. "I wanted to cut my hair and look good, but the producer wouldn't let me. He said it was distinctive."

That summer, chess players became celebrities. "People would pull me over on the sidewalk and ask whether it was better to open with the king pawn or the queen pawn," Pandolfini said. "Once, I was walking on Sixth Avenue and a stretch limo pulled up. Out jumped a gorgeous woman shouting, 'Bruce Pandolfini. Bruce Pandolfini! Oh, wow!' Shelby Lyman and I were in a restaurant in Manhattan, and Dustin Hoffman came up and said, 'Shelby, how are you?' 'Fine,' Shelby replied. 'Do I know you?' Now that I had been on national television, even my father was secretly proud that I had taken up chess."

In the middle of the Fischer-Spassky match, Lyman told Pandolfini that he no longer had the time to coach some of his private students. "I want you to take over the lessons," he said.

"But I'm not a chess teacher," Pandolfini told him.

"Don't worry. You'll be great. It's nothing. Just be yourself," said Lyman.

Pandolfini gave it a shot. After a couple lessons he found that he and the student enjoyed it, and he asked Lyman what he should charge. "Fifteen dollars an hour," said Lyman, "three bucks more than I'm charging."

" 'How can I charge more than Lyman?' I asked myself," said Pandolfini. "Well, the fellow ended up cheerfully paying me fifteen dollars." One day during the match, Channel 13 told Pandolfini that three hundred people had called requesting chess lessons. He gave fifteen of them lessons and passed the other names to fellow indigent masters. "That's how many chess teachers in New York got started," said Pandolfini. The Marshall was also getting calls from people caught up in Fischer mania who just had to know the truth of the Poisoned Pawn Sicilian, and Pandolfini received their names, too.

Besides these private students, Pandolfini took on requests to give group lessons to the blind, the deaf, and the handicapped. "I even taught people who couldn't leave their homes," he said. "For a Jewish Community Center on Long Island I developed a program where I taught eight to ten shut-ins at a time over the phone. It was kind of like a talk radio show."

He also taught a weekly course at the Manhattan House of Detention. "We met in the library," Pandolfini recalled. "There were mass murderers in the class. One day there was a riot, and the guards sealed the building, trapping me in the library with twelve people, any one of whom could have killed me in a second. I was afraid that someone would say, 'Let's take the chess guy hostage.' I continued the class as if nothing had happened, and they all sat there in rapt attention." In 1973, he taught the first chess course in the country for college credit—the class my father took—at the New School.

Three months after Pandolfini gave his first private lesson, he was charging as much as $135 an hour. "When people in the chess world found out what I charged," said Pandolfini, "they couldn't believe it. 'Who the hell is he? He can't play chess anymore, so he teaches.' Well I didn't try to justify the rates. I knew I could teach well." Most chess books were hard to follow because they were written by chess masters who never bothered to teach anyone. Many strong players are poor instructors because they don't realize how little chess their students know—they talk over their heads. Or else they have such combative personalities that it is not within them to be nurturing and they end up competing with their students.

As more and more children learned the rules of chess, having caught the bug from their Fischer-enthralled older brothers and parents, Pandolfini took them on, dropping his older students. "I felt I could do more with them," Pandolfini said. "I was starting with tabula rasa, so to speak. I didn't have to push them hard at first. Their memories were good, and they were learning by leaps and bounds." In the 1970s, parents were willing to give their kids chess lessons because of the beauty of the game, with no expectation of Pandolfini pushing them to win this or that tournament. "My, has that changed," Pandolfini said. "You've heard of stage mothers? They're wallflowers compared to chess parents who think their kid is the next Bobby Fischer."

ONE FRIDAY IN NEW YORK JUST BEFORE CHRISTMAS IN 2000, I WATCHED PANdolfini give lessons to two of his students. I met him first at the East Village apartment he has had since 1976—"my inner sanctum," he calls it—a ten-foot-by-ten-foot room with an attached kitchenette and a small bathroom and closet. The kitchen is unusable, the stove and refrigerator blocked by a three-foot-high mound of running shoes, baseball cards, philosophy books, chess manuals, and posters from *Searching for Bobby Fischer*. The main room is a nest of papers, books, and stacks of video- and audiotapes—lectures on everything from the theory of general relativity to the origins of Romantic poetry—that reach three-quarters of the way to the ceiling. During the day, Pandolfini keeps his mattress in the closet so that there is room to move around. The answers to most questions you could ask about chess history are somewhere in his piles. This time he was rooting through the mess trying to find a 1964 chess magazine with a cover photo of George C. Scott playing chess with Stanley Kubrick on the set of *Dr. Strangelove*.

"I gave a copy of the photo to Mrs. George C. Scott," Pandolfini said. "She now wants another copy to give to Tom Cruise. He wants it because he has fond memories of playing chess with Kubrick on the set of *Eyes Wide Shut*. Kubrick was good, but Bogart was probably Hollywood's best player." Although Pandolfini couldn't find the photo, he unearthed a Spanish comic book about love slaves, which Bobby Fischer had translated into

English. As we examined Fischer's childlike writing, Pandolfini realized that he was forty-five minutes late for his first lesson. It is not unusual for him to miss appointments. Once, he failed to show up for a birthday party his friends threw for him at the Marshall. He always goes to a student's home to give lessons; it is less inconvenient for the student when he runs late.

Fabiano Caruana, the top-ranked player in the country under the age of eleven, was happy to see Pandolfini when we reached his parents' Park Slope apartment. Fabiano folded up his scooter and plopped himself down at a chess table in the front room. He was small for his years—he was eight—and had curly brown hair and bright, alert eyes. Pandolfini was eager to show Fabiano some new rook and pawn endings, but Fabiano insisted on playing a game. Pandolfini chose a cramped formation called the French Defense, a favorite of Botvinnik's. Fabiano, a tenacious attacker, couldn't sit still while he played. He stood up or slung both legs up on the table, and stared off into space while Pandolfini was thinking. When Pandolfini moved, he responded instantly with a move of his own.

"The little machine is eating me alive," Pandolfini said, "but that pawn move can't be right. It weakens the dark squares."

"No, it doesn't," Fabiano said.

"Of course it does," Pandolfini said.

"No, it doesn't," Fabiano repeated.

"Fabiano's greatest strength," Pandolfini told me later, after Fabiano had lost the game, "is that he has the courage of his convictions. He is stubborn and sticks to his ideas, come hell or high water. That serves him well in tournament play—you need to believe in yourself—but it makes him harder to teach. When he has a misguided idea, it's not easy to talk him out of it."

CHESS IS A PURSUIT, LIKE MUSIC OR MATHEMATICS, IN WHICH NATURAL TALENT is essential but must be cultivated. No one is born knowing how to checkmate a lone king with just a bishop and a knight, or when the exchange can be sacrificed advantageously in the Dragon. These are the kinds of skills Pandolfini teaches, customizing problems so that they stretch the student's ability and imagination but aren't so difficult that the kid gives up in frustration. He also reviews the student's recent tournament games, asking him why he made each move and what he would have done had his opponents responded with different, stronger moves. Pandolfini is out to correct errors in thinking, positions in which the student is convinced that he has pulled off a clever maneuver but has succeeded only because both he and his opponent missed the refutation.

In New York, it's easy to find a financially strapped chess master willing to give chess lessons, but finding one who likes to teach very young children—and has Pandolfini's talent for it—is another matter. Most parents are relieved that Pandolfini is not bent on creating a chess champion. "Before Bruce, we had the type-A spouse of a grandmaster," the mother of one of his third-grade students told me. "Then the brooding grandmaster himself. They were obsessed with the idea of making a prodigy."

Pandolfini's second lesson of the day was nearby, in Windsor Terrace, at the home of Giancarlo Roma. A fourth-grader, Giancarlo was more respectful of Pandolfini than Fabiano was, though his playing style was no less aggressive. They did a "postmortem"—chess lingo for postgame analysis—of a game that Giancarlo had recently played on the Internet. He had used the Traxler Counterattack in the Two Knights Defense, a highly tactical variation in which both sides were walking a fine line between victory and defeat. "You can get away with taking his pawns," Pandolfini said. "Pig out if you wish. There's nothing wrong with a little piggetry."

"When Bruce comes, we put out wine and cheese and then leave the two of them alone," Giancarlo's father, Tom, told me. "But I once sat at the top of the stairs and listened to the whole lesson. I find extreme beauty in the way Bruce describes chess moves, in the way he creates a story out of each game. I'm a photographer, and I teach photography, and I've always told my students that chess is one of the highest art forms. In our culture, which promotes a short attention span and instant gratification, there's something delightfully old-fashioned about chess. There's also something frighteningly narcotic about it." Giancarlo's father hopes that chess will always have a place in his son's life—"maybe he'll be the best chess-playing shortstop on the Yankees"—but he doesn't want chess to overwhelm his life. "There's always that danger," he told me. "Fischer cheated himself by taking the game too seriously. He robbed himself of his own humanity by despising the very existence of his opponents. There was a period in my own life, when I worked on Wall Street before I became a photographer, when I drank a lot and stayed up late playing through the chess games of old masters. I read Nabokov's chess novel then, and it certainly was a cautionary tale."

ONE AFTERNOON IN 2001, PANDOLFINI CANCELED HIS CHESS LESSONS AND joined me for a screening of *The Luzhin Defense*. In a Hollywood ending to an otherwise dark and arty movie, Luzhin's fiancée, who does not play chess, discovers his notes on how to dispose of Turati and takes his place at the board to make the stunning and decisive rook move. On the scale of cinematic incredulity, it is as if Rocky's girlfriend hopped into the ring and delivered the knockout blow.

It is understandable that it took seven decades to turn Nabokov's novel into a movie: there is little action, other than the self-defenestration, as much of the story takes place in Luzhin's head as he goes mad. The irony is that movies figure heavily in the novel, the first talking pictures having appeared at the time Nabokov wrote it. Despite the efforts of Luzhin's fiancée to keep his mind off chess after his breakdown, they happen to watch a film that includes a chess game, with the pieces set up in a way that, Luzhin amusingly declares, could not actually occur in a real game. And Valentinov doesn't exactly kidnap Luzhin in the book. He says he is making a movie that includes a chess game and for verisimilitude wants Luzhin to appear in the film. The movie set is a ploy to get Luzhin to sit down again opposite Turati and finish the game.

As the credits rolled, Pandolfini joked that he suspected he would not get any new students from the film, as he had from *Searching for Bobby Fischer*. "Let's face it," Pandolfini said, "there are more unbalanced people in chess than in your average profession or activity, although perhaps no more than in other arts. But that's because the chess community is wonderfully accepting—everyone is welcome to play and you don't need any social skills to succeed." And, indeed, everyone is welcome. Chess may be the only sport or game in which a talented nine-year-old can face a seventy-five-year-old master and it's not clear who'll win. "The game is a great equalizer," said Pandolfini. "Go to Washington Square Park and you'll see Wall Street brokers playing kids from Harlem."

Because chess culture has turned a blind eye to how chess players dress or speak (or whether they can speak at all), chess culture is a haven for social misfits. For those who are inclined to escape from the rest of the world, chess offers its own rich world. Devoted competitors replay games from top tournaments, and these are virtually inexhaustible: a single CD-ROM called *Mega Database 2007* contains more than 3.5 million games played between 1560 and 2006, with more recent games available on a weekly basis from the Web site The Week in Chess. Chess clubs on the Internet allow anyone, even in the most remote location, to find a strong opponent at any hour. One night, for instance, I played blitz chess online with a lonely biologist at a research station in Antarctica; instant-messaging software allowed us to review the game afterward and chat about penguins.

"People whose sense of self derives from how they do at chess, because they have so little else going on in their lives, are the ones who are likely to crack up from the pressure of tournament play," Pandolfini said. "Fischer was a case in point."[4]

Fischer was once asked in a television interview what his interests were besides chess. "What else is there?" he innocently replied. And yet Fischer dropped out of chess and the public eye after beating Spassky in 1972. He joined a fundamentalist religious sect in California, became a zealous anti-Semite, and had various run-ins with the law. The chess world waited for him to return, or at least to publish his favorite games, but all they got was a candy-cane-colored booklet called *I Was Tortured in the Pasadena Jailhouse,* an incoherent diatribe about his brief incarceration after being mistakenly arrested for a bank robbery. In 1992, Fischer was back in the spotlight, earning $3 million for a rematch against Spassky in Yugoslavia, in violation of the State Department's ban on Americans conducting commerce there. The games showed little of his earlier brilliance.[5] Fat and slovenly, Fischer himself was also unrecognizable. Once a Cold War hero, he now uttered a bunch of obscenities and spat on a letter from the State Department that protested his play. Again he vanished, only to emerge occasionally as a call-in guest on talk radio venting about Jews.[6] He lived as a fugitive in Yugoslavia, the Philippines, and Japan.[7]

In July 2004, Fischer was arrested by Japanese immigration agents in Tokyo's Narita Airport on the grounds of being illegally in the country with a revoked U.S. passport. Washington pressed for his extradition, but Fischer was one move ahead of the American authorities and persuaded the Icelandic parliament, which fondly remembered the attention he brought to Reykjavík in 1972, to grant him Icelandic citizenship and a passport. After nine months in a Japanese detention center, Fischer boarded a plane to Reykjavík with his new fiancée, the head of the Japanese Chess Association, and went into hiding yet again.

WHETHER CHESS IS A PRECURSOR TO PSYCHOSIS IS NOT SOMETHING THAT the parents of Pandolfini's students want to think about. They are caught up in the more immediate issue of helping their kids adjust to defeat and victory. Today there are thousands of children around the country who play in scholastic chess tournaments, far more than there were in my youth and Pandolfini's. "You see the same kids and their parents at tournament after tournament," Fabiano's father told me. "Chess gives you a big extended family."

"Some parents used to discourage their kids' interest," said Pandolfini, "but not because they saw chess as a hotbed of insanity. In my day, in the 1960s, the game was disparaged as a shady activity, something that street hustlers did. It wasn't taught in any school then. Maybe just a few hundred kids played tournament chess, and many of them were, well, strange." Chess is now mainstream. None of his current students, he said, "want to live in a house shaped like a rook." They want to play baseball and hockey, go to summer camp, and practice the piano.

To succeed at tournament chess, you need to be aggressive. "The only goal in chess is to prove your superiority over the other guy," Kasparov once said. "The most important superiority is the superiority of the mind. I mean, your opponent must be destroyed. Fully destroyed." For Pandolfini's students to make it to the highest echelons of chess, they must have the determination to win at any cost—and they must be able to tolerate this unbridled ambition in themselves without being destroyed by it in their opponents. Pandolfini had that determination, but he could not reconcile it with his image of himself.

"Chess is war," Pandolfini said. "And it is also very hard work. You have to master on the order of one hundred thousand different chess ideas and concepts, patterns of pawns and pieces. You're going to lose a lot of games in the process, so you'll have to be able to make your peace with that, which isn't easy. Kids have as much trouble as adults facing the fact that they've lost because their opponents outwitted them.[8]

"Ninety percent of my students give up tournament chess when they get into junior high school," Pandolfini continued, "and the main reason is that they can't stand losing. There are other reasons, too, like they discover girls. But they'll miss competitive chess. I still sometimes wonder whether my quitting was the right decision. I definitely miss the rush from wiping out an opponent. I wish I didn't have the bloodlust deep within me."

THROUGHOUT MY CHILDHOOD, I STRUGGLED BETWEEN WANTING TO BE unique and wanting to blend in with the crowd. Even in grade school, I felt different from the kids around me. In fact, my family and I *were* different, starting with our physical surroundings. My friends' homes were white, freshly painted, and ringed by well-manicured lawns. Our house was pale lime, the paint flaked, and we had no grass worth mowing. We lived in the woods on the edge of a steep ravine at the end of a dead-end road. If the Addams Family had lived in a cottage, it might have looked like this. The roof leaked, fungus spouted from the floorboards, and squirrels ransacked the attic.

Our house was completely cluttered, overrun by my dad's reams of paper and my mother's collection of found objects. A gigantic egg-shaped L'eggs panty-hose display, which she rescued from the trash bin of a local pharmacy, had a prominent place in our living room for years while she pondered what to do with it. Visitors mistook it for an avant-garde lamp and fumbled to find the switch. My mother also salvaged twelve-foot cardboard tubes from the garbage of a fabric store. The tubes lay in our downstairs hall for half a decade, with guests tripping on them, before they, too, defeated her and she had me strap them on the station wagon and haul them to the town dump. A large enclosed porch was too crowded to sit in; it housed her button and seedpod collection, which numbered in the thousands and served as the raw material for necklaces and bracelets that she intended to make. I could never decide whether all the clutter was a sign of life compared to my friends' comparatively empty and sterile homes, with their armchairs wrapped in stain-resistant plastic, or whether the disorder was a complete embarrassment.

Our religion, or rather our lack of it, also distinguished us from other families. We were atheists—there is no religion recorded on my birth certificate—and this did not sit well in elementary school. During the pledge of allegiance in first or second grade, the teacher noticed that I quietly skipped the words "under God." She ordered me to say them. When I didn't comply, she banished me daily to the hall during the pledge. The teacher stopped punishing me only after my father visited the principal and threatened to involve the ACLU and sue the school. Still, many kids refused to sit with "the atheist" in the lunchroom. Initially, I was reserved about my beliefs and was ostracized for them, but as I got older, I fought back by telling everyone how foolish they were to believe in a God who did not exist.

By junior high school, I stopped saying the pledge of allegiance altogether because I had become a self-proclaimed World Federalist who believed that countries should do away with national borders. But I wasn't a little Ted Kaczynski. I had close friends, and my outré politics did not stop me from being elected class president. I like to think that my schoolmates were responding to my self-deprecating humor, my intelligence, maybe even my courage in holding unpopular beliefs; they were also seduced by my fanciful campaign platform about students wresting more control of the school from the administrators.

School sports were where I suffered most as an outsider. I was gawky and uncoordinated. When teams were picked in gym class, it was a toss-up whether I or a hapless fat kid would be the last one chosen. Then I'd be assigned to some inconsequential position—in softball, I'd back up the right-fielder—where I'd see little or no action. If I dropped the ball or otherwise muffed a play, our gym teacher would punish me by yanking me from the game and making me run laps or do push-ups, and then he'd ridicule me because my push-up form was horrible. When, with his tacit encouragement, one lug in the class roughed me up, my response was to skip class. I didn't tell my parents about the sadistic teacher because I was ashamed.

My father never came right out and said that he wanted me to play sports. Nor was he, at three hundred pounds, exactly running around with me in the backyard tossing a football. Nevertheless, he liked to tell me stories about his college triumphs as a boxer and a tennis player. He said that when he attended the University of Wisconsin at Madison, he was the heavyweight champion in his college division. On the tennis court, he said, he held his own against Pancho Gonzales, in the days before the self-trained legend became the best player in the world. These stories only made me feel more inadequate.

I made the best of my differences, but it was exhausting: I longed for once to be part of a team or a clique. When I entered Staples High School, a sport was obviously out of the question; I fantasized instead about being in a rock band, but I wasn't musically talented. I was even envious of a small marauding gang of juvenile delinquents in my otherwise tony high school who flunked their classes, walked around with cigarette packs stuffed between their T-shirts and their biceps, and patrolled the town in old cars with souped-up engines and no mufflers. And so, in tenth grade, I signed up for the chess team, naively hoping that it would bring some camaraderie into my life.

Unfortunately, chess wasn't much of a team sport—even though, at the scholastic, national, and international levels, there were occasional events billed as team competitions. Staples had four students who signed up for the chess team. Our faculty adviser, an AP chemistry teacher named Mr. Lawrence, would find another high school that had a chess foursome. As our best player, I would square off against their top guy, our second-best would play their second-best, and so on. But my teammates and I couldn't consult one another during the games, and so it was still essentially an individual competition. I was also stronger than my teammates, and so I didn't play training games with them in anticipation of our matches. It wasn't even an organized chess league. We played maybe two or three times a year. We had no spectators, no cheerleaders, and no groupies. When we won, we weren't rewarded with a ticker-tape parade or even a warm hand-shake from the school principal. In fact, nobody at school except the four of us and Mr. Lawrence even knew that we had played.

I nearly always beat the other kids in these matches. When we played home games, in Mr. Lawrence's classroom, I tried to defeat my opponents quickly so that I'd have more time to peruse his mail-order catalogues for chemistry equipment. This was in the days before Victoria's Secret. His Bunsen burner catalogues were nearly as hot. Braless women in unbuttoned white lab coats were shown holding Erlenmeyer flasks and demonstrating sterile pipettes.

CHESS WAS FAILING ME IN DIFFERENT WAYS IN CONNECTICUT AND NEW York. In Westport the chess was easy and boring, and my steak-and-potato teammates were largely uninteresting. The Manhattan chess scene was stimulating and challenging, but the tournaments themselves were very stressful. During the nights between tournament games I did not sleep well. I dreamed about chess—and the chain of mental events was often the same. First I'd see a chessboard, the pieces perfectly centered on their original squares. Then I'd concentrate at length on this familiar, initial setup, trying to make sense of the beauty—and the horror—of the game that mesmerized me. When I was finished pondering the initial position, I'd see the chessmen slide gracefully across the board as they repeated, move for move, part of a game from out of my past or from the annals of chess history—often a fragment of a game I didn't realize I had committed to memory. (The odd thing was that when I was awake I had difficulty playing chess in my head.) The first game would be followed by another, then another, and so on through the night.[9]

Mental chess has been depicted in literature as putting an intolerable strain on the mind. (And not just in literature: the Soviet Union banned blindfold chess exhibitions in 1930 on the grounds that they were a health hazard.) Dr. B, the protagonist of Stefan Zweig's 1942 novella, *Chess Story*, is held by the Gestapo in deprived, solitary confinement. He is able initially to maintain his sanity by playing chess with himself in his head. But ultimately Dr. B has a schizophrenic breakdown because the part of his mind that is playing White is bent on annihilating the part that is playing Black.

Of course I fared better than Dr. B, even if the mental chess made me woozy. The pace of the games in my head gradually picked up throughout the night, reaching a manic crescendo at daybreak. When it was time for me to get out of bed, I was not in a good condition to play an actual game. I never fell asleep at the board—I was too keyed up—but I had to find strong moves while battling a headache and feeling lousy. It wasn't fun.

Even though my game continued to improve, the rate of improvement had slowed, and I was not satisfied with my play. Most of my games seemed marred by the absence of a coherent plan or even outright blunders. The games that ran through my head seemed purer. I enjoyed playing chess with myself. On each move, I took a fresh look at the board and followed what seemed to be the objectively correct plan. My judgment seemed better than in tournament play, when the endorphin rush or mental demons interfered with my appraisal of the position. The self-imposed pressure to win can be so intense that it forces the intellectual faculties to a standstill, like the effect of car headlights on a deer.

I shouldn't have been so hard on myself. I already knew enough about chess to realize that even the world's best players made mistakes. The twenty-one-game match between Fischer and Spassky was heralded as the "match of the century," but it was full of blunders. In a lifeless position in the very first game, Fischer made one of his worst mistakes ever. On the twenty-ninth move, he greedily snatched a flank pawn with his dark-squared bishop, but the pawn proved to be toxic. Fischer thought that he could extricate the bishop if Spassky tried to ensnare it by hemming it in with adjacent pawns. He had miscalculated, however, and Spassky subsequently trapped the cleric. But my awareness of the fallibility of the top masters didn't make me any more tolerant of my own lapses. Instead, it made me feel that something was rotten at the core of the game.

Chess also became increasingly solipsistic for me. Although it challenged my intellect in a way that nothing else had, it did not help me feel part of a group. Certainly the Staples chess team was no substitute for the basketball team, and even at the tournaments themselves, with dozens of people crammed into the playing hall, I still felt lonely. And while in principle I liked that the larger chess world was not judgmental about the misfits who flocked to it, I felt too ordinary to count myself one of them, either. I suspected that the kids I met in the 1970s in Manhattan tournaments really *did* want to live in rook houses. I simply wanted to live in a house where the paint didn't peel. In Connecticut I was too different to be normal, and in New York I was too normal to be different.

During my junior year at Staples, I defected from chess to tournament bridge. I learned the card game from a book along with my friend Josh, who was so good at mathematics that while in high school he was receiving private instruction in number theory from a Yale graduate student. I was good at math, too—although not that good—and bridge involved the quick computation of odds. Bridge wasn't nearly as stressful as chess—it didn't take as much work or preparation, and I didn't dream about the hands I played. For me what distinguished bridge the most from chess was that it was an intimate partnership game. It was like doubles in tennis or ballroom dancing: you had to coordinate your moves. There were also true team competitions in bridge. Josh and I taught the game to two of our friends, Richard and Victor, and the four of us spent part of the summer traveling to regional tournaments. We had a blast competing as a team and reviewing the hands afterward—and we stayed up late playing cards among ourselves.

We had no money to pay for a room in the hotels where the tournaments were held, so we improvised. At a competition at Grossinger's, a well-known Borscht Belt resort in the Catskills, we simply slept on the floor in a new wing that was under construction and we were awakened the next morning by bewildered workmen. In another hotel we slept in the playing hall itself, under four rectangular, cafeteria-style tables that had been used for tournament registration. We simply pushed the tables flush to the wall and, for an element of privacy, realigned the tablecloths so that they extended all the way to the floor. The night watchmen did not detect us when they shined their flashlights around the room. Once we got some rest on the pews in an unlocked church—after getting into the sacramental wafers and dressing up in purple robes. In bridge I finally found some camaraderie: my teammates were smart and fun and didn't want to live in a house adorned with the ace of spades. Our group dissolved only when we all went off to different colleges.

FISCHER'S MISANTHROPIC GHOST STILL HAUNTS CHESS, BUT NOW, AFTER THE turn of the twenty-first century, the game has an improved image thanks in part to the rock-star status of Garry Kasparov, world champion from 1985 to November 2000. Kasparov has worked tirelessly to establish scholastic chess programs in dozens of countries. He is an urbane, well-spoken millionaire who retired from tournament play in March 2005 to plunge into Russian politics as the front man for Free 2008, an organization that was intent on blocking Vladimir Putin from amending the Russian constitution so that he can seek a third term in 2008. (Kasparov subsequently founded United Civil Front, a social movement dedicated to stopping Russia from returning to totalitarianism.) Kasparov is to chess what Tiger Woods is to golf, Wayne Gretzky is to hockey, and Michael Jordan is to basketball—except that he dominated chess longer than these men ruled their respective sports. For a fifth of a century he was the number one rated chess player in the world. He is so well known that Pepsi once made him the focus of a Super Bowl commercial, in which an elevator and a vacuum cleaner attacked him after he defeated one of their mechanical confederates, a computer, at chess. Pandolfini's students think Garry Kasparov is a god. "Unlike Fischer or Morphy, Kasparov does not behave like he is on leave from an asylum," Pandolfini told me.

And yet even Kasparov isn't entirely able to abide by social conventions. Like Fischer, he can barely conceal the contempt he feels for his opponents. I once watched him play thirty-four games simultaneously against teams of school children in Manhattan's Puck Building. It took him just two hours to defeat all of these beginners. And yet even though his opponents were only a fifth to a third his age, the world's highest-rated player could not restrain himself from his fabled glowers and glares. In one game, he was impatient when two eight-year-olds who were collaborating did not resign in a hopeless position. He rolled his eyes and shook his head whenever he reached their board. Finally, as he marched two pawns deep into his adversaries' home territory where he could soon promote the foot soldiers into queens, he growled, "How many queens do you think I need in order to win?"

I first met Kasparov through Pandolfini in November 2000, when Bruce was the master of ceremonies at a Manhattan charity event in which the Russian played twenty-one games simultaneously against amateurs. Kasparov had been dethroned as world champion two weeks earlier by his protégé Vladimir Kramnik, and this was the first time he had played in public since. Kasparov grimaced and grumbled when a boy offered him a draw in a position in which the boy stood much worse. Pandolfini tactfully warned the crowd that if any draw offers were to be made, the champion would make them.

After nearly two hours, Kasparov had disposed of everyone except Nelson Farber, an attorney in his late thirties. Farber had managed to frustrate Kasparov's efforts to pull off one of his trademark flashy attacks. At one point, the Russian stared, squinting, at the ceiling for several minutes, shaking his head disapprovingly. Farber sat there stoically, only to subsequently blunder in a position that looked dead even; when he finally acknowledged defeat, Kasparov broke into a wide grin and pumped his hand.

Pandolfini and I went to dinner with Kasparov afterward, and I asked him whether Farber could have drawn the game if he hadn't made the error. "Of course," Kasparov replied, as if I had asked the world's dumbest question. "For a moment before he blundered, I thought of offering him a draw. But I didn't like the way he looked. He was too smug and self-confident. I wanted to crush him."

Later, I contacted Farber and told him that Kasparov hadn't offered him a draw because he looked too confident. "Confident?" Farber said. "That's ridiculous. I was scared shitless. It was a Walter Mitty moment with everyone crowded around the board and Kasparov staring off into space for ages. I thought etiquette required me to move instantly, but here he was taking a lot of time. There was a moment when we exchanged smiles. My smile was 'I'm happy to be here, amazed I lasted this long.' His smile was 'I'm going to kill you.'"

KASPAROV'S AGGRESSION EXTENDS WELL BEYOND THE CHESSBOARD. HIS APproach to casual conversation is as vigorous as his chess. When he learned early in our first dinner that I had run Encyclopaedia Britannica, he tried to seize the initiative by displaying his knowledge of U.S. history.

Even though we were now ostensibly on my terrain—he was playing Black, as it were—he stumped me with a series of obscure questions, on Civil War battles, I think. When he told me the answers, his bemused grin said, "Ha, I'm a Russian and I know more about the Civil War than the American-born president of the most prestigious encyclopedia!" Kasparov was unrelenting with the trivia interrogation, and finally, to silence him, I joked that I had only read volume A. I encouraged him to ask me anything about Angola, aardvarks, or *Antigone*. He laughed, and I changed the subject to Russian politics, a topic he could not expect me to know much about.

By the end of the meal I was sick to my stomach, and when I got back to my hotel room and took off my shirt, I saw that my chest was a topographic map of welts and hives. This was my first outbreak of idiopathic angioedema in the half year since I had left Chicago. I had been so involved in talking to the chess god, even as he tried to upstage me, that I'd ignored the warning signs. My chest and legs had started itching at dinner, but I'd tried to suppress the urge to scratch them by concentrating on what Kasparov was saying. Two hours later, however, I was checking myself into an emergency room—a crazy end to a crazy evening.

After the ER docs stabilized the swelling, they questioned me about what I had eaten for dinner. I couldn't think of anything unusual. I now wonder if it was possible that my allergic reaction was exacerbated by my emotional state. I had intense, conflicting feelings about the evening. I was thrilled, of course, to meet Kasparov—he was smart and engaging on subjects far afield from chess—but I was also unnerved by his insane competitiveness, directed first at Farber and then at me.

Our dinner stirred up all sorts of issues. I have never gotten along with alpha males and am unsure about the line between acceptable competitiveness and nasty aggression. I had difficulty in gym class not just because I was inept but because sports seemed too brutal to me. When is the urge to win not just about performing optimally and more about breaking your adversary, physically or psychically? Assuming your opponent is not a jerk, is it immoral to want to destroy him? To me this kind of attitude, which is common in chess, detracts from the nobility of the game. Chess is said to be a safe way to sublimate aggressive impulses. But is it harmless just because the aggression isn't physical? The idea of "healthy competition" may be a myth when it comes to chess. Can you really play a friend, go for each other's jugular, and be buddies afterward?

I have watched thoughtful chess players wrestle at different levels with these issues. Pascal Charbonneau avoids playing chess with his girlfriend, who is an international master. Nor will he play a game with me, although he'll happily help me for hours with my own chess (although I must wonder if he is actually conflicted about the reverse possibility— that he'd derive unwholesome pleasure from trouncing me). Nigel Short has eliminated the possibility of playing chess with his wife by humiliating her the first time she asked him. He insisted on doing it blindfolded with just fifteen minutes on the clock while she could take all the time in the world while looking at the board.

As for my own attitude toward competition, I can play card and board games with people I love, but I can't do it casually. I like to go all out in games. So if I think people I care about are going to misinterpret my determination as aggression, I won't play. Ann has tried to interest me in Scrabble, but I've turned her down because I don't want to risk upsetting her. She probably has a better vocabulary than I, but I'm convinced I'd consistently beat her because I'm a better strategist. I also have the infuriating habit of appearing as though I don't give a damn. So she might be deflated to lose to someone who doesn't seem to be trying.

My health took a scary turn after my night in the hospital. An allergist in Woodstock ran some tests for obscure disorders and one came back positive for a rare form of neuroendocrine cancer. He tried to calm me by explaining that the result might be wrong, because the test was so strongly positive that my symptoms should be even worse. I reminded myself, though, that my symptoms were disturbing enough for him to test for the cancer in the first place. It was a hellish two weeks while I waited for the result of a retest and occupied myself reading horrific accounts on the Internet of people who had died from the disease. I also read that people undergoing the test should avoid Tylenol, tomatoes, and avocados in the preceding days. As it happened, I had consumed all three the first time around. This time the result was negative. We repeated it a third time for safe measure: I wasn't going to die.

My allergist reviewed what we knew about my strange condition. We knew I was highly allergic not just to aspirin but to the whole related class of drugs known as nonsteroidal anti-inflammatories, and we also knew that the facial swelling and hives occurred, too, when I wasn't taking any of these drugs. Now the chemical basis of aspirin is salicylic acid, an old natural remedy found in the bark of willow trees and other plants. Hippocrates, the father of modern medicine, recommended willow-bark tea to ease the pain of childbirth, and Native Americans used it to treat muscle aches and fever. My doctor consulted the medical literature and found that a tiny fraction of people who were allergic to aspirin also had adverse reactions to fruits and nuts that were high in salicylates. Because this extreme kind of allergy was rare, the literature was rather old and unreliable on the precise salicylate levels in various foods, and so I eliminated most of the suspect ones from my diet. I cut out almonds, apples, oranges, and strawberries. Thankfully, the episodes of idiopathic angioedema decreased in severity and eventually ceased altogether.

I was also doing better with my hand. Before I returned east, I saw a neurosurgeon in Chicago about my chronically tingling fingers. He said that he could operate on my elbow to relieve the pressure on the pinched ulnar nerve but that the surgery could leave my elbow unstable. He told me to wait eighteen months because aggravated nerves generally heal at the rate of an inch a month and the distance between my numb pinkie and my elbow was approximately eighteen inches. Some of his patients, he said, insisted on the surgery because they found the numbness too distracting. I decided to wait. My main difficulty was that I couldn't sense where exactly my pinkie was. It would protrude at odd angles from my hand and I'd smash it on door frames and the edges of tables. But the tingling was declining and pretty much disappeared according to the surgeon's forecast.

As I recovered my full health, Pandolfini gave me chess lessons whenever my work took me from Woodstock to New York. We would dissect my recent tournament games, and he'd point out plans and ideas that I had not considered. We also worked on a psychological issue. My games exhibited the kind of dramatic swings on the chessboard that Sosonko had described—my opponent is winning, he screws up; I'm winning, I blunder; it's drawish, he's winning again. We worked on my being Zen, on my smoothing out my internal reactions so that I could stay focused on the game. I had particular difficulty not capitulating if the game suddenly swung in my opponent's favor. Rather than making my adversary work for the full point, I would in effect pout and roll over. With Pandolfini's guidance, I tried to arrest my self-defeating attitude. Even a theoretically winning game doesn't win itself; a fallible human being must correctly marshal his forces move after move if he is going to bring home the victory. If I put up sufficient obstacles, it was not inevitable that my adversary would win "a won game." Most games, Pandolfini said, are won by the player who makes the next-to-last blunder.[10]

I had a chance to apply this lesson when I faced nineteen-year-old Noah Siegel in the second round of a rapid tournament at the Marshall in August 2001. Siegel was a seasoned junior player who was rated nearly four hundred points more than me, at 2333. If our ratings accurately reflected our respective playing strengths, he should beat me 92 percent of the time. I had White and played the Exchange Variation against his French Defense. This variation, in which White initiates a pawn trade on the third move and brings about a symmetrical pawn structure, seems a timid treatment of the French. But no less a player than Bobby Fischer was successful with it.

Of course I was no Fischer, and Siegel achieved a strong position, with pressure on my queenside. My position was far from lost, but it was the kind of game, with his rooks bearing down on my weak queenside pawns, in which I usually mentally gave up and engaged in ineffectual wood-shifting. This time I concentrated and resisted. We both thought too long in this thirty-minute game, and in the resulting mutual time scramble, I contrived to divert his attention by a desperate attack on his king.

We each had only half a minute left, and he made a couple of inaccurate moves. My fingers were shaking, and we both clumsily knocked over pieces as we struggled to beat the clock. When we both went under ten seconds, our hands collided. I didn't know who stood better. Indeed, I had no idea at all what was happening. I was just blindly pushing pieces, playing anything that came into my head, to avoid losing on the clock. I started checking his king. If I was lucky, I thought, maybe I could escape with a draw by perpetual check. He extended his hand and I shook it. "Nice," he said, and I thought he was monosyllabically congratulating me on my wily achievement of a draw.

Siegel left without a postmortem. I also exited the playing hall, and took a moment to compose myself. During time pressure I'm not usually aware of feeling nervous—my pulse doesn't race or my stomach ache—but I get brain-lock. I can't think clearly. Once the pressure ends and the game is over, the tension overtakes me and I'm scared I'm going to vomit. My antidote is to drink a couple of glasses of water. That cured me quickly this time, and I proceeded to write ½—the numerical value of a draw—on the official scoreboard. Only after I recorded the game as a draw did the final position flash through my mind, and I had the strange thought that I had improbably checkmated him. Not that I could have mated him if I had played a better move but that I *had* actually mated him. Impossible, I thought. It would be like having sex with a woman I had long coveted and not realizing it. Could I really be that stupid? I ran back into the tournament hall to see if the final position was still on the board. Sure enough, it was. I had hunted down his king, just as I had envisaged. And then I realized he must have been congratulating me on my unexpected victory and had exited abruptly because he was upset.

The tournament director had already removed the scoreboard on which I had posted "the draw." I found him and told him, without going into the embarrassing details, that I had incorrectly marked the result. I presented the situation as if I had made the handwriting equivalent of a typo. He raised his eyebrows, and said, "OK, I'll change it because I know Noah will protest if he didn't actually lose." Of course I knew Noah wasn't going to protest—he knew better than I did that I had won.

Chess was an insane game. When I lost, I was unhappy. And yet it was necessary to play and risk defeat if I was ever going to win and relish victory. Here I had succeeded in checkmating the highest-rated player I had ever defeated so far in a tournament, and I couldn't enjoy it. I was both amused and disheartened by the absurdity.

RUSSIAN DOMINATION

"Whether you like it or not, history is on our side. We
will bury you."
—NIKITA KHRUSHCHEV

"The loss of my childhood was the price of becoming
the youngest world champion in history. When you have
to fight every day from a young age, your soul could
become contaminated. I lost my childhood. I never
really had it. Today I have to be careful not to become
cruel, because I became a soldier too early."
—GARRY KASPAROV

LIKE OTHER AMERICAN DEVOTEES OF THE GAME, I REALIZED
that Russia was master of the sixty-four squares when I first cracked
open a chess book and stumbled on its intimidating litany of exotic Slavic
names—Shcherbakov, Nezhmetdinov, Gurgenidze, Kholmov, Yusupov,
Psakhis. All serious chess players in the West live in the shadow of Russia,
which has towered over the international chess scene for more than sixty
years. There is a joke in chess circles that you don't stand a chance of becoming world champion unless your name is Russian and starts with a
K: Kramnik, Kasparov, Karpov, Kasimdzhanov, and Khalifman were
all world champions during the past twenty-five years, and another K,
Korchnoi, was the strongest challenger to the throne. Russia was such a

chess powerhouse that in 1970 a Soviet team defeated the rest of the world's top grandmasters in an event called the USSR vs. the World. If I had attended high school in Moscow in the 1970s, I would not have made the chess team, let alone played top board. I would have been lost in a crowd of other mediocre fifteen-year-old players.

In tsarist Russia, chess was played by the political and intellectual elite. "Thank you, darling, for learning to play chess," the great nineteenth-century poet Pushkin wrote to his wife. "It is an absolute necessity for any well-organized family." After the revolution, with Moscow's encouragement, the game exploded and became a national pastime. The man who convinced the fledgling Communist state to support chess was a midlevel bureaucrat named Alexander Fyodorovich Ilyin-Genevsky. As a player he was not among Russia's very best (although he was skilled enough to be the three-time champion of Leningrad and to defeat Capablanca once in 1925), but he had the curious distinction of being the only known master who'd had to learn the game *twice* from scratch, because a brain injury in World War I erased his memory of how the pieces moved. During the Russian Revolution, when food shortages, power outages, and sub-zero temperatures brought Moscow to a standstill, Ilyin-Genevsky buried himself in chess. Even after the central chess club—along with the city's theaters and other venues of entertainment—had been destroyed, he would hike through the frigid, blacked-out city to play against a dozen other chess addicts in a basement apartment illuminated by match light.

In 1920, Ilyin-Genevsky organized the first Soviet Championship. He was the head of an organization of military reservists and he introduced chess as an activity to build discipline among his men. The success was conspicuous, and swiftly replicated across the Soviet Union: chess instruction became a required part of pre-conscription training in factories, mills, and sports clubs. Ilyin-Genevsky went so far as to proselytize that chess was more important for a soldier than sport, because it helped develop not only boldness and willpower, but also the ability to think strategically.

By the late 1920s all of Russia had adopted the slogans "Take chess to the workers!," "Chess must be a feature of every peasant reading room!," and "Chess is a powerful weapon of intellectual culture." The game was found to increase literacy because chess-crazed workers learned to read so that they could study chess books and newspaper chess columns. Communist leaders also believed that the game combated religious superstition by promoting critical reasoning. The fact that what happened on a chessboard seemed to be within the players' control appealed to Communist sensibilities and was seen as a welcome antidote to Russian writers like Gogol and Dostoyevsky, who emphasized chance and fate.

The daily papers were full of praise for the game that was sweeping the Soviet Union. The theoretical virtues of chess aside, Kremlin bureaucrats and the press were comfortable promoting the game because they knew that the fathers of Communism were themselves fanatical players. "Our great teachers, Marx and Lenin," *Pravda* explained, in 1936,

> devoted themselves enthusiastically to chess in their leisure hours. They saw in it primarily a means of strengthening the will, a training-ground for resolve and nervous energy. Lenin's chief struggle in chess lay in the stubborn struggle, in making the best move, and in finding the way out of a difficult, sometimes almost hopeless situation. The fact of winning or losing meant less to him. He enjoyed his opponent's strong rather than his weak moves and he preferred to play with strong opponents.[1]

Chess also became a means for the new Soviet state to triumph on the world stage. In 1936, Mikhail Botvinnik tied for first place at Nottingham, ahead of a very strong field of American and European players.[2] It was the first success for a Soviet player abroad, and it was celebrated back home as a great political victory. Botvinnik, twenty-five, was savvy enough to dispatch a telegram to Stalin from England. "I am infinitely happy to be able to report that a representative of Soviet chess has shared first place in the tournament with ex-champion of the world Capablanca," he wrote to the man whom he addressed as "beloved teacher and leader."

Pravda ran a photograph of Botvinnik on the front page along with a rousing account of how the victory was not accidental:

> Sitting at the chess table in Nottingham, Botvinnik could not fail to sense that the whole country was watching every move of the wooden pieces on the board and ... from the most remote corners to the

Kremlin towers was wishing him success and giving him moral support. He could not fail to sense the powerful breathing of his great motherland. That is why he played so calmly and confidently, that is why he could allow himself the luxury of playing aggressively, moving away from old, stereotyped patterns of play.

Twelve years later, in 1948, Mikhail Botvinnik became world champion. Since then, a Russian player has always held the classical world title with the sole exception of Fischer, from 1972 to 1975.[3] It wasn't just the Russians' command of the moves that made them superior at the chessboard, it was also their practiced steeliness. Botvinnik, for example, overcame an aversion to tobacco smoke by forcing himself to play training games with a chain smoker who purposely exhaled in his face while at the same time hammering away at his French Defense.

Moscow gave stipends to grandmasters, enabling them to earn a middle-class living. The profession of chess master was appealing to worldly intellectuals because they were granted the rare freedom to travel abroad for tournaments, even during the darkest days of the Cold War.[4] In the West, the Soviet chess system was romanticized—and demonized—as a program that identified toddlers who had exceptional talent and spirited them away from their parents to special chess boarding schools. In fact, the children lived with their families, and the chess instruction was conducted after school. A few very gifted kids were invited to chess summer camp for a couple of weeks.

The Soviets dominated international chess not because they snatched children from their homes and drilled them in the Leningrad Dutch Defense and the Volga Gambit, but simply because they had, as the world champion Anatoly Karpov once put it, "such a lot of people playing chess."[5] The game also had a social status that made it far more than a pastime: cultured Muscovites might spend a Sunday afternoon at a chess match instead of the Bolshoi. If a society exposes *everyone* to chess and values the game, more people are going to catch the fever and pursue it until they're world-class.

It is intellectually irresponsible to generalize about national temperament, particularly for a place as large and ethnically diverse as Russia, but that hasn't stopped Western commentators from asking whether the popularity of chess there can be ascribed in part to national character. If a paranoid personality is an advantage in chess—and that's a big *if*—the Russians would seem to be naturals at the game, these commentators argue. Lord Taylor, writing in the London *Sunday Times* in 1962, caused a small uproar among chess players, who resented being described as pathologically suspicious, when he observed:

> Pure paranoia is a rare mental illness whose synonym is systematised delusional insanity. Its essence is that it combines suspicion with organised tortuosity. All of us are apt to become paranoid at times, to think others are talking about us, or even scheming against us. Almost always we are wrong.

Taylor described the rare situations in life when paranoia may be beneficial.

> In business and litigation, politics and war, a small measure of paranoia may be a useful protective mechanism. But as a rule paranoid feelings are a disadvantage to both parties in the situation. There is only one place, where as a temporary expedient, a paranoid approach is a positive advantage—on the chessboard.

In chess, of course, your opponent really is out to get you from the very first move. Owing to Stalin's Great Terror and Moscow's official encouragement of neighbors spying on neighbors, "it will be obvious at once," Lord Taylor concluded, "that the Russians have more than their fair share of paranoia." Taylor's view was shared by Russian grandmaster Valery Salov, who told *New in Chess* in 1991: "This may sound strange, but probably this habit of always looking for enemies, this persecution mania, is not bad when you're playing chess."

The father of modern Soviet chess, Mikhail Botvinnik, a taciturn and robotic personality, certainly had this habit. When he was negotiating the rules of engagement for his 1951 World Championship match with his young compatriot David Bronstein, whose passionate, unpredictable personality was the opposite of his, Botvinnik tried to change the rules governing adjournments. A game was traditionally played for a maximum of five hours a session. Whosoever's turn it was at the five-hour mark did not make his move on the board but instead wrote it down, sealed it in an envelope, and handed it to the arbiter, who would open it in front of the players when the game was continued another day. After adjournment, the competitors and their seconds would pore over the game for hours before resuming play.[6] Botvinnik was worried that a partisan arbiter might surreptitiously open the envelope, change the move, and reseal the envelope, so he insisted that the move also be recorded in a second envelope for backup.

"The Soviet chess world was aghast at this peculiar degree of suspicion from the world champion," Harold Schonberg wrote in *Grandmasters of Chess*. "There was a month-long negotiation over this alone, and Bronstein finally gave in." But Botvinnik continued his paranoid behavior by misleading his own second about the move he had sealed in a key adjourned game.[7] In subsequent matches, Botvinnik did not even employ grandmasters to assist in opening preparation. He feared that they might leak opening innovations to his opponents.

Whether or not Russians in general have been unfairly tagged as paranoid, it is hard to deny that many of the world's top chess players have a suspicious mind-set. They worry that their adversaries are reading their minds and poisoning their beverages. Hikaru Nakamura, the 2005 U.S. champion, did not have a grandmaster coach or second because, like Botvinnik, he felt there was no one he could trust. "Almost all of the top players in the U.S. are foreign-born," Nakamura said. "That makes it very difficult because if you want to study with them, there's a possibility that they'll go on and show everything to their friends." Even the most levelheaded players can become unusually suspicious during a heated match. After Spassky fell behind in his 1972 match with Fischer, the normally even-keeled Russian asked that his chair be X-rayed and dismantled to make sure that Fischer hadn't implanted a harmful radiation emitter inside it.

IN THE TWENTY-FIRST CENTURY, RUSSIA IS STILL A CHESS SUPERPOWER, ALthough the luster of the game has diminished since the collapse of the Soviet Union. After Moscow discontinued many of the perquisites traditionally given to grandmasters, they emigrated in large numbers to the West, causing considerable resentment in their new countries. Everyone on the 2004 U.S. men's team—Onischuk, Shabalov, Goldin, Kaidanov, Novikov, and Gulko—was born in the USSR, and all but one member of the 2004 U.S. women's team was too. Chess instruction in urban centers like New York may have benefited from the influx of Soviet players and trainers, but many Americans resented the Moscow-on-the-Hudson contingent, who started appropriating what scanty money and opportunities were available in U.S. chess. Worse, they suspected Soviet émigrés of colluding—throwing games to each other—in the weekend open tournaments that were the bread and butter of U.S. masters. The American chess scene became polarized, with ex-Soviet players branded as scheming opportunists who knew how to circumvent every regulation and law. As British GM Nigel Short told a journalist, "Those who were brought up under [the Soviet] system all have the same warped outlook: 'You fuck with my wife—I kill you. I fuck with your wife—you keep quiet if you know what's good for you.'"

Unfortunately, it doesn't take long to stumble upon someone in the chess world who conforms to the stereotype of the conniving Russian. On a trip to the Marshall Chess Club, I had difficulty parking. One of the Russian regulars, who was outside smoking, saw me drive past three or four times. After I finally found a questionable place to leave the car and entered the Marshall, he took me aside and offered to sell me physician license plates, which would attach magnetically to my own plates and allow me to park legally anywhere in New York.

AT ITS PEAK, IN THE EARLY 1980S, THE SOVIET CHESS FEDERATION HAD FOUR million members; the United States Chess Federation, by comparison, never boasted more than 95,000. With the top Russians facing insufficient competition abroad in those days, they were left to beat up on one another, and the two who did it with the most gusto were Karpov and Kasparov. To date, theirs has been the bitterest rivalry in chess.

Karpov, who is twelve years older than Kasparov, was the darling of Brezhnev, while Kasparov was an advocate of democracy before the USSR collapsed. The U.S. media portrayed their world title bouts as the bad Russian—the Communist automaton whose nickname was the Fetus because his head seemed oversized for his small body—versus the good Russian—the friendly face of *glasnost* and *perestroika*. Hans Ree, a Dutch grandmaster who watched their title match in New York in 1990, was entertained by the American television coverage. "When Karpov is being mentioned, you see tanks and portraits of Stalin," he observed. "When Kasparov is featured, the screen shows young mothers with children."

Karpov became champion in 1975, when Bobby Fischer refused to defend his title and slipped away to become the Howard Hughes of chess. Kasparov first opposed Karpov for the crown in 1984, and won it the following year. All in all, the two men played a record 144 games in five title matches. Although Kasparov continuously held the title after 1985, the cumulative score in the twelve dozen games played over six years put him only two games ahead. He won twenty-one, lost nineteen, and drew 104. "The games were fantastic," recalled Pandolfini, who followed them closely at the time. "It was a clash of two playing styles. Karpov was the wily defender who could nurse small advantages in pawn structure and piece placement into victory. Kasparov's play, like his personality, was more aggressive. He always pressed for the initiative."

Karpov and Kasparov's clashes were not confined to the chessboard. "Each K had a team of trainers and coaches," recalled Pandolfini, "and there were charges that each side had paid off the other to learn their secret opening move preparations." And then there was the war of the so-called parapsychologists—accusations that the teams had hired hypnotists to sit in the playing hall and hex the opposing player. (Such wars were nothing new: In the 1978 World Championship, in Baguio, the Philippines, Karpov asked a parapsychologist to sit in the audience and jinx his opponent, Soviet defector Viktor Korchnoi. But Korchnoi responded in kind; he recruited two saffron-robed mystics, Didi and Dada, who were under indictment for attempted murder, to meditate in the tournament hall.)

In the 1984–85 match, when Kasparov first tried to wrest the title away from his predecessor, whoever won six games first was supposed to be crowned the champion. The ensuing struggle became the longest and most controversial contest in the history of chess. The purgatory began on September 10, 1984, in central Moscow's prominent Hall of Columns and ended five execrable months later on the city's fringes in Hotel Sport, to which the punch-drunk combatants had been moved when the Hall of Columns was needed for the state funeral of General Ustinov. The chess press joked that the good general "had been waiting long enough and had given Karpov every chance to finish the match."

Indeed Karpov had sprinted ahead 4–0 (with five draws along the way) and apparently made the decision to desecrate his would-be usurper by preventing him from ever getting on the scoreboard. So Karpov stopped taking risks and waited for Kasparov, who had been dismissed by the pundits, to make a mistake. In response, the younger man also started to play solidly, hoping that the longer he resisted, the more he would erode the stamina of the physically frail champion. But Kasparov, too, had underestimated his adversary. The two men drew seventeen consecutive games and then Karpov won again, pushing Kasparov to the precipice at 5–0.

Kasparov, wrote Dutch grandmaster Hans Ree,

> knew that should he lose the next game, he would never again find the strength to play Karpov. No one who loses a world championship match by the score of 6–0 should ever try again. He should consider gardening. Kasparov's seconds lapsed into total silence, because no one wanted to be responsible for the fatal advice that could cause the end of Kasparov's chess career. Kasparov ended up sleeping in his mother's room, so that at any time during the night he could hear her comforting words.

In the thirty-second game, after four more draws, Kasparov finally got on the scoreboard with a much-needed victory. There were another fourteen draws and then the Azerbaijani challenger had two consecutive wins, bringing the score to 5–3, with the champion still leading. Even though the match score on paper continued to look bleak for Kasparov, the momentum after forty-eight games and five months of play had swung in his favor. Karpov looked like a ghost: his physique had shriveled and he apparently needed sedatives to sleep and amphetamines to come to the board. On February 10, 1985, FIDE President Florencio Campomanes, under pressure from Karpov's acolytes in the Soviet Chess Federation, abruptly canceled the match, on the ground that it was injurious to the health of *both* players. At the closing press conference, Kasparov puffed himself up to look his most robust and decried the unlawful cancellation. In the nasty recriminations that followed, both players claimed that FIDE's dramatic decision had favored the other.

Hindsight suggests that Karpov's supporters were misguided in orchestrating the cancellation—he only managed to hold onto the World Championship for another eight months. After all, both men were exhausted, and Karpov was one game away from victory; his best chance was to continue the match, propped up by the finest in Soviet pharmaceutical science. Had he managed to win the match, he might well have knocked out Kasparov for good. Ree also pointed out that Karpov was forced to live with the knowledge that

> whoever gets such a chance and misses it never gets another, because something inside him has been broken. Kasparov, on the other hand, had looked his own death as a chess player in the eyes, and became hardened by the experience.

Kasparov and Karpov then curiously reversed roles in the chess world. The new champion

> wasn't just chess player, but also chess politician, granting and receiving favors, forming coalitions, making other players dependent on himself, sometimes meting out punishments. It was the same game Karpov had always played so brilliantly, infuriating Kasparov.

The struggle between the two men was also played out in their respective autobiographies. In *Karpov on Karpov*, the older Russian voiced his disapproval of his adversary's behavior at the board. Kasparov was known to make dismissive faces, shrug his shoulders, wave his hands, stare at the ceiling, and pace wildly. Sometimes he leaned over the board and crowded his opponent's physical space.

> Each time before I sit down with him at the board, all I have to do is remember that he'll begin to perform his theatrical pieces, he'll affect a deep meditation, torments, and hesitation, even though he knows every move in advance and is only performing during a game. You can be sure this spectacle is not for me—Kasparov understands that I know his worth—but for the public, and yet I can't deal with the annoying fact that I have to be part of it.

In *Child of Change*, Kasparov acknowledged his own behavior but denied it was deliberate:

> Some people seeing my intense concentration at the board, with my
> head in my hands and a fixed look in my eyes, think this is all an act
> designed to frighten or intimidate my opponent, like Tal's famous
> glare.[8] That is not so, though I admit that sometimes it could have that
> effect on a weak or impressionable opponent. It is all for my own ben-
> efit really, to exclude all outside distractions and force myself to dig
> deep inside my mind for the right combinations. You have to keep
> your thoughts together, not allow them to scatter under pressure.

Other world chess champions, Kasparov argued, also had "strange habits"
at the board. But these, too, he said, were simply a means to release tension
rather than a calculated effort to unnerve the opponent. "Steinitz, the first
world champion, used to hum Wagner," Kasparov wrote. "Alekhine would
twist his hair, Botvinnik his tie, Lasker smoked cigars. Morphy never
raised his eyes to his opponent until he had made the decisive move."

But if Karpov was more convincing than Kasparov on the subject of
his rival's "strange habits," he was not at all believable when he tried to
paint him as an agent of stagnation because he was once a member of
the Communist Party (which Karpov himself never was). Recent events
have confirmed Kasparov's commitment to Western-style democracy.
To the dismay of his family and friends, who are worried about his
physical safety, the man who was once invincible in chess has become
one of the loudest voices in Russia objecting to Putin's turn toward
totalitarianism and the widespread business corruption and cronyism
throughout Moscow. Journalists in Russia who said a lot less are now
dead—in improbable car accidents, mysterious gas-stove explosions, or
apparent contract slayings—and businessmen who crossed Putin are
now in jail.

In his mission to checkmate the former KGB chief-turned-Russian
president, Kasparov may be guilty of megalomania—believing that he
won't be defeated in life because of his overwhelming success in chess—
but the genuineness of his effort is unimpeachable. Kasparov has always
been politically active, and now he has given up chess and chosen the per-
ilous course of guiding his country toward an open society and a free-
market economy. Karpov, meanwhile, has showed his old Bolshevik
stripes by publicly supporting Putin.

IN DECEMBER 2002, I HAD A FRONT-ROW SEAT WHEN KASPAROV AND KARPOV came together for old times' sake for a two-day match in the ABC Studios in Times Square. The two veterans played two games of rapid chess a day, at the brisk time control of twenty-five minutes apiece with ten seconds added for each move. Each man received an appearance fee, said to be $200,000 for Kasparov and $50,000 for Karpov, but there was no cash prize for the winner. "It doesn't take a prize to get the two of us to go at it," Kasparov told me before the match. "I want to maintain my winning streak against him and demonstrate once again that he and I are much different when it comes to morality and politics."

The organizer of the match had invited me because he liked the chess articles I wrote. He asked me if I knew a celebrity who understood enough about the game to be able to make the honorary first move. (The first move is, in fact, chosen by the player with White, but you still want someone who can perform it without, say, pushing the king pawn an extra square or making a knight hop in the shape of a *V* instead of an *L*.) I am friends with David Blaine, the magician and endurance artist—we've played chess together—and I thought he'd enjoy meeting Kasparov. "Chess is like magic," David once told me. "You always have to stay one step ahead of your opponent—or your audience."

The television cameras were rolling when Kasparov and Karpov swaggered up to the board and watched David pick up a White pawn. With an agonizing expression on his face, David grunted and squeezed the pawn, like the strongman at a carnival, until he'd crushed it into a cloud of dust. The match arbiter started berating David on camera because the pawn he destroyed was irreplaceable. Like each of the other chessmen, it was uniquely equipped with a microchip so that the electronic circuitry in the chessboard could sense what square the pawn was on and broadcast the full game position over the Internet to hundreds of thousands of chess fans around the world. The arbiter was angry, but the champions were laughing—a rare display of levity for them at the start of one of their matches. Needless to say, David made the crushed pawn rematerialize and the match, and Internet transmission, began without a hitch.

Kasparov easily won the first game and seemed on his way to victory in the second after winning a pawn. But both players were short of time, and in the ensuing struggle, Karpov started to hunt down the younger man's king. In desperation, Kasparov sacrificed his queen to stop the mating attack. When he subsequently lost another piece, he resigned and left the playing hall. And so the score was 1–1 after the first day.

On the second day of the match, Karpov overslept during an afternoon nap and arrived for the third game a few minutes late and out of breath. He asked the tournament organizer for a ten-minute delay to compose himself, but Kasparov insisted that the game start immediately. It was Kasparov, though, who soon fell several minutes behind on the clock, and his old rival outfoxed him in the endgame, after most of the pieces and pawns had been exchanged. Karpov was now ahead 2–1; with only one game remaining, he could not possibly lose the match. Kasparov had to win to secure a tie.

In the fourth game, Kasparov had the advantage of moving first, but after twenty-eight moves he could do no better than reach a sterile, even position. He shook his head in disgust, looked up at the ceiling, mumbled something inaudible—as if he was asking God why he had been put through such agony—and offered Karpov a draw. And so Kasparov lost the match 2½–1½. He had told me that whenever he loses he's in deep physical pain.

The organizer invited David and me to dinner with the two players and their teams. Going to a fancy hotel restaurant with Karpov was probably the last thing Kasparov wanted to do in order to put the defeat behind him, but he forced himself to attend because he knew the organizer was planning other lucrative chess events. He sat at a table with only his entourage and lowered his head to his plate for most of the meal. His team of seconds spoke quietly among themselves while their boss picked at his fish. At Karpov's table, the victor and his team were getting smashed. David went over to Kasparov and pulled him, literally pulled him, to his feet. The Russian tried to push him off, but David led him forcefully by the hand to where Karpov was sitting and performed a mentalist card trick for the two champions. Karpov was fooled—he laughed loudly and appreciatively at the outcome. Kasparov was tricked, too, but he was so withdrawn that he couldn't even force himself to smile. David's girlfriend, a tall model with perfect teeth and an incandescent smile, winked at the world number one, who was normally a ladies' man, but even she couldn't elicit a response. Kasparov slunk back to his table, sagged into his seat, and left the restaurant soon afterward.

I stayed behind and had too many vodka shots with Karpov. He was not a large man, although the small body of his Fetus days had swollen a bit. Karpov started making fun of how dejected Kasparov had looked at the meal. He imitated his rival by putting on his best hangdog expression and resting his head on a dinner plate. Then he stopped the impersonation, started slapping the table, and told me how happy he was to see Kasparov so miserable. "I've waited for this," he said. "I've waited long for this. He deserves to suffer." Karpov had never won a match against Kasparov before. In fact, the last time he'd defeated him in an individual game had been twelve years before, in 1990.

After he downed another vodka, Karpov looked a bit wistful. "I know Kasparov as well as I know anyone," he told me. "I know his smell. I can read him by that." Indeed, the two men had sat face-to-face for more than six hundred hours, their foreheads sometimes only millimeters apart as they leaned in over the chessboard. "I recognize the smell when he is excited and I know it when he is scared. We may be enemies, but we are intimate enemies." And then Karpov reverted to imitating his rival by laying his head on the table.

KARPOV'S IMPERSONATION OF KASPAROV WAS FUNNY, BUT HE HIMSELF IS not a model of good sportsmanship when he is defeated. In fact, he is known on the grandmaster circuit as a very sore loser. He runs a chess school in Lindsborg, Kansas, where Pascal Charbonneau used to be an instructor. One summer evening Pascal arrived at the school, weary from a full day of car rides and plane flights from Baltimore. When he entered the building, he saw Yuri Shulman, a grandmaster and fellow instructor, playing blitz with Karpov. Karpov won the game, and Shulman looked exasperated. He got up from the table and said, "Pascal, you play."

Pascal put down his luggage and took Shulman's place. The Canadian was excited because he had never faced a world champion before. He had White in the first game. Soon he had a slight advantage in a Taimanov Sicilian, and he was ahead on the clock, too. Toward the end, he was two pawns up with a clear win on the board and an overwhelming time advantage of twenty-five seconds to Karpov's six seconds. "Karpov just let his clock run out," Pascal told me, "and announced to the assembled spectators, many of whom were weak players, 'I lost on time.' He said it in a voice that made it sound like he had a great position, but he was completely lost." Shulman, who had stepped away, returned and asked in Russian who won. "I was quiet," Pascal said, "and Karpov didn't respond. Shulman repeated his question, and Karpov said, 'It was not bad for Pascal.' Only when Shulman asked a third time did Karpov clearly admit that I had won.

"I played the second game very badly," Pascal recalled. "I lost without putting up a fight. Maybe subconsciously I thought that if I lost there was more chance Karpov would play a lot of games with me"—which is indeed what happened. Pascal played better in the third game and was up a pawn but still managed to lose. "At that point," he said, "I told myself to stop playing like an idiot. Next I tried the Paulsen Sicilian as Black. He didn't respond very accurately, and I didn't give him any chances." Pascal evened the score with another win. "In a subsequent game I was better the whole time, but he defended well," Pascal recalled. "And with each of us having twenty seconds left, I offered a draw. To my surprise, he turned me down and played on. He tried to blitz me and wanted to beat me on the clock, but he played terribly. When he had only eight seconds left and there was no hope for him because I was about to queen a pawn, he said, 'OK, it's a draw,' and swept all the pieces aside and then set them back up. Of course it wasn't a draw."

All in all, the two of them played fifteen games, and in the end Karpov was ahead by only a single one. "I was extremely happy," Pascal recalled. "I quit after a game that he won because I didn't want him to hate me."[9]

I NEVER GOT TO PLAY KARPOV, BUT I DID FULFILL EVERY CHESS PLAYER'S dream—nightmare, really—of facing Kasparov, in a simultaneous exhibition over the Internet. The six-board event was sponsored by the high-tech firm ZMD, and Kasparov's opponents were stationed in the company's various offices and factories around the world. Because of the different time zones involved, it was difficult to schedule the event at an hour when all of the participants were fully awake. I played at 6:00 A.M. from an office in Long Island. ZMD had kindly put me up in a hotel a few blocks away, so that I could get a proper night's sleep before the match. Kasparov was playing from somewhere in Europe.

A few days before our game, I had watched Kasparov give a simul against twenty-four traders on the New York Stock Exchange. He had limited the event to people who were rated below 2000. The same rating ceiling applied to the Internet simul, and his agent had questioned me to make sure I wasn't too strong for the event. The emphasis on rating seemed strange, because Kasparov had achieved godlike status in 1998 by demolishing the entire Israeli national chess team of grandmasters and international masters—players rated in the 2500s and 2600s—in simultaneous play. At the stock exchange, the opponents were complete amateurs and he disposed of them all, 24–0, in only an hour and forty-five minutes.

Although the competition was weak, I was impressed by how earnestly he had taken the event. To make it interesting for himself, he had been determined not to concede a single draw, let alone a loss. One of the games stayed with him. "If he had played better," Kasparov told me afterward, "I'm not sure I could have won. I'd have to play like Karpov." He chuckled at the thought. "Yeah, like Karpov, grinding him slowly, slowly down in an agonizingly long game." We were wolfing down a buffet dinner at the stock exchange because he was about to fly to Germany, but the conversation kept returning to this particular game. "Maybe if I played f5, I could have broken through," he said, interrupting some non-chess story that I was relating. Kasparov could not stop thinking about the game until he had determined the truth of the position. It was remarkable how the greatest mind in chess managed to turn an informal encounter with an amateur into a rich intellectual challenge.

As Kasparov left for the airport, he asked me whether he'd be playing me in the ZMD simul.

"Yes," I said.

"Do you know if I have White or Black?"

"I'm afraid you have White."

"Oh, goody," he said, gleefully rubbing his hands together, and we both laughed. He was a good sport to pretend that he needed White.

If Kasparov could act as if the color mattered, I could fantasize that I had a chance of victory and prepare for him by examining his games in detail. I ended up putting in almost as much work as I had for Larsen. I concentrated on the few hundred recorded games that Kasparov had played against amateurs in simuls, and I studied move for move each of the ones in which he'd had White. I saw that he shunned all sharp, mainstream openings, preferring quieter systems in which confrontation was postponed until the middle game.

This was the opposite of his approach against grandmasters, and it made perfect sense. In a simul he wasn't going to repeat a high-level game in one of his favorite openings and risk a well-prepared amateur coming up with an improvement (as I had against Larsen). He would then have to show the world how he'd counter the novelty. It wasn't worth it—he wanted to save all theoretical battles and secrets for important games against strong opponents. Against unskilled adversaries like me, he could afford to develop his pieces in a more leisurely fashion. He knew he could simply outplay us from a level position later on—not through showy tactics but through a complete understanding of the subtleties of the game.

In preparation for our encounter, I hired Alexander Baburin, a convivial Russian grandmaster living in Dublin. Working on a shared board over the Internet while we spoke on the phone, Baburin helped me devise responses to the calm systems Kasparov had previously adopted in simultaneous play. Even though these systems were designed to tamp down early Black counterplay, in a few cases we came up with ways to unbalance the situation, giving me at least the remote hope of avoiding the slow death to which Kasparov would otherwise subject me. And in cases where we couldn't drum up counterplay, Baburin helped me comprehend some of the nuances of the resulting middle-game structures so that—if I played exceptionally well and Caissa smiled at me that morning and Kasparov happened to be having a rough day—I might, just might, earn a draw.

I was so absorbed in my fantasy of preparing for Kasparov that I actually contacted the few players in the world who had recently beaten him and asked for their advice. Teimour Radjabov, a young player from Kasparov's hometown of Baku, Azerbaijan, gave me a pep talk about not getting discouraged if the game did not seem to be going in my favor. It was the same kind of advice Pandolfini had given me about not capitulating prematurely. Radjabov could speak from experience. At the 2003 Super Tournament in Linares, Spain, the so-called Wimbledon of chess, the fifteen-year-old Radjabov found himself in a much worse position—on the Black side of a French Defense—against the world number one. Rather than just submit to inevitable defeat, the tenacious teenager muddied the situation by offering up a knight on the twenty-first move. Kasparov declined the gift horse and went astray in the ensuing complications. With his twenty-sixth move, he blundered a piece—and with it, all hope of saving the game. After Radjabov's thirty-ninth move, Kasparov purposely let his time expire and left the playing hall without doing a postmortem with his opponent, or even shaking his hand.

At the closing ceremony at Linares, Radjabov was awarded the most-beautiful-game prize by a vote of the international journalists in attendance, many of whom were strong players themselves. While Radjabov's mother videotaped her son receiving the prize, Kasparov took over the microphone on the podium and shouted, "How could you give the beauty prize to a game in which I lost a piece because of a stupid mistake? It has been selected only because it was the only game that I lost and I consider this to be a public insult and humiliation."

Later he confronted individual journalists, like the Australian grandmaster Ian Rogers, and demanded to know how they voted. When Rogers conceded that he supported the choice, "Kasparov launched one of the most violent verbal assaults I have ever experienced," Rogers wrote. "With a crowd of spectators gathering, including Linares officials, Kasparov, with his hand not far from my throat, launched into a ten-minute volley of abuse and then turned his fire on a local journalist. Eventually Kasparov's mother succeeded in dragging her son away." Malcolm Pein of London's *Daily Telegraph* wryly summed up the incident: "It saddens me that the world's greatest player should behave like a child after losing to one."

In my game with Kasparov, his manners were irreproachable. Of course, there was an Internet connection and four thousand miles between us, so that I did not have to endure his physical presence. Mig Greengard, a chess journalist and friend of Kasparov's, was at the Long Island playing site. When the games began, Mig did his best to stick out his chest and imitate the Russian's imposing demeanor. My first surprise was that I, and not Kasparov, was playing White: some software glitch prevented the organizers from giving me Black as they had promised. It was normally an advantage to have White, but now all my preparation as Black was useless, and my opening moves were unadventurous. The software had other problems too: the kid who was playing next to me watched one of Kasparov's rooks mysteriously turn into a knight. The boy was screaming about this while I was trying to concentrate on my own game. The time control was a swift twenty-five minutes a side plus an increment of ten seconds a move, the same as in Kasparov's rapid match with Karpov. Kasparov's other five opponents were considerably weaker than I. After fifteen minutes they had all lost, and I was left to play one-on-one with the great man.

Kasparov had adopted a relatively obscure variation of the Sicilian and fluidly developed his pieces. My development, on the other hand, was aimless and phlegmatic. I fell behind by shuffling my light-squared bishop a ridiculous five times to a place it could have reached in a single move. I found myself trying to anticipate threats of his that weren't even there, adopting a batten-down-the-hatches, curl-up-like-a-porcupine strategy. It was as if I was imitating my young son's play—he is new to the game and hates to move any of his pieces beyond the fourth rank for fear that they will become targets. I muttered something aloud about my inert position, and Mig consoled me by saying that even top grandmasters find themselves playing passively against Kasparov.

The thirteenth world champion then orchestrated the exchange of queens and tortured me in the endgame by increasing his stranglehold on my wobbly position, confidently marching his king into the game along the exposed dark squares on my queenside. My weaknesses metastasized as the game continued. With only four seconds left on my clock, I lost a bishop on the forty-sixth move and resigned. I was upset by my blunder at the end: I wanted Kasparov to know that I was a better player than this game showed and worthy of writing about chess.

I talked to him a few days later on the phone in Moscow. "You didn't stand a chance because of your teammates," he said. "They weren't too good." He was being both truthful and charitable. "Your play of course was much too passive," he continued matter-of-factly. "You must try to do more with White. But somehow you reached a position that wasn't all that bad. You could have made me work for the win."

I was still worried that Kasparov thought I was a *patzer*, and I complained to one of my friends. "Look on the bright side," he said. "Whenever you play in a tournament for the rest of your life, you're never going to face anyone stronger." It was a good point.

FOR PLAYERS OF KASPAROV'S STRENGTH, COMPUTERS ARE THE NEW FRONTIER, and the day is near when machines will totally dominate human players. "They'll win every match," Kasparov told me. "And then the challenge will be: can the top player, on his very best day, when he's rested and has no distractions from his personal life, still win a single game from the machine?" In other words, it will be a success for humans if they get on the scoreboard at all, losing a six-game match, say, 5–1 instead of being wiped out 6–0. This will require a remarkable shift in thinking for the world's top grandmasters, cocky competitors who thrive on destroying their opponents. The silicon adversary may take the odd blow, but it will never go down.

How soon this day will come, whether it's next year or five years from now, is hard to predict, but it's certainly not decades away. The best machines already play world-class chess and have fared well against the likes of Kasparov and Kramnik. Aside from the machines' success in high-profile matches, their very existence is revolutionizing the way all serious players approach the game.

In the mid-1960s, before the invention of the personal computer, a master prepared for an opponent by going through back issues of chess magazines and books trying to scrounge up any games that the adversary had played. If the master was lucky, he'd locate a few, which would provide limited insight into the opponent's strengths and weaknesses and the openings that he preferred. Except in the case of a very famous adversary, the number of games available would generally be insufficient to discern the full scope of his opening repertoire.

Players in the early 1960s studied chess openings, of course, but because they had access to all of their own previous games and few of their opponents', they tended to work more on expanding their knowledge of their own opening lines than on looking for flaws and improvements in their rivals' games. If a player was fortunate to come up with a killer innovation on the thirteenth move of a well-trodden path in the Dragon, he could spring it on an unsuspecting opponent in Buenos Aires and then surprise another adversary three weeks later in Budapest who reached the same position—news of the innovation would not have traveled that quickly. Now the word spreads immediately, thanks to the Internet, and any serious player who checks major tournament Web sites will know about the improvement; he will therefore either avoid the opening line in his own future games, or welcome it because he has worked long into the night and developed a refutation that the innovator overlooked.

The modern information revolution in chess actually began long before the Internet. In 1966, a thick Yugoslavian periodical called *Chess Informant* began to anthologize games from top tournaments and annotate them with symbols so that readers around the world could follow the analysis without knowing Yugoslavian or English. (For instance, *?!* indicated a move that was considered dubious but interesting and + − showed that White had a winning advantage.) The *Informant* soon became indispensable to top players. Tigran Petrosian was the world champion then, and he contemptuously called the new generation of players "the children of the *Informant*."

Kasparov himself helped to pioneer the next explosion in chess information, two decades later. During his matches with Karpov, in the 1980s, he encouraged a group of programmers in Germany, who were the progenitors of ChessBase, to develop a computerized database that stored the games of major players and allowed him to categorize them, subgroup them, and slice and dice them in all sorts of ways. Kasparov could then examine, for instance, all the rook endgames that Karpov had reached, or all the middle games Fischer had played in which the American had two bishops and his opponent had two knights. The database was coupled to strong chess-playing "engines," or programs, which would review the games, particularly the openings played, in search of better moves and chess truth.

Today, every tournament regular has access to the huge game collections and engines, with names like Fritz, Shredder, and Junior, distributed by ChessBase. Their flagship, *MegaBase* CD, includes 2,500 games of Kasparov's, 580 of Pascal's, and 22 of mine among its millions of games. (My games are pathetic blitz efforts, unsuited for preservation, from an online tournament in which IMs and GMs gave me a harsh schooling in time management.) A search in *MegaBase* on the Sicilian Dragon, the opening in which Pascal craftily defeated the Bulgarian, turns up thirty thousand games.

A top-tier chess game in the twenty-first century therefore begins long before the antagonists actually take their places at the board. Each cerebral gladiator, assisted by a team of human seconds, the sous-chefs, dissects the other guy's previous efforts and puts his own favorite openings through the engines in search of innovations that he can unleash during the upcoming contest. As a result, the playing field is completely different than it was in Fischer's day, but it is a level field nonetheless, because virtually all dedicated players have access to ChessBase software.

Not every competitor, though, has the temperament to stare at a computer screen for days, studying hundreds of games, assimilating what's been played before, and guiding the machine to search for opening innovations. Pascal, for one, hates this sort of preparation and would prefer that the databases didn't exist. Fischer himself believed that the vast game collections were robbing chess of spontaneity. To de-emphasize the role of memorization, he proposed a whole new variation of chess, called Fischer random chess, in which the initial set up of the pieces varies from game to game and is established just before the game commences. I, however, might have enjoyed those additional hours in front of the computer; after all, I always found studying chess more rewarding—and less stressful—than actually playing the game.

KASPAROV MAY HAVE HELPED USHER IN THE COMPUTER AGE IN CHESS, BUT he is also its most conspicuous victim. In 1997, he played a highly publicized match in New York City, touted as "the last stand of the brain," against the IBM supercomputer Deep Blue. Not since Fischer-Spassky in 1972 had a chess match garnered so much media attention worldwide.

Deep Blue was a 1.4-ton, refrigerator-size calculating monster, with 256 processors, or mini-brains, working together to outsmart its human opponent. Even the normally ruthless Russian looked vulnerable when up against this unflappable silicon Goliath, and despite the fact that his faults were on full display during the match—his hotheadedness, his moodiness, his paranoia, his inability to be gracious in defeat—no one wanted to see him lose to a machine. Kasparov had triumphed over computers before, including a weaker progenitor of Deep Blue the previous year, but he let this one get under his skin from the start.

Machines like Deep Blue are typically very materialistic—they'll happily grab a pawn or a piece, even if they have to wait out a blistering attack, provided they don't foresee themselves actually getting mated. A human grandmaster, on the other hand, will generally avoid snatching material if the price is being on the defensive for a dozen moves—he knows that a single oversight may lead quickly and irrevocably to checkmate. It's like inviting someone to fire a gun at you: if you fail to dodge a bullet, it's all over immediately. But if you can stand the pressure of being under the gun (and who could stand this other than an emotionless automaton?), this may be a great strategy: when your enemy has exhausted his ammunition, you start firing back and he is defenseless. Most human players, however, find it easier to attack than to defend: if you're the gunman and you fire a bullet wide, you won't lose on the spot and may even have time to recover before the counterfire.

Kasparov handily won his first game against Deep Blue in 1997, but was suffering in the second. At one juncture in the middle game, he clearly expected Deep Blue to penetrate his home territory with the White queen and pick off a pawn or two. This materialistic maneuver would have allowed Kasparov a modicum of counterplay—not enough, perhaps, to save the game, but more than he had. But the machine did not operate according to expectations: instead of going after the pawns, Deep Blue quietly clamped down on prospective counterplay by a simple shift of a bishop. Kasparov was dumbfounded that the machine was capable of playing such a refined, effective move. He resigned in disgust eight moves later. Subsequent analysis revealed that as bad as Kasparov's position appeared, he could have achieved a draw with a long sequence involving a rook move that he had not considered. This was the first time, he said, that he had ever resigned a drawn position. Not only was he dismayed by his own colossal misjudgment, he was also confused by the computer. How could the same machine that had played so brilliantly earlier, foregoing a pawn meal in favor of a quiet bishop shift, now mistakenly allow him to wiggle away with a draw? Deep Blue's erratic play was more characteristic of a human being, he thought, than of a machine.

Kasparov was also clearly frustrated that it was impossible to get a psychological advantage over Deep Blue, because the computer was simply playing pure chess: it didn't care whether it won or lost. He could have spat at the machine or taken off all of his clothes and stood on his head, and it wouldn't have made any difference—Deep Blue couldn't be distracted. The machine kept coming at him, and Kasparov collapsed under the pressure of an opponent that he knew would never tire. It was the most stressful chess he had played since the aborted marathon with Karpov in 1984 and 1985.

He lost the sixth and final game—and with it the match, by the score of 3½–2½—in only nineteen moves, his shortest loss ever. The game had lasted only a little over an hour, and Kasparov was pummeled the whole time because he had suicidally chosen a known inferior and passive line of the Caro-Kann Defense—a particularly odd selection given that he himself had defeated the Caro-Kann when Karpov previously played it against him in four key games. By the end of the match with Deep Blue, Kasparov was a broken man, a bloodied, knocked-out boxer who could barely crawl out of the ring. "The pressure got to me early," he told me years later. "By the last game I was in no condition to play chess—or do anything else."

His recollection was an understatement: at the time he had been so wounded that he lashed out and suggested that Deep Blue might have cheated—a charge that IBM denied—by getting advice from human chess masters during the games.[10] That's apparently the only way he could justify to himself its humanlike play. Did he really suspect that IBM had secretly enlisted Karpov or another GM to feed moves to the machine? The world's number one human player demanded a rematch. IBM, which was offended by his accusations, turned him down, ordered its programmers to clam up about how Deep Blue worked, and mothballed the machine. The press joked that Deep Blue had turned Deep Yellow.

EVEN PEOPLE WHO DIDN'T KNOW HOW TO PLAY CHESS TOOK KASPAROV'S DEfeat personally, as if it had been a terrible defeat for humankind. Editorials lamented the triumph of a machine in an area that had been widely regarded as a hallmark of human intelligence. And Wall Street rewarded IBM: the stock shot up 7 percent during the ten-day match, adding $11.4 billion to the company's valuation. In fact, though, Deep Blue had merely demonstrated that computers were good at what they have always been good at—calculation. The fact that a car can outrun a human athlete doesn't detract from the New York marathon; why, then, would we let a machine's success at chess somehow diminish human chess performance?

When electronic computers were in their infancy in the 1940s, pioneers in the nascent field of artificial intelligence set the goal of building a machine that played high-level chess. Unlike many other intellectual endeavors, the game was appealing to programmers because the machine's competence at chess could be judged precisely by pitting it against rated human players under controlled conditions; the machine would earn a rating, and subsequent improvement could be quantified by how its rating increased. To measure a machine's ability as a poet, say, would have involved subjective judgments. AI researchers hoped that, by building a chess computer that played as well as the world's elite, they would better understand the nature of human intelligence.

The irony in Deep Blue's success is that it provided no insight whatsoever into human chess playing; man and machine actually approach the game completely differently. Deep Blue chewed through three million moves per second, while Kasparov looked at, perhaps, one to three. Even at a speed of millions of moves per second, Deep Blue could not usually look very far ahead because the number of possible continuations was staggering. There are, for instance, more than 10^{40} (that's the number 1 followed by forty 0s) conceivable legal chess positions—and even more possible chess games. "There are more chess games," Kasparov likes to point out, "than there are atoms in the universe."

The strength of world-class human players lies in their ability to decide who stands better in a given position, and this ability—general chess knowledge, if you will—is hard to build into a machine. According to popular wisdom, a grandmaster is a kind of human computing machine: when he chooses a move, he explores numerous continuations in his mind's eye—if I push the king pawn, he'll fork my rooks, but then I'll trap his queen—at lightning speed with incredible precision. But this view is wrong: calculation is not the only, or even the main, secret of the master's success. He depends much more on pattern recognition than on the exploration of a mind-numbing aggregation of moves. "Calculation," wrote Father William Lombardy, a grandmaster and Roman Catholic priest, "most often comes after the goal is achieved, the moment when a winning position converts into a mathematically forced win."

The Dutch psychologist Adrian de Groot found that of the thirty-eight legal moves possible in the typical position, the master ponders an average of only 1.76. In other words, he is generally choosing between two candidate moves that he recognizes, based on the hundreds of thousands of positions he has played himself or seen others play, as contributing to the immediate or long-term goals of the position. Humans are better than computers at long-range strategic planning, where delicate, methodically executed maneuvers ultimately carry the day. Deep Blue and its silicon heirs excel in hand-to-hand combat, tactical dogfights in which brute computational strength prevails. Rather than despair that *Homo sapiens* has been somehow belittled by Deep Blue's victory, we could rejoice that human beings uniquely possess knowledge and intuition that computers are not yet close to approximating. After Deep Blue, grandmasters who battled machines often defanged them by the deliberate anti-computer strategy of avoiding messy brawls.

Although the match with Kasparov showed off Deep Blue's computational prowess, it did not actually settle the million-dollar question of whether man or machine plays better chess. The event was stacked against Kasparov, and not for the spurious reason that the machine was a fraud. The contest with Deep Blue was inherently unfair because, unlike high-level encounters between humans, Kasparov had the huge disadvantage of playing without having seen a single game of his opponent's, while Deep Blue had for examination hundreds of Kasparov's games. The match had been sponsored by IBM itself, and Kasparov believed that the company had a conflict of interest in ensuring that it was conducted fairly.

MAN-MACHINE ENCOUNTERS SEEM TO BRING OUT THE WORST IN TOP grandmasters: they self-destruct in ways that they never would against fleshy opponents. In the fall of 2002, Vladimir Kramnik, Kasparov's successor as world champion, sought revenge for humanity in an eight-game match against Deep Fritz, one of Deep Blue's mechanical confederates. (The "deep" means that the machine has more than one processor, unlike most desktop computers, which have only a single brain.) The match rules were designed to eliminate the inequities inherent in Kasparov's encounter, but they swung too much in the other direction, in the human's favor. Well in advance of the play, Deep Fritz's handlers had to provide the world champion with a copy of the software and promise not to change it subsequently. The latter requirement put the machine at a deficit: human competitors, after all, are free to adjust their playing style anytime they want.

"It was a terrible thing," said Frederic Friedel, co-founder of Chess-Base, the manufacturer of Deep Fritz. "Kramnik had Fritz's brain in a bottle. He could figure out what Fritz would play in a given position. Imagine that you and I are having a debate tomorrow. And today we practice first. You say something stupid and I completely refute it. Well, tomorrow you'll be on your guard and won't say the same thing. But a clone of you would repeat the same stupid argument. Kramnik had a clone of Fritz."

Even with that edge, however, Kramnik couldn't beat the computer. Throughout the match, he let himself be psyched out by the knowledge that his opponent was looking at millions of positions per second—even though he knew that it was doing ineffectual busywork, because the vast majority of those positions were nonsense and didn't warrant examination at all. Nonetheless, there was always the theoretical possibility that a counterintuitive continuation, which a human master would normally not even consider, let alone play, might turn out to be best. Kramnik became obsessed with this remote possibility and couldn't stop himself from considering improbable moves. And yet he knew that this approach was self-defeating; in the precious finite time his plodding human brain had to study the position, he should have been trying to assess which of the few natural-looking moves was actually the strongest. If Kasparov had convinced himself that Deep Blue couldn't have beaten him without human aid, Kramnik had succumbed to the delusion that he could outcalculate the calculator.

Kramnik still might have won had he consistently played the cautious, largely defensive chess for which he was known: at the start of the sixth game, he was ahead by a full point. But he then threw his lead away when he imprudently launched a sacrificial attack that the supercomputer easily rebuffed. "I wanted to be a hero," he told me later on the phone. "I had fallen in love with the sacrifice. I was seduced by the apparent beauty and at the time I thought that I was playing the most brilliant game of my career." But the machine came up with a nimble defense that he'd missed. The eight-game match ended in a tie.

IT TOOK KASPAROV SIX YEARS TO RECOVER FROM HIS MATCH WITH DEEP Blue and publicly jump back into the ring with a machine. Now that Kramnik had had the guts to take on a computer and play it to a tie, Kasparov was eager both to avenge his own humiliation by Deep Blue and upstage Kramnik by performing better than him. In early 2003, Kasparov faced a program called Deep Junior in six games in New York City. This time, the organizers tried to strike a balance between the computer-friendly conditions of the Deep Blue competition and the pro-human rules of Kramnik's contest. The programmers had to provide Kasparov with a current copy of the software in advance, but they were then allowed to tinker with it all they wanted—except during an actual game.

Friedel predicted Kasparov would triumph as long as he was cautious. "Junior is a street brawler," Friedel told me before the match. "You remember *West Side Story*? It's the Jets. It will be constantly taunting Garry, 'Do you want to fight with knives? Whips? Pistols? Machine guns? You choose the weapon.' If he knows what's best for him, he'll say, 'Let's stay in the ring and keep these big soft gloves on.' But it's not his nature to duck a challenge."

Indeed, initially Kasparov did not play it safe. In the first game, he came out swinging with a hyperaggressive pawn thrust on the seventh move and won decisively. By the start of the sixth and final game, the machine had fought back to tie the match—winning a game when Kasparov blundered in a better position and drawing the three other encounters. In the final game, Kasparov sacrificed the exchange on the twenty-third move, and the few hundred spectators cheered and rose out of their seats. Five moves later, though, Kasparov blinked: at his instigation, man and machine agreed to a draw, not in a lifeless position but in a knotty unbalanced situation full of fight. Against a human opponent, he would certainly have continued and in all likelihood clawed his way to a win. The carbon-based chess fans were disappointed that, just as they were beginning to smell the kill, the alpha male of their species had chickened out. The audience hissed and booed. "Kasparov's a pussy!" one kibitzer shouted.

"I was exhausted," Kasparov told me afterward. As with Deep Blue, he had once again let an encounter with a machine play games with his head. He had been obsessed with idea that Deep Junior would never tire. "The machine is never distracted by an argument with its mother," he told me, "or a lack of sleep. My goal was simple—not to lose."

LATER THAT YEAR ESPN INVITED ME TO BE THE COLOR COMMENTATOR FOR Kasparov's final effort at proving himself against a machine—this time, X3D Deep Fritz of Hamburg, in a four-game match at the New York Athletic Club in midtown Manhattan, just below Central Park. (The number of games in these matches had progressively fallen from eight when Kramnik took on Fritz, to six when Kasparov faced Junior, to four here—so that human fatigue would be less of a factor.) My fellow commentator was Seattle GM Yasser Seirawan, four-time U.S. champion. The host was Jamaican-born Maurice Ashley, a charismatic grandmaster whose e-mail handle "FirstBlackGM" aptly encapsulated his groundbreaking chess career. Ashley, who lives in Brooklyn, has a brother and sister who are both kickboxing champions. "It's scary to see them sit around and watch videos of their fights, vicariously reliving every brutal moment. I prefer to take my hostilities out on the chessboard. Step out-side," Maurice joked, "and I'll smash your Sicilian."

The New York Athletic Club was a strange venue for a chess match. It was a stuffy members-only institution whose name was incongruous with the formality of the place. Even though I was covering the match for ESPN, I was initially barred from the athletic club because I had the audacity to wear running shoes. Many scruffy chess fans were never ad-mitted because they were not wearing—and did not own—the requisite attire. Maurice and I joked about the irony of the match being held at a club that not so long ago would have refused to admit both him and Kasparov, a Jew. Given that I don't play sports or watch them—I couldn't tell you the rules of football—it was also ironic that I was now an ESPN commentator.

The match would air live on ESPN2, after a show on the World's Strongest Man Competition. Besides the Fischer-Spassky contest thirty years earlier, there was not much precedent for live televised coverage of chess in the United States, and the ESPN show had its bugs. My Telestrator was broken for all four games, so that I was unable to demon-strate moves on the on-screen board. Yasser's Telestrator worked fine, but I couldn't do my job of interrupting him and asking Everyman questions— "Why doesn't he just retreat the queen there?"—when his grandmasterly analysis went over the heads of the audience. Fortunately his explana-tions were good, and Maurice kept things moving by trotting out every sports analogy, and then some, to get across what was happening on the chessboard. I had memorized every juicy chess anecdote I could find, every nugget of chess history, and all the dirt I could turn up on Kas-parov, so that I was able to fill the airtime when the Russian went into a long think. The three of us had fun interpreting Kasparov's body lan-guage: When he took off his watch, the position was complicated and he was getting down to business. When he took off his jacket, things were very serious. When he put his watch back on, it was a signal that he was about to finish off his opponent.

There were operational difficulties besides the Telestrator. The rest-room at the New York Athletic Club was inconveniently located several hundred feet from the ESPN set, and so our producer prohibited us during commercial breaks from removing our earpieces and mikes and running to the bathroom. He feared we might not make it back to our seats and get wired up in time. He ordered us not to have caffeine or other diuretics on the morning of the show. He thought that holding our bladders during the first game might be a problem, because we were scheduled to be on the air on ESPN2 for three hours.

The game was a thrilling slugfest with the machine opting to give up a rook for a bishop in order to slow down Kasparov's attack. Maurice, Yasser, and I scrupulously avoided the bottled water on our anchor table until the last commercial break, when the control room said through our earpieces: "Drink up, boys! Soothe those parched throats! We're off the air in six minutes." We each downed a large bottle of Poland Spring. With only two minutes remaining and the game still going, the controller announced that there had been a change of plans: the show's ratings were so good that we were going to preempt the scheduled programming and continue live coverage until the game was over. Maurice and I looked at each other in disbelief—the game, which seemed quite complicated, could last a few more hours. "Try to hold it, guys," the controller barked into our ears. "You don't want to short-circuit the set!"

Call it special prejudice—we had wanted our human confederate to win the game, and he had a material advantage on the board, but his king was suddenly under assault. Now we found ourselves improbably rooting for a quick draw so that we could make it to the lavatory. Caissa, the goddess of chess, evidently understood our dilemma: six moves and twenty-five minutes later, the machine cleverly forced a draw by perpetual check.

The computer won the second game after Kasparov missed a simple tactic in time pressure. Then Kasparov evened the match in the third game by strangling Fritz with classic anti-computer play: as White, he steered the game into a closed position, where normally powerful pieces were limited in their mobility, and long-term planning was more important than calculation. The last game was anticlimatic: Kasparov as Black selected a defense in which the majority of pieces and pawns were quickly exchanged, and he played carefully to a draw on the twenty-seventh move. The best human player ever, and arguably the most battle-hardened, had once again chickened out.

After this event, the competitions between man and machine lost their novelty and allure. The chess world had grown weary of watching

Kramnik and Kasparov muddle their way to ties in three successive matches. Chess fans turned their attention back to the stressful struggles at the board between flesh-and-blood players. The rhythm of intraspecies games was more familiar, and there was always the chance for added excitement if the players spun out of control, like NASCAR racers, and injured themselves, their opponents, or the furniture in their hotel.

IN THE FALL OF 2006, VLADIMIR KRAMNIK PUT HIS WORLD CHAMPIONSHIP on the line in an event that had long been anticipated, a match that would, after thirteen confusing years, finally unify the two competing world titles—Kramnik's classical one, whose lineage included Kasparov, Fischer, and Botvinnik, and FIDE's "cheaper" title, which was granted in a shorter match at a faster time control. The FIDE champion was a reserved Bulgarian named Veselin Topalov, whose playing style was anything but reserved. Kramnik was the stolid, risk-averse defender—his nickname was Iceman—and Topalov was the dreamy tactician who dramatically sacrificed pawns and pieces with ease and seemed to cook up kingside assaults out of thin air.

The twelve-game match in Elista, Kalmykia, promised to be a battle royal. More people seemed to be rooting for Topalov, because they preferred his unrestrained approach to chess. They also held it against Kramnik that, unlike his predecessor Kasparov, he had been somewhat invisible in his half decade as world champion—never appearing, for instance, in the United States to promote the game.

Despite Topalov's chessboard aggression, he was known for having unsteady nerves. He was capable of mysteriously collapsing even when he had a large advantage. Playing Black in a Catalan Opening, Topalov could have achieved a draw in the first game by repeating moves, but instead he pressed for a win, blundered, and lost after seventy-five moves and six and a half hours. In the second game, he missed a winning combination on his thirty-second move, gave Kramnik too much counterplay, and lost a tricky endgame. After two successive draws, Kramnik had a commanding lead of 3–1.

The playing area in Elista had been designed to minimize the possibility of cheating. Both combatants were routinely searched, even the heels of their shoes examined, to eliminate the possibility that they were receiving assistance through cell phones or miniature computers. The live audience at the tournament was separated from the players by a glass wall, and there was supposedly even an electromagnetic interference signal designed to block wireless communication to any concealed earpieces that they might be wearing. (At the 2006 World Open in Philadelphia, a few months before the Kramnik-Topalov match, a player was found to be wearing a tiny wireless earpiece through which he was suspected of receiving advice about the moves a computer would make in his position.) Each player was provided with a private rest area and an adjoining bathroom to which he could retire as often as he liked, but these rooms were searched before the games; in addition, a closed-circuit video system enabled the match arbiters to observe what each player was doing in the rest area (though not in the bathroom) during the play.

After the fourth game, Topalov's manager improperly obtained the videotape of Kramnik's rest-area activity and protested to the appeals committee that the Russian had gone into the bathroom, where he could not be observed, a suspicious fifty times. The implication was that he was somehow cheating. Topalov's manager demanded that Kramnik's private potty be made off-limits, and the appeals committee—which had been handpicked by Kalmykian and FIDE president Kirsan Ilyumzhinov, who favored the FIDE champion Topalov—locked the bathroom before the fifth game, while also conceding that Kramnik's visits to the loo were not quite as numerous as Topalov's manager had alleged.

"I was lying on my couch next to my toilet and was furious," Kramnik recalled. "I did not think about the World Championship or the score. And then there was a new problem: I had to go to the bathroom, urgently. I asked the arbiter to open my toilet. He just shrugged and offered me an empty coffee cup."

Even though the appeals committee had essentially supported Topalov, his manager went one step further by demanding that an attendant now accompany Kramnik whenever he visited their now-common crapper—or else Topalov would refuse to shake his hand. Kramnik, a man of quiet dignity, found himself in the uncomfortable position of explaining his hydration and evacuation habits to a prying press and addressing the unspecified smear of foul play. Dubbed Krapnik, he quickly became the butt of jokes made by late-night comics and journalists around the world—a photo was posted on the Web in which Kramnik's pants were stained in a spot that suggested he had actually visited the bathroom one time too few. Kramnik had had enough and refused to make a single move in the fifth game. FIDE promptly forfeited him.

Top grandmasters, who had hoped that a unified world title would bring much-needed sponsorship dollars to the game, were crestfallen. "Once again chess has shot itself in the foot," British GM John Nunn wrote on the Internet. "Who will want to sponsor a top-level chess match if the whole thing can grind to a halt over a dispute about a toilet? At least when the 1984/5 Karpov-Kasparov match was controversially terminated . . . , the players had managed to entertain the chess public with forty-eight games before everything collapsed in chaos. Apparently today's players only have the stamina to manage four!"

When Kramnik was forfeited, Toiletgate became an international incident. Ilyumzhinov happened to be meeting with Putin at the time, and the Russian leader made clear his support for his confederate Kramnik and his displeasure at the whole unseemly incident. Ilyumzhinov rushed home to Kalmykia and fired the appeals committee. He unlocked Kramnik's privy but added an attendant who was supposed to monitor what the Russian was doing. Putin then called Kramnik and urged him not to quit (as Henry Kissinger had similarly urged Fischer during his 1972 match with Spassky). Kramnik resumed the sixth game "under protest," and, facing Topalov's Queen's Gambit, achieved a draw as Black. The seventh game was also drawn.

Topalov's manager then increased the psychological pressure by releasing a statement claiming that Fritz would have made 78 percent of the moves Kramnik had made so far, implying that the Russian had unlawful access to Fritz during the games. (Of course Kramnik and Fritz are world-class players with similar ratings in the 2700s, which is the simplest explanation for the commonality of their moves.) The assault on Kramnik's integrity was now too much for him: with his nerves frayed, he collapsed in the next two games, allowing Topalov to pull ahead for the first time in the match, by one point. Now the grandmaster community was firmly in Kramnik's camp, with many well-respected GMs releasing an open letter in which they condemned Topalov's deplorable psychological warfare and urged Kramnik to soldier on and try to win despite the unjust forfeit of a key game. In the tenth round, Kramnik, with most of the chess world cheering him on, recovered his equilibrium and decisively disposed of Topalov on the White side of a Catalan. The match was now tied, and when the final two encounters both ended in draws, the contest was sent into an overtime series of rapid games. Kramnik defeated Topalov twice in the fast play and won the unified crown. Putin was pleased: Kramnik had beaten back the latest, nefarious threat to Russian domination of the World Championship.

Kramnik must be a masochist. On November 25, 2006, with not even two months' rest after his stressful victory over Topalov, he jumped back into the man versus machine fray by taking on a new and improved Deep Fritz in a six-game match in Bonn, Germany. The first game was drawn, and then in the second, in a position that would likely have led to a draw, Kramnik made the most basic and catastrophic error in chess. In a position in which he had plenty of time on the clock, Kramnik succumbed to *amaurosis scachistica*—chess blindness—and failed to see that the machine was threatening to mate him on the spot. When he didn't simply parry the threat, the machine pounced and checkmated him.

"I cannot really find any explanation," a stunned Kramnik said after the match. "I was not feeling tired. I think I was calculating well. . . . It's just very strange. I cannot explain it." By overlooking a mate in one, the fourteenth world champion now has the dubious distinction of making the worst blunder ever in the history of championship chess. Not surprisingly, for an activity in which a player's psychological readiness is as important as his knowledge of the Sicilian, Kramnik did not recover. He never beat Fritz once and lost the match 4–2.

5

AN AMERICAN IN MOSCOW

"In Russia, truth almost always assumes an entirely fantastic character."
—FYODOR DOSTOYEVSKY

DURING THE ESPN MATCH, THE ELEVATORS AT THE NEW York Athletic Club were a good place to hear chess gossip. An acquaintance of mine named Andrew, who was a newcomer to chess but fascinated by the scene, rode them frequently in the hope of meeting famous players who had come to watch Garry Kasparov confront the computer.

"I met Jennifer Shahade," he gushed to me. "You're friends, right?"

"Yep."

"Is she the U.S. women's champion?"

"Last year she was. Now it's Anna Hahn, a trader on the Nikkei."

"I need to meet her, too," said Andrew. "I Googled Jennifer. Her favorite book is *The Brothers Karamazov*. I'm going to read it this weekend. Does she give private lessons?"

"Yes, and she's looking for students."

"How good do I have to be before she'll coach me?"

"She works with beginners."

"OK, but I don't want to embarrass myself. I'm heading to a Village chess shop tonight to work on my game."

After another elevator ride, Andrew told me that he had overheard a young man in a dark suit explaining how to beat Kasparov. "What nonsense!" Andrew said. "I can't believe the guy was so arrogant."

"Kasparov has been known to lose," I said.

"Not to this guy. No way. He was a businessman. He wasn't Russian. He looked too normal to be a strong player. He was just a braggart."

Andrew was mistaken. The man was Joel Lautier, a thirty-year-old grandmaster from Paris and full-time chess professional, who is one of the few human players to achieve a plus score against Kasparov in classical chess. During the Russian's reign as world champion, they played ten games and Lautier ended up one game ahead. Three of the encounters had been decisive, with the Frenchman winning two of them.[1]

I corralled Joel between games at the New York Athletic Club and interviewed him over drinks. I was impressed by his intensity, self-confidence, and total devotion to chess. "I've had very strange dreams," he told me, "in which the entire universe operates not by physical laws but according to the rules of chess. A person says good-bye, turns into a rook, and moves off horizontally the way a rook does. I like Nabokov because of the very real way he portrays how the game can take over your life."

When Joel was thirteen, he trained with Yacob Murey, an untitled player who emigrated from Russia to France via Israel.[2] Murey was a walking chess encyclopedia who had a wealth of original ideas about the openings. "He looks like a tramp," Joel continued. "He dresses badly and is not too clean. He doesn't know how to properly eat what's in front of him. He speaks only about chess, as if it is the most important thing in the world, and he talks about the game even with nonplayers who can't follow what he's saying. They think he's a madman. If you spend a couple of days with Murey, you forget that anything else exists in the world besides chess—it's a wonderful feeling. It is important to meet such people because then you realize how rich and deep the game actually is."

I asked Joel what it was like to face Kasparov. "Obviously I enjoyed myself," he said. "Garry is an anxious player. He absolutely hates losing, and that fear of defeat drives him to work extremely hard and play well. He's a comedian at the board, and I think he knows that. He makes all these faces. In our games he was not too emotional until he was losing. Then he'd start swearing and muttering to himself in Russian. I understand the language so I could really enjoy the show. Russian is very rich when it comes to curse words. What he said cannot easily be translated into English."[3]

Joel first beat Kasparov at Linares 1994 in a thrilling encounter in which Joel had two queens. "It was absolutely crazy," he recalled, "with three queens on the board." After Kasparov lost, Joel asked him if he wanted to analyze the game.

"There is nothing to analyze," Kasparov responded, and he bulldozed his way out of the room.

"Some unfortunate fan approached him for an autograph," Joel recalled, "but Garry shoved him up against the wall. A defeated Kasparov is a serious beast." Kasparov had calmed down by dinner, however, and he proved willing to discuss the game in the dining hall. Then he invited Joel back to his hotel suite, where they analyzed the game for two or three hours. "Garry is a very complicated, two-sided person," Joel told me. "He can be extremely combative and hostile, and then he can do something unexpected and very generous, like going over the game with me for an evening. You have to admire his genuine love for chess."

I asked Joel what their relationship was like these days. "Not good," he said. "I don't think he likes people who have a plus score against him." Joel may also be on Kasparov's bad side because of his suggestion that the champion's on-and-off-again relationship with FIDE strongman Kirsan Ilyumzhinov was governed less by what was good for chess and more by what was good for Kasparov. "There's a joke chess players tell," Joel told me. "Kasparov once said, when he broke with FIDE, 'I will not take Ilyumzhinov's dirty money.' After Kasparov had a rapprochement with FIDE, he was asked why he was now taking the dirty money. 'Ah,' he said, 'it's because I discovered the money was laundered.'"

Joel's role as one of Vladimir Kramnik's seconds in the 2000 World Championship can't have helped his relationship with Kasparov either. "He probably sees me as the enemy because I assisted the man who dethroned him. I don't have bad feelings toward him. He's a great, great player."

JOEL NEVER WORKED SO HARD IN HIS LIFE AS THE TIME HE HELPED TWENTY-five-year-old Kramnik prepare for Kasparov. For six months before the match in London, he and two other grandmasters aided Kramnik full-time. "Vladimir was incredibly organized," Joel said. "He divided the openings he was thinking of playing among the three of us and had us analyze them individually for days." Joel initially worked from home in Paris. "Sometimes I looked at chess for ten hours a stretch," he said. "Kramnik would rotate among the three of us, visiting me for two or three weeks at a time to go over my analysis and push it even further."

The match itself, which lasted three and a half weeks, was even more grueling. Each game started about 2:00 P.M. and finished by 6:00 or 7:00 P.M. Afterward, Kramnik would do a brain dump of everything he'd thought about during the game, and the three seconds would write it all down, to dissect it later in case a subsequent game followed the same course. Then they'd go for a walk and eat dinner. At 10:00 P.M. they'd resume preparation. Kramnik stayed with them until 2:00 A.M. They continued analyzing through the night, until Kramnik rejoined them between 10:00 and 11:00 A.M. Then they'd show him what they'd looked at.

"I was impressed that in one hour he could go through all of our analysis—eight or nine hours of it—checking every line, learning the moves by heart in the process, and actually exercising his critical eye on them," Joel said. "At some point, he'd say, 'I don't like this particular line. You should check it again before the next game.' It was amazing that he could instantly spot the critical places without our having to tell him." Then they'd take another stroll, eat lunch together, and walk Kramnik to the board. Game time was when the seconds were finally free to sleep, but of course they wanted to be awake for the finale of each encounter.

Joel's work with Kramnik did not translate immediately into his own chess success. "I actually played much worse," he told me, "because it was very depressing. I saw that he was so much faster than me and could instantly feel things on the chessboard that took me time to figure out for myself. There were many occasions where he wouldn't trust a variation before he even did any calculations. He is a very intuitive player. He often decides immediately on his next move and spends his thinking time confirming his choice. When I play, I make a lot of my decisions by vigorously calculating everything. I close in on the right move by methodical, step-by step analysis. Instead he feels the right move. That skill is very hard to learn—it's more of a gift."

World-class players generally make tough bosses, but Joel found Kramnik to be pleasant and kind. "Most strong players are completely self-centered," Joel said, "because they are used to doing things alone. They are blind to how other people feel or else simply don't care. Garry can be charming, but he can also behave terribly, especially after a defeat. Vladimir is extremely well balanced and almost never loses his composure. There were tense moments in the match—like when Kasparov shifted to the Nimzo-Indian Defense, for which we were not as well prepared—but Vladimir didn't take it out on us. He remained calm."

The secret of Kramnik's victory in the sixteen-game match, in which Kasparov astonishingly did not win a single game and lost twice, was his deep understanding of his opponent's psychology and his ability to translate that knowledge into an opening for which Kasparov was not temperamentally suited. It wasn't a question of busting one particular line in the Najdorf that Kasparov liked to play, or one specific line in the Grünfeld—it was a question of employing a whole new opening system that would take the world champion out of his comfort zone. It had to be a system that Kasparov had not faced before in match play and one that Kramnik himself had never employed, so that it would be a complete surprise. Moreover, it had to be a system that would be hard for Kasparov to master during the match, with his team of seconds and computers in overdrive. The so-called Berlin Defense to the Ruy Lopez met the criteria and had the additional promise of getting the queens off the board on the eighth move, making it harder for Kasparov to play his signature attacking game. Kramnik knew that Kasparov would suffer psychologically without his lady.

"There was one big problem with the Berlin," said Joel, laughing. "It's absolutely horrible. It's very passive and unnatural. It takes a long time to get your king to safety. White pushes back your pieces with his pawns. It's hard to coordinate your rooks because they're not connected. You have to make funny moves to even get the rooks out. White definitely has an advantage, but it's not so easy for him to play. You reach an endgame right in the opening, so Black's loss of time isn't that bad.

"We kept telling Vladimir that the Berlin was crap. But he kept insisting that we look at it. Vladimir has a classical chess upbringing and normally he wouldn't even consider playing such a passive defense. But he knew Garry would hate the tortuously slow pace even more than Kramnik himself did. Vladimir kept ordering us to explore the Berlin further." Kramnik discovered many subtle ideas and nuances and convinced himself to like the defense. By the start of the match, he had played the defense in training games with Joel and his other seconds, and it had been very hard for them to draw him with White. "His match strategy was brilliant," Joel said. "Garry was tortured—but for me the Berlin is one of the most depressing things in chess. I'd give up the game if I were forced to play it."

JOEL LAUTIER WAS BORN IN TORONTO, IN 1973, TO A JAPANESE MOTHER AND a French father, both computer specialists. His first language was English because his nanny, and the rest of Toronto, spoke English. "My parents talked to me in French," he recalled, "but I responded to them in English, which was a strange way of communicating." When he was three, his family moved to France, and he started playing chess six months later. Joel's father was obsessed by the Fischer-Spassky match, which had taken place just before Joel was born. His mother taught him the moves and his father helped him improve. "In a sense I already had the routine of a chess professional when I was five," Joel said. "Every day I played a long match against my mother when she came home from work." In the morning, his father would help him prepare for the match; later that evening, the two would go over the games. "The fact that chess is my career," Joel said dryly, "was not an improvised choice."

Joel's first chess memory, from the age of five, was his father bringing home a board without any coordinates on the sides. "He'd point to a square and say, 'Pretend you're White and tell me the coordinates,'" Joel recalled. "And I'd say, 'e4.' 'Now pretend you're Black,' he'd say, and he'd point to a different square and ask me the coordinates. That's how I started learning blindfold chess." Joel mastered mental play when he was ten, during his two-hour commute to a new school. Each day he brought a book of chess puzzles with him and solved them in his head on the long ride.

Joel said that as he became increasingly involved in the chess world, his father's only concern was "whether I could make a living." In 1988, when Joel became world junior champion at the age of fifteen—the youngest person ever to do so—his father realized that it was a realistic possibility. (Although Joel had skipped a grade in school because he was academically gifted, he never graduated from high school, because his senior-year final exams in Paris in 1990 were inconveniently scheduled at the same time as the World Championship Qualifying Tournament in Manila.) In January 1995, Joel's ranking in the world peaked at number twelve. When I first interviewed him in November 2003, he was number thirty-two. "My ambition is to break into the top ten," Joel told me then. "I'll be sad if I don't at least try." Joel conceded that he can't calculate as fast as he could when he was twenty years old, but believes he can give younger players a run by concentrating on aspects of the game that they've neglected. "With their computer databases," he said, "they may know the latest opening wrinkles. But after the opening, the gods have placed the middle game. And after the middle game, the endgame."

Joel's holistic approach and his emphasis on fundamentals are very Russian, which is no surprise since he learned the language when he was twelve so that he could read Russian chess books, immerse himself in Moscow chess culture, and study with a top Soviet coach. His high forehead is topped by a thick black coiff; my first impression of him was that he could have passed as an apparatchik in the Brezhnev-era politburo. "If you're going to be a great classical chef," he told me, "you must learn French. If you're going to be an opera singer, you have to know Italian. If you're going to be a chess player, you must learn Russian." Joel added that while there may be many drawbacks to Communism, the Soviet system produced "many damn good players."

LIKE JOEL, I HAVE ALWAYS BEEN FASCINATED BY RUSSIA, AND CHESS WAS JUST part of it. I was in first grade in 1962 when Nikita Khrushchev stationed nuclear warheads ninety miles from Florida. I remember the "duck and cover" drills during the Cuban Missile Crisis, in which we practiced hiding under our desks. (The whole country was then subscribing to the delusion that this would protect the children of America from nuclear attack.) For me, though, Russia has a mystique beyond Cold War intrigue, because my father was a disillusioned Communist.

Some of my earliest memories of my father involve his flirtation with Communism. When I was four, I accompanied him to the polling station in Westport for the U.S. presidential election in 1960. We went early in the day, and when he emerged from the voting booth, I asked him whether he had chosen Kennedy or Nixon. He leaned down to whisper in my ear, and the old ladies who were manning the polling station on behalf of the League of Women Voters moved forward to overhear. "Eric Hass," my father stage-whispered.

"Eric Hass?" they buzzed. "Eric Hass?" The ladies were all aflutter trying to figure out who he was. Alas, my father had not started a trend. When the ballots were tabulated later in the local paper, there was only one reported vote for the Socialist Labor Party candidate. Some years later my father cast a vice-presidential vote for the Black Panther activist Angela Davis. I don't know whether he voted for her because she was the Communist Party candidate or out of neighborly affinity: she had been incarcerated a couple of blocks from his Village apartment, in the infamous Women's House of Detention, which we often walked past on my weekends in the city. The inmates would press their faces to the tiny barred windows, shout obscenities, and describe in violent and sexually graphic detail what they wanted to do to the men on the street. The women made me nervous and my father laugh. They were like characters in the novels he taught at the New School.

My dad was drawn to Communism because of its promise of equality for the working class. He had been influenced by a series of demeaning, poorly paid jobs in high school, such as shoveling horse carcasses into glue-factory ovens, and he became a labor organizer in his late teens. (My mother had a photograph of him in high school leading a student demonstration in support of workers' rights.)

Then World War II forced radical intellectuals of his generation to reassess their commitment to Soviet Communism. My father felt betrayed in 1939, when Stalin signed a nonaggression pact with Hitler and allowed Germany to invade Poland. Stalin's subsequent slaughter of his own people confirmed my father's decision to align himself with Leon Trotsky, the banished Bolshevik leader (and, incidentally, a chess fanatic who purportedly planned the details of the Russian Revolution by moving pieces around on a chessboard). Trotsky was not as authoritarian or ruthless as Stalin; he objected to appeasing fascist countries and called for a democratic worldwide socialist revolution. Over time my father mellowed into a New Deal Democrat.

There were other Communist sympathizers in my family, like Aunt Molka, the mother of the ex-husband of my father's sister, who was a colorful presence at Thanksgiving. My father dismissed her as a closet Stalinist and warned me to stay clear of politics while we ate turkey lest the mealtime pleasantries erupt into an internecine feud between Communist splinter groups. Molka was a world-renowned marionettist, and my dad was particularly distressed by a puppet show she performed in which she reenacted, with unrestrained enthusiasm, the fatal ice-picking of Trotsky when he lived in exile in Mexico.

Although my dad had renounced Communism before I was born, my friends and I still knew him as a political and social activist. As a child, I was both proud and embarrassed by my dad's utopian and leftist views, just as I had conflicted feelings about our cluttered house. My dad was an early opponent of the Vietnam War—he was active in the War Resisters League—and I admired him for challenging my friends' and their parents' belief that they had to support the President of the United States.

Years before I was eligible to be drafted, my father was scheming about how I could avoid Vietnam. As an atheist, I would not be able to receive a conscientious objector exemption to military service on religious grounds. And so he started dragging me, at the age of seven or eight, to Friends Meeting Houses, so that I would be able to claim that I was raised as a Quaker pacifist; he made sure I signed the guest book at the meetings. To create a further paper trail of my opposition to the war, he also took me to peace rallies in the hope that I'd be arrested, or at least end up in the newspaper. And he sent me to a radical sleepaway camp near the submarine base in Groton, Connecticut.

We spoke Esperanto there, painted ban-the-bomb signs, and stuffed envelopes with antiwar brochures. I became very good at drawing mushroom clouds. In the evening our long-haired counselor would abandon us: he'd take the signs we had made and join other peaceniks in blocking access to the nuclear subs. Every few days we would get a new counselor after the previous one had been arrested for trespassing on military property. Late one night, pro-war townies set the camp on fire. The barn burned and horses stampeded. I begged my parents to retrieve me.

Still, the frightening experience did not sour my father on doctrinaire summer camps. For the next three years he sent me to an all-boys Quaker camp in Vermont. I enjoyed the outdoor activities—swimming, canoeing, hiking, lean-to building—but rejected the religious underpinning, subdued as it was. I did not like singing "Kumbaya." I resisted weaving Eyes of God. I started skipping the morning meditative Quaker services, to the consternation of the camp's earnest director, and played chess instead with a friend.

The counselors in Vermont were not arrested in demonstrations. They supervised us closely all summer long, although they occasionally coerced us into doing questionable things like hoeing in the nude. A dozen of us would walk around naked on a hillside, in various stages of pre- and post-puberty, turning over soil, pulling weeds, and harvesting carrots. I may have learned a bit about gardening, and the need to apply sunscreen, but I was ashamed to take off my clothes again in front of anybody for the next decade.

My father's radicalism extended to his ideas about primary-school education. He was the president of the Summerhill Society of America, an organization devoted to establishing alternative, progressive schools modeled after A. S. Neill's controversial Summerhill in England, where kids were not confined to classrooms and could run around doing whatever they pleased: playing chess all day, or even nude hoeing, if they were so inclined. Given my dad's affiliation with Summerhill, my own education—public schools in affluent Westport, Ivy League college—was surprisingly traditional. My parents disagreed about where to send me, and so their solution was that my mother chose the elementary and secondary schools, my father selected the summer camps, and I picked the college.

My father wanted my education to include Marxism. When my parents were lying in bed late at night and my mother couldn't sleep, he would explain *The Communist Manifesto* to her. It was the perfect cure for insomnia, she told me, although that of course was not his intention. My turn to understand *The Communist Manifesto* came at Harvard when, with my father's approval, I took a large lecture course on Marx from the celebrated ex-socialist neocon thinker Daniel Bell. We had to read twelve hundred pages of Marx, not just the published works but drafts of them. I found the writing tedious—much of it was detailed description of every conceivable job in Industrial Age England—and two days before the exam I had managed to get through only a measly two hundred pages.

In the end, it required drugs—the first I had ever taken—for me to conquer Marx, please my dad, and retain my summa cum laude grade point average. One of my college buddies had received a prescription for Dexedrine from his physician father, who assumed his son would be buying amphetamines from street peddlers in Harvard Square and preferred that he obtain pure stuff from a pharmacy instead. But he warned his son not to take Dexedrine after exam week. He had too many patients, he said, with high-powered jobs, many in government, who were addicted and needed ever-increasing, destructive doses to achieve the same effect.

My studious compulsiveness required me to spend a day in the Science Center Library researching possible ill effects of Dexedrine in obscure medical journals—time that would have perhaps been better spent reading more Marx. I ended up taking the minimum dose and found that I could concentrate with laser focus on whatever I wanted. Anything I turned my mind to seemed to be the most exciting subject in the universe. I spent a long day in the Winthrop House Library scanning one thousand pages of Marx. I took the five-part final on speed. When I received my exam books back, the teaching assistant had written, "A, A+, A, A+, A. Superb work!! Too bad you didn't talk more in section—we could have used your insights." I think I received the top score. I could have been the poster child for Dexedrine. I hadn't felt like I had taken a drug. I wasn't jittery or manic at all. I felt totally rested and alive. I was having the best day of my life. It was scary how great I felt. I sensed Dexedrine's addictive appeal and never took amphetamines again.

I recently found my Marx exam in the attic. When I review it now, and see the teacher's approving red check marks next to my essays, I am mystified that I was ever able to discourse, to my father's great delight, on Hegel, Montaigne, Feuerbach, *homo faber*, *lumpen proletariat*, and the Eighteenth Brumaire.

Today there is a debate in the chess world about drug testing. FIDE officials dream of chess becoming an official Olympic sport, and so, in compliance with International Olympic Committee standards, they have introduced random drug testing at tournaments (prompting one wag to suggest that FIDE officials are the ones on drugs if they truly think that chess will ever be played in the Olympics). Critics of the testing point out that chess has never had a drug problem. They also claim that there is nothing to test for because no medicine is known to boost chess or other intellectual performance. My two days on Dexedrine suggest otherwise. Amphetamines, I'm certain, could make you more alert and focused at the chessboard and help you cram the latest twists in opening theory just before the critical game, even if you forgot them a day later. OK, your brain cells will eventually sizzle if you do too much speed, but by then you will have played moves that will immortalize you in the chess hall of fame.

IN LATE JANUARY 2004, JOEL LAUTIER ENTERED THE ANNUAL AEROFLOT OPEN in Moscow, along with 163 other grandmasters from thirty-two countries—a world record for most GMs in a single tournament. There were 650 competitors in all, playing in three sections, for $150,000 in prizes. For nine straight days they would play a game a day, each one lasting typically between four and six hours. Lautier, with a stratospheric rating of 2676, was the sixth-highest rated player in Aeroflot, with a mere two dozen rating points separating him from the number one seed. Consequently Joel hoped to win one of the top prizes—uncontested first place paid $25,000.

At Joel's suggestion, I traveled to Moscow for the second half of Aeroflot, accompanied by my college friend Matt, an artist and keen observer of the human condition (particularly mine). Matt doesn't play tournament chess but appreciates my enthusiasm for the game. At Harvard, more than a quarter century ago, he watched me confront one of the first desktop chess computers, at the Boston Chess Club; it played so slowly that I abandoned the game in the middle.

On our Russian adventure, I made the tactical error of requesting aisle seats opposite each other on the plane. That left the seat next to Matt free for occupation by a Russian master from Brooklyn who's been known to walk ten miles to a chess club just to get a game. He has a very aggressive playing style—he likes to develop his queen as early as the second move, in violation of chess common sense—and he has a camel's overbite and lips that are always twitching. How he could afford to go to Moscow was anyone's guess; maybe he had cajoled someone into backing him. He spent the nine-hour flight mumbling to himself while shifting flat, button-size chess pieces around on a dingy magnetic board and doing mathematical puzzles from a book for clever children. Every so often Matt shot me a reproachful look. While the plane was taxiing to the gate, the Russian master could not contain his hyperaggressive impulses. He was the only one who prematurely removed his seat belt and stood up.

"Sit down!" the Aeroflot stewardess commanded.

"*J'adoube!*" ("I adjust!") he responded, as he stumbled back into his seat. This common chess expression is what players say when they want to suspend the touch-move rule so that they can adjust a piece without having to move it.[4]

Matt and I sped in a jalopy of a taxi from the airport to the massive Hotel Russia on Red Square. The hotel, which billed itself as the largest in Europe, was both the site of the tournament and the place we were staying. We arrived during the fifth round and went straight to the playing hall, which was crammed with hundreds of competitors. Suspended from the ceiling was a large, dusty inflatable plane with a faded Aeroflot logo. Matt's first impression of the tournament was that it reeked of testosterone, like a high school locker room after a basketball game. I had become inured to this familiar tournament smell.

We peeked at Joel's game against Artashes Minasian, an Armenian GM in his mid-thirties, and I tried to explain to Matt how Joel was beating back the do-or-die King's Indian, a counterpunching response to his queen-pawn opening. Joel won the game in thirty-four moves, and now, midway through the tournament, he had a score of three wins and two draws, putting him in a tie for the lead with seventeen others. Over the next two days, he went on to draw his sixth game and then, in the seventh round, demolish another King's Indian. "Petrosian once said that the King's Indian paid his rent," Joel gleefully told me, "and now it's paying mine."

In the evenings after his games, I had expected Joel to hit the chess books, but he wanted to party and show us late-night Moscow. Our second day there was a holiday called Defenders of the Motherland Day, a kind of Russian equivalent of Veterans Day. What remained of the Communist Party held a nostalgic, boisterous, red-flag-waving rally; elderly men paraded through the streets in ill-fitting army uniforms from their youth. After Joel's seventh-round rout of the King's Indian, he took us to an artsy supper club where twenty-year-old women in ersatz military fatigues held a runway fashion show to mock Defenders of the Motherland Day. With their breasts exposed, they wielded grenades and marched down the runway to the blasting tune of "You're in the Army Now."

I liked the new Russia: I had not expected this degree of open, cheeky dissent, the women engaged in the kind of performance art I might see back in New York. Even in the incessant snow and freezing temperatures of February, Moscow was surprisingly vibrant, with its mix of proud old-world Bolsheviks and the cavorting representatives of a skeptical new generation. After dinner, Joel and I went to a subterranean rock club and had another beer. "This one is for the King's Indian Defense!" I said, raising my stein. "May foolhardy Black players continue to venture it!"

I felt guilty keeping Joel out late when he had to play chess the next day. With two rounds remaining, his score of 5½–1½ put him in a six-way tie for second place, only a half point behind the sole player in first. Joel was in an excellent spot to win substantial money—even to garner first prize, if Caissa smiled and paired him with the current leader and Joel knocked him out. "It's good for me to party," he explained to me at 1:30 A.M. "If you weren't in Moscow, I'd be doing too much chess and there'd be diminishing returns. Soon I'll be hungry for chess. I'll prepare a couple of hours, to 4 A.M. or so. Then I'll get a decent sleep because my game is not until the afternoon."

We got back to the Hotel Russia at 2:00 A.M. and Joel immediately checked the next-round postings. "Damn!" he said, "It's the worst possible pairing. I get Pavel." Joel was scheduled to play White, and I imagined Pavel Tregubov to be a fearsome Russian heavyweight, a World Championship contender who'd learned chess at the age of two and actually knew how to marshal the Black forces in the King's Indian. The Russian-born Tregubov turned out to be a close friend and neighbor of Joel's in Paris. They had studied chess together for hours, trusting each other to the point where they knew each other's opening secrets. It would be psychologically difficult for Joel to go all out against his chess helpmate, and vice versa—and it might risk undermining their friendship—even though a win in the penultimate round would bring Joel that much closer to a lucrative first-place finish.

It was no surprise the next day when Joel and Tregubov—by tacit or explicit agreement—played a quiet, bloodless draw. And yet, going into the next and final round, Joel remained only half a point behind the leader—and therefore was still in contention for first place. Thousands of dollars—and priceless prestige—were at stake.

JOEL'S OPPONENT WAS A SEASONED PROFESSIONAL, RAFAEL VAGANIAN, FIFTY-two, the first great player to emerge from Armenia after Tigran Petrosian, the ninth world champion. In the 1980s, the heavyset Vaganian had been among the chess elite, and yet he had never ascended to the very pinnacle. Botvinnik regarded him as a natural but lazy talent and once said "that Vaganian played as though chess did not exist before he came along." This was a backhanded compliment: Botvinnik admired Vaganian's verve at the board but disapproved of his reluctance to study the games of his chess forebears.

GM Genna Sosonko, writing in a book called *The Reliable Past*, interpreted the fact that Vaganian wasn't a World Championship contender as a deliberate choice:

> [He] lacked the obsessive desire to become not just one of the best, but the very best, to subordinate everything in life, if only for a time, to those little wooden figures.

To ascend that final step in chess, Vaganian would have had to give up a life filled with friends, long sessions at the dinner table often lasting far into the night, dates and parties, cards and dominoes, jokes and tricks. . . . He was too fond of all the joys of life . . . to trade them all in for immortality in the form of his photograph hung up for posterity amongst the apostles on the chess club wall.

In the heat of a tournament, though, Vaganian had the killer instinct. At Aeroflot, he and Joel were both braced for a fight to the death. "The only way to go was all out," Vaganian wrote afterward, "because a draw would yield both of us nothing but a small amount of cash. A win, however, would yield to a high placing, probably a tie for first (which is what happened) and, if everything fell into place, even the first prize would be within reach."

Unfortunately for a night owl like Joel, this fateful last game was scheduled for early in the morning, instead of in the afternoon like the previous eight rounds. The game was one of six conducted on a roped-off, elevated stage at the front of the playing hall—an arrangement that was frustrating for the spectators. From beyond the ropes, I could watch Joel but not see the board clearly. The moves of the game were posted on monitors in a nearby press room and on the Internet. In the press room, I could see the position but not him, so I went back and forth between the monitors and the tournament hall.

Joel had White, and the game began as a Queen's Gambit Declined, Exchange Variation, with Joel developing his dark-squared bishop to the fourth rank, as he liked to do in this line. This was no surprise to Vaganian, because he had reached this very position against Lautier three years before in a blitz tournament and defeated him. On the seventh move, however, Joel varied from their earlier encounter by moving a knight instead of a pawn. They sheltered their respective kings on the same side of the board and staked out territory in front of their monarchs, Joel with pawns and Vaganian with pieces.

On the seventeenth move, Vaganian made an impressive rook sacrifice to break up the advanced pawns in front of Joel's king and launch an attack. I had noticed that Joel reflexively tapped the floor with his right foot when his game was complicated. But here, after his twentieth move, his foot was still. In fact, his whole body was fatalistically tranquil and subdued— because the outcome of the game was now apparently beyond his control.

I returned to the press room to study the position. Vaganian was pounding Joel's king and could always force a draw by perpetual check, but there was no reason for Vaganian to bail out with a draw if he could find a knockout blow. The assembled journalists realized that the Armenian had an easy win if he simply shifted his light-squared bishop to the edge of the board and forced an exchange for the opposing cleric. It was an obvious move. The chess reporters, me included, were much weaker than the players on the stage. If we found the move, surely a grandmaster of Vaganian's caliber would, too. I rushed back to the tournament hall to watch the expected denouement.

Joel was still sitting there stoically, and his opponent was lost in thought. Ten minutes passed and Vaganian had not found the move. Joel, for sure, had seen the winning continuation because his normal poker face was now grim; he was waiting for the guillotine to drop.

My head started to ache, as if my own game had gone awry. I didn't want to watch him suffer. I had asked him once how he handled losing.

"Very badly," he said. "Very, very badly."

"What do you do?" I asked.

"I smash the pieces. I send them flying. At least that's what I did when I was a kid. I remember playing a very respected international master, a nice old man in his seventies. I was sure I was winning, but somehow I made a mistake and lost. I was pissed off. The man saw that I was unhappy and tried to console me, saying that I had played well. I told him to go to hell and smashed the pieces. Of course, what's allowed when you're about twelve doesn't look good when you're a grown-up. So I had to stop that. Losses still affect me a lot but I'm quieter about them now. Which may be a bad sign, actually. You have to really hate losing to play your best."

Another ten minutes passed and Vaganian was literally scratching his head. I thought I detected a fleeting look of bemusement on Joel's face. Could it be that his opponent would not find the coup de grâce?

Five more minutes passed—twenty-five minutes in all—and still Vaganian had not played the "obvious" move. Joel was pallid again. The tension was too much. Joel was a take-charge kind of guy—someone who taught himself Russian at the age of twelve because he knew he was going to be a chess professional—and here he was in the uncomfortable position of having no influence at all on his destiny. His fate was in the hands of an opponent who, after playing well earlier, was now apparently having trouble concentrating. Yet another minute passed before Vaganian, his neurons finally synchronized, shifted his bishop to the flank. The Armenian grandmaster stood up and paraded around the stage, confident of victory.

Seven moves later Joel extended his hand in resignation. He did not abuse the chessmen or tell Vaganian where to go. In fact he did not say anything at all. He looked dazed. His eyes were watery, and there were beads of sweat on his forehead. He rose quietly and paused to look at the other top games on the stage.

Then Joel descended into the main tournament hall and walked slowly into the adjoining espresso lounge, where other competitors who had finished their games were imbibing beer and vodka. An attractive woman asked Joel if a friend could take a picture of the two of them. A Russian television crew cornered him for an interview. Another journalist turned on a tape recorder and asked him a series of questions. I could not follow the conversations—they were in Russian—but I could see that he was straining to smile and appear upbeat.[5] He was in demand for interviews in Moscow because of his language skills, his reputation as a strong player, and his new role as president of the Association of Chess Professionals, an organization dedicated to getting more money and better playing conditions for tournament regulars.

When the last journalist was finished, I put my hand on Joel's shoulder. "You're a sport," I said. "I don't know how you do it."

"Fuck this!" he said. "It's horrible to have a long tournament come down to one game and everything blow up in your face." He walked away to decompress, and I went off to have lunch with his friend Pavel Tregubov.

"I know how Joel feels," Tregubov said, "to play on the stage and have your game collapse in front of the entire chess world."

I SAW JOEL A FEW HOURS LATER AT THE CLOSING CEREMONY. PLAYERS, journalists, fans, and friends all came together for rounds of cheap champagne. A few of the players still wanted more chess after nine days of tournament play; they commandeered the computer monitors in the espresso lounge and played bullet chess (one minute per side) on the Internet. Magnus Carlsen, a thirteen-year-old Norwegian wunderkind, was taking on all comers in person in five-minute games.

Joel, on the other hand, was eager to abandon chess for the evening and invited me to join him for dinner with Misha, a friend and lapsed tournament player from St. Petersburg who had come to watch the game. First, though, we had to wait an hour until 8:00 P.M., when Joel was supposed to receive his prize-fund check of $800. The loss to Vaganian had cost him dearly: if he had won, he would have received about $18,000. Joel did not get his check until 10:00 P.M.—waiting is still a national pastime in Russia—by which time we had spent too much of it on pricey beer in the hotel bar.

When Joel excused himself to get a jacket, Misha asked me where Joel's chess game had gone astray. Let's just ask him when he returns, I said. By this time, six hours had passed, and I was eager to hear Joel's dispassionate analysis of the game. "No," Misha said, "He'll go ballistic. We need to give him time to recover." As the evening unfolded, the time Joel needed would prove to be even more considerable than Misha had anticipated.

Misha took us to Taras Bulba, one of his favorite Ukrainian restaurants, in the inner ring of the city. Like most dinners in Russia, the meal began with vodka. The waitress presented us with a flask of vodka, cranberry juice, *kvas* (a thick brown nonalcoholic beer made from wheat), and a plate of small pickles each wrapped in snow-white lard. The custom is to clink shot glasses, swallow the vodka in one gulp, chew the lard, and wash everything down with large quantities of cranberry juice and *kvas*. When Misha passed around the lard, he offered a toast to Dr. Atkins.

The meal in Moscow improved after the lard. We consumed flaky cabbage and meat pies shaped like empanadas, three varieties of wild mushrooms in a garlicky cream sauce, crispy chicken croquettes, and a thick potato casserole—with vodka after every few bites. Joel excused himself to go to the restroom, and while he was gone I pressed Misha on when we should bring up the chess game. "You have to be patient, Paul," he said, "or he'll chop your head off. Police interrogators don't just ask a suspect if he murdered his wife. They win his confidence first and then spring the question."

When Joel returned, Misha explained that he was studying French. Joel begged him to say something, anything, in French. Misha became sheepish and refused. It was easy to be intimidated by Joel's command of languages—fluent French, English, Russian, German, Spanish, and a smattering of Japanese. If you closed your eyes, Misha said, and listened to Joel speak Russian, you'd think he was a native speaker. (His English was also free of any trace of a French accent.) His Russian was so good that when the Moscow police stopped him once for a routine check of his identity papers, they became suspicious when he produced a French passport. They apparently wondered if he might be a spy, but he talked his way out of the situation by claiming that he taught Russian at a French school. Misha said that in Soviet times Russian children were told that their language was the most complicated in the world. He had learned from his French lessons that this wasn't true: his French-to-Russian dictionary was three times the size of his Russian-to-French one, and the English-to-Russian dictionary was even thicker.

It was past midnight, and with all the champagne, beer, and vodka in us, the meal degenerated into a series of bad jokes and tasteless toasts. "We tell Estonian jokes," Misha said, "the way Americans tell Polish jokes." Historically Russians have considered Estonians to be *politicheskaya prostitutki* ("political prostitutes") because they switched sides during World War II and the Russian Revolution.

Two Estonians are sitting on a bench, Misha said. After half an hour, one of them says, "I really like New Year's. Yes, I like New Year's a lot." A half an hour passes and the other one says, "I really like sex. Yes, I like sex a lot." Another thirty minutes goes by and the first man says, "I prefer New Year's to sex because it happens more often."

It was 1:00 A.M., and Joel seemed to have unwound. I looked at Misha questioningly. Was this the moment? Misha shook his head. He proposed we retire to a special club he knew. "Joel," he said, "you'll like the place because you think you've been everywhere in Moscow. Paul, you'll love it because you're from Woodstock. It's a private druggie club for the snowboarder and cliff-jumping crowd. You won't find it in any guidebook."

"OK," Joel said. "Let's go."

We left the restaurant and followed Misha to a large building, constructed in the Khrushchev era. It was the headquarters of FAPSI, one of the intelligence agencies affiliated with the KGB. "They make the eaves-dropping devices," he said, "and do the high-tech cryptography shit."

The guard station near the building was unoccupied. Behind the building was an empty parking alley with a rope stretched across it to discourage access. "Very high security," Joel said, as he lifted the rope for Misha and me to duck under.

Misha led us down an icy alley to a plain metal door in a windowless section of the building. "This is it," he said. Without Misha, I wouldn't even have noticed the door. It was not lit, there was no identifying sign or number, and it was blocked in part by a small mound of snow and litter plowed from the alley. It was also diminutive, like a shed door or the entrance to a Hobbit hole.

Misha looked around to make sure no one had followed us. Then he slid a tiny panel aside, revealing an electronic combination lock. He punched in three numbers and struggled to release a pin next to the lock. It wouldn't move.

"Damn," he said, "they must have changed the combination. I could call my friend but it's too late. He has a kid."

"Do you know his cell phone?" Joel asked.

"Yes."

"Well, call it," Joel said. "He'll have turned it off if he went to bed."

"I suppose you're right," Misha said. Joel was good at applying to life the kind of coldhearted analysis that served him so well at the chessboard.

Misha phoned his friend, who said that the combination had not changed. Misha tried again and still the pin wouldn't budge. Joel took over and, with a firm yank on the pin, managed to open the door. We went inside and pulled the door shut behind us. I heard it lock in place.

We were now in a dark tunnel, descending, I imagined, into Middle-earth. We came to another door with an electronic combination lock and a tiny pad to which Misha pressed his thumb. It must be reading his fingerprint, I thought. Perhaps the thumb pad, as well as contributing to security, was an inside joke—a reminder that we were in the bowels of an intelligence building. Misha had no trouble with this door, and we found ourselves navigating a smoky hall. "There used to be a big picture of Osama bin Laden on the wall," Misha said. "It made me uncomfortable."

There are times at the chessboard when your opponent makes a move and you're not sure whether it is a feint or a real attack. You can work yourself into a paranoid sweat imagining that the move is the start of a brilliant plan known only to your adversary. You can frantically re-arrange your chessmen in the hope of somehow parrying the nebulous threat. Alternatively, if you're in a confident mood and can't figure out the purpose of his move, you can assume it has no purpose and jauntily proceed with your own game.

I was similarly conflicted as we made our way along the dark passage. Where were these guys taking me? I didn't know them well. I had only spent a few hours with Misha and a couple of evenings with Joel. And why *was* his Russian so good? I had promised my wife that I was going to be cautious in Moscow, and here I was letting two drinking buddies lead me to a secret club under the KGB. What if I had been in Washington, D.C., and two men I barely knew offered to take me down a concealed passageway to an opium den under the Central Intelligence Agency? I would have dismissed the existence of such a place and thought them mad for even suggesting it. And if they persisted in leading me to a base-ment door in the back of the CIA building (although how, with no guards in sight, could it really be the CIA?) and insisted there was a nir-vana drug haven inside, I would not have entered. And this was lawless Moscow, not American-friendly Washington. Why hadn't five days of watching Joel launch sneaky attacks on the chessboard honed my sense of danger?

Even if the promised club lay at the end of the hall, I feared that all those cigarettes, bongs, and joss sticks would surely make it a firetrap. If a clumsy celebrant knocked a candle over, would there be a way out of the underground inferno other than this narrow hallway with its elec-tronic locks? And what if the club was raided? Had I suffered through *Midnight Express* for nothing?

I considered my options. I could scramble my chessmen in a feeble at-tempt to guard against these vague threats. Or I could charge blithely ahead. I reminded myself how often, at the chessboard, I had hunkered down against attacks that never materialized because they weren't actu-ally in the position. After all, I was working on overcoming my inner chicken. To overcome my overly cautious habits, I had also recently switched my opening-move repertoire to such explosive crowd-pleasers of yesteryear as the King's Gambit, in which White offers a pawn in return for easy development and control of the center. After you've given up material—the proffered pawn—you don't have the luxury of making prophylactic moves against nonexistent threats. If you don't make the most of your position, your opponent will quickly catch up in development, consolidate his position, and, after judiciously swapping pieces, win in the endgame when his extra pawn advances to the far side of the board and morphs into a mighty queen.

The King's Gambit should be assayed only by White players who press forward full throttle and never second-guess themselves. And so, in a similar spirit, I chose to put aside my anxieties and enjoy the rest of the night. Later, when I told Matt about my adventure, he agreed that I had done the right thing. "Joel projects total self-confidence and control," Matt said. "I'd follow him over Niagara Falls in a barrel if he proposed it."

The club was a warren of windowless rooms. First, we entered a small theater. The seats came from vintage Soviet-era Aeroflot planes whose propellers were mounted on the walls and ceiling. A half dozen hipsters were watching an American war movie that involved a daring helicopter rescue. The crowd looked pretty upscale. "These people have money," Misha whispered, "but they think Russia is too commercial. Instead of spending a hundred thousand dollars on a Mercedes, they buy a Range Rover."

Next we passed through a cozy dining area where a woman in a bright red dress was eating a crepe. "They serve food twenty-four hours a day," Misha said. We walked through a billiards parlor and a small room with two twin beds. "Any member can spend the night here," he said.

We ended up in the tearoom and settled into low cushy chairs next to a bookcase crammed mostly with French literature. Joel approved of the reading selection. We had the tearoom to ourselves except for a young woman in dreadlocks who was curled up on a couch writing in a journal. The décor was 1960s college chic—beads, netting, candles, incense, and large regal hookahs that rivaled any I had seen in Woodstock or the Village: I could have been sitting with my dad at a poetry reading on Bleecker Street. Misha suggested that we start with Paraguayan tea, which was sipped through fancy straws from individual spherical pots. The tea was not for the faint of heart; it tasted like tobacco.

Next Misha ordered us a hookah. "Are you going to join us, Paul?"

"I'm thinking about it."

"It's quite mild," he said.

"All right."

"Will melon be OK?"

I said sure, not really knowing what I was agreeing to.

Three young women in long batik dresses started to prepare the water pipe. They treated it as a valuable totem, and they handled it gracefully and deliberately, as if they were enacting choreographed roles in a religious ceremony. One woman carried water in a silver pitcher. Another removed tobacco from an ornately embroidered bag and gently tamped it down in the bowl of the pipe. The third lit a foot-long match with great flourish. The women took turns adjusting the fire in the bowl and puffing on the long tube that snaked from the pipe. When they were satisfied that the draw was right, the most blissful of the three brought the hookah to our table.

"Whenever I come here," Misha said, "the women always look the same to me. I'm never sure if I've seen them before. They always prepare everything in the same exact way. I guess they all went to tea-and-hookah school."

The smoke was as mild as Misha promised. I would not have described it as melon, but it was vaguely fruity. It left a heady buzz that swept away any residual worries I had about the wisdom of my subterranean adventure.

"I like it here," I told Misha. "I want to be the first American member. But how can this place exist under the intelligence building without the authorities knowing? They must see people coming and going."

"Of course they know. I'm sure there are members who are informers. The place is certainly bugged. I'm sure they hear everything we say right now."

"Really?" Joel said. "Then we should say something interesting. Perhaps, Paul, you want to share your impressions of Putin with our larger audience."

I laughed and inhaled more melon.

"This is the new Russia," Misha said. "No one cares if you hate Putin. You can criticize the government all you want, even denounce it."

"You sound suspiciously like a government agent who is trying to trick us into revealing our true feelings," Joel said. He was used to looking for traps on the chessboard.

"An agent? Good guess," said Misha. "But even the KGB doesn't care whether you're pro- or anti-Putin."

"So what are they looking for?" I asked.

"They're looking for people who aren't who they claim to be. You say you're a chess writer from New York. They'll check that out, and if they discover you're actually a greeting card salesman from Langley, they'll observe you further or haul you in."

"Maybe it's you, Paul, who's actually the problem," Joel said. "We don't really know you. You could be CIA. How clever to pretend you don't speak Russian when you understand everything."

"*Do svidaniya*," I replied.

We talked about spying and politics for another hour, and how the Moscow business scene, in its embrace of capitalism, had become more lawless than America in the robber-baron days, with cutthroat businessmen slaying one another and paying friends in the Kremlin to cause tax difficulties for their competitors. At Britannica we had wanted to come out with a Russian edition but were discouraged by stories of Moscow publishers who torched one another's warehouses to keep rival books from reaching the stores. My father would have been profoundly disturbed that the dream of a Communist paradise had come to this.

Then our conversation turned back to the club itself. Misha told us that he was friends with two of the founders, now deceased. One of the founders, Aleksei, died the year before when he jumped off a cliff with a parachute. He opened the chute in time, but a strong wind blew him back and battered him against the rocks. As a memorial tribute, dozens of his friends and fellow club members jumped off Ostankino, the huge television tower in Moscow.

The other founder, Max, died before the club opened on New Year's Day, 2001. He had $60,000 in cash on him and was driving a Jeep Cherokee to the club so that he could pay the contractor and builder. But he never made it. The car was found intact sometime later on the outskirts of the city. The money was gone, and his body had been shot and burned, a gruesome flourish that was typical of many murders in Moscow. Only one trusted confidant knew he was carrying $60,000, Misha said, so it couldn't have been an inside job. With that much money on him, he would not have stopped for hitchhikers. He would have stopped only for the police. And the murder investigation was perfunctory—all the more reason, Misha said, to suspect that the authorities themselves were behind it.

Misha looked at his watch. It was 4:00 A.M. "We should go soon," he said. "Even though I came to Moscow to see you, Joel, I'm also here on business. I'm expected to show up in our office tomorrow." But then as Joel and I reached for our coats, Misha seemed to change his mind. "Let's stay awhile longer. I can always call in and tell them I'm coming in late because I drank too much. Many places expect that you're going to miss at least a day a week because of hangovers."[6]

Misha offered the hookah to Joel again. He was smiling impishly as he guided the tube toward Joel's mouth. "You look good and relaxed," Misha said, winking at me, "so now I can ask you what's really on my mind." He looked at his watch again. "I have waited patiently now more than twelve hours, a respectable amount of time, without asking you what went wrong in your game."

Joel stiffened. "If you've been that patient," he said testily, "you can surely wait another twelve hours."

"We're your buddies," I said. "Both of us came all the way to Moscow— me, thousands of miles—just to watch you play."

"You saw me play."

"Yes, but I need to understand it."

Joel took a deep toke on the water pipe and blew smoke rings across the table. There was an uncomfortable silence. Finally Misha said, "Maybe we should really go."

"It's OK," Joel said. "We can stay. What happened is not so complicated." I leaned forward, in anticipation of Joel's explanation.

"I knew what defense he was going to play," Joel continued. "He always responds the same way to d4. I had two basic choices. I could try to grind him down in a long game in which I try to build up small positional advantages. Or I could go for a quick kill. I chose the quick kill but it backfired. He came up with a quiet, effective move, putting his bishop out of harm's way, so that it wouldn't be a target for my advancing pawns. Then it was my pawns that became his target and I was really fucked." The hunter had become the hunted.

JOEL RETURNED THE NEXT MORNING TO PARIS, AND MATT AND I SPENT AN extra day in Moscow. I visited the famous Central Chess Club, an old baroque building, where generations of Russians had discovered the secrets of the sixty-four squares. The club was in sad disrepair; the tiles on the hall floor were so loose that they'd clack and distract the players whenever someone walked down the hall. Support for chess infrastructure in Russia was an unfortunate casualty of the fall of Communism. In front of the club was a man who wore a tie clasp in the shape of Karpov's silhouette. He was peddling Russian chess books for 30 cents each, and I bought as many of them as I could carry with me back to the hotel.

After I dropped off the books and resumed walking around Red Square, two cops stopped me and told me, in broken English, that there was something wrong with my passport. They apparently expected a bribe, but I pretended I didn't understand English, and they let me go. A few blocks later, a small child dropped a thick wad of bills and gestured toward it, indicating that I should pick it up and return it to him; I had been warned that this was a common scam in which you'd be accused, if you were a good Samaritan and picked up the money, of removing some of the bills. I ignored the boy—although I knew that my father, a fan of three-card monte and other street hustles, might well have played along, just to see what would happen. A T-shirt vendor sold me a nice bright red shirt with a black hammer and sickle. I eagerly bought it—I wear mostly T-shirts—and after I paid him, he sneakily tried to substitute a ratty threadbare shirt for the higher-quality one that I had paid for.

Moscow was starting to seem like one big con game—and it extended even to the chess. I went to an Internet café in an underground shopping mall below Red Square, where I saw that Lautier's loss to Vaganian had been published on chess sites across the Web. I was irritated to read commentators suggesting that the Armenian deserved a brilliancy prize because he had worked out the whole long bloody combination in advance, from the initial rook sacrifice to the clinching bishop shift. Anyone who had witnessed the game knew that this clearly not the case: in fact, it had taken Vaganian some twenty-five minutes to see a conclusion that even those in the press box had quickly spotted. If Vaganian deserved a beauty prize, it was for the intuitive sacrifice itself, not for his ability to foresee every move that followed.

There is a long tradition in chess of dressing up a game after the fact. The great Alexander Alekhine, world champion for all but two years from 1927 to 1946, was adroit at rewriting history. He presented his games as inevitable marches toward victory in which the losers were able to offer only inadequate resistance. When his real games were far too messy for him to describe this way, he changed the endings to demonstrate his cleverness and passed them off as ones he had actually played. He apparently also invented entire elegantly played games and claimed that they were real. While I was reading about the Aeroflot Tournament on the Web, I noticed that Joel was online, so I instant-messaged him the silly comments about Vaganian's foresight.

"That's ridiculous," he shot back. "I'm sure he saw that the rook sacrifice wasn't risky because he could always force a draw by perpetual check. He obviously found the winning move later on."

"The comments suggest that he saw everything in advance," I typed back.[7]

"My God, what crap!! If he saw everything, he wouldn't spend twenty-five minutes on the bishop move. I'm gonna kill him the next time I play him!"

I LEFT THE INTERNET CAFÉ AND HEADED TO TVERSKAYA STREET, MOSCOW'S equivalent of Manhattan's Fifth Avenue. I found a fancy coffee shop and ordered a cappuccino and tarte tatin. A middle-aged man was sitting there at a wooden chessboard with a gnarly hand-carved set. I smiled when he looked at me, and he motioned enthusiastically for me to join him. He gave himself the White pieces and placed a large Soviet-era chess clock next to the board. He conveniently adjusted the minute hands so that he had a full five minutes and I had closer to four. I wasn't going to argue with him—we didn't share a common language—and in any event, I was having such a stimulating time in Moscow, I really didn't care. Whenever he moved a piece, he would not put it down in the middle of the square, as was customary, but in one corner so that it protruded confusingly into two neighboring squares. If I adjusted the piece so that it was more centrally located, he'd push it back so it was off kilter again. He smiled demonically whenever he captured one of my men. He was a clock banger, too, and toppled my coffee in his excitement—fortunately I had already sipped most of it.

In the face of his annoying behavior, I found myself serenely happy because I was able to play the so-called Slav Defense—and in Moscow, of all places. It was as if I had made a clever visual pun. I was even happier when, despite the one-minute deficit he had given me, I beat him in the time scramble. I had a rare surge of patriotism, or maybe it was just animalistic delight at demolishing this annoying cheater. I had fared better than Napoleon. I had defeated a Russian on his own soil.

ANATOMY OF A HUSTLER

"Amberley excelled in chess—one mark, Watson, of a
scheming mind."
—SHERLOCK HOLMES,
The Adventure of the Retired Colourman

"One time, before a game with Najdorf, Tal casually
went to the beach, but carefully left his shoes outside
his hotel room so that the excitable Argentinean star
would think he was busy preparing an opening!"
—ANTHONY SAIDY,
The Battle of Chess Ideas

AS CHILDREN WE HARBOR ALL KINDS OF ILLUSIONS. THAT
Santa Claus and the tooth fairy are real. That our parents are omniscient
and invincible. In my case, I grew up believing two convenient fictions:
that chess was a moral, contained world void of hypocrisy and deception, and that my engaging storyteller of a father was forthright and
honest, at least with me. I held onto the latter illusion much longer than
the former.

Back in the 1960s, my father and I had watched disreputable characters in Washington Square Park begin a chess game with an outlandish
pawn thrust called the Grob, or the Spike. (Henri Grob was a Swiss
painter and chess aficionado who explored this wickedly strange opening

move and published the first treatise on it.) White begins with g4, unnervingly shoving his king-knight pawn forward two squares, in contempt of basic chess principles. The flank advance weakens the position of White's king, doesn't take possession of the center, and leaves the pawn, which can't be advantageously defended, subject to immediate attack. White in fact often cavalierly jettisons the pawn, immediately throwing the game into bewildering complications in which the startled and unprepared Black player has to think for himself.

My father once played the Grob against me, when I was eight or nine. After he made the peculiar pawn advance, he couldn't remember what to do next and we both started laughing. I loved that he was bad and naive at chess, because he was so skilled and conniving at other games. When I was small, he would drag me to a seedy Ping-Pong and pool hall in Times Square. Sometimes we'd play billiards together, but I usually found it boring because he'd run through a whole rack of balls before I got a turn. I had more fun watching him play table tennis. He was a giant bear of a man, and younger guys in their twenties and thirties eagerly took him on for $100 a game. But this fat guy had sharp reflexes and a surprisingly strong serve, and even when he was huffing and puffing he could volley from way off the table. To enliven the game, he'd then talk the suckers into a rematch of obstacle-course Ping-Pong, in which beer and Coke bottles were randomly positioned on the table—and he invariably won that, too.

On our trips to Times Square, we'd also visit a place known as the Flea House, where rumpled men played chess and checkers. Although my dad knew that it was foolish for him to play chess for stakes, he'd get in on the action by placing side bets on who would win—and he had an uncanny ability for backing the victors. As for other board games, he played Scrabble for money, but his real preference was cards: bridge, rummy, and, particularly, poker.

I think my father did well at poker, but I can't be sure. The train ride from Westport to Manhattan was an hour and five minutes. When we were still one family, my father sometimes commuted to Manhattan on a particular, early morning train where a bunch of men played high-stakes seven-card high low. The game apparently agreed with his wallet, because after my parents separated and he moved to the Village, he occasionally took a predawn train to Westport—not to see my brother or me, but so that he could turn right around and catch the poker train back to the city.

During a long weekend at Grossinger's, some Orthodox rabbis paid him to teach them poker. To make sure that they understood the lessons, he engaged them in training games for real stakes. My dad won so much money from them that on the way home to Westport he stopped at an auction and bought my mother prints by Miró and Chagall.

When I received a term bill from Harvard my freshman year, my father told me that he didn't feel like writing a check. He went out and won seven grand that evening and handed me the wad of bills to take back to Cambridge. The Harvard bursar was aghast when I showed up with cash. But my father also lost big: when I was a high school sophomore, my brother and I accompanied him to Europe aboard the S.S. *France.* (My dad was afraid to fly and never took airplanes.) Dizzy Gillespie was the featured performer on the ship, and after my father made sure that we were asleep, he played poker with Gillespie and his band. My dad was the only stranger in the game, and I was not surprised when he returned with an empty billfold. Fortunately, our meals on the cruise had been paid for in advance.

DURING THE SUMMER OF MY SOPHOMORE YEAR IN COLLEGE, WHEN I WAS living with my father for the first time in New York, he invited me to watch him shill in a three-card monte game on Fourteenth Street. The dealer was a thirty-year-old ex-con who had perfected, during his long days in prison, the sleight of hand required to host the game profitably. Unfortunately for his business, he looked like the ex-con he was. That's why he employed my dad—white, obese, and pushing sixty—to make the game seem safe for Village tourists who wanted to impress their dates by gambling.

Their three-card monte game was played on the sidewalk, atop an overturned cardboard box that functioned as a makeshift card table. The dealer would put three queens—the two black ones and the queen of hearts—faceup on the box for everyone to see. Then he would turn over each card, mix them up, and position them, still facedown, in a row. The object was to guess the position of the red queen. Any bystander could plop down $20 or more and be paid two to one if he guessed correctly. So in theory it was an even bet—maybe the odds were even in the player's favor because he knew the initial location of the red queen. But of course a skilled dealer has all sorts of misdirection techniques to steer the bettor wrong. For instance, while shuffling the cards, he "accidentally" sends the red queen flying. The shill—in this case, my father— retrieves the card from the ground. Before returning the queen to the dealer, he gets a passerby's attention and shows him, and not the dealer, that he has put a little crease in the corner of the card. Now when the dealer shuffles the cards, the mark thinks he can identify the queen of hearts by the unobtrusive crease and, in his excitement, shells out big bucks. He is devastated, of course, when the creased card is revealed to be a black queen. During the shuffle, the dealer had surreptitiously un-creased the red queen and made a similar fold in the corner of a black card. That summer I learned not only the secrets of three-card monte but also discovered, unfortunately, that my father's deception was not confined to cards and Ping-Pong.

I was working as an elevator operator that August in an exclusive res-idential high-rise on the Upper East Side. The job paid well; I'd obtained it by referral from an orthodontist friend of my father's who felt guilty because the experimental New Age braces he'd imposed on me had failed to straighten my teeth. The atmosphere in the building was absurdly for-mal. Housekeepers and nannies who were not accompanied by children were barred from the main lobby and directed to a dilapidated service el-evator. As the operator of a lobby elevator, I had to wear white gloves and was instructed not to speak to a tenant unless spoken to first. The building's rules required that I wedge myself into a corner during the el-evator ride and look discreetly at the wall. Regal old heiresses enforced the rules, but thankfully there were also liberal nouveaux riches who warmed up to me after word spread that I was attending Harvard.

The building had a large staff of Yugoslavian doormen who cheerfully called out "*Pitchka!*" to any attractive woman who walked by. The woman would invariably smile, unaware that the word meant *whore*. On top of the lockers in the basement of the building, where we would change into our starchy uniforms, was a kind of museum display of dildos and other em-barrassing objects that my coworkers had fished out of the residents' garbage. Each object was labeled with the name of its former owner so that we would know where to direct our ridicule. I was amused, and a bit stunned, by how much my coworkers knew about the private lives of the residents who trusted them. I liked how the Yugoslavians banded together, but I was an outsider to their locker room high jinks: my summer job was clearly not going to relieve my sense of isolation in life.

Once I worked an onerous double shift straight through the night. At least I received a hush-money tip from a woman who was cheating on her traveling husband—and a podiatrist's wife who felt sorry for me summoned me to her apartment and handed me a glass of wine and a plate of shrimp scampi and lobster tail, prepared by her cook. After sixteen hours in the elevator, I returned to my dad's apartment at ten in the morning. It was drizzling, and I told him that I wasn't feeling well and wanted to get a milkshake. I asked him where the nearest Baskin-Robbins was. He said there wasn't one nearby. But we went to one last week, I reminded him. Where was it? Oh yes, he said, but that Baskin-Robbins doesn't have milkshakes. That's strange, I told him, because I remember seeing people sipping shakes. And how could an ice cream store not make a milkshake? Maybe, he said, but that particular Baskin-Robbins only sold premade shakes that weren't very tasty. Premade shakes? I've never heard of that. They're bad, my father said, because the ice cream has freezer burn. The conversation continued in this surreal vein, with my father digging himself in deeper with increasingly convoluted rebuttals to my attempts to probe his explanations.

Since then, I've replayed our conversation dozens of times in my head. His intentions, I now think, were not malicious. When I told him that I was feeling bad, he must have thought that I meant I was coming down with a cold and he didn't want me to go back out in the rain. Another father might have said, "I'm sorry you're getting sick. Maybe you should stay inside and skip the ice cream." And I would have responded, "Oh, no, I'm not ill. I feel shitty because I've been in an elevator for hours, and the fresh air, even if it is drizzling, will do me good. A milkshake will cheer me up." Although my dad was apparently operating out of concern for me, he couldn't simply suggest that I stay inside. He didn't want to contradict my wishes. He had to be liked every second of the day, and he feared that if he objected to *anything* I wanted to do—even something as inconsequential as getting a milkshake—I might be unhappy with him and reject him. (Of course, the whole uncomfortable conversation could have been avoided if he had simply offered to get the milkshake for me.)

Because he couldn't handle potential friction about a stupid milkshake, perhaps it isn't surprising that he also spurned conflict on all matters of any real importance. Rather than being direct with me, he would try to influence my behavior by inventing baroque stories that had obvious morals and object lessons. That summer, though, I was still oblivious to all of this, at least at a conscious level, and I responded by doing what I had always done. I convinced myself that I was somehow mistaken— maybe I had misunderstood him about Baskin-Robbins—and that he was right. He was my dad after all, and if he claimed that the dog had eaten his homework, he must be telling the truth.

WITH HINDSIGHT IT IS EASY TO SEE MY LIFE AS A GRAND FREUDIAN CASE study. Long before I was clear about my father's inability to tell the truth, I had an academic interest in deception. As a kid, I was fascinated by the age-old liar's paradox, in which a person declares, "I'm lying to you right now." Well if he's a liar, his statement is false, but that means he's not lying to you right now, which means he's a truth teller. But if he's a truth teller, his statement is true and he's lying to you, which makes him a liar. This self-contradictory spiral has occupied philosophers since the time of the ancient Greeks. Bertrand Russell, for one, explored the ramifications of the so-called Barber of Seville, a relative of the liar's paradox. Imagine the Barber of Seville who shaves every man who does not shave himself. Does the Barber of Seville shave himself? If he does, he doesn't, and if he doesn't, he does. Another contradiction, Russell wrote in his autobiography, "can be created by giving a person a piece of paper on which is written: 'The statement on the other side of this paper is false.' The person turns the paper over, and finds on the other side: 'The statement on the other side of this paper is true.' It seemed unworthy of a grown man to spend time on such trivialities, but what was I to do?"

In my youth I spent many evenings solving and inventing brain teasers that were trumped-up versions of the liar's paradox, many involving a missionary captured by island savages, each of whom either always tells the truth or always lies. The savages plan to kill the missionary either by roasting him over an open fire or throwing him to crocodiles. They will free him if he can determine with a single yes-no question how they intend to kill him. The missionary doesn't know whether any individual savage is a liar or a truth teller, and so if he asks one of his captors the direct question "Do you plan to burn me?" he won't be able to judge the veracity of the answer. I was proud of myself when I realized the missionary could win his freedom if he asked, "Is it true that either you tell the truth and you want to burn me or you are a liar and you want to toss me to the crocs?" (This academic interest in truth telling persisted through college. For my honors thesis in history and science at Harvard, I wrote a 130-page essay on a very abstruse debate in twentieth-century philosophy of science about how to categorize different types of truths.)[1]

In late elementary school I invented a sly game that would have horrified my mother and greatly entertained my father. My friends and I would slip items into strangers' carts at the local supermarket and hope they'd buy them. I developed an elaborate scoring system in which each item in the store was assigned a point value. Small, inexpensive items, such as a candy bar or a pocket-size box of raisins, were worth only a point or two. Small, expensive things such as a tin of smoked oysters were worth four points because even though they were easy to slip into someone's cart, they would make the cash register clink and were therefore often detected and immediately returned. A large item such as kitty litter was worth seven points, and a big, expensive item such as a two-pound steak or a leg of lamb, even more. The most points were reserved for a large, inappropriate purchase, such as a jumbo box of tampons placed in the cart of a seventy-year-old man. The best way to achieve a high score was to wait for a shopper to rush off to retrieve a forgotten item while her purchases were rung up. I would sidle up to the checkout counter, smile cherubically as if I were the shopper's son, and place the high-scoring item near the front of the queue so that it would be scanned and bagged before the shopper returned. My friends and I played the game for a couple of months, and the store, which was huge and had perhaps a dozen checkout counters, never stopped us. Maybe they even knew and tolerated us: after all, we moved hundreds of dollars of merchandise.

Two of my principal hobbies in adolescence, magic and acting, also reflected my obsession with false appearances. For a while, I thought about being a professional magician. I spent many afternoons at Tannen's, a celebrated magic store and salon in midtown Manhattan where masters of legerdemain swapped trade secrets. For a magician to be great at sleight of hand—at cards, coins, or rings—he must practice thousands of hours, putting in even more time than chess demands. I had too many other interests to find the time. I was more serious about acting, though, and took after-school classes. (Westport—home to Paul Newman and Linda Blair of *The Exorcist*—had many fine acting programs.) It appealed to something primal in me because I enjoyed escaping from my own world. I liked pretending to be somebody else. Acting was also therapeutic. I allowed myself to get angry on stage in a way that I never could in real life. Magic and acting seemed like benign forms of deception—or maybe not even deception at all, because the members of the audience have given the performers license to fool them.

I HAD MANY HOBBIES AND INTERESTS, AND IDEAS FOR MAKING A LIVING, before I settled on writing. During my senior year in college, I thought I wanted to be a lawyer. My father hated attorneys—he demonized them as money-grubbing stooges of big business—but I had no intention of being a corporate lawyer. I wanted to work for the ACLU and argue freedom-of-speech cases before the Supreme Court. I wanted to stop schools from ostracizing child atheists. I thought my dad would think that this was a noble career choice. Indeed, at first he acted as though he approved. Yet the day before I went to take my LSATs at New York University, he told me about various people he knew who were unhappy with their lives. Each of these depressed individuals happened to be a lawyer. He didn't bother to point out their shared profession—that would have been too obvious—he simply left it to me to draw the appropriate conclusion.

Later that evening I discovered on his desk the partial manuscript of a book called *How Not to Raise Your Child to Be a Lawyer*. I asked him what the hell he was writing. He told me that I shouldn't be snooping around his office. I said I was always in his office and that the manuscript was in plain view, perched on top of the typewriter. He said I shouldn't have looked at it. I said he knew I always used his typewriter, and so he must have left the manuscript there because he wanted me to see it. And the topic, I said, could not be a coincidence. What the hell was the manuscript? I repeated. It was nothing, he said, just something he happened to find. Nothing, I said. How could it be nothing? I told him I could tell from the font and the paper that he was the one who had typed it. You're right, he conceded, but he claimed that the manuscript didn't reflect his sentiments. He said he was ghostwriting a book for a famous female attorney. I was furious, and yet I could not get him to admit, no matter how much I pressed him and how agitated I became, that he did not want me to be a lawyer. He retorted that the famous female attorney might not want me to be a lawyer, but that he felt differently. It was *she* who had the problem. He was just a hired gun, he claimed. Law was a fine profession. In fact, I'd make a great lawyer, he said, because I was good at arguing.

The next day I couldn't concentrate on my LSATs. During the test, my head and stomach ached, and instead of focusing on the questions, I kept obsessing about the events of the night before. Accept that he's ghostwriting a book, I said. Accept that its subject matter is just a coincidence. No, another part of me said, recognize that your father is a disturbed man who will make up anything if it suits his purposes. Acknowledge that he is a pathological liar. I hated that harsh label, but I suddenly realized that that was what he was.

I started thinking about various fibs that I had told in my own life. Usually I had been fooling myself rather than anyone else, but I still wondered whether it was fair of me to be angry with him. Even though I was a direct person who did not shy away from confrontation the way he did, was I fated to follow his example in conflating truth and fiction? I was also extremely troubled that I hadn't consciously recognized his lying sooner. I knew that it was not easy for me to remember hurtful events involving someone close to me. I tended to reinvent the other person's behavior, sanitizing or legitimizing it, and then, after I replayed the invented behavior enough times in my head, I'd get confused about whether the real, unsettling stuff had actually occurred.

I thought about other things that he must have made up. I remembered that once, when my Harvard roommates were trading stories of their athletic successes, I proudly told them about my father's boxing because I had no story of my own to share. I boasted that at the University of Wisconsin my father had been the division champion in his weight class. One of my roommates subsequently looked my dad up in the record book but couldn't find his name. I told my father about this, and he said that it had been one of the saddest days of his life and an awful miscarriage of justice. He said he had won the championship, but for a half second the referee had been befuddled and mistakenly lifted the other guy's hand, depriving my dad of his rightful place in history. How could it be that I was only now, in the middle of my LSATs, recognizing the obvious duplicity of this incoherent explanation? It also seemed particularly cruel that my father had boasted about his triumphs as a jock, given how tormented I myself had been about sports.

His sabotage worked—I never became a lawyer—but it also destroyed our relationship. From that moment on, I was never comfortable around him again. He lived just six more years, and I periodically asked him about dozens of stories that I now believed were false. Not once did he concede that he had ever lied to me.

My father succumbed to cancer in 1982. Afterward, my mother told me that on one of their first dates, in the mid-1950s, he claimed that he was dying of an incurable disease, some kind of kidney disorder. That explained why the old friends of his whom I had run into in the past expressed amazement that he was not yet dead. At the time I thought they were referring to his obesity and chain-smoking, but now I realize that he had duped them, too, with tales of fatal nephritis. My mother said that many of his friends stopped seeing him because he told them one lie too many.

ALTHOUGH MY FATHER HAD EXPOSED ME TO CHESS HUSTLERS WHEN I WAS A kid, I always regarded these skanky tricksters as betraying the true spirit of the game—much like doctors who take the Hippocratic oath and go to work for tobacco companies. I thought that the game's exalted status demanded that you try to win by making objectively strong moves. The hustler's modus operandi, on the other hand, is to play sneaky, third-rate moves, which give him an edge only if his adversary gets bamboozled. But he is gambling: he will be left with an inferior game if his opponent is able to keep a cool head and sidestep the dangers.

As an adult, I was eager to understand deception at the chessboard. In 2003, I read a multivolume book called *Chess Openings for Hustlers* written by perhaps the greatest chess con of all time, a man with the evocative name of Claude Frizzel Bloodgood III. "The game of chess is the second most entertaining diversion ever created by the mind of man," wrote a friend of Bloodgood's in the introduction to the first volume. "It is second, of course, only to chess *with money on the table.* If you've ever played under the gun, with your cash at stake and the clock ticking, you know what I mean."

The author of these words proudly identified himself as a hustler and said that players like him existed in all walks of life:

> You might run into a chess hustler almost anywhere; at the local park on a sunny summer afternoon, in the last booth in the back of a dark bar, beside you on a cross country flight, or down at the neighborhood filling station. Practically anywhere chess is played, you'll find someone willing to play for money. Whether your cash flow is positive or negative in these encounters depends a great deal on how well you're prepared for combat.

In speed chess for money, Bloodgood advocated avoiding mainline openings and assaying obscure but sharp gambits which, though ultimately unsound, often defeat adversaries who cannot make their way through the minefield of traps before the clock runs out. Bloodgood himself was especially successful with the Grob.

To understand the appeal of these sketchy openings, I visited Tom Plenty, a pseudonymous Grob lover and protégé of Bloodgood's, who asked me to withhold his real name because his conservative, blue-chip employer might not appreciate his circle of chess junkies. Plenty was a clean-cut man a decade younger than I, and we met in a Cajun restaurant in his hometown. Before the waitress could take our order, he set up a chessboard and challenged me to speed chess. "I'm not very good," he said, "but I'm good at setting traps. Maybe I can intimidate you with my tricky play."

As a rule, chess players who cheerfully announce that they're going to intimidate you don't usually succeed. Plenty was no exception—I beat him easily. I wish we had been playing for money. I didn't tell him that I had spent the two-hour plane flight earlier in the day looking at Grob games in my computer database and memorizing published refutations. I wanted to out-Grob him by coming across as an untrained talent. In the second game I had White and trounced him with a dubious line of the age-old King's

Gambit. The openings I favored, like the King's Gambit and the Budapest, were less flaky than the Grob, but still far from mainstream.

Now that I had earned his respect, Plenty told me the story of his chess life, starting with the Fischer-Spassky match. "I was a diligent student then," he said. "I studied openings and endgames. I read books. I studied pawn structure and really tried to understand the game. Then I fell in with the wrong crowd." In his early teens his parents dropped him off on Thursday evenings at a college chess club forty-five minutes from their home. It was a college club only in name, because it was open to anyone and drew "chess bums" from the community at large. "I played chain-smoking, pizza-eating, beer-swilling alcoholics," Plenty recalled, "and these guys introduced me to a drug which I'm now hooked on. It's called speed chess. It's superficial chess, but I realized halfway through high school that I sucked at slow chess. I gave up my dreams then of becoming world champion. I knew I'd never be anything more than a Grand Patzer, the upper level of bad players." But Plenty really loved the game, and he drifted into the hustler world of unsound openings. He discovered that he got the most pleasure in chess when he beat someone in twenty moves with a weird little trap that he was booked up on and his adversary wasn't.

Plenty's introduction to hustling was a book called *200 Traps in Fianchetto Openings* ("fianchetto" is a term for the development of a bishop on the long, corner-to-corner diagonal). "I remember being astounded that all these sweet traps were out there," Plenty said. The very last page of this book discussed the Grob. "I knew this was the Holy Grail, the magic bullet that was going to take me to the next level," he said. "The Grob was full of really sleazy stuff. When Black responds logically, White just comes in and murders him. I've developed a taste for the quick kill. Life would not be as wonderful without the Grob."

Plenty researched the opening and located Henri Grob's widow in Switzerland. He wrote to her and obtained a copy of the German text her late husband had written. He learned German chess notation and memorized the move sequences in the book. "The first night I played it at the club was beautiful," he said. "I had everyone on the ropes. All the best players were waiting in line to play me, and I was disposing of them one by one. The Grob is a street fight. You say, 'Look at my thumb!' and if he does, you sucker punch him. Of course if this doesn't work, you're out of luck. You get one shot at the guy and that's about it."

His opponents at the club soon learned how to avoid the pitfalls. "The novelty wore off," Plenty said, "and they tore me to pieces. But the love affair was still there. I just needed fresh victims. There's nothing better than when a Grob virgin takes the gambit pawn, and I think to myself, OK, buddy, now you're in my world."

Plenty tried to track down everything that was known about the opening. Michael Basman, an international master in England, was the strongest player to employ the Grob in serious tournaments. Plenty examined Basman's games but judged them tepid: "I didn't think he was a real Grobster because he wouldn't gambit the g-pawn, but quickly defended it with another pawn. He's a wimp—no, I don't want to say that because I'd be insulting wimps. Defense is for women. It's the ladies' variation. Real men sac the g-pawn."

Plenty came across an inspiring booklet called *The Tactical Grob* by Claude Bloodgood. "As I read it," Plenty told me, "I thought, My God, this guy is exactly like me. He analyzes like me. He likes cheapos. He seemed to be my mental twin. For all I knew this guy could be my illegitimate father. I began stalking him." First he tried to contact the publisher, but like so many chess publishers it had gone out of business. Then he posted messages on computer bulletin boards (this was in the Usenet days before the Internet) letting the chess world know he was looking for Bloodgood. He eventually received a tip that Bloodgood might have been incarcerated in Virginia in the early 1970s.

Plenty called the Virginia penal system in 1990 and asked if they had a forwarding address for someone who might have been in prison twenty years ago. They told him Bloodgood was still there, at the Powhatan Correctional Center in State Farm. "I thought, That's not a good sign," Plenty said. "He obviously wasn't there for jaywalking." They started corresponding. "Soon I found myself playing postal chess," Plenty said, "setting and evading sordid little traps, with this man who had committed an awful crime." Bloodgood had beaten his mother to death with a baseball bat after she prosecuted him for forging her signature on a tax refund check.

Plenty then located another Grobster, a gadfly chess journalist named Sam Sloan whose claim to fame was starting a sex cult in Berkeley in the

1960s (and who, in the summer of 2006, would be elected to the board of directors of the United States Chess Federation). "I learned of this incredible coincidence," Plenty told me. "Sloan also served time at Powhatan, although he and Claude apparently never met. Something to do with a messy custody fight." They had other things in common: Sloan had also been on unofficial death row—in an Afghan prison, where people were routinely executed. "I started to worry," Plenty said. "Powhatan, death row—there seemed to be so many problems associated with this opening. Maybe it was like King Tut's curse. If you touch the opening, bad things happen to you. But I thought maybe you have to play the Grob really well before shit happens, and I wasn't at that stage."

Plenty first visited Bloodgood in prison in 1993 or 1994. "He was wheeled out attached to oxygen tanks," Plenty recalled. "He had emphysema and lung cancer and looked older than the hills. It was easy to believe him when he said he was born in 1924," although he was in fact born in 1937. Plenty described Bloodgood as bald and stocky, "an evil Uncle Fester," but admitted that, despite his ailments, he was charismatic.

Bloodgood's illness did not stop him from playing decent speed chess. "He crushed me game after game in prison," Plenty said. "I think he was maybe master level. He was always very scrupulous about the rules. He never cheated or took back a move. He always played touch move. To him, chess was the only thing in his life that he was honest about. It was probably the only thing he really excelled at as a result of his own hard work."

In prison Bloodgood wrote three books on the Grob and other hustler openings, but these did not bring him fame. They appealed largely to the subculture of street players who inhabited places like Washington Square Park. But in the rarefied world of correspondence chess, in which each contestant has three days to ponder a move before he dispatches it by mail to a faceless opponent, Bloodgood was a minor celebrity because of the sheer number of games he played. There was a time in 1970 or 1971 when he conducted an astonishing twelve hundred postal games at once, surely a world record. It was ironic that Bloodgood, who earlier had served time for robbing a post office, had unlimited free postage at Powhatan—a peculiar perquisite of being on death row for first-degree murder.

Bloodgood was a member of the so-called Class of '72, the group of death row inmates who received a reprieve when the Supreme Court outlawed capital punishment in 1972. Despite the fact that he had to start paying for stamps—he used money from his veteran disability checks—he continued to play hundreds of correspondence games. His name showed up occasionally in British and American chess periodicals along with the moves of over-the-board games he claimed to have played in the 1950s against Humphrey Bogart (who tried what Bloodgood dubbed the Maltese Falcon Gambit), Clark Gable, Marlene Dietrich, and Charlie Chaplin. In 1996, he finally became famous in the chess world at large when the USCF published the April ratings of tournament players. There on the Top 50 list was Claude Bloodgood with the astronomical, grandmasterly rating of 2655. Although he had no international title, he was listed as the number nine player in the country, his name in klieg lights between two famous grandmasters in the number eight and number ten spots.

Bloodgood himself never claimed to be of grandmaster strength. In fact, he had written repeatedly to the USCF warning them of a problem in the rating system. In a closed pool of players, like a prison chess club, the rating of a player who is much better than the others can steadily climb because he will pick up a point or two for every victory, even for wins over rank beginners.[2] And prisoners, because they are not pressed for time, can play more than one game daily, and the one- and two-point gains add up. Bloodgood played seventeen hundred rated games in 1995—that's four to five games a day—and his rating soared 421 points in just two years.

The USCF was in a quandary in 1996 because it had ignored Bloodgood's warning. The organization had promoted prison chess as a way of intellectually stimulating inmates and fighting recidivism, but now its own rules seemed to require inviting a convicted murderer to the U.S. Championship. Of course, he wouldn't be able to attend in person, but he was miffed at the USCF for not responding to his letters, so he cantankerously suggested that they accommodate his special circumstances by letting him play by phone or fax. Chess had enough of an image problem without the USCF being seen to coddle violent criminals.

The USCF knew it had a public relations disaster for another reason: in 1974 Bloodgood had used chess as a means of escaping from jail. The

1970s were liberal times, when America believed in the idea of rehabilitating prisoners, even murderers. The governor of Virginia and the head of the prison system gave Bloodgood and a fellow inmate, who had stabbed a woman seventeen times, permission to stage a chess tournament outside the correctional facility. They vanished for a month, and the FBI issued an all-points bulletin describing Bloodgood as an "armed and dangerous homicidal psychopath with homosexual tendencies."

Of course, the USCF did not invite him to the U.S. Championship. Like the Soviet Chess Federation, which punished players who defected or fell from grace by bowdlerizing their names and games from chess books, the USCF simply omitted Bloodgood from future Top 50 lists, but incongruously continued including him on the alphabetical list of *senior masters*, players with ratings over 2400. On the June 1997 list, his rating reached a stratospheric 2722, which made him the second-highest-rated player in the country, behind World Championship hopeful Gata Kamsky.

"I get mad," Plenty told me, "when ignorant people say Bloodgood was fraudulent about chess. He gave me copies of more than a thousand games. He played four or five rated games a day because he had nothing to do but sit around and watch paint peel off the wall. Bloodgood saw his rating go through the ceiling. He knew he was overrated. I called the USCF many times on his behalf trying to warn them before it became a scandal."

As their friendship developed, Bloodgood told Plenty about his past life as a Nazi courier, shuttling across the Atlantic, delivering instructions to German agents on American soil. "The stories were really outrageous," Plenty said. "They couldn't be true, but I don't think Claude lied to me. He concocted a very elaborate history which I think he truly believed. He told me he met Himmler in a German military school and played chess with him in their leisure time. He put so much detail into the story—how Himmler parted his hair—that for a moment you'd buy it." Plenty suspected that Bloodgood had met a German spy in the United States after the war and basically appropriated his identity. Bloodgood taught himself German to add credibility. He showed Plenty the moves of the games he'd played against Himmler and Goering.

Bloodgood also told Plenty about his Hollywood years, which began when Bogart came to cheer up the patients in a California VA hospital where Bloodgood was recuperating from a foot injury sustained on a military base. He said that he befriended Bogart and was briefly married to Kathryn Grayson, the MGM actress who starred in *Show Boat* and *Kiss Me, Kate*. She was, in fact, fifteen years older than Bloodgood (but only two years older than the age he claimed to be). He said they were wedded in Mexico and that Grayson subsequently had the marriage annulled.

"I thought, No, you weren't married to her," Plenty told me. "Then I did a Freedom of Information search on Claude. It took a couple years and I get this large file from the FBI that says he may have married Grayson." Plenty also found an article by a journalist who tracked Grayson down and said the actress did not confirm or deny if she knew Bloodgood.

PLENTY ASKED ME FOR ONE LAST BLITZ GAME. HE TOOK WHITE AND AN-nounced, as he pushed the g-pawn, "This is going to be ugly." This time he was right. On the fifth or sixth move he made a bishop lunge for which I was not prepared. I got the worst of the opening, but toward the end, when we were both low on time, he blundered away a winning position.

"Damn!" he said. "You were on the ropes. See the attraction of the opening? It's exciting. The people who gravitate toward the Grob actually have a different mind-set on life. We look for cheap instantaneous grati-fication. We don't like to work."

He cited examples from his own background. In engineering school he had entered problem-solving contests that were run by the mathe-matics department. He always won the weekly contests by employing a mainfame computer to number-crunch all the possible solutions. "The math department hated engineers, and I really pissed them off," Plenty recalled. "So they changed the rules so that you couldn't use computers. Grob players are pathologically pragmatic."

He asked me to guess how he met his wife.

"I have no idea," I said.

"I met her at a lesbian bar."

"Uh—OK?"

"I was thinking like a Grob player. I want to pick up girls, and there's no guys at a lesbian bar. I'll have no competition. So the odds are already in my favor because mathematically there's a probability that some are at least bisexual. I don't look like Tom Cruise. I'm not this real macho guy. So if this girl likes other girls, she's not looking for a macho guy. So this increases my chances. This is the Grob mentality—I'm either going to win real quick or be shot down real quick. I'm not going to have to sit there all night and talk to these girls and buy drinks and wonder if they're playing me for a sucker. They're either interested in me or they're not." He met a straight woman that night and they were married six months later.

After this story I felt that it was time for me to leave before I, too, was afflicted by King Tut's curse.

BLOODGOOD DIED IN PRISON IN 2001. PLENTY ENCOURAGED ME TO MAKE A pilgrimage to the public library in Cleveland, Ohio, where his papers were housed. One floor of the library was devoted to the John G. White Chess and Checkers Collection—seventy thousand books and magazines, the largest chess collection in the world. The library had recently acquired twenty large moving cartons of Bloodgood's papers and personal effects, such as a pocket magnetic chess set, an unfilled prescription for a steroid inhaler, a senior-master certificate from the USCF, and Christmas cards from Bill Clinton and George and Barbara Bush because his name had erroneously made it onto a list of model prisoners.

Of course I was interested in Bloodgood not just because he had taken chess obsession to extreme levels but because he was a compulsive liar. He was also a pack rat like my dad. He kept thousands of postcards from his correspondence games. He had carbon copies of the hundreds of complaints he'd sent to prison officials about inadequate medical care. He filed dozens of lawsuits against people who he thought had wronged him, and the library had copies of all the legal briefs he had written. The Powhatan officials got tired of responding to his nuisance suits and tried to thwart his efforts by taking away his typewriter. He continued the legal actions by laboriously writing the briefs by hand.

The boxes in the library were not yet catalogued, so I went through the thousands of papers one by one. I wasn't looking for anything in particular but was hoping to gain insight into Bloodgood's mind. After reading his correspondence and the hundreds of briefs he wrote, it became clear to me how suspicious he was: everywhere he looked, he saw people conspiring behind his back. The absence of a vegetable dish at a prison meal was evidence of the penal system deciding to weaken him by depriving him of important nutrients. A knight missing from his chess set meant that the warden himself must have sneaked into his cell and stolen the piece while he was sleeping.

Among the hundreds of letters I examined were two that he received from someone I knew. I immediately recognized the name. I had played him in two rapid tournaments at the Marshall and he'd behaved abominably. I was White and Bloodgood's correspondent, a nervous and twitchy man, adopted a kind of Grob in reverse with Black.[3] He slammed the pieces, knocked them over at key moments, and incessantly banged the clock. Sometimes he stood up and played from a standing position, so that he had greater leverage in smashing the chessmen and the clock. How, I now wondered, did all these lowlifes come to play the same ridiculous opening?

In one of Bloodgood's boxes, I found an unpublished novel typed on more than a ream of paper. I skimmed the text. It was a potboiler about American spies in Nazi Germany just before the war. The prose was fairly coherent if overheated. Along with the novel were copies of letters in which Bloodgood expressed disappointment about not knowing how to get the book published.

The similarity to my father was eerie. One of my dad's biggest frustrations in life was not being able to write the Great American Novel. He had committed so many novels to memory, and had studied and taught literature for decades, that he was sure he could write a stellar one. He once took a year off from the New School, the magazine business, and poker in order to complete a novel. A millionaire friend of his named Mike even lent him a year's pay so that he could continue to support all of us. Toward the end of the year, my dad told me that his apartment had been ransacked and the TV, stereo, and typewriter stolen. He said that the draft of the novel was missing. He kept it in the typewriter case, he said, along with the typewriter. The crooks had walked off with the case. My father was tearful, and I accompanied him to Greenwich Village pawnshops to see if the typewriter might be there. He had already looked in trash cans in the neighborhood and posted reward notices in the diner and Laundromat.

I could tell that he was devastated, but much later I wondered whether he might have discarded the novel himself because it fell short of his expectations. My father was completely disorganized, so that it was hard to imagine him tidily keeping the manuscript in the typewriter case; all of his other writings were scattered around his office. Besides, I doubted whether there was room in the case for both the typewriter and a book-length manuscript. And he had made a carbon copy of everything else he wrote, so what happened to the copy? It still makes me sad that I cannot trust his woeful story.

My father, I hate to say, was a Grobster in life. He always wanted immediate results. He was brilliant and talented, but apparently didn't have the patience or discipline to complete a project as demanding as a novel.

WHEN I RETURNED HOME FROM CLEVELAND, I RESEARCHED BLOODGOOD'S family and located his sister, who was five years his junior. She told me on the phone that she had learned only recently of his death, months after it had happened. She had tried to separate herself from her brother out of psychological necessity and fear that she could be Bloodgood's next victim. "I wish there had been an autopsy," she told me, "to see if his brain was wired funny from birth. He started at such a young age with all the lying and stuff. Maybe he did it because he was so smart and bored to crap in school."

She recalled how their mother was mortified when one of Claude's elementary school teachers called and said, "Mrs. Bloodgood, if you can't afford to feed your child, we have special programs." He had pocketed his lunch money and told people in school that his parents were poor. "He skipped school all the time," his sister said, "and my parents always told me what a brilliant genius he was. It was only years later after he killed my mother and I was in therapy that I understood I wasn't stupid."

Claude often physically tormented his sister. He was on the wrestling team and liked practicing his moves on her. "He had me down on the floor," she recalled, "with his foot against my neck and his other foot under my arm. He was pulling my other arm out of the socket. I was screaming because I thought he was going to break my arm. The neighbors heard me and came over. My mother was mortified. His role in the family was to be the troublemaker and my role was to be the good girl and shut up. But now the neighbors knew."

When Bloodgood was fifteen, he robbed a convenience store. His father kept a German Luger as a war souvenir, and Bloodgood used it in the robbery. "There were no bullets in it," his sister said, "but he was tried as an adult because of the gun."

Bloodgood finished his first prison term when he was seventeen. He hated returning to school and continued to get in trouble. "My father yelled at him to apply himself and took a belt to him once," she said. "They always got in each other's face—testosterone plus—and Claude would threaten to burn the house down. He would sit for hours at the chessboard with all his chess books. That drove my father crazy." He wanted Bloodgood to find a job and do something with his life. He convinced him to commit himself voluntarily to a mental institution, in Williamsburg, Virginia. "It was a pretty gruesome place," his sister recalled, "where everyone was drugged like crazy and had bracelets on their feet. Everyone was on the ground. It was upsetting for me to see him there. The doctors said that he was a psychopath, that he had no conscience, and would do whatever he wanted."

Soon Bloodgood went into the marines—first to Parris Island, South Carolina, and then to Okinawa, where he was trained as a sharpshooter. He beguiled his sister with wild stories of geishas. When he returned home to Virginia, he told his family that he had tricked the Mafia by selling them a nonexistent call-girl ring. "Now my father was really worried," she recalled. "He'd walk around the house with a gun and keep the shades drawn in case the Mafia came for their money."

I asked her if Bloodgood might have met Bogart in a California VA hospital in the 1950s.

"Hell, no."

"So he was never in a VA hospital?"

"He was in 1955, I think, but not in California."

"Did he have friends in Hollywood?"

"Of course not."

"Could he have been married to the actress Kathryn Grayson?"

"That's a joke."

"Not according to his FBI files. They don't rule it out."

"Well, there you go. One of the things about my brother was that there was always a very tiny thread of truth in these goddamn wild stories. Just enough to pique you and make you wonder about everything else."

She said that their father loved Claude despite his criminal behavior. His brother would take the family credit cards and go on vacation in Mexico. "My father always welcomed him back," she said, "and tried to find him a job and get him back into society." In 1968, Claude cashed their parents' IRS check. "They reported this," she said. "My father told my mother and me that he worried Claude was going to kill one of us. But I was worried that he was going to kill my dad—they were the ones who fought. My father soon had second thoughts and said that he couldn't put his own son in jail. Two weeks later, Dad died. My mother went ahead and testified against Claude, and he turned to her in the courtroom and said, 'You'll never live to spend Dad's money.' He went to jail for one year, came out, and killed her.

"He could be really vicious and cruel. When I asked if Mom had suffered when he killed her, he said, 'Yeah, she suffered.' But he could also be very generous and protective. He stood up for me when other kids harassed me. I remember how one Easter I knocked over my parents' radio and broke it while looking for my Easter basket. I was terrified by what my father would do to me. Claude saw I was scared and he told my father that he did it. Claude was so bright and he exposed me to a lot of things that were way beyond my parents. He had me reading Dostoyevsky when I was eleven or twelve. He taught himself Russian from audiotapes and then he taught me.

"I'm glad he did the chess thing in prison. It gave him something to do with his mind. I have to laugh because this sounds gross, but that's really what he wanted to do with his life. Just sit there and play chess. He didn't want to get a job. I'm sure it was horrible to be in jail for thirty years, but he made the experience what he wanted it to be.

"Recently I read some of the chess books he wrote. They're interesting. I haven't played since he was a kid. He was much better than me. Maybe I'll get back into chess now."

ONE EVENING, AFTER I HAD SPOKEN WITH BLOODGOOD'S SISTER ABOUT HIS childhood, I had a postmortem with my own mother about my father's difficult upbringing. His mother, Charlotte Dinter, had been a bon vivant, a strong, independent woman who owned two chic dress boutiques in New Jersey. My father was haunted throughout his life by the identity of his own father, who had left before he was born. There was a name on his birth certificate, James Smith, which he suspected might have been made up. He never met his father, and his mother refused to tell him anything about Smith. When he occasionally asked, she'd cry and not respond. She was married four times, and her boyfriends were too numerous for my dad to keep track of their names. She would gallivant around the world with these men, spending months at a time at resorts in Germany. I do not know who took care of my dad back in New Jersey when she was in Europe; his sister would be shipped off to a Catholic boarding school within walking distance of their home.

Some of the husbands were losers. Husband number three showed up at her front door and threw a bottle of acid in her face after she broke off their relationship. My father summoned the paramedics, and his mother was basically OK because she had ducked in time. Husband number three went to prison, and Charlotte changed her name and switched residences out of fear that he might return after his release.

In my father's senior year in college, he took the name of husband number four, the new man in his mother's life, whom he liked better than the others and hoped against hope was his real father. The timing made that unlikely: Charlotte and number four would have had to have first met nineteen years earlier, before the three intervening husbands. Number four was a Russian-born Jew who became an officer in the U.S. Army and won a medal for his heroism in Cuba during the Spanish-American War. After the war, he ran hotels in Miami. His army awards plaque indicates that he was a short, thin man—a fact that also argued against his being the father of someone as tall and big-framed as my dad.

I didn't like Charlotte. We'd visit her once a year for Thanksgiving at her home in Plainfield, New Jersey. My dad would always coax me beforehand to hug her enthusiastically. I didn't like her because on Thanksgiving she'd have me sit on her lap and talk through me to my parents as if I were a ventriloquist's dummy. "Mommy, you've aged a lot," she'd say in a squeaky voice. "You have new wrinkles on your face." And to my dad, "You should have me wear a nice suit to Grandmother's, not dress me like a slob." At least she wanted me to wear men's clothes. My father claimed that every Halloween when he was a boy, Charlotte had forced him to dress up as her.

Charlotte was born in 1898 in Görlitz, Germany. Her mother died when she was in her early teens, and in 1913, at the age of fourteen, her father shipped her off by herself, speaking no English, to be raised by relatives in Pennsylvania. She apparently learned English quickly, because two years later her high school report card showed her getting good marks: Plane Geometry 88.6, Chemistry 93.1, Cicero 90, Latin Prose 92, English 86.5, Spelling 99, European History 92.2.

I told my mother that some time after my father died, Charlotte had confided in my cousin, who was the unofficial family historian, that she had been raped by one of her Pennsylvania relatives. My mother was surprised. "Now I understand," she said. "Once I made an off-color joke about rape and Charlotte got very angry." My cousin speculated that the man could have been my dad's father. That would explain why Charlotte became distraught and withdrawn when my dad raised the issue of his paternity.

"Did I ever tell you that your father told me about how the lying began?" my mother asked.

"He admitted he lied?"

"Yes."

"What did he say?"

"I can show you," she said.

"You can show me?"

"Yes. The lying started with a high school English composition. He made it all up. The teacher praised him, and he realized how easy it was to fool people and be rewarded for it." Because of the lying, my mother said, he later became a patient of Fritz Perls, the legendary founder of Gestalt therapy.

My mother left the room and returned with the composition, which was written in the form of a letter to his teacher. A weathered Post-it note was attached to it on which my mother had written: "Jim Hoff-man's composition re: his family. Age 15 with scarcely one true fact."

The letter began:

> 940 Kensington Avenue
> Plainfield, New Jersey
> September 24, 1934
>
> My dear Miss Gilbert,
>
> It is with a feeling of joy that I write this letter to you. It always gives me great happiness to tell anyone, whether by word of mouth or in writing, about my family. My father came to this country at the age of eight.

I felt queasy as I read the letter to myself. Of course, the first yarn he told would be about the father—and a heroic father, too—that he never had. It made sense. The letter continued:

> He and his people were poor hard working Germans who came to this country looking for honest work and a home of their own. When dad was twelve, his father died leaving him the soul [sic] support of the family. From but a school boy of twelve to a sweat shop is one long jump. Slowly, however, he lifted himself and his family out of their environment by hard work. From the factory he advanced to a newspaper office. Gradually he worked his way upward to the ranks of reporters. Then he met, fell in love and married my mother. When I was four years old, I distinctly remember his appointment as a columnist on the "Times." In this new position he had a column of his own in which he could write about anything of current interest he wished. A small struggle between two minute republics in South America, "The Twenty Four Hour War," broke out. Anticipating the war, the "Times" sent dad down to the war zone. Although the war lasted but twenty-four hours and he was a non-participant, he was one of the twelve people killed in the war. Since that time, mother has worked hard to support my younger sister and myself. She owns a dress shoppe and is getting along fine. For a woman who never worked before his death ten years ago, she's doing a great job.
>
> Sincerely yours,
> *James Williams*

Below the letter, the teacher had written in red pencil: "A perfectly fine letter. I was <u>greatly</u> <u>moved</u> by it. Be as fine a fellow as you appear to do justice to such parents!"

I didn't know what to think. On the one hand, I was glad that my dad felt safe enough with my mother to confess his deception. My impression of their marriage was that it had been absent of such intimacy, and I was comforted to learn otherwise. It would have meant so much to me, though, if he had admitted to me before he died that he had manipulated me, too.

I also didn't understand why my mother had kept the letter and why she'd never told me about it before. She knew how troubled I was by my father's behavior—she and I had spoken about this many times over the past twenty-five years. Why had she been holding out on me? And what compelled him to keep the letter in the first place? The substance of the letter was also disturbing: it was calculated to control the emotional response of his audience. My father had gone for the quick hit of an engaging, targeted lie by which he could engender a sympathetic reaction from his teacher rather than risk the uncertainty of how she might respond to the untidy truth.

IT IS EASY TO DISMISS BLOODGOOD AS AN ABERRANT FIGURE IN THE CHESS world. After all, it's not as if chess masters make a habit of bludgeoning their mothers. But it is a truism in research psychology that behavior carried to a grotesque extreme may reveal, by its very excess, essential aspects of normal behavior. What should we make of Bloodgood's pathological lying? Is it characteristic of chess players?

Tom Plenty said that chess was the one activity in which Bloodgood was scrupulously ethical and that he never violated the touch-move rule. But Bloodgood was dishonest in chess in a fundamental way. He invented games—not just the result but all the individual moves—played against people whom he presumably never met: John Wayne, Gary Cooper, Peter Lorre, and Henry Fonda. He went so far as to publish fictitious games and dress them up with elaborate stories about the context, such as the particular Hollywood restaurant in which they were played.

In my youth, when I frequented Washington Square Park, I often faced *patzers* who fabricated stories about how they'd once trounced Bobby Fischer at blitz. They'd even point to the particular table on which the purported victory took place, and some would show me the moves of these alleged miniatures. If Fischer had lost that many games back then, he would have given up chess.

The undeniable truth is that deception is everywhere in the world of chess. When chess amateurs describe their ability, they are prone to add a couple of hundred points to their peak rating. And when they tell you the score of a lengthy blitz match against a stronger player, the score tends to shift in their favor with each telling. Players of all strengths often let their time elapse, like Karpov did when he played Pascal, because they find it more palatable to lose on time than on the board.

In addition, there are whole tournaments recorded that simply never occurred. For example, according to the Web site for the "Heroes of Chernobyl" tournament in April 2005, three grandmasters, five international masters, and six other players conducted a round-robin near Kiev. The Web site showed photographs of the players and even provided all the moves of their games. But the tournament itself turned out to be faked in order to elevate the ratings of the designated winners.[4]

Allegations of rating fraud even extend into the equivalent of the chess "White House." Zurab Azmaiparashvili, a tough-looking grandmaster from Georgia and vice president of the World Chess Federation, has long been dogged by rumors of paying opponents to throw games.[5] In a tournament in Macedonia in 1995, which GM Nigel Short called "highly irregular" because there were questions about whether any of the games were ever played, the Georgian reportedly won fourteen games, drew four, and lost none—a spectacular performance that netted him forty rating points and made him ranked number seventeen in the world. Azmai, as he is known, wondered why Short and other grandmasters were skeptical of his success when, in 1993, he had already been ranked number eleven. The Macedonian tournament took place in a restaurant, he said, and most of his opponents were too relaxed to care about their games.[6]

In many tournaments there is scuttlebutt about fixed games in the final round, players agreeing to throw games to each other in order to maximize their collective earnings, the loser receiving a kickback from the monetary prize granted the winner.[7] In individual games with peculiar results, such rumors are hard to prove or dispel. A player who lets his clock run out in an easy, winning position might not have thrown the game but been the victim of fatigue and simply misread or misjudged the clock. There are strong players such as Bobby Fischer who suspect that most top games are fixed. When he played in the Candidates Tournament in Curaçao in 1962, some of the Russians drew quickly with each other—under instruction from Moscow—so that they could save their energy for their encounters with him. But Fischer takes the accusation of arranged games to a ludicrous extreme, maintaining that Kasparov purposely lost the World Championship to Kramnik so that the title would still be held by a Jew. (Not only is there no evidence for a rigged match but there is a fundamental problem with Fischer's theory: Kramnik is not Jewish.)

Viktor Korchnoi, the outspoken Soviet defector who challenged Karpov for the world title in 1978 and 1981, wrote in *Chess Is My Life* about the extent of cheating in Soviet chess.[8] In the Chigorin Memorial Tournament in Leningrad in 1951, Korchnoi admitted to earning a national master norm in an underhanded way. He needed a win in the last round against an experienced master but found himself in "a dead drawn position" at adjournment.

> Being a young player, I had a number of supporters, including some of the organizers of the tournament. They put strong pressure on my opponent, threatening not to hand over the cash prize due to him, if he did not agree to their demands. In the end my opponent succumbed to this blackmail, and he found a way to lose the drawn position. I must admit that throughout this unsavoury episode I behaved quite improperly. I made out that I knew nothing of what was happening, and laughed at my opponent.

Five years later Korchnoi tied for first at Hastings in 1956. He said that his compatriot, grandmaster Mark Taimanov, persuaded him privately to agree to a draw before they faced each other at the board. Later Korchnoi was stunned that Taimanov wrote a book in which "he went into raptures about how brilliantly we had played—but in fact the whole game had been worked out beforehand!"[9]

Although cheating in chess is an old phenomenon, the advent of chess-playing software that can easily fit on a concealed computer or a PDA now makes it simpler for dishonest amateurs to make strong chess moves. In 1993, an unrated first-timer to tournaments entered the World Open in Philadelphia under the name John von Neumann (the same name as the celebrated pioneer of artificial intelligence). After he drew with a GM and defeated a strong master, "von Neumann," whose pocket bulged suspiciously with something that was making a buzzing sound, was interrogated by a tournament director who concluded that he knew very little chess strategy.

Chess engines have only gotten smaller since 1993, and the time will soon come when Fritz will run on a cell phone or an iPod. Von Neumann had to leave the board to consult his pocket computer, drawing attention to himself by constantly getting up and down and making it impractical for him to get assistance on every move. The development of tiny wireless transmitters embedded in the ear canal and miniature cameras concealed in a sleeve or disguised as a shirt button means that a weak player, aided by an accomplice who is located remotely and equipped with a computer, can have grandmaster-strength software making all of his moves for him. Computer-assisted cheating is now such a threat to the integrity of amateur chess that a town meeting on the subject was held on December 4, 2006, at the Marshall. The conclusion of the meeting was that such chicanery is nearly impossible to prevent. Tournament organizers fear that casual players may stay away from the game if they are subjected to the same stringent anti-cheating measures—metal detectors, bathroom attendants, a prohibition on iPods and music headsets—to which highly paid chess pros like Kramnik and Topalov are now forced to submit. Moreover, it is questionable whether such measures would eradicate all cases of silicon-aided cheating. Wireless devices need not be metallic and could be so small that they'd elude all methods of detection except for invasive strip searches, and in the United States—unlike in Kalmykia—it is against the law to jam wireless communications.

GIVEN MY EXPERIENCE WITH MY FATHER, I MIGHT BE EXPECTED NOW TO have a sixth sense for exaggeration or deception. Instead I'm not at all skeptical, at least on a conscious level. I habitually believe that people are telling the truth. It is simply too disturbing for me to think that they're not. In the chess world it is particularly hard for anyone to separate fact from fiction because many seemingly over-the-top chess stories turn out to be entirely or partially true. Or we simply don't know enough to be able to judge their truth.

On August 17, 2003, ChessCafe.com published a remarkable interview that Susan Polgar, a former women's world champion, conducted with Paul Truong, her business manager and friend. Truong revealed that when he was five—yes, five!—he won South Vietnam's first National Junior Championship for players under the age of twenty-one. "All of a sudden, I became a sensation, a child prodigy," he told Polgar. And he followed up this success by winning his first national championship when he was eight. "I thought I had a chance to showcase my talent on a world stage," he continued, but then, when the North Vietnamese occupied Saigon on April 30, 1975, his life "came tumbling down."

Truong said that because his father had worked for the U.S. Embassy in Saigon, his family was singled out by the Communists. His father went into hiding, and the new government prohibited Truong from continuing his chess training and traveling abroad, although he was permitted to defend his title four times. On the fourth anniversary of the fall of Saigon, Truong and his dad escaped from Vietnam by boat.

The tale he told Polgar was harrowing: six hundred people were crammed into a small wooden boat with no food, no water, no bathrooms, no ventilation. The overworked engine exploded. Truong and his father were fortunate to be rescued and towed back to Vietnam and thrown into jail. After bribing officials to release them, they left by boat again, but were attacked five times by different bands of Thai pirates, who looted their possessions, raped the women, kidnapped the young girls, and finally sank the boat. People drowned and were eaten by sharks. A U.S. oil tanker rescued the survivors and brought them to

Malaysia, where they were confined in a primitive, overcrowded refugee camp on an abandoned soccer field.

The Malaysians eventually forced Truong, his father, and seven hundred other refugees onto a boat that was equipped with inadequate supplies of water and gas. After weeks at sea, watching their fellow passengers perish, Truong and his dad found themselves on a

> wild and deserted island. . . . But we still had no food. I had to hunt and fish with my bare hands, and find fruits from the jungle. . . . This was a real survivor experience, not the game you see on TV. Many more people died as a result of malnutrition. We stayed here for about 5–6 months, I think. Then finally, we came to New Jersey on December 1, 1979. I spoke no English. I was frail. I was very rusty in chess. It was a disaster.

In the United States, he said, he struggled through high school because he didn't know the language, while working seven part-time jobs to earn money to send to his mother and sixty other relatives in Vietnam. He played chess again but couldn't afford the entry fee of big tournaments. In 1982, at the age of seventeen, he decided to give up his dream of "being a grandmaster and even world champion" to pursue college and a career in business. "How could I be a world-class player," he said, "if I did not even have the opportunity to train or play?" After succeeding in unnamed business ventures, Truong decided to devote himself to giving every child who wants to play chess the guidance and support needed "to pursue his or her dream. . . . I want to bring respectability to chess. I want to bring chess to the same level as golf or tennis. . . . If I can survive everything I've went through in life, why can't I do this?"

The ChessCafe interview concluded with the following exchange:

> SP: Have you thought about putting your inspirational life story into a book, maybe even a movie? I know that there are a lot more incredible details (including an episode where you had a gun pointed right at your head and you refused to back down to the Communists, you would rather die for what you believe in) that you did not want to go into. Your story can rank right up there with the Anne Frank story and many other WW/Holocaust stories.
>
> PT: I would love to but I don't know how to go about and do that. Maybe someone can help me. But if and when it happens, I would like

to use the money from book sales or a movie deal to help chess. I will only do it for a meaning, not just to make money for myself. . . . I will only re-live this painful part of my life if it can benefit millions of children and women.

When the interview appeared on the Internet, it received a lot of attention. I found the story very moving and shared it with others. These people had a different reaction: they were completely skeptical. They thought that it was a calculated attempt, like a carefully laid swindle on a chessboard, to land a movie deal. Still, I couldn't help wondering if the story was true (and, even now, I don't know that it wasn't). Or if it wasn't literally true, maybe it was emotionally accurate, with a basis in reality at its core. I liked Paul Truong—he had sent me photos that he had taken of me at the ESPN match and at other chess events, and I admired his efforts to promote the game—and so I didn't even want to consider the possibility that he was stretching the facts. I was disillusioned with the number of dishonest men and Grobsters I had met through chess, and in the larger world, too. So I closed myself off to the idea that he might be yet another one.

But not totally, it seems. Because in the many months since the interview appeared, I've been tempted occasionally to investigate the accuracy of Truong's story. I asked Truong once if I could speak to his father to get his view on what had drawn his son to chess. What I said was true, but I particularly wanted to speak to his father to see if he would support Truong's life story. Truong responded that he would put me in touch with his dad, but then he never sent me his father's phone number. Nor did I pursue it. I actually preferred to avoid talking to his father. I wanted to believe Truong. And if he wasn't telling the truth, I didn't want to use his father to expose him and drive a wedge into their relationship. I knew how destructive it could be when deception comes between a father and a son, although here the roles would have been oddly reversed.

TWO MONTHS AFTER MY OWN FATHER'S DEATH, I CLEANED OUT HIS APARTMENT in the Village. It was a Herculean task—he had so much junk. But I welcomed the job because I wanted to find clues to who he really was. I was hoping that I might be able to figure out whether he had ever been an athlete, whom he had dated besides my mom, and how much money he actually made from gambling and hustling. In the end, though, after I had gone through all of his papers, I felt that I hardly knew him any better than before.

I was overwhelmed to discover that my father had kept carbon copies of every letter and handwritten note he'd ever sent me, including one-sentence thank-yous. The "Paul file" of these copies, and all the letters that I had ever sent him, filled a deep unlocked drawer in his office. Why had he kept all this? Because he was lonely and liked to reread his mail? Because he was paranoid and had to document everything? Because he had an exaggerated sense of his place in history and wanted to leave his correspondence as a record for posterity?

I found the last letters I had written to my father particularly difficult to reread. I had finally confronted him in writing about his lying, because my attempts to do so in person had been too tearful and frustrating; he would twist what I said and try to persuade me that I was the one who was misperceiving reality and needed psychiatric help—the same suggestion he had made to my mother years ago when she'd tried to talk to him about problems in their relationship. I wrote these letters when my father was dying of prostate cancer that had spread to his bones and, ultimately, his brain, reducing his 300-pound frame to half its former bulk. I should have been comforting him during his final months—my mother, after barely seeing him for a decade, had taken him into her home to care for him at the end of his life—but instead my letters were angry and contemptuous. Was it weirdly admirable, masochistic, or simply a sign of compulsion that he had kept these letters along with the others instead of simply tossing them in the trash?

Aside from the "Paul file," the drawer contained four curious items. The first was a long handwritten list of two- and three-letter words, compiled by my dad in the days before there were strategy books on Scrabble; he was so competitive with me when I was young that he had concealed the fact that he had memorized these particular words. I could only hope now that he had learned them not specifically for the purpose of beating his ten-year-old son but also because he played Scrabble for money.

The second was a sealed manila envelope on which he had written, "BURN IT! JIM'S JUNK. PLEASE DESTROY WITHOUT OPENING,

AFTER I DIE. IF YOU DARE OPEN THIS ENVELOPE, MY HAND WILL GROW OUT OF THE GRAVE AND CHOKE YOU!" He was taunting me even after he was gone. I put the envelope aside, postponing the dilemma of what to do with it.

The third item made me laugh. It was a series of contact sheets of photographs that had been taken in the apartment. Each image was a group of lounging nude women. Way to go, Dad, I thought. His story that he had rented out his apartment as the set of a porn film was apparently true; the fact that some of his outrageous tales were credible only complicated my efforts to make sense of his life.

Finally, under all of the papers, I found three chess pieces from my childhood set, on which we often used to play together. I don't know whether he had intentionally kept these pieces as a reminder of better times between us or whether they had just settled, like pennies and paper clips, at the bottom of the drawer. The two White bishops were sooty and oily from tobacco smoke, almost as dark as the Black pawn.

I realize now that I was drawn to chess because there can be no doubt about the result—there is no room for deception. Nothing is clearer than checkmate, the king threatened with execution with no place to go that's not controlled by the enemy. In the postmortem you can debate your adversary for hours about what *might* have happened if you had played differently, but there is no avoiding the fact that the actual game ended in a win, loss, or draw. Because my father was my main opponent when I was young, the unambiguousness of the result was important to me, although at the time I didn't know why. When my father lost a game, he couldn't worm his way out of the defeat. I had witnessed the loss myself—indeed, I had inflicted it—and so he could not claim that a confused referee had raised the wrong guy's hand.

There is truth on the chessboard in other ways, too. The opponent can try something tricky, as Pascal did in the Dragon game against Drenchev, but everything is there for both players to see. In poker you need to judge whether an adversary is bluffing without knowing his cards. In chess nothing whatsoever is concealed. Both players analyze the same configuration of pieces and pawns.

Emanuel Lasker, the world champion from 1894 to 1921, famously said:

On the chessboard, lies and hypocrisy do not survive long. The creative combination lays bare the presumption of a lie; the merciless fact, culminating in checkmate, contradicts the hypocrite. Our little chess is one of the sanctuaries where this principle of justice has occasionally had to hide.

Lasker further claimed that chess was not merely a substitute for life but a way of rekindling interest in the larger world.

Many a man, struck by injustice as, say, Socrates and Shakespeare were struck, has found justice realized on the chessboard, and has thereby recovered his courage and his vitality to play the game of life.[10]

When I was immersed in chess as an adolescent, my sentiments were similar to Lasker's. I thought the game's special decisive nature made it a rare bastion of truth in a world filled with confusing falsehoods. I was wrong. The irony is that chess, which seems so pure in the abstract, is a magnet for deceptive people. I moved away from the game not because I lost interest in what was happening on the board but because I could not tolerate the dishonesty and psychic aggression all around me in the tournament hall.

As an adult, I have met many top players who are unable to maintain close friendships. "The longer you play chess, the more self-centered you become," said Aleksander Wojtkiewicz, a Polish-American grandmaster. "It's necessary in chess to put yourself first," Wojtkiewicz told me. "It's easy to forget that anyone else exists. That attitude doesn't work in the rest of life. That's why few of us chess players can hold marriages.[11] Look at Karpov and Kasparov."[12] If I was going to remain in the chess world, I wanted to find strong players, chess role models if you will, whom I admired not only for how they guided their cavalry and clerics, but also for how they conducted their lives.

FEMALE COUNTERPLAY

"They're all weak, all women. They're stupid compared to men. They shouldn't play chess, you know. They're like beginners. They lose every single game against a man."
——BOBBY FISCHER

"Women could be just as good at chess, but why would they want to be?"
——MARGARET MEAD

"I believe chess can bring me closer to the spiritual part of this world in a way that simple material stuff can't."
——IRINA KRUSH

"DO YOU WANT TO KNOW THE TRUTH, PAUL?" KASPAROV asked. We were having dinner at a sleek French restaurant a few blocks from his Manhattan hotel. "Or do you want me to be politically correct?" The latter question was, of course, theoretical: even if I had opted for the sanitized version, he still would have steamrolled me with his version of the truth. Kasparov was about to tell me why there would never be many women in the top echelons of chess. This disquisition had been prompted by our waitress, a tall young woman wearing a slinky black dress and a jeweled stud in her nose, who was now across the room getting our drinks. Kasparov was obviously intrigued by her beauty—her charcoal-black, waist-length hair, her high cheekbones, her sallow lips—and confounded by her conspicuous lack of interest in chess, which emerged after she'd recited the seafood special in a detached, listless voice. Kasparov, ever observant, had noticed on the back of the menu, in small type, a list of regular weekly events at the restaurant: a jazz brunch on Sunday, a string quartet on Monday, and so on. Tonight was "chess night." He asked her when people would start playing.

"Chess," she snorted, "you've got to be kidding. It may say that, but I've worked here three months and never seen anybody play."

Kasparov forced himself to smile. It must have been a novel experience for him to talk about chess with someone who had no idea who he was. He seemed both humbled and disgusted, and when she left to fill our drink order, he shook his head as if he were confounded by an unexpected development at the chessboard.

"Most women are not contemptuous of chess," he told me. "They admire what we do, the force and passion with which we throw ourselves into the battle. How we destroy our opponents." I liked how Kasparov was using the collective *we*, including me in the brotherhood of chess players, but I didn't agree with where he was going. "But there's a reason why women themselves do not excel at the game," he continued. "Chess is a combination of war, science, and art, areas in which men dominate and women are naturally inferior. Not by choice but by design. I tell the truth, even if it is not what people want to hear."

It was a truth Kasparov had been telling since 1987, when he wrote *Child of Change* and pondered why "the female is much less deadly than the male" in chess:

> Botvinnik believes there are physiological reasons why women will always play less well than men, that a woman's nervous system is designed to cope with her function as a mother of children, leaving her with less natural aptitude for making decisions. This, of course, is a contentious subject, especially in these days of women's liberation. But I have to say that I think Botvinnik is right.

Kasparov then observed that in areas of abstract thought like music, mathematics, and chess, women have historically shown less talent than men.

> There are no women grandmasters at composing music or painting. Women's minds cannot handle the concepts of Euclidean geometry.

> They do better in areas with a human dimension, such as medicine or writing fiction. Also, I think top-level chess requires a degree of natural aggression which does not come naturally to many women.

He went on to note that modern scientific research supported Botvinnik's view:

> Men do much better in tests to measure spatial-visual ability, such as breaking up patterns into smaller units, a key factor in chess. [Moreover] a woman's train of thought can be broken more easily by extraneous events, such as a baby crying upstairs. This is not part of their environmental conditioning, but organic, part of their genetic molecular structure. The effect, in computer terms, is to overload their memory bank with a series of little events to which they are programmed to respond, thereby limiting their powers of concentration.

Kasparov concluded by apologizing to women for his seemingly chauvinist views:

> Only in fiction (*Queen's Gambit* by Walter Tevis) does a woman take a game from the world champion. I'm sorry, ladies, but there it is!

When Kasparov wrote these words, there were no women ranked within the top one hundred players in the world. And now, two decades later, there is one, Judit Polgar, who got as high as number eight. Kasparov believes she is just the exception that proves the rule. "An individual woman may play well," he told me, "but as a group, they'll never succeed."

KASPAROV'S ACQUAINTANCE WITH JUDIT POLGAR BEGAN INAUSPICIOUSLY. Born in 1976, she is the youngest and strongest of three chess-prodigy Hungarian sisters who were homeschooled by their psychologist father. Laszlo Polgar believed that genius was not innate but could be taught through rigorous conditioning in early childhood. Like B. F. Skinner before him, he tested his controversial theory on his daughters. He chose chess as the medium not because he loved the game but because his first daughter, Susan, liked chess and he knew his educational theory would command attention if he could create female stars in an activity that had long been dominated by men. He reportedly arranged for the girls to wake up to chess problems that he posted next to their beds. Each morning began with spirited bouts of Ping-Pong for physical exercise, followed by six to eight hours of chess. His wife, who also stayed at home to help with the instruction, taught the girls languages and occasionally shepherded them to museums.

Hungarian officials objected to Laszlo's experiment; they threatened to commit him to a mental institution and they dispatched armed policemen to his home in Budapest to try to force the girls to attend school. The Hungarian government retreated when Laszlo promised to send his daughters to school once a year for standardized testing. "We learnt what we needed very quickly and forgot it as soon as the exams were over," Judit Polgar told London's *Daily Telegraph*.

The training regimen also dismayed prominent members of the chess world whose own self-images were invested in the idea that chess genius was more than rote learning. Kasparov, for one, famously dismissed Judit Polgar as a trained dog, and Nigel Short christened her "Lassie." Kasparov claimed later that the epithet was not intended to denigrate her as a person but to disparage the mechanistic way in which her father had instructed her.

However Judit and her sisters were taught, the chess world could not ignore her amazing accomplishments. At ten, she made headlines in the United States by winning the unrated section of the New York Open. At twelve, she became the world's youngest international master. And at the age of fifteen, she bested Bobby Fischer's record by a month as the youngest grandmaster ever.[1]

JUDIT POLGAR WAS SEVENTEEN WHEN SHE AND KASPAROV FIRST FACED EACH other at the chessboard. The year was 1994, and the occasion was the annual Super Tournament at the Hotel Anibal in the Spanish town of Linares. On Kasparov's thirty-sixth move, in a position in which he was winning, he confidently picked up a knight, advanced it to the c5 square, released it completely for a microsecond, and then swept it back up with three fingers—after presumably noticing that the move was a blunder that would allow Polgar to fork his queen and rook. He showed little emotion as he thought for a few minutes and then moved the knight to a different square, one that ruled out the fork and maintained his advantage. Polgar was stunned. She struggled to process both the fact that, in a split second, she had gone from losing to winning to losing again and her suspicion that the world champion, a veteran twice her age, had cheated her.[2] He appeared to have violated one of the most sacred and irrevocable rules in tournament chess: touch move.

This rule has two parts: first, if you touch a piece you have to move it, and, second, if you release it, you cannot pick it up again. Touch move is drilled into all chess students, and every player can remember losing games because he intemperately touched a piece or put it on the wrong square. (Or winning games because he improperly retracted a move, as I did in the Harvard Open.) The honor code knows no exceptions—not for world champions, not for enfant terribles.

Polgar was unsure how to respond. Standing nearby were both the arbiter and the owner of the hotel, who was the sole and generous sponsor of the tournament. She looked at them, as if appealing to them for confirmation, but they didn't react. (It is the arbiter's job to enforce the touch-move rule if he sees a violation.) Polgar resigned after another ten moves and then quietly asked Kasparov whether he had in fact released the knight. He gave her a patronizing smile and responded: "Come on, what do you think, with a few hundred spectators as witnesses?"

Polgar still suspected that Kasparov had cheated her. Her middle sister, Sofia, urged her later to ask him again, but she rejected the suggestion, imagining the possible consequences.

> He's only got to say that it's not true and who'll believe my story then? I can see it. How very unsporting of such a young girl. You can tell she is very young. She is in time trouble, she is lost and tries such a cheap trick. And against Kasparov too, who would be the last to permit himself such a thing. In plain view of the arbiter, of the whole crowd, and, as if that were not enough, of a camera crew as well.

A Spanish television crew was filming Linares, but they returned to their Barcelona studio before Judit Polgar—or anyone else at the tournament—could see if the questionable knight maneuver was on videotape. A few days later, however, rumors swept the Hotel Anibal that the television producers had reviewed their reels of tape and found incriminating footage of Kasparov taking his hand off the knight. The tournament organizer released a statement saying that any such suggestion was a scurrilous besmirching of both the champion and the tournament's good name, and he ordered that the tape not be shown anywhere in his hotel. Of course his order just stoked the controversy, and when a copy of the tape surfaced at the playing site, it was passed around and viewed repeatedly like a bootlegged video of Paris Hilton or Pamela Anderson. There was no mistaking that Kasparov, who had retreated to his hotel suite, had indeed released the knight.

The chess press took the champion to task. "You bring down shame on yourself if you break this code of honour," wrote *New in Chess* journalist Dirk Jan ten Geuzendam:

> Young Bobby Fischer, for instance, concentrating deeply in a game against German grandmaster Unzicker, happened to be fiddling with his h-pawn [the kingside rook pawn] in the assumption that it had been captured and taken off the board. When he realized to his dismay what he was doing, he didn't have to think twice before accepting the consequences of his mistake. He moved the h-pawn, causing irreparable damage to his position, and lost quickly.

The groundswell of support for Judit gave her courage. When she spied her former opponent leaving the hotel, the teenager caught up with him and asked point-blank, "How could you do this to me?" The consequence of her boldness, she told Geuzendam, was that Kasparov didn't speak to her for three years.

Although the world champion eventually apologized, he continued to insist that he did not realize at the time that he had released the knight—a view that his critics do not believe. "I shared a ride with Judit right after the game," Karpov told me, "and she was so distraught not just by what he had done but by the fact that his body language at the board—his sitting there still and quietly, as if trying to disguise his crime—gave away that he knew he had wronged her." Karpov, of course, was hardly a disinterested observer and always offered the worst possible interpretation of his rival's behavior.

I was not at Linares, but I would not read too much into reports of Kasparov's unusual stoicism at the board. Whether or not he thought he'd released the knight, he certainly knew that he had almost committed a colossal blunder, and this knowledge would have distracted him.

Maybe he was sitting there impassively mulling over his near-death experience and clearing his head so that he could continue the fight. My own belief is that Kasparov is guilty, but not beyond a reasonable doubt: it is conceivable he released the knight without really knowing it. I've witnessed many games in which the atmosphere was so charged that the players were not aware of the obvious. I was guilty of this myself in my game with Noah Siegel. If I was capable of winning a chess game and not knowing it at the time, I imagine it is entirely possible that a world champion could momentarily release a knight from his grip in the middle of a tense battle and not realize it. But there was also no denying that Kasparov would have found it especially humiliating to be beaten by a seventeen-year-old girl.

Forty years ago Bobby Fischer, who described all women as "weakies," boasted that he could beat any female player in the world at knight odds (handicapping himself by starting the game without one of his steeds). In an interview with *The New York Times* in 2002, Kasparov conceded that women's chess had improved to the point where it would be rash for him to repeat Fischer's boast. "Now I wonder if I could be so prudent to give a pawn," he cockily told the *Times*. Ironically, his own question had already been answered in the negative by the time the interview was published on September 22, and if the *Times* editors had followed chess news, they would certainly have scotched his comment. On September 9, the "trained dog" Judit Polgar, after losing ten games to Kasparov over a period of eight years, had finally defeated him in Moscow in the Russia versus the World rapid match.

In our conversation at the restaurant, Kasparov was focused on the absence of women at the very top. From my own perspective as an amateur, I was more interested in the fact that there were more women now playing in tournaments in New York than there had been when I was a child. OK, the raw numbers were still relatively small, but in the 1970s many of the tournaments I'd entered were all male. The girl whom my father described my playing in *Lithopinion* was one of only three, I think, in a competition involving a few hundred kids. I would have enjoyed the game more as a teenager if girls had played it in greater numbers. Not just because I was developing an interest in girls then, but because their very presence might have served as a brake on the arrogant frat-boy antics of the male players.

ON THE THIRD THURSDAY IN MARCH 2003, WHEN MANY ART GALLERIES across Manhattan were holding their monthly openings, seventy-five art connoisseurs and chess fanatics milled about the Viewing Gallery on Seventeenth Street, sipping wine, eating cookies, and occasionally glancing at the confetti-like landscapes on the walls. A little after 7:00 P.M., two elegantly dressed young women, one wearing only black, from her gloves and sleeveless dress to a black flapper wig, and the other all in white, emerged from the unisex restroom and took their places on opposite sides of a chessboard at the front of the gallery. They planned to play two games, at the fast pace of twenty-five minutes a side per game. They shook hands, and the woman in the white wig began by confidently advancing her queen pawn two squares and depressing the dual chess timer next to the board. The crowd nodded approvingly. "I would not have given up chess," a disheveled man in his sixties announced, "if my opponents had looked like this." I had to admit that the all-male flea-infested chess parlors I frequented with my father in Times Square were a world away from a chic art gallery in which two smart and beautiful women were playing the ultimate intellectual game.

The woman in black was Jennifer Shahade, twenty-two, the strongest female chess player in history to be born and raised in the United States. She grew up in Philadelphia, where she learned chess at the age of five or six from her father, Michael, four-time champion of Pennsylvania. She was also inspired by her brother, Greg, two years her senior, who became a master when he was fourteen and at twenty earned the prestigious Samford Fellowship for the country's most promising college-aged player. Jennifer's big break came in 1996 at the so-called Insanity Tournament at the Marshall Chess Club. "It's a crazy event," she said. "You play, I think, nine games. You play all night with the rounds starting at odd times like 2:11 A.M. and 4:23 A.M. I was about to turn sixteen and I managed to get it together and do well with no sleep." She came in first and joined her father and brother as a certified chess master.

Jennifer's opponent at the Viewing Gallery, nineteen-year-old Irina Krush, a petite brunette and Pascal Charbonneau's girlfriend, was certainly no chess slouch, either. Irina had emigrated from Ukraine in 1988 before she turned five, the age at which her father taught her the game. At fourteen she became the youngest U.S. women's champion ever, a record that still stands. In 2000, she continued to break records by becoming the first American woman to earn the title of international master.

Of the 80,000 members of the United States Chess Federation in 2003, some one thousand had earned the coveted rank of national master, but only fifteen American women, Jennifer and Irina among them, had that distinction. Although the two women were friends—they were teammates at the 2002 Chess Olympiad in Bled, Slovenia, and classmates at New York University—they were also fierce competitors, and at the art gallery they went all out.

Jennifer responded to Irina's queen-pawn opening with a provocative defense known as the Grünfeld, favored by both Fischer and Kasparov. Black goads White into placing pawns in the center of the board, normally an important goal, but figures that she can undermine the center with well-placed blows from the flanks. Here the plan failed because Jennifer overlooked the fact that Irina could win a key center pawn. Later Irina infiltrated with her knights and launched a decisive mating attack. You could sense Jennifer's desperation as she struggled to shelter her king. As she pondered the position, she leaned over the board and their heads almost touched. She cradled her face in her hands—a characteristic posture she shares with Kasparov—and squeezed so hard that her fingers left red marks on her cheeks. She squirmed in her seat and twisted her feet in her black boots. There was no defense, and she resigned on the forty-second move.

"This really sucks," she said to me after she got up from the board. "All your close friends show up to drink wine and enjoy themselves while you lose in front of them." Twenty minutes later, however, she had composed herself and sat down for the second game. This time she had the advantage of moving first. She advanced her king pawn two squares, a more aggressive opening than Irina had employed in the first game. Jennifer needed to win to even the score, and she planned to press Irina from the onset. Irina did not shy away from the battle, and steered the game into an obscure line of the Richter-Rauzer Variation of the Sicilian Defense. The two players positioned their kings in opposite corners of the board and launched all-out assaults on the opposing monarch.

Irina's attack netted her two pawns, and she could have won immediately by sacrificing a rook, but Jennifer set a trap on the thirtieth move. If Irina misjudged the position and made the seemingly natural response of offering the exchange of queens, Jennifer could win a knight—a decisive material advantage—through a simple four-move combination. At classical tournament chess, where each player can take three to five hours for a game, Irina would presumably have never fallen for such a swindle, but here, faced with her time running out, it was possible that she would go wrong. The people next to me in the audience, even with wine in them, recognized the trap. "It's Jennifer's only chance," whispered her brother Greg. He turned nervously away from the board, as if staring at it might jinx his sister's subterfuge. Pascal, who of course was rooting for his girlfriend, started pacing. Irina fell for the trick and, unlike her emotional opponent, sat motionless as she lost the knight and subsequently the game.

It was almost 10:00 P.M., and the spectators chanted, "Tiebreak! Tiebreak!" hoping that the two women would play a sudden-death game (five minutes a side) to determine the winner. But Irina had a late-night engagement, and Jennifer, who was drained, seemed content to call it a tie.

"People sometimes ask me if chess is fun," Jennifer told me afterward, as we sipped white wine in the gallery. "Fun is not the word I'd use. Of course, I enjoy it, or I wouldn't play. But chess is not relaxing. It's stressful, even if you win. The game demands total concentration." She surveyed the young, natty crowd that had just watched her play. "It's now cool to play chess," she said. "The game is finally shedding its image as a magnet for geeks."

Female celebrities now proudly associate themselves with the game. Madonna reportedly took chess lessons from the Scottish national champion (her husband, filmmaker Guy Ritchie, is Scottish). Carmen Kass, a *Vogue* model of the year and the face of L'Oreal, is president of the Estonian Chess Federation. Kass told *Vogue* that she doesn't know anyone else in her profession who plays the royal game. Although Kass has entered tournaments, she is not so committed to chess, she joked, as to have "a regular Tuesday-morning game with Kasparov or an IBM computer."

Jennifer herself was a model of coolness. Her brown curls, when they weren't stuffed under a black pageboy wig, were streaked blond and pink. She lived in a loft in Williamsburg, Brooklyn, where Internet cafés and Thai restaurants have displaced mustard and girdle factories. She played basketball, air hockey, and Ms. Pac-Man. She stayed out all night at clubs and bars.

WHEN I PLUNGED BACK INTO THE CHESS WORLD, I KNEW JENNIFER ONLY from afar. She played in the top section of many of the tournaments I attended, and I was intrigued by the contrast between how nervous and anxious she appeared at the board and how relaxed she looked between games. She has a boisterous, infectious laugh that can fill a large playing hall and a gentle conversational manner that puts even the most socially awkward male master at ease. I liked her evident passion on and off the board.

Jennifer has a mischievous side, too. When she tires of telling people she has just met that she is a chess champion—because that inevitably derails the conversation into a long Q and A about chess, and she has answered the questions time and again—she says she's a circus performer. "I'm not a good liar," she told me, "but I'm thrilled when people believe me."

After the match with Irina, I interviewed Jennifer in her Williamsburg apartment for an article I was writing for *Smithsonian* magazine. I noticed that her interest in wigs extended beyond the black hairpiece she'd worn at the Viewing Gallery. On the wall were photos of her solidly built father (he competes in Iron Man triathlons) and her brother wearing pink shoulder-length wigs. "I love the color," she told me, as she showed me a campy self-portrait in which she explored the idea that a woman can be both a sex goddess and an intellectual. She was wearing a pink wig, pink gloves, and a slinky pink dress. She had made herself up to look like a vampish Marilyn Monroe. She was dressed to party, but was reading a book with a pink cover called *Secrets of Chess Tactics,* a classic Russian text that is serious even by the erudite standards of chess literature.

We spoke for an hour about her interest in chess, and then I asked if we could play a game of blitz. There was a board already set up across the room, and she agreed. If I had been a player of her caliber, our first game would have been monumentally important as we each jockeyed to win and establish a trend that would prove who was better. Here, of course, there was no question that she was much stronger than I, but the game was psychologically loaded nonetheless. I expected her to win, but I still wanted her to respect me: I didn't want to play like an idiot. I wanted to demonstrate that I had some command of the pieces. And if I was fortunate, I might make a move or two that she found interesting, if not inspired. My biggest fear was that I'd bore her.

Jennifer was also clearly less relaxed than she'd been during the interview. She was playing with her hair, twisting its pink and blond streaks, and adjusting her pawns so that they were in the center of their starting squares. Despite my desire to impress her with a cunning combination, I also felt sympathetic; if I made the most horrible blunder in the history of chess, it would be our little secret. If she made a similar error, the five million readers of *Smithsonian* might be party to her humiliation.

I looked across the table and wondered what was going through her mind. I knew she didn't want to screw up, but what exactly was her strategy? Would she try to wipe me out from the start? Probably not, I thought. Her eyes were kind, and I imagined she was the type of woman who'd want to beat me but leave me feeling good about myself. There was also a double standard. If a man went straight for the jugular, he'd expect to be admired. Was she concerned that if she blew me away, I might be one of those unenlightened guys who would describe her in print as an aggressive bitch? Or could it be that she actually wanted to be described that way? I didn't know her well enough to judge.

She shook my hand, I started her clock, and she casually pushed her king pawn forward. I steered the game into a Najdorf Sicilian, and she responded with the fashionable English Attack, which leads to positions that are among the wildest in the rough-and-tumble world of the Sicilian. In many variations of the Sicilian, White soon advances her kingside pawns toward Black's king; in the English Attack she launches the pawns particularly early.

On the eighth move, I advanced the rook pawn on my kingside, in defiance of conventional thinking. I intended to shelter my king on that side of the board. Chess students are taught not to move pawns in front of their castled king because they can become targets or leave weak squares around the king. But I had seen some recent grandmaster games in which the rook pawn was advanced in this exact position, in the hope of slowing White's anticipated pawn onslaught. She smiled and stiffened a bit in her chair. She knew from my move that I had at least a passing familiarity with modern opening theory. I hoped that I was lucky and she hadn't faced this prophylactic pawn push before.

She made natural moves on her next ten turns, continuing to maintain the advantage that the White pieces gave her. Then, on the eighteenth move, she pushed a pawn deep into my king's front yard—so deep, in fact, that it was knocking on the palace door. She had dispatched the foot soldier on a kamikaze mission to pry open lines to my king. Whether the sacrifice was objectively warranted wasn't clear, but it was pure Shahade, and no doubt intended in part to intimidate and confuse me. She liked to take risks on the chessboard and throw the game into chaos.

For the next dozen or so moves, we had a thrilling, tit-for-tat slugfest. First we traded dark-squared bishops, although this improved her position by bringing her queen closer to her quarry, my king. I picked up my light-squared bishop and captured her knight, which was also poised to invade the king's palace. She in turn captured my bishop. With one of my rooks I chopped off a juicy-looking pawn, with a motion of my hand that was unusually aggressive for me, and she replied by jauntily executing one of mine.

I paused to evaluate who stood better. I had weathered her attack—hallelujah!—and, after all the exchanges, remained a pawn up. I thought I had the advantage, although maybe not enough to win against a player of her caliber. There was no reason I should lose, though. Then I checked the clock and saw to my delight that I had a luxurious twenty-five seconds remaining to her paltry fifteen seconds. She was notorious for getting into time pressure in her long tournament games, and now she had done that—perhaps fatally—here.[3] If I could just move instantly and avoid blunders, she would surely run out of time before I did.

I was pleased that I had more than acquitted myself on the board—she respected me now, I hoped—but I was conflicted about impending victory. I started to worry that it was self-serving if I beat her in an off-hand game and wrote about it. She seemed to be playing hard, but what if she was just a fine actress and going easy on me out of some unusual sense of chivalry? I looked up at her face. She was pressing her temples and squeezing her cheeks. No, she certainly didn't look as if she wanted to lose. I checked the clock again. All this introspection had cost me ten seconds; we were now even, at fifteen seconds apiece. I panicked and mindlessly repositioned my knight.

I was ahead again in time after two more moves, seven seconds to four. But she did not collapse. Instead, she went out swinging by trying to sacrifice a rook for my knight. Her hand was shaking when she picked up my knight, and it slipped out of her grip and went careening into the wall. I hesitated to capture her rook with my pawn. She would then take the pawn with her queen, bringing that mighty piece very close to my king, whose protective pawn fortress was now completely denuded. And yet I didn't see a killer follow-up for her. But I gave her the benefit of the doubt by assuming that I was missing something diabolical that she had seen. Why else would she want to part with her valuable rook? So I declined the rook and captured a knight of hers instead. It was not a bad move; it kept my advantage.

Two moves later she reached out and stopped the clocks and announced with obvious relief that I had lost on time. My dreams of triumph were reduced to fantasy. I saw that she had just two seconds remaining on her clock. I asked her if I could have captured the rook and lived. I don't see why not, she said softly. She had outwitted me not by the objective strength of her final moves but by the clever psychological ploy of making an unexpected, intimidating-looking capture that caused me to think when I could not afford to. A good player, I learned, never gives up until she has exhausted every conceivable weapon in her arsenal.

I ASKED JENNIFER IF KASPAROV'S VIEWS ON WOMEN HAD DETERRED FEMALE players from pursuing the game. "You have to laugh," she said. "Does he really think that women can't play well because we all hear babies crying in the back of our minds?" She joked about staging a tournament above a nursery to see if men would handle the noise better than women. "I don't really care what Kasparov thinks," she continued. "He's not a sociologist, and he's not going to stop me from playing. I'll listen to him when he analyzes chess positions."

I remembered Irina Krush telling me that she thought being a female player was an advantage. "You get more invitations to exclusive tournaments," Irina explained, "because you're considered to be something of a novelty. Male players sometimes claim that I have an advantage because they are distracted by how I look. I don't buy that, though. When chess players lose, they always come up with an excuse."

Jennifer's own views on this particular excuse mirrored my feelings when I played her. "If you find someone attractive," Jennifer said, "you don't play worse. You buckle down and try to play better because you want to dazzle them with your brilliance."

The chief impediment to more women playing tournament chess seems to be cultural. "If you're going to become very good at chess," Jennifer told me, "you have to pour yourself into it." In our society, we approve if a boy plays chess. We see it as a sign of intelligence. But we consider it weird if a boy is obsessed with chess, if he spends the bulk of his waking hours playing and studying the game. "Now if a girl does that," Jennifer said, "it's not just weird, it's downright unacceptable to most parents. Women are usually discouraged from pursuing chess and other intellectual activities that require time-consuming devotion."

In her own case, she said, she was free to be obsessive. Jennifer had the blessing, and the example, of her mother, who was both a success in the traditional male field of chemistry (she is a professor at Drexel) and an avid games player—of blackjack, poker, and, to a lesser extent, chess. "There were periods in my life," Jennifer told me, "when chess was the most important thing to me. It's not that I did chess all day—I took time out to be with my friends or to exercise—but I justified the time with my friends and the exercise as being good for my chess. Today my life is more balanced."

UNLIKE JENNIFER'S LIFE, IRINA'S REVOLVES AROUND THE GAME. "I AM VERY chessy," she told me. Irina is uncomfortable giving interviews—she'd rather be playing chess than talking about the game. But one morning at 3:00 A.M., when I was driving home from a tournament with her and Pascal, she was unusually philosophical. Of all the top players I know, she is the most idealistic about the power of chess to give meaning to life. "Chess is a gift that civilization handed us," she told me. "I believe chess can bring me closer to the spiritual part of this world in a way that simple material stuff can't." She sees no intrinsic reason why women can't play as well as men but doubts whether there will ever be many women in chess. "You have to be obsessive to play the game well, and women aren't as obsessive as men," she said. "I'm not fanatically crazy about chess. I like the game but I'm not going to study it ten hours a day like many male grandmasters did when they were teenagers."

"I think it's a matter of choice," Pascal interrupted. "Women haven't chosen to devote themselves to the game."

"Biology can get in the way," said Irina. "A lot of things change for girls when they're thirteen, fourteen, and fifteen. Things change for boys, too, of course, but not as early so it's easier for boys to concentrate on chess in their early teens when playing and studying the game has the biggest payoff. During those years, interactions with the opposite sex matter more to girls. Their first crushes, their first kisses, when they first fall in love. . . .

"I think girls are more emotional than guys. Lots of my mistakes happen because of how I emotionally respond to a position." She told me about one of her games at the U.S. Championship against a player named Tatev Abrahamyan. "I had a shitty position," Irina said, "and was being outplayed. I saw that she had a move that would give her a great position. I was very unhappy. But she didn't think long and made a move that was one hundred times worse than the move I expected." Irina was so shocked that she did not adjust to the new situation and immediately made a losing retreat with her queen. "It was horrible," she recalled. "The position was certainly not beyond my understanding. Immediately afterward, I realized the retreat was bad. I had made a very emotional blunder because my shock blinded me for a moment." Irina paused for a minute. "You never hear male players saying they're shocked. Maybe it's because men are not as honest."

"What?" Pascal interrupted.

"Men never say the truth. If a male player panicked, he'd deny it."

"What?" he teased.

"Be quiet, Pascal." Irina turned back to me. "Is a woman more likely to panic than a man? I don't know. Are the top men naturally calmer, or have they just trained themselves regardless of their personality not to panic because that's what it takes to be a top GM? Regardless, I need to work on this."

FOR MOST OF THE GAME'S LONG HISTORY, WHEN WOMEN PLAYED CHESS IT was in the context of courtship. When Benjamin Franklin was an old man in Paris, he tried to seduce women over the chessboard by playing them in their boudoirs. A favorite partner was Madame Brillon de Jouy, an acclaimed harpsichordist and composer who lived with her older philandering husband on a fancy estate not far from where Franklin was staying. She met Franklin in 1777, when she was thirty-three and he was seventy-one. Although they never consummated their relationship, the two exchanged more than 130 steamy letters over an eight-year period, in which he suggested that his penis was a stallion ready to invade her stable. When they got together in person, she'd sit in his lap and they'd play chess.

Apparently his seduction technique did not include letting her win. "She is still a little miffed about the six games of chess he won so inhumanly," wrote Madame Brillon about herself in one of their letters, "and she warns him she will spare nothing to get her revenge."

Another time he kept her playing chess in her bathtub until late at night, for which he apologized the next day in a letter: "Never again will I consent to start a chess game with the neighbor in your bathing room. Can you forgive me this indiscretion?"

She certainly did. "I get so much pleasure from seeing you," she replied, "that it made up for the little fatigue of having come out of the bath a little too late."

In Franklin's time, women were not welcome in the chess clubs of Europe or America. It was not until the mid-1880s that a club in Turin, Italy, allowed the wives and daughters of its members to join them at the chessboard, a practice that was applauded by world champion Wilhelm Steinitz. "This is as it should be," Steinitz wrote, "and we hope that this example will be followed by other chess societies, it being evident that, if we engage the queens of our hearts for the queens of our boards and if we can enlist the interest of our connubial mates for our chessical mates our intellectual pastime will be immensely benefited and will pass into universal favor." But change was slow. When the first women played in an international tournament, in London in 1897, a commentator cautioned that they "would come under great strain lifting the leaded, wooden chess sets."

WHEN KASPAROV HOLDS FORTH ON THE SCIENTIFIC EVIDENCE FOR WHY FEW women play world-class chess, he is carrying on a long tradition. There is a rich psychoanalytic literature on the unconscious motives governing chess players and the lack of women in the game. Freudians say that an unresolved Oedipal complex is responsible for driving male chess masters to kill the king, the father figure. Because women do not have the same unconscious desire to murder their dads, the argument goes, the game does not have the same symbolic appeal. Psychoanalysts have also doubted women's ability to muster the competitive impulses necessary to play topflight chess. But the papers in the psychoanalytical literature do not cite scientific research or case studies to support this view. They provide no more insight than Tal's quip that women can't play chess because they can't keep their mouths shut for five hours.

Typical is "The Psychology of Chess," by Dr. Ben Karpman, from a 1937 *Psychoanalytic Review*. In describing women's behavior at the chessboard, Dr. Karpman repeats dubious anecdotes from a 1931 book called *Chess Potpourri*:

> Miss Muller Hasting's first play was with Miss Eschwege, with whom she played until fifty-four moves had been made, when she resigned for no more serious reason than that, first, because she was tired, and second, because she preferred to lose her first game and win the latter one! . . . At another board a king was moved into check and several minutes had elapsed before either side discovered the error!!!! In one case, a lady with a simple winning ending offered a draw, which was accepted. Upon being shown that she had an easy win, it was perhaps excusable that she was not sure whether she had really offered a draw!!!

Dr. Karpman's selective choice of evidence was particularly lame because he was writing at a time when Vera Menchik, a Moscow-born master living in England, was storming the bastions of male chess. In 1929, in Karlsbad, Czechoslovakia, she became the first woman to play against men in top international tournaments. Albert Becker, an undistinguished Viennese master, had objected to her participation and derisively said that anyone who lost to her should be forced to join what he called the Vera Menchik Club. He expected the club to have no members, but he became the first inductee when she defeated him at Karlsbad. He was joined by Max Euwe, future world champion, whom Menchik beat at Hastings in 1931, and by Samuel Reshevsky, the American phenom, who, though up a pawn against her at Yarmouth in 1935, ran out of time. "I didn't expect her to see so much," an admiring Euwe said. All in all, though, she played timidly against men compared to the verve she showed in games against female adversaries. She became the first women's world champion, in 1927 in London, and she defended her title six times, scoring an overwhelming eighty points in eighty-three games. She died in 1944 in an air raid on London.

IN CONVERSATION, JENNIFER GETS IMPATIENT DISCUSSING THEORETICAL reasons why more women don't play chess. "I'm more interested in doing something about it," she told me, "than in debating hypotheticals." She and Irina are working to increase the presence of women in chess, not just through their own play but also by helping young girls master the game. There are many good reasons to teach kids chess, Jennifer told me: it helps them learn to concentrate, to think ahead, to see that their actions have consequences, to cope with defeat, and to be gracious in winning.

On a Sunday afternoon in early January 2003, I joined Jennifer and Irina in the midtown New York offices of a foundation called Chess-in-the-Schools for a program called Girls Academy. Once a month, a couple of dozen girls, many from disadvantaged neighborhoods, come together from across the city for six free hours of intensive instruction from Shahade and Krush. The two champions know that they are role models for girls who dream of reaching the higher echelons of chess.

The attendees at Girls Academy, who ranged in age from nine to thirteen, broke into two groups that afternoon, and Jennifer spent the first couple of hours showing her group the moves from well-known games in which strong women defeated male grandmasters—"Play like a girl!" was her charge to them. She wanted them to play like Judit Polgar. "I love her uncompromising approach," Jennifer explained. "Just when you think the position is sterile and drawish, she stirs up complications by sacrificing a piece and launching a blistering attack. It's awesome."

Jennifer herself also favors bold, tactical moves. She is a much more aggressive player than her father and brother—something you wouldn't guess from her soft, compassionate voice and the almost balletic way that she carries herself when she is not huddled over a chessboard. "By comparison, I play like a real wuss," her father told me later. He explained that his own style is more positional. He accumulates tiny advantages until he wins in the endgame. "She goes for the jugular immediately," he said, "and reaches positions that are so complicated they give me a headache to look at. I don't know how she does it. Even Greg, whose play is much sharper than mine, doesn't take the kinds of risks Jen does."

Her father had been the one to accompany her to the Insanity Tournament, and on the train ride home to Philadelphia, he told her gleefully, "No one could ever say you play like a girl." In her book *Chess Bitch*, published in 2005, Jennifer reflected on her dad's comment:

> At the time, I considered it a compliment. I didn't see any reason for my violent style except that I liked attacking chess. However, I was aware of the stereotype that women were more patient and passive while men were supposedly braver, and I wanted to be a hero too. In retrospect, I see my chess style was loaded with meaning—to be aggressive was to renounce any stereotype of my play based on my gender.

She was purposely trying to copy the attacking style of the world's number one female player, Judit Polgar.

> For a while, I played recklessly, and at first I lost many games because of my one-dimensional style. Many opponents altered their strategies when playing against me, choosing quiet systems—such as the English opening—in order to derail the tactical melees at which I excelled.

Ironically, as Jennifer's familiarity with the chess world grew, she saw her notion of gender stereotypes turned inside out:

By the time I was nineteen, I started to mingle in the higher ranks of international chess, playing in world championships and the biennial chess Olympiads. I realized that to play like a girl did not have the same meaning at the top as it did in parks and scholastic tournaments. It turned out that to play like a girl meant to play aggressively! This was most vividly demonstrated to me when a Russian coach looked at some of my boldest games and said derisively, "I see women's chess hasn't changed. Women have no patience; they always want to attack immediately."

That afternoon at Girls Academy, Jennifer shared with her students one of her own disappointments at the chessboard, from the 2002 Olympiad in Bled, where teams from eighty-nine countries competed in the women's division and the United States was in medal contention until the end. "You can always learn more from your losses than from your wins," Jennifer told them. "If you lose, it's because you missed something. You need to understand what that something is so you don't make the same kind of mistake again." She set up the key position from the final round against Ukraine and explained how she went wrong. "I had a choice of two ways to capture," she said. "I could have taken with the pawn or the rook. If I took with the rook, it would lead to a draw. I took with the pawn and quickly lost. Taking with the pawn was a radical misjudgment. Why did I do it? There was probably a psychological reason. Earlier I thought I had stood better in the game, so I didn't want to settle for a draw and admit that I hadn't been able to press my advantage." The girls were listening respectfully to Jennifer.

"I also learned from Bled," Jennifer continued, "that I didn't have enough stamina." This was a startling confession from a woman who made her mark in the Insanity Tournament. "I'm used to American weekend tournaments in which four or five rounds are crammed into two or three days." The Olympiad lasted two weeks. She won five of her first six games but then sadly had a big slump so that she ended up with six wins and five losses. "I can play chess twelve hours a day for a weekend on sheer adrenaline and then crash," she said, "but I can't sit at the board with peak concentration for days at a time." She told me later that she was running, lifting weights, and shooting baskets to build up her endurance.

Toward the end of the afternoon, Jennifer and Irina's students came together for joint instruction. Irina set up a position on an oversize demonstration board in front of the room. She asked the girls to study it and then pair off and play the position out, with chess clocks ticking as if this were a tournament. Later the girls would compare their moves with the continuation favored by the chess titans who had actually reached the position. Jennifer glanced at the demonstration board and exclaimed with mock horror, "That position was never reached by a woman!"

"It's OK," Irina responded, with a straight face, "because one of the players was a homosexual." The class cackled, and Jennifer flinched at her colleague's lack of political correctness.

The position Irina selected was reached after the sixteenth move of the famous 1895 game between world champion Steinitz and the gay German master named Curt von Bardeleben—the model for Nabokov's Luzhin. On White's seventeenth move—which the girls were asked to find—Steinitz boldly sacrificed his queen pawn so that a path would be cleared for his knight to join in the hunt for the Black king. When Irina eventually showed the class the sacrifice and the subsequent play, the girls marveled at the depth and beauty of Steinitz's mating attack. What Irina didn't tell the students was the fate of the two men. Steinitz eventually went mad, claiming that he could play chess with God over an invisible phone line and beat Him even after giving Him the handicap of an extra pawn. And von Bardeleben, of course, leaped to his death from a window. But the fact that chess has a long history of association with obsession and eccentricity is emphatically not part of the curriculum at Chess-in-the-Schools. Earlier that same day, when a student asked Jennifer what became of Bobby Fischer, she responded, "Never mind! Let's just appreciate his games!"

Between the two women, however, the crazy competitiveness of their world was a running joke. During a break at Girls Academy, Jennifer put aside the remains of a large tossed salad. She had eaten none of the sun-dried tomatoes, which were scattered across the bowl. Irina was eyeing the salad dregs, and Jennifer offered them to her.

"Why didn't you eat the tomatoes?" Irina asked. "Are you trying to poison me?"

"You never know," Jennifer playfully responded.

"It would be a good trick," said Irina. "I wonder if anyone has ever tried it—making their opponent sick just before an important match."

LATER THAT WEEK JENNIFER AND IRINA WERE COMPETING IN SEATTLE, ALONG with fifty-six other players, for the 2003 U.S. Chess Championship. Jennifer was the defending women's champion, and Irina wanted a shot at the title, which she had won once before, in 1998. When Jennifer won the title in Seattle in 2002, it was the first time women and men had ever played together in the 157-year-old national championship. No female player had ever qualified for the championship, and in 1937 a separate women's division was created in which female players competed among themselves for the title of U.S. women's champion. In 2002, the women's section was abolished, and players of both genders were thrown together. Jennifer, who never faced a single female in the tournament, nonetheless became U.S. women's champion by virtue of achieving the highest score of all the women. At the players' meeting before the 2002 tournament, some of the men complained that the participation of women would degrade the quality of the play, but Jennifer proved them wrong. In the very first round, she disposed of Gennady Sagalchik, the grandmaster who had been particularly vocal in objecting to the inclusion of women; she now had a Vera Menchik club of her own. Later, back in Brooklyn, Jennifer celebrated in a blue wig at an all-night warehouse party with a childhood friend who was wearing a T-shirt that was supposed to say, "Jennifer Shahade is a Man Eater," but the friend's Magic Marker had run dry after she wrote Jennifer's name.

"I was delighted to beat Sagalchik," Jennifer told me, "because I had a pattern of reaching good positions against grandmasters, getting nervous, and making inaccurate moves that let them slip away."

And yet Jennifer is not entirely convinced that having a coed championship is in the best interest of women's chess. While the top-ranked women are strong enough to give the men a good fight, or even beat them, the lower-ranked women who qualify for the championship are much weaker than the weakest men. "Is it good for a young woman's confidence and chess career if she has a horrible result in the U.S. Championship?" she said. "Maybe it would be better for her to play in an all-women's event? But I can also argue the reverse—that it is motivating to play in a championship with the country's best players, and that women will get better as a result."

JENNIFER GOT OFF TO A SLOWER START IN THE 2003 CHAMPIONSHIP, BUT AFter a victory in the seventh round she was tied for first among the women and consequently was in a good position to retain her title. Her brother was also competing in the championship—the first time since 1969 that two siblings had played in it—and he, too, had an important win in the seventh round.

The Shahades had radically different methods of preparation. Each evening at about 10:00 P.M., they'd learn whom they'd face the next afternoon and whether they were going to have White or Black. Before going to bed, Jennifer would turn on her notebook PC and search through her database of more than two million chess games for those that were played by her opponent. She'd scan the relevant games and make a quick decision as to what sequence of opening moves she thought would give her adversary the most trouble. But she would save the bulk of her study for the morning. "I can sleep better," she told me, "after I select the particular opening. Otherwise I'll toss and turn and mull over it during the night."

Greg's approach was less disciplined. He routinely went to bed at four in the morning and rose only minutes before the 1:30 P.M. round. He, too, possessed a PC with two million chess games stored on it, but the database apparently received less use than his sister's. Instead he pressed the computer into service to play online poker and kung-fu chess, at which he was the number one player in the world. (Kung-fu chess is an Internet action game in which multiple chessmen rush forward as fast as you can move them.) Greg also kept himself busy with a Sony PlayStation, a TV season's worth of *The Simpsons* on DVD, and a Dance Dance Revolution Pad (an electronic dance mat), all of which he'd hauled out to the West Coast from New York.

I visited Seattle for the last few rounds of the tournament. I happened to occupy the hotel room next to Greg's, and on the night before the final round, when he could have been preparing for one of his toughest opponents—fifteen-year-old Hikaru Nakamura, who was about to break Bobby Fischer's 1958 record as the youngest American grandmaster and go on, in 2005, to become the youngest U.S. champion since Fischer—I awoke at 4:00 A.M. to the sound of Bart Simpson's voice and Greg laughing loudly.

"How's the Nakamura preparation going?" I shouted through the wall.

"Not well," said Greg. "I haven't started yet."

The next day was not a good one for the Shahades. Greg lost to Nakamura, and his sister was ground down by Benjamin Finegold, whose rating has occasionally gone high enough to make him the top-rated American-born player. Greg and Jennifer both finished the nine-round tournament with an even score of 4½–4½. Jennifer had tied for first among the women with Irina and Anna Hahn, a Latvian émigré. The next day the three of them would play a round-robin match of speed chess (fifteen minutes per side per game) to decide who would become U.S. women's champion.

"I departed from my usual, more methodical style of preparation and tried to study every opening under the sun," Jennifer said. "I knew it was a crazy, stupid thing to do—you can't possibly master numerous opening lines in one evening—but I couldn't help myself. I wanted to be prepared for anything they might play, and then all night I dreamed about the possibilities." She arrived at the board exhausted, and lost her encounter with Irina. Hahn, twenty-six, whose national ranking made her the underdog, managed to beat both of them and walk off with $12,500 and the title. "It all ended much too quickly," Jennifer said, "after ten grueling days of chess." Although she was no longer the U.S. women's champion, she had done well enough in Seattle to earn the second of three norms toward the title of international master.

JENNIFER GRADUATED FROM NYU ONLY A MONTH BEFORE THE CHAMPIONSHIP, and in Seattle she was in a reflective mood about what she was going to do with the rest of her life. "I majored in comparative literature," she told me. "It's a toss-up," she joked, "about whether comparative literature or chess will be more useful in paying the rent. I'm struggling right now with how much I want to make the game the focus of my life or whether I want to do something in the arts. I love chess, but it's the height of decadence. The positions you reach in a well-played game are beautiful, but the beauty is inaccessible to those who haven't mastered the game."

In addition, Jennifer worried that the game itself doesn't have a lot of social purpose. "You can understand if someone is spending sixteen hours a day trying to cure a disease or to write a novel," she said, "but to play better chess?" As a feminist, she also hadn't completely made her peace with the brutality of the game. "Chess is patriarchal—I sound like a college student—it's a war game that rewards ruthlessness, not cooperation." Yet she is drawn to the intensity of the game and obviously excels at it.

Jennifer's views on chess and gender evolved over the next two years as she worked on her book, *Chess Bitch*, about women who play the game. "I would no longer describe chess as patriarchal," she told me recently. "It's chess culture, not the game itself, that needs to change. The culture is extremely competitive and may turn off people who are interested in playing for fun. If the media focused more on unusual personalities and the beauty and art in chess, less competitive types—in particular women, who are generally not encouraged to be competitive—might play the game."

IN 1994, SUSAN POLGAR, TWENTY-FIVE, THE OLDEST OF THE THREE HUNGARian sisters, moved to New York. Judit, seven years her junior, was already eclipsing Susan in international tournaments, but it was Susan who had first broken gender barriers in chess and confronted institutionalized discrimination at tournaments, paving the way for younger female players like Judit. Their father had decided that the reason women didn't make it to the top in chess was that they didn't have much practice against strong men. And so he encouraged Susan not to restrict her play to women's tournaments. At the age of seventeen, she became the highest-rated player in the world her age or younger, but the Hungarian Chess Federation was not ready to let a woman represent her country in the

World Junior Championship and sent a lower-rated boy instead. In 1986, she qualified for the overall World Championship, but FIDE banned her participation, claiming that it was an all-male affair. FIDE, under pressure from the Soviets, whose domination of world chess was threatened by the Hungarian star, did her further injustice by blatantly awarding all of her female adversaries in the world an extra 100 rating points.[4]

In 1991, Susan was able to thumb her nose at FIDE by becoming the first woman ever to meet the requirements for the "male" grandmaster title.[5] (Later that year Judit, not to be outdone, achieved the spectacular distinction of becoming the youngest grandmaster ever. Judit would take their father's prescription about playing chess with men to an extreme: she'd play exclusively with men, forgoing women's-only tournaments that she could have easily won. The middle sister, Sofia, after meteoric success on the tournament circuit, moved to Israel and gave up the game.) In 1996, Susan—while living in America but still playing for Hungary— won the Women's World Championship and retired from competitive chess to raise her two children.

In a tremendous coup for American chess, Susan Polgar decided to come out of semiretirement seven years later, in 2003, and play for the women's team that would represent the United States in the 2004 Olympiad in Calvia, Spain. The U.S. women had never won a medal in thirty-six previous Olympiads, and Polgar was determined to change that. She and Paul Truong, her manager (who was also the chess player with the disturbing boat-person tale), organized a rigorous training program for the prospective team members and obtained funding from the USCF and the Kasparov Chess Foundation. In another break for America's chances, Kasparov himself decided to coach the team. His views on the inherent inferiority of women at chess obviously did not stop him from helping individual female players succeed. His personal involvement in the U.S. effort upped the ante because he expected the team to win a medal.

Jennifer Shahade was one of the candidates for the team, and I accompanied her to a training session with Kasparov over the Memorial Day weekend in 2004. Besides Jennifer and Polgar, the prospective "Dream Team" included Irina and two strong immigrants from countries where chess was taken seriously: Anna Zatonskih, twenty-five, from Ukraine, and Rusudan Goletiani, twenty-three, from Georgia. Only Goletiani, who was visiting family back in Georgia, missed the session with Kasparov.

Kasparov had worked with these same women once before, a year earlier, and Jennifer was apprehensive then because of the things he had said about women. But he quickly charmed her, she told me, by claiming the press had distorted his views and saying that he saw no reason there couldn't be ten Judit Polgars. This time Jennifer was nervous because of the assignment Kasparov had given them. He had asked each woman to select two of her recent games and show them to him in front of the others. The idea was not to show their best efforts but to present games in which they had gone astray and were still unsure now about the correct strategy and needed the world champion's guidance. Jennifer planned to discuss two games from the recent Women's World Championship in Elista, Kalmykia, where she had been eliminated in the first round by a Georgian. The first game ended in checkmate on the thirty-sixth move, a rarity at Jennifer's level because a master player usually resigns before her king is decisively cornered. She was embarrassed to show him the game, not because of the mate (she doubted he'd want her to play it out that far) but because she'd missed a simple tactic earlier. "I'm afraid of boring him," she told me, "but I do have questions about it. I'd much rather show him one of my better games in which I crushed someone with a clever attack."

Jennifer got a four-hour reprieve because Kasparov asked Irina to demonstrate her games first. Irina showed him a drawn game from Elista against Ketino Kachiani of Germany, who knocked her out in the second round. Irina was White and Kachiani defended against Irina's usual d4 opening with a newly popular defense known as the . . . a6 Slav. Irina built up a strong positional advantage by posting all of her pawns on dark squares, including two well-supported pawns she had advanced into her opponent's territory, thereby blunting the mobility of Kachini's dark-squared bishop.

"Her bishop is in a zoo behind bars," Kasparov said approvingly. "How does she save the game?"

"She doesn't save the game," Irina responded. "I screwed it up."

"Ah. You saved it for her. Just keep the bishop caged on the kingside. Then crush her on the queenside. What can she do?"

"Maybe Irina lost on purpose," Truong joked. "Otherwise she might still be playing in Elista and not have made it back for the training with you."

"That's the answer I wanted to hear," Kasparov said.

"I was trying to play on the kingside," Irina said, as she demonstrated how she advanced two pawns in that sector of the board.

"You shouldn't move those pawns. You've already won on the king-side. You've cut her bishop off there. So leave it trapped and switch your dreams to the queenside."

Irina showed him how the actual game petered out to a draw after she allowed Kachiani's bishop to escape. "It's a pity," said Kasparov. "You were so close. Were you optimistic during the game?"

"Yes," Irina replied. "I thought I might win."

Irina showed him a second game in which she had Black and was hell-bent on pressing a kingside attack that never succeeded. At one point he stopped her and pointed to her opponent's weak pawns on the other side of the board. "You have to widen your horizon," he said, "and look at the opposite side. Don't just look at the king. Look at weak pawns. Win-ning a pawn is as good as creating a mate in three! Remember, Irina, there are two sides of the board. You need a constant reminder that the game can be won on the queenside as well as the kingside." Kasparov changed the subject. "How will you respond to e4?" When he'd trained her the previous year, she was not sure how she'd defend against the king pawn.

"I've learned the Petroff."

"What if White avoids the Petroff with the King's Gambit?"

"I'm hoping no one plays the King's Gambit against me."

"Hoping? You must do more than hope," Kasparov scolded. Then he cited a recent catastrophic miniature: "Bologan also didn't study the sidelines and he lost to Shirov in twenty moves. You must avoid that fate!"

Before breaking for lunch, Kasparov bedazzled the women with behind-the-scene tales of his own games. He also told them how he was working on a book about Karpov and offered the controversial view that

Karpov would have beaten Fischer in 1975 had the American champion chosen to defend his title. "Fischer put a lot of pressure on Spassky in 1972. Spassky fell apart after Fischer forfeited the second game by failing to show up. Karpov would have gleefully written a book called *How I Won Game Two.* Karpov would have said, 'Mr. Fischer, make an appointment with your psychiatrist.' He was like a mirror: All of Fischer's psychological attacks would have backfired." The older generation of Russians like Spassky felt like rabbits in the grip of a boa constrictor when they played Karpov. "Fischer looked at Karpov's games," Kasparov said, "and got scared. The only way Fischer would have survived is if he had lasted twenty-five games, when Karpov's fatigue might have set in. But it is unlikely he could have lasted that long. Trust me. I can be accused of being anything except being a friend of Karpov's. His chess did not progress from 1975 to 1983. He could have used Fischer. Just as I needed Karpov for me to become as strong as I am. I despise Karpov as a person but admire him as a chess player. I look back with fondness on some of our games." Kasparov's voice softened, and he looked dreamily past the women. "He and I were the only two people in the world who knew what was happening on the chessboard."

There was a long silence while everyone thought about the implications of what Kasparov was saying: that he and Karpov were a class apart from all other chess players. That even other top grandmasters couldn't really appreciate the finer points of how the two Ks marshaled their pieces and pawns.

Finally Susan Polgar spoke. "I saw Fischer in Budapest," she said. "He analyzed your 1985 match with Karpov very deeply. He is convinced it was prearranged because he couldn't believe the mistakes."

"Look at all the mistakes in his match with Spassky," Kasparov shot back. "I'm not saying his match was fixed. And look at his matches with Petrosian and Taimanov—all the blunders there."

I was impressed that Polgar had the temerity to raise Fischer's absurd charge. I assumed that she was simply needling Kasparov for his grandiosity. Later, however, when I told Pascal about her inquiry, he suggested that Kasparov himself might have planted the subject so that he'd have a forum to address it. I had forgotten that I was in the bizarro world of chess, where little can be taken at face value.

"Do you see yourself playing twenty years from now?" Polgar asked Kasparov.

"Maybe I will be moving pieces then," he responded, "but I'm not sure I'd call that playing."

The women went off to lunch with Truong, and Kasparov asked me to join him at a deli with Owen Williams, his manager, and Michael Khodarkovsky, the head coach of the Olympiad training effort and the director of the Kasparov Chess Foundation. "I'm worried about Irina," Kasparov told Khodarkovsky as we sat down at the table. "She is not making much progress. Her problem is that she can be attracted to a certain idea, stick with it even when the circumstances change, and lose control of the board. She plays move by move and loses track of the big picture."

Before Khodarkovsky could defend Irina, Kasparov was berating our Hispanic waiter, whose English was poor, for bringing a glass of tap water. "I only drink bottled water," Kasparov declared. While the waiter scurried away to correct the situation, Kasparov explained that his mother had taught him never to drink tap water. I wasn't about to argue with him, but this was New York City in 2004, not Moscow in 1974. The waiter returned with a bottle of sparkling water. Kasparov opened it and poured himself a glass. "I didn't ask for bubbles," he said as he shoved it back toward the befuddled waiter, who took it away and returned with an ice-cold bottle of Poland Spring. Kasparov screwed up his face, and Williams interpreted the expression: "He wants room temperature water." The waiter enlisted the help of the cashier, and the two searched unsuccessfully for unrefrigerated bottled water. "Maybe you can heat it a bit," Williams suggested, but Kasparov had run out of patience. As he got up to leave the restaurant and go in search of water elsewhere, he pointed to the sandwich column of my menu and said, "Order a chicken salad for me."

Five minutes later Kasparov returned with his own bottle of water, and the waiter put a chicken salad sandwich in front of him. "I don't want a sandwich," Kasparov growled. "I asked for chicken salad." This time, he left the restaurant and didn't return. Williams, Khodarkovsky, and I ate our meals in silence. When the waiter cleared the plates, I asked Khodarkovsky what we should do with the uneaten sandwich. "We'd better take it with us," Khodarkovsky said. "If he asks for it, you don't want to be the one to tell him you threw it out."

When the training session resumed, Kasparov was charming and vivacious again, as if the awkward lunch had never happened. Jennifer finally presented her games. "I expected my opponent to play the Najdorf," she said. "She's been playing it her whole life—there were fifty games in the database. But she surprised me by playing the Richter-Rauzer instead"—the same defense Irina had played against her in the art gallery.

"How old is she?" Kasparov asked.

"Seventeen."

"So she's played the Najdorf for seven years," he scoffed, as if he thought that was insufficient time to master this complex opening. "Now, I've been playing the Najdorf my entire life."

Jennifer played through the game, and they agreed that she could have been more aggressive in the opening but had an advantage in the middle game. She was nervous as she showed Kasparov how she overlooked a simple threat and blundered away a rook for a bishop. The thirteenth world champion was supportive. "I understand why you blundered," he said. "You were better the whole game. This was the first time she had a threat. She had played passively move after move and you forgot that she could attack." Changes of pace, he explained, are difficult even for seasoned pros.

"What would a woman play in this position?" Truong piped up, trying to be funny.

"What would a man play?" Kasparov responded.

"We were both in time pressure," Jennifer added, "although she had even less time than I did."

"Let me give you some advice," Kasparov said. "Never look at the opponent's clock. After the first match with Karpov, I realized that I should never look at his clock. I would get too excited when he was running low. But I couldn't control his moves. Karpov was capable of making three consecutive 'only moves' with just thirty seconds left." *Only move* is chess lingo for a situation in which a player has just one continuation that will allow him to survive; in other words, he'll lose immediately if he does anything else.

Kasparov did not make Jennifer play out the game to the mate. "The opening was equal," he said in summary. "From a roughly equal position you outplayed her. That's good."

The Dream Team took a break, and Truong and Kasparov went on the Internet to review the games that had been played earlier that day in the semifinals of the Women's World Championship in Elista. Kasparov studied the photographs of two of the contestants, Humpy Koneru, seventeen, of India, and Ekaterina Kovalevskaya, twenty, of Russia. "By ChessBase criteria," Kasparov said. "These women do not qualify for pictures." It was not clear whether he was putting down how they looked or lampooning ChessBase, the leading Web site for chess news, for publishing photographs of gorgeous young women who aren't very good players.

"Typical women's chess," Truong said, as they glanced at the games. "There they go again, pushing their a and h pawns—premature aggression. Do you see also how some of these women are mad enough to keep playing when they are down a rook?"

Jennifer was delighted to work with Kasparov and Susan Polgar, but was dismayed by all of the jokes about women's chess and what she saw as the surprising sexist views of Polgar herself. Writing in *Chess Bitch*, she described one of the first training sessions with Michael Khodarkovsky:

> Michael began his session with us by saying, "I know that feminism is popular in the United States, but in Russia we understood that women and men play differently." Michael advised us: "With this in mind, you should never be ashamed to tell your trainers most intimate details . . . or when you may not be able to play one hundred percent." Paul Truong, a fuzzy-haired Vietnamese ball of energy with a tittering laugh, clarified Michael's statement for the team: "Does everyone know what Michael is talking about? . . . Menstruation!"

The training sessions, which had seemed like a great idea for advancing women's chess in America, were turning into a feminist's nightmare.

> I thought I had entered the twilight zone, an impression that was furthered when Susan Polgar, one of my childhood heroines, joined forces with Michael: "Now, menstruation may not require that someone take a day off, but it might affect, for instance, the choice of

opening." Michael mentioned a computer program that a Soviet friend of his had developed, which would determine how, at any given day, the menstrual cycle would affect play.

Other meetings they had were equally surreal. Truong was the bubbly marketing whiz behind the Dream Team, and like many marketers, he promised the moon. "He told the women that there were millions of dollars involved in the project and that they would all become stars in America," recalled Pascal Charbonneau, who often accompanied Irina to the training. "He said they'd all be wearing designer clothes because designers would sponsor them. He said they'd have a speech coach to teach them what to say in public and help them handle the pressure of being celebrities and all the journalists who'd be chasing after them. He said if they won a medal they'd go to the White House for sure." Truong did come through with some promises, like persuading IBM to donate laptops to each of them so that they could run chess software.

Truong entertained the women with stories of his chess and gustatory prowess. "Truong claims to be part of a special private club that eats the hottest hot sauce in the world," Pascal said. "Only thirty people are members. And he said the hot sauce was made out of this ridiculous amount of peppers—I think it was thirty thousand tons, but I could be wrong. His point was that it took thirty thousand tons to make a tiny bit. He said that if normal people like us tried the hot sauce we'd probably die. And we'd say, 'Really, Paul, dying is a bit much.' And he'd say, 'Well you'd at least end up in the hospital with very serious stomach problems.'"

UNFORTUNATELY, THE DREAM TEAM'S SENSE OF CAMARADERIE WAS UNDERmined almost from the beginning by a controversy over which four women would actually be included; women's chess is not exempt from the ugly bureaucratic intrigue that seems to infect the game at both the national and international levels. These backroom deals—such as those made in the late 1980s to stop Susan Polgar herself—advance or retard the careers of individual players. Here, the three highest-ranked women,

Polgar, Krush, and Zatonskih, were certain to represent the United States in Calvia, but only one of the two other players, Shahade or Goletiani, would join them. The squad was supposed to have been selected by the time Kasparov trained them over the Memorial Day weekend. Whichever player, Shahade or Goletiani, had been ranked higher by the USCF on the April 2004 rating list was supposed to make the team. Before the April rating list was issued, preliminary calculations suggested that Shahade was going to edge out Goletiani by a few ratings points, but Khodarkovsky complained to the USCF that Goletiani's rating did not include her first-place performance of 7½ points out of 9 at the Women's Continental Championship in Venezuela in September 2003.

The USCF did not routinely rate foreign tournaments—it was the United States Chess Federation after all—but apparently there was an old, little-known precedent for rating certain international tournaments provided the player made a request beforehand. The USCF claimed that Goletiani had not made such a request, and Khodarkovsky said she had. The USCF backed down and decided at the eleventh hour to include the tournament in Venezuela, and Goletiani's rating then eclipsed Jennifer's by seventeen points, 2376 to 2359.

Irina, who is known to be vocally indignant about behavior she perceives as unethical, lodged a protest in support of Jennifer. There was no paper or e-mail trail to substantiate that Goletiani had made a request beforehand, and it seemed unfair to her that Khodarkovsky, who was the coach of the whole team, was advocating on Goletiani's behalf. Moreover, if the Continental had been rated in a timely manner, back in 2003, and not at the last moment, Jennifer could have chosen to enter additional tournaments to try to regain her lead over Goletiani. As it was, she found out that she had relinquished the lead only when it was too late to do anything. Jennifer was disappointed that Polgar, who had faced such overwhelming discrimination in her own chess career, did not speak out publicly against the injustice of including the Venezuela rating.

That spring, the USCF worked behind closed doors to address the Shahade-Goletiani controversy. The chess federation hastily scheduled a seven-person 2004 U.S. Women's Championship for late June at St. John's University in New York City and declared that the winner would take the fourth spot on the Olympiad team. "It's annoying," Jennifer told me then, "because I think I would have beaten out Rusa if the ratings had been legitimately calculated. But what can I do? I'm tired of arguing. Chess politics is a huge distraction from my enjoyment of the game."

Over the next month Jennifer prepared for the 2004 championship, more than she ever had before. She worked with her old coach, Victor Frias, and her brother. She studied all of her adversaries' games and cooked up an opening surprise for each of them. One of her opponents, Tatev Abrahamyan, liked to play the French Defense, against which Jennifer had had trouble in the past. Greg knew the pseudonym that Abrahamyan employed when she played games on the Internet Chess Club. Her pseudonymous games with the French Defense were stored in cyberspace, and Greg and Jennifer saw that Abrahayman did especially poorly in one particular line. Jennifer decided to repeat the line in the tournament and won easily. "I felt naughty doing this, like I was taking advantage of some deep dark secret," Jennifer confided later. "But it felt good."

By the penultimate round she had already clinched the title of U.S. women's champion and the fourth spot on the Olympiad team. *Chess Life* magazine ran a close-up of her face on the cover along with the one-word title "UNSTOPPABLE."

I wish I could have watched Jennifer win the championship, but I was not in the United States at the time and had to content myself with checking the Internet to follow her progress. A week after her victory, I met her in the Village for a celebratory drink. A stranger approached us on the street and asked her if she remembered playing him. "Not really," she admitted.

"It was a few years ago," he said. "We played three games."

"Did we?" she said. "What was the result?"

"I won one of them," he said.

"That's funny," she said, grinning. "I only remember two of the games."[6]

The man left, and Jennifer told me about the conclusion of the championship. "I was guilty of all sins the evening I knew I won," she explained. "Pride—I was calling all my friends and telling them I won. Gluttony—I went to a French restaurant in Williamsburg and stuffed myself with wine and mussels. Sloth—I never prepared for my last-round game with Irina. And, oh yes, vanity—I was thinking about what I was going to wear the next day. I went over to Greg's house and showed him the game that clinched it for me. He said I was a great champion." She called her coach, who told her the last game with Irina was still important. Of course, she had thought a lot about playing Irina before the tournament. "I knew I'd have Black," she recalled, "and she's tough with White—I don't do so well against d4. But with the title in the bag I was wired. I was too excited and blissed out to care.

"When I lose, I'm in pain. It's not depression but a crappy why-am-I-so-dumb? feeling. It passes quickly if I get away from the tournament hall and watch a movie, have a glass of wine, or spend time with friends who aren't in the chess world. When I win, though, the glow stays with me."

For a week after winning the championship she was on a high. "I wandered around the streets and parks of the East Village, sipping an iced coffee," she wrote later. "My victory made everything appear to be shot in Technicolor: the emotional content of every experience was heightened. Every joke became funnier, every conversation more satisfying, and every dessert sweeter."

She was delighted that she had overcome enormous hurdles to fight her way onto the Dream Team, a club that had not been eager to admit her. Still, she remained an outsider on the team. She was less chess-centric and politically and socially more liberal than her fellow players and coaches, and the only one among the eight of them—Polgar, Krush, Zatonskih, Khodarkovsky, Truong, Kasparov, and Alexander Chernin (an opening theoretician who was brought in to assist the women)—who was born in America.

The Dream Team came together for one final training session six weeks before the Olympiad. For Jennifer it was the most uncomfortable meeting of all. It coincided with the Republican National Convention in New York, in which George Bush was nominated for a second term. The Kasparov Chess Foundation asked each of the women to sign a contract that prohibited them from writing or talking publicly about their experiences at the Olympiad without first clearing it with the foundation. The contract also required them to forgo alcohol for the entire event. "I avoid drinking during tournaments," she told me at the time, "but what if the occasional glass of wine helps me relax? Besides, I don't want to be told how to conduct myself away from the chessboard. As for the gag order, it's outrageous. I'm not going to sign away my freedom of speech." She was finishing her book and planned to write about the Olympiad.

What irked Jennifer most, though, was a lecture Polgar gave the team that she thought was directed at her in particular. Polgar began on an innocuous note, reminding the women that they were a team. They were sisters, she said, united in the common goal of winning a medal for America. She then said that they were role models for girls and should always dress, speak, and act appropriately. Jennifer was wearing a John Kerry T-shirt from an anti-Bush rally a day or two before. The black T-shirt said "PROTEST IS PATRIOTIC" in magenta lettering. If they had daughters, Polgar continued, they should behave in a way that would make their daughters proud. Jennifer was so offended that she skipped the next day's training.

IN OCTOBER 2004, THE DREAM TEAM TRAVELED TO CALVIA, WHERE THEY squared off against squads from eighty-six other countries. Each four-person team fielded three players in a given round, and there were fourteen rounds in all. I followed the games on the Internet and was disappointed to see that Khodarkovsky only allowed Jennifer to play twice. She was permitted to compete in the first round against Venezuela, in which she drew with Black against a weaker opponent. Then she was benched for the next four rounds. Khodarkovsky played her for the last time, as Black again, in the fifth round. Against a Swedish opponent whose rating was two hundred points lower than hers, Jennifer did not play her usual tumultuous Grünfeld, but tried to play it safer and recover her bearings by assaying the tamer and more solid Nimzo-Indian Defense. Still, she was less practiced in the particulars of the Nimzo-Indian and was unceremoniously routed by a blistering kingside attack. "They should never have started her with Black," her brother told me. "She's much better with White, and that would have given her confidence."

"One of the team meetings was very awkward," Pascal recalled. "Khodarkovsky said something about having to play 'full force' the next day. We all looked at each other uncomfortably. 'Full force' was a code phrase for playing without Jennifer." Khodarkovsky never fielded Jennifer in the remaining nine rounds.

"She stayed outwardly upbeat and supported us through all fourteen rounds," Irina told me. "That was important to our success but it couldn't have been easy for her."

The Dream Team won the silver medal behind China's gold, the best performance ever for the U.S. Women's Team. Before Calvia there had been Internet gossip and chess club speculation about whether former women's world champion Susan Polgar could still be at top form, after her voluntary eight-and-a-half-year absence from international competition. In Calvia she played all fourteen rounds and achieved the highest score, 10½ points, on Board One, with seven victories and seven draws. She had the best rating performance (2622) of all the women in the championship. And Polgar had now played fifty-six games in four Olympiads (in 1988, 1990, 1994, and 2004) without a single loss.

IRINA PLUNGED FURTHER INTO CHESS AFTER CALVIA, PLAYING DURING THE next two years in important events in Montreal, Edmonton, Chicago, San Diego, Philadelphia, France, England, China, Siberia, Kalmykia, Italy, Germany, and Israel. After she graduated from NYU in 2006, she chose to devote at least the next year to chess, postponing the decision of how she would make her living. "I need to run with chess," Irina told me. "It's the activity I enjoy most in life."

Jennifer never completely hit her chess stride after Calvia. She played in the 2005 U.S. Championship in San Diego, but had a disappointing performance. "I miscalculated something early on," she told me, "and then, because I had lost confidence, in subsequent games I crazily rechecked my calculations four, five, maybe six times. You can't waste time like that—particularly with my playing style, which is all about calculation." As a result, she found herself in even worse debilitating time pressure than she normally faced. After San Diego she started playing less chess and buried herself in completing *Chess Bitch*. The writing life agreed with her, and in the summer of 2006 she became full-time editor of the USCF's new Web site, for which she wrote news stories and a blog and posted photographs she'd taken of American players. She had found a way to meld her interests in chess and the arts into a job.

Paul Truong must have gone heavy on the hot sauce after Calvia because he went into hyperdrive helping Susan Polgar become one of the most recognized chess celebrities in the world. The media reported that, in August 2005, she set a world record for most games played simultaneously. For sixteen and a half hours, from 10:30 A.M. to 3:00 A.M., she faced 326 opponents in Palm Beach Gardens, Florida. She beat 309, drew 14, and lost to only 3. All in all, she walked 9.1 miles from board to board.

I was praising Susan Polgar's performance at a dinner when Pascal, whose deeper immersion in the chess world makes him more skeptical than I am, started to calculate how fast she would have had to play each game: sixteen and a half hours, or 990 minutes, divided by 326 games comes out to about three minutes a game—including the time walking from board to board. And Pascal, who has given many exhausting simultaneous exhibitions himself, with far fewer opponents, was not the only one who found the three-minute figure suspiciously quick. A few days later, international master Andrew Martin of England, who had set the previous record of 321 games, came forward and publicly questioned whether her feat was physically possible in only sixteen and a half hours.

"I just don't understand this," he wrote on the ChessBase Web site, in a long piece on the difficult circumstances of his record-setting simul. Of Polgar, he asked, "How can one play so many games in such a short time? . . . That's less than 1 min per game overall!" But Martin did not explain how he had gotten the three-minute calculation down to one minute (presumably he was attributing two minutes a game to the walking of 9.1 miles, but why?). "How long were these games, how many moves . . . How do you persuade so many people to sit there for so long waiting for the moves to be played?" he asked. "Susan is a great player, so of course she is capable of a great result. But has the marketing gone too far on this occasion? What credibility can we attach to these figures?"

Polgar responded on ChessBase with photographs of the event and a very detailed description of the arrangements. She accepted his one-minute-per-game estimate but claimed she had actually played that quickly. "There is one fact I would like to clarify," she wrote.

Each game did not take a minute to complete by both sides but only by me. While I was walking, my opponents had plenty of time to think. We did not allow any pass. Therefore, a move must be made as I arrive at the board. Then I responded basically instantly. My moves against the weaker players did not take more than a second or two at most. If each game averages 30 moves or even less, it would take about a minute or less to complete.

Even after this extensive rebuttal, there were still those who felt that questions had been left unanswered. Did all of Polgar's opponents really move the very moment she reached their boards? What about the time she presumably lost to bathroom breaks during the sixteen-plus-hour marathon? Perhaps the chess world is so competitive that even the best players will occasionally give in to pressure to appear even more invincible than they are. Or perhaps it is simply that there is so much jealousy in top-level chess that accusations of impropriety are inevitable. The principal complainant, Andrew Martin, was hardly a disinterested observer, but a man whom Polgar intended to displace in the record books. Either way, these messy disputes that seem to occur at all levels of play are far from the spiritual aspects of chess that drew Irina to the game. Even players as accomplished as Kasparov and Polgar can't remain totally above the suggestion of scandal.[7]

"I'M NOT THE WORLD'S BIGGEST GEEK"

"On the college chess circuit, there are certain maxims:
Advance your pawns, protect your king—and don't be
surprised if your opponent has gray hair."
—*THE BALTIMORE SUN*

EARLY IN 2004, BEFORE JENNIFER SHAHADE KNEW OF THE
rating shenanigans that might rook her out of a spot on the U.S.
Olympiad team, her brother gave me a seven-hour chess lesson. We concentrated on openings because my knowledge of them was extremely
thin. Now, a day-long lesson was obviously not optimal—by the fifth
hour my head was foggy and my hand cramped from writing down
moves and entering them in my computer—but it was the best we could
do given Greg's busy schedule and mine. Greg Shahade, twenty-five, was
once one of the country's leading junior players, but after the 2003 U.S.
Championship he cut back drastically on tournament chess. He still
played late-night blitz on the Internet and gave the occasional chess

lesson to a friend, but he had switched his allegiance from I-can-barely-pay-the-rent chess to I-can-buy-the-building poker. He played Texas Hold'em online and maximized his earnings by playing four to six games simultaneously. (Jennifer would eventually follow her brother into the world of online poker. "It's not as challenging as chess," she said, "but the money makes it interesting.")

In our chess marathon, Greg showed me some sharp, unorthodox responses to various lines in the Sicilian, and a couple of weeks later I had a chance to use one of them—an audacious queen move in which White ignores Black's attack on his knight—at a rapid tournament at the Marshall. My twenty-something opponent was a relative newcomer to the tournament scene, and I was favored to beat him easily. He was clearly uncomfortable with the rapid time control (twenty-five minutes a side for the whole game) and moved too fast early on when he should have taken more time to think. By the tenth move I had sacrificed a knight and a bishop and had to shelter my king from check, but I was poised to capture his rook and assault his king.

All this was according to plan: Greg had showed me this very position in the final hour of our lesson. As I stared at the board at the Marshall, I wished I had been more than a stenographer when Greg and I looked at the position; I should have questioned him about the subtleties. I faced the choice of retreating my king to the left or the right. I remembered writing down that Greg had chosen the left, but now, with the clock ticking, the move looked suspect. I feared that my opponent's attack on my king would come faster than my counterattack. Could I have written down the wrong move or did Greg screw up? Damn, I thought. Forget the lesson and just analyze.

I decided to move my king to the right. Within a few moves I had a winning game and was cheerfully pursuing his king. There were many ways to culminate my attack, but I had consumed too much time determining the very best way of proceeding instead of just making natural, albeit perhaps second-best, moves that would have won anyway—that's how strong my position was. Soon I was in danger of losing on time but made what I deemed a brilliant move. I slid my rook forward and chopped off his centrally posted bishop that was defended by his king pawn. I had noticed that the king pawn was overworked as a defender;

when it recaptured my rook, it would no longer be defending the Black knight, which I'd then merrily execute with my queen.

But the neophyte sitting across from me found a hole in my plan. He didn't immediately recapture my rook with the pawn, but first moved his knight to check my king and then used the knight, not the pawn, to take my rook. I was horrified that I had missed the powerful intermezzo—the in-between move of the knight check—and a few seconds later made a worse howler by losing my queen to another knight fork. I resigned in disgust. It was the first time in my life that I had blundered away my queen in a tournament game, and I was embarrassed to do it in front of two of the stronger players at the Marshall who happened to be watching.

My opponent wanted to review the game. I agreed, even though I was simmering inside. In the postmortem he kept earnestly suggesting horrible continuations, overlooking mates in one and mates in two. That made me feel even worse. I had lost to this studious *patzer* because of my own stupidity. I knew better than to equate intelligence with chess success, but at the time I felt like the world's biggest idiot.[1]

I had been working at chess as an adult for three years now. Although I certainly had a more sophisticated understanding of the game than I did when I was a child, my response to losing was hardly more mature. Not only was I still finding the game too stressful, I was encountering a problem that I didn't remember having in my youth: unless my opponents were total schmucks who taunted me or otherwise misbehaved, I had trouble defeating them if I knew they'd get upset.

One evening I faced a small nine-year-old boy in another rapid tournament at the Marshall. He was a nice kid who was shy and respectful. On the twentieth move, I won a key pawn. I was also ahead on the clock, and it should have been a simple matter to land the knockout blow. All the bishops and knights had been exchanged, and I could immediately infiltrate his back two ranks with my queen and rooks.

But he looked so distressed when I won the pawn. His eyes were tearful, his shoulders sagged, and he slumped in his chair. I empathized with him and started spending more time on my moves because I had trouble focusing on the position. Instead of taking over his home ranks, I dallied and advanced a rook pawn. He tried to drum up counterplay by advancing his pawns toward my king, but I still had an objectively winning position although I was now perilously short of time. When I finally got around to dominating his home rank with my queen, he sobbed and sank even further into his seat. His discomfort was so visible that I lost whatever remained of my concentration and wasted additional time trying to recover it. I didn't follow through by piling on my rooks, but captured another pawn with my queen. This, too, should have won, but I now had less than twenty seconds. We traded pawns on the kingside—I was still winning—and then, Zap! He grabbed a pawn near my king with his rook, offering the rook as a sacrifice. I saw, as my clock ran down, that he could force a draw by perpetual check if I took the rook. So instead I preserved my advantage by seizing another pawn and checking his king. He retreated the king into the very corner of the board.

I could have now forced the exchange of queens, bringing about a two-pawn-up endgame that I could win without effort, but instead I harassed his queen by attacking it with my rook. He ignored the attack and instantly responded with another rook sacrifice near my king. This time I could not turn down the rook (because he would have mated me on the next move), but after I captured it he could clinch a draw by perpetually checking me. I started to propose a draw, but before I could finish my sentence, he gently interrupted me and pointed out that my flag had fallen. I had lost the game on time. I was crestfallen and annoyed by this defeat, even though I had brought it on myself.

I spoke to Greg afterward. "You did what?" he said, incredulously. "You felt sorry for him when you were beating him? You're crazy, Paul. You're completely crazy. You should crush these kids and make them really cry." Indeed, I was a head case, the tormented duelist who draws his pistol first but can't get off a shot. We humans are supposed to learn from our mistakes, yet here I was repeating the same self-destructive pattern I had followed when I played Greg's sister. I was ahead on the clock and on the board but allowed myself to be flummoxed by my opponent's eleventh-hour, desperado sacrifices and my reservations about winning.

The boy who beat me did not gloat. He just looked relieved and a bit embarrassed by his unlikely victory. You can tell a lot about a person's character by how he acts after a chess game. I admired the boy because, like Jennifer, he did not display his glee at the change of fortune in his favor. In a world full of Grobsters, this attitude was rare.

Overall, I was playing better chess—my rating was two hundred points higher than when I had quit in college—and yet I still felt out of place in the chess world and might have given up the game entirely if I had not met Pascal Charbonneau. Although I did not know it at the time, he would change the way I thought about chess.

EVER SINCE I HAD GONE TO AEROFLOT, AND WITNESSED FIRSTHAND HOW Joel Lautier had responded to victory and defeat, I wanted to get further inside the head of a top player to understand the full range of his emotional responses to the game. I wanted to know how he prepared for each opponent, how well he slept before a critical encounter or after a bruising loss or a triumphant win, and how he psyched himself up at game time. Of course, I had interviewed various players about their pre- and postgame rituals, but in the world of chess, with its endless posturing, I could never be sure of the answers. I asked Joel once if I could watch him prepare for an opponent. He said to ask him again after he had had a few vodkas. I did ask again and he politely declined. I assured him that I would not reveal anything about the openings he prepared or new ways he might concoct to bust the King's Indian. I think he trusted me but was understandably concerned that my presence in his hotel room— even a quiet presence at three in the morning—might interfere with his routine. When I approached Kasparov about watching his preparation, he screwed up his face and looked at me in total disgust.

My interest in observing one of the top players prepare behind closed doors was more than academic: I wanted to understand whether my responses to the game made me a freak or whether other players had the same experiences. I was curious to learn if my internal reactions to the game were typical of a chess amateur but not of a world-class player. I knew that my mood greatly affected my play: a slightly strained conversation with my wife, never mind a full-fledged argument, could throw off my game. I knew that I did not sleep well during tournaments because I was too plagued by all the chess variations that raced through my head—not to mention the strange dreams in which attractive women moved like knights and sinister men like bishops.

In the spring of 2004, I had all but given up on finding a player who would let me shadow him at the upcoming FIDE World Championship

in Tripoli, Libya. Then, in May, my wife and I attended a press conference in New York announcing a match in the city between Irina Krush
and Almira Skripchenko, the French women's champion (and Joel Lautier's former wife). Ann usually passes up chess events, but this time she
joined me because the venue was the legendary Russian Samovar, the
Manhattan restaurant co-owned by Mikhail Baryshnikov and patron-
ized by Russian artists and Soviet defectors. Ann is more sociable than
me, and while I was standing around the buffet table nibbling *pelmeni* and
caviar, she was across the room introducing herself to Pascal. When he
told her that he was going to Tripoli in a month to play for the World
Championship and was nervous about traveling by himself, she told him
that I was considering attending but didn't want to go alone, either.

Pascal and I started talking. He explained that Irina couldn't accompany
him to Tripoli because she had a sudden chess commitment of her own: the
2004 U.S. Women's Championship that had been hastily arranged to solve
the Shahade-Goletiani rating controversy. Between bites of gravlax, Pascal
asked me if I wanted to come along. I expressed interest, but warned him
that I'd want to observe absolutely everything he did to prepare for his
games and hoped my presence wouldn't be a distraction. "That's fine," he
said. "I don't really have a preparation routine so there'll be nothing for
you to disturb. I've been to tournaments alone, with strangers, with my
dad, and with Irina, and I haven't noticed a correlation between how I do
and who accompanies me." This last remark, I'd learn, was vintage Charbonneau: he was the consummate rationalist. And so, in the course of a
three-minute conversation, we had agreed to travel together to a country
that did not have diplomatic relations with the United States.

Both of us, however, harbored doubts about our trip. Although Pascal
was glad he wouldn't be traveling alone, he later confessed that he wondered whether an American journalist was the safest possible companion
during the U.S. occupation of Iraq, when anti-American sentiment in the
Arab world was at its zenith. "I was a little concerned," he said, "but
somehow I was happy. I thought we'd get along. You seemed interesting. I
knew you were accomplished, and I hoped we'd become friends."

My concerns revolved around how little I knew about him. I had a sense
that he was a nice guy because I had eavesdropped, fourteen months earlier,
on a postmortem he'd done with Irina at the 2003 U.S. Championship in

Seattle.[2] He had gone to Seattle to support Irina, and I had gone there to watch Jennifer. Pascal was camped out in the press room for much of the tournament because it had a high-speed Internet connection and he was typing commentary on the games, which was being Webcast. He had another window open on his computer in which he was playing blitz chess online as he typed the commentary. He had a serious demeanor about him, but I could tell from the awful puns he wove into his commentary that he also had a silly side. Once, when Irina's game ended early, the two of them went over it, move for move, in the press room. I noticed how gentle he was when he suggested improvements in her play and how he consoled her when she got mad at herself for blundering.

Kindness is a wonderful attribute in a traveling companion or a friend, but it is not a sufficient, or even necessarily a desirable, quality in an interview subject. One of my writer buddies, Bernard, got me worrying about whether Pascal might be too bland: "Your passion is mad geniuses," Bernard said. "What if he's neither crazy nor a genius?" I started to wonder whether I'd have anything to write about if his preparation for his chess adversaries was uninteresting. Or if his games were dull. Or if he couldn't articulate his feelings about chess. And what if he was not stirred by victory or defeat—what if chess playing was no more eventful for him than brushing his teeth? Then I worried about what this young man, half my age, might think of my play. What if he decided that I was a complete moron because my chess rating was comparatively low? Or a total loon because of all the emotional baggage I brought to the game? What if he concluded that I should renounce chess, get out the Preparation H, and watch *On Golden Pond*? It would cost me a couple of thousand bucks to go to Libya—it was not as if Southwest Airlines flew from White Plains to Tripoli—so the trip needed to be productive.

AS IT HAPPENED, ONLY THE DOUBTS OF THE MORE RATIONAL ONE OF US proved to be warranted.

In the week after the Russian Samovar, I started to play through the 456 games of Pascal's on the *2004 ChessBase MegaBase* CD, including youthful efforts of his going back to 1996, when he was all of thirteen. I noticed immediately that many of his games were high-wire acts. He habitually put himself at risk, courting dizzying complications that might conceivably backfire, but trusting his own ability to see through the thicket of possibilities more clearly than his opponents. I was particularly delighted that he occasionally employed the same crazy opening, the King's Gambit, that I had intemperately made the core of my own repertoire as White.

The King's Gambit, a rarity in top-level and amateur chess today, was an adventurous reversion to the nineteenth century, when the prevailing playing style was to go straight for the other guy's monarch almost from the first move, sacrificing pawns and pieces with abandon to open lines for the attack. Indeed, the King's Gambit begins with the offer of a pawn, the king bishop's pawn, at White's earliest possible opportunity, on the second move. The pawn sacrifice helps White grab the center and develop quickly, but it also has the drawback of immediately weakening a key dark-squared diagonal leading to White's own king. Moreover, a pawn is a pawn, and if Black survives the attack and everything is swapped off the board, the extra foot soldier will win the game for Black in the end.

The art of defense was primitive in the nineteenth century, and so White's early provocations often succeeded in bamboozling Black and mating his king. When Black eventually learned such defensive techniques as returning the pawn at the proper moment in order to advance his own development, White had less success and the opening was largely abandoned by the middle of the twentieth century. Only a few intrepid romantics, such as Boris Spassky, the tenth world champion, continued to play it.

In the 1960 USSR Championship in Leningrad, Spassky trounced David Bronstein, a fellow practitioner of the King's Gambit, in a twenty-three-move miniature after a brilliant knight sacrifice. The game was so beautiful—and so famous as chess encounters go—that the position after Black's twenty-first move was reproduced in the James Bond film *From Russia with Love* as a game between "Kronsteen" and "McAdams." In 1960, a dozen years before their legendary world title bout, Spassky defeated sixteen-year-old Bobby Fischer with a King's Gambit at a tournament in Mar del Plata, Argentina, spurring the disbelieving youngster to search for a refutation of the opening, which he published to much acclaim the following year.[3] Fischer's analysis had the effect of further thinning the already depleted ranks of King's Gambit partisans.

I was a fan of Spassky's aggressive style, and my interest in the gambit grew after I read that he had employed the opening some fifty times and never lost with it. I once asked Garry Kasparov whether Spassky's record could be seen as an endorsement of the opening. "No," Kasparov said, "it's an endorsement of Spassky. The King's Gambit is rubbish! Spassky was so strong that he could succeed even after handicapping himself with a dubious opening."

Joel Lautier, too, was not keen on the King's Gambit. "You play that?" he said to me. "I prefer to start the game with as many pawns as the other guy."[4]

Any second thoughts I had about accompanying Pascal to Tripoli evaporated once I studied his games. I couldn't imagine having a dull time with someone who played such a wild opening. And the fact that I was going with him to not just any tournament but the World Championship only added to my excitement.

PASCAL WAS ONE OF 128 MEN FROM FIFTY-SIX COUNTRIES WHO'D CONTEST A series of knockout matches in Tripoli. The knockout format promised to be suspenseful, even if, as some chess commentators argued, it was an imperfect way of crowning a world champion. In seven rounds, a single winner would emerge. The early rounds would consist of only two games, and so if someone had an off day and lost the first game, he didn't have any time to recover his confidence by playing a safe draw—he had to win the next game. In Fischer's time, the matches between prospective World Championship contenders were at least six games, so that one slip or blunder wasn't necessarily fatal.

The pace of the games in Tripoli would be spellbinding for the spectators and harrowing for the players. The time control—forty moves in ninety minutes and then fifteen minutes for the conclusion of the game, with a thirty-second bonus after each move—was fast for a World Championship, and it was one with which Pascal and the other contestants had little experience. When the players finished the first time scramble and reached their fortieth move, they would not be able to take a long coffee or bathroom break without cutting into their precious last quarter hour. Normally the second time control was a full hour, giving players a chance to recover their bearings and leisurely complete their games. Fifteen minutes was not much time to figure out how to nurse an advantageous but difficult endgame to victory or how to hold a dubious position if you were on the defending side.

Pascal, with a rating of 2474, was seeded number 114 among the 128 players bound for Tripoli. He was paired in the first round against a French player his own age, twenty-one-year-old wunderkind Etienne Bacrot, the number 15 seed, rated 2675. Bacrot learned chess at the age of four and became an international master when he was thirteen, five years before Pascal, by defeating, among others, two former world champions, Vassily Smyslov and Anatoly Karpov. "I thought I was playing a child," a stunned Smyslov said, "but I am certain I played a grandmaster." In March 1997, at the age of fourteen years, two months, Bacrot officially received his GM title, setting a record as the youngest grandmaster ever. The French representative was the on-paper favorite to beat Pascal, but the relatively fast time control and shortness of the match could work to the Canadian's advantage. Still, to score a major upset, Pascal would have to pull everything together.

PASCAL CHARBONNEAU EARNED THE RIGHT TO REPRESENT HIS COUNTRY in the World Championship when he won the 2002 Canadian Chess Championship at the age of eighteen, by scoring an upset victory in a two-game playoff match against forty-eight-year-old Kevin Spraggett, the highest-ranked grandmaster in Canada, who was once among the top eight players in the world. *The Vancouver Sun* reported that the normally reserved teenager jumped up from his chair, "lifted two clenched fists into the air in a victory signal and strode around the room as if emerging from a boxing ring instead of the sport of mind-flexing."

The same paper hailed Pascal's win with a front-page headline: "I'M NOT THE WORLD'S BIGGEST GEEK." To prove that he really was, the article showed a series of head shots of him taken in the heat of play. He was seen scowling, sucking his left hand, shoving a finger into his right ear, putting a thumb in his mouth, and rubbing his left eye after pushing up his glasses. The *Sun* must have worked hard, sorting through rolls of film, to find such unflattering photographs: in reality, Pascal was a handsome, sociable kid with a sturdy athletic build, stylish undersize screw-less glasses, and dark hair that he used to wear on the slightly shaggy side.

It was only five months after winning the championship that Pascal was caught up in the particular ugliness of Canadian chess politics, with its divisions between Quebecois and native English-speaking players. By the time he played on the Canadian team in the 2002 Olympiad in Bled, in October, a non-Quebecois player had begun a campaign to diminish Pascal's reputation in the chess world. He suggested that Pascal's rating was inflated because his father had paid a Serbian grandmaster from Greece, the 1993 world junior champion, to throw a six-game match to him in Montreal. Accusing someone of buying games, even when there is no evidence, is like accusing someone of child abuse; damage is done when the allegation is made, and there is little an innocent person can do to quiet the rumor mill and emerge with his reputation unsullied. Pascal was fortunate that many players ignored the accusation. The effort to cast him as a monomaniacal schemer, like the *Sun's* attempts to portray him as the quintessential geek, fell particularly wide of the mark: in fact Pascal was an unusually well-rounded player who had always been as de-voted to sports as he was to chess.

PASCAL WAS BORN ON MAY 6, 1983, IN MONTREAL. HE HAS TWO GORGEOUS sisters, Veronique, five years his junior, a volleyball enthusiast and late-night partier who won't go near a chessboard; and Anne-Marie, two years his junior, an actuary who was the third best female chess player in Canada (and, according to Internet chatter, also the most beautiful). His Quebecois parents chose his name because it reflected their respective in-terests. His mother, Danielle, was a professor of computer science, and PASCAL was one of the first programming languages. His father, Yves, was a mathematician turned actuary, and Blaise Pascal was a seventeenth-century French mathematician and theologian who was known for the elegance of his mathematics—particularly for a pyramid of numbers called "Pascal's triangle."[5]

Pascal Charbonneau's parents taught him to play chess when he was five, and at the age of seven he entered his first scholastic tournament, the Quebec Provincial Championship for First Graders, and placed third. "I was very happy," he recalled. "I got a big trophy. Chess is full of trophies." When he was eight, he won the Provincial Championship for the Second Grade, and he repeated that success year after year in higher grades. Before he left elementary school, he had achieved the rank of expert in the Quebec rating system, the equivalent of a master rating on the U.S. scale. And yet chess was just one of his many interests, which included judo, piano, basketball, and most of all tennis, a game he would play throughout his twelve years of education at French-speaking Catholic schools.

In school, the nuns often scolded him for talking disruptively in class. "I was a big gabber," he recalled, "but I grew into being the teachers' pet. In high school, my classmates voted me the suck-up award." Pascal had plenty of academic success, coming in second place in the National Latin Verse Competition and doing well in a national mathematics contest organized by the University of Waterloo.

Pascal began playing tennis at the same age he learned chess, and soon did well in tournaments at the local and provincial levels. "I don't know whether I could have been a grandmaster at tennis," he said, "but I could have tried." The tennis coach took his father aside and told him that Pascal should give up chess so that he could spend more time on tennis and turn pro. The chess coach lobbied just as hard for the reverse.

Pascal attended an all-boys high school. "They're great," he said, "as long as you have social contact with girls. You feel so much freer to say and do what you want. As soon as girls are in the picture, the boys try to upstage each other and don't make the same kind of jokes." Most of Pascal's socializing was through the chess world. He met his first girlfriend at a tournament when he was fourteen. Like him, she not only played chess but was an overachieving generalist. She was a straight-A student, a gymnast, a figure skater, and a pianist who had perfect pitch. But she lived five hundred kilometers away in Toronto, and so they saw each other only at chess events.

AT FOURTEEN, PASCAL PERSONALLY EXPERIENCED CHEATING FOR THE FIRST time at chess. In the last round of an open tournament, he faced an international master, and the two of them were in contention for $1,500 Canadian for the best performance of a player rated under 2400. "In the middle of the game the guy took out this peculiar little bottle that had a strong herbal smell," Pascal recalled. "I didn't know whether it was a drug or what. He looked nervous and started drinking it and he got pissed off when I smiled." They reached a position in time pressure where Pascal had no winning chances and his opponent was a bit better. "He repeated the position three times," Pascal said, "and I stopped the clock and claimed a draw by three-fold repetition. He said, 'No, no, it's not a draw.'" Pascal proposed calling the arbiter, who'd review the score sheets to see if the same position had indeed occurred three times, but his opponent objected. "He had tears in his eyes," Pascal recalled. "He was agitated and said, 'How can you do this? We should have made a deal and split the money.'" By drawing and scoring only ½ point each, they allowed another player to leapfrog them and win the $1,500. "He didn't propose a deal before the game—I'll give you $600 if you lose—because he thought he was going to beat me," Pascal said.

Afterward, the master challenged him to speed chess at $5 a game. Pascal refused, and the master tried to entice him by offering him time odds of five minutes to two. Still he turned him down. "My father was so offended," Pascal said, "that he got out his wallet and was ready to back me. I had to restrain him. Now that I'm older, I understand the guy's behavior, even though I don't approve. The money meant a lot to him, and many chess professionals like him were just scraping by."

BECAUSE PASCAL'S WEEKS DURING HIGH SCHOOL WERE FILLED WITH HOME-work and tennis and basketball practice, he didn't have much time to socialize. Even though he was incredibly busy, he was also lonely. He'd spend a couple hours each evening playing blitz on the Internet Chess Club and instant-messaging people. "I met this girl on ICC," he recalled. "She didn't play chess but hung out there, chatting. We messaged each other daily and then we started talking on the phone." She was a chess groupie, and for more than a year Pascal, seventeen, considered her to be his girlfriend, even though the two had never met. "She lived in the United States and was three years younger than me," he explained. "At that age, we couldn't just pick up and travel." Her parents were Jehovah's Witnesses, and they didn't approve of the relationship. They were afraid that Pascal was going to pull their daughter away from the faith, and once when it looked like the two of them might actually meet, her parents nixed the idea, the girl went into hiding, and her father reported Pascal to the police.

In August 2001, after graduating from twelfth grade, Pascal played in an eleven-round international chess tournament in Montreal and scored a respectable but less-than-exciting 4½ points out of 11. Afterward he was supposed to join his family on a vacation in Maine, but instead he remained behind, telling his parents that he was working at a tennis camp. To the astonishment of his friends, who were envious of his conspicuous accomplishments as a student, an athlete, and a chess player, Pascal then ran away from home—first to Toronto, and then clear across the country to British Columbia. He was eighteen years old. He left his parents a note, but did not tell them where he was going. He stayed in touch with them by e-mail and first disclosed his whereabouts on September 11, in case they were worried that he was in lower Manhattan. Pascal was gone ten months. He missed the last year of school (there are thirteen grades in the Quebecois system), derailing his admission to the best universities in Canada and the United States.

"I'm not proud," he said, "but I had to leave. If I had told my parents beforehand, I would not have gotten out of the house. I hurt them a lot." He left home, he said, because he felt that his life was too routine and predictable; he needed to see if he could make it on his own. "I had no time for myself with chess and sports and school," he recalled. "Everything seemed the same from day to day, with my life controlled by these activities. I felt that I was a tennis- and chess-playing robot. I was programmed to succeed. My parents were not pushy about what particular things I did, but I always felt pressure to succeed since the time I was small." The fact that Pascal's year-long relationship with his Internet girlfriend had gone nowhere also contributed to his sense of discontent.

Pascal wanted a more adventurous life than his parents, who were rooted with their families in Quebec: "I knew from my chess travels that there was an exciting world out there." He respected his father, who had worked since the age of thirteen and became an actuary in Canada at a young age, but he felt that his father's life was too staid. "He is very proud that he's never been drunk," Pascal said, "that he's never had more than three glasses of wine. He talked to me a lot about his work, but never about girls before my mom. I don't know if he was with any. I don't think he lived outside his home until he got married, and that was at twenty-eight. He had reasons, of course, but I was afraid I was aiming for something similar."

Pascal found a room in the home of an elderly chess organizer in Victoria, on Vancouver Island. "I made her day," he said. "She'd be happy if I stayed forever, but it wasn't the adventure I was looking for." Soon he took an apartment share in Vancouver with two strangers, one of whom became his girlfriend.

"She was different than the girls I knew in Montreal," he said. "She was very artsy. She was into writing, design, wearing pretty clothes, and going to galleries. She liked beautiful things and was beautiful herself." She was twelve years older than he and an actress in *Terror Firmer*, a Troma send-up of a slasher film. "She murders men while having sex with them," he said. "I'm glad I didn't see it before we got involved."

In Vancouver he continued playing chess for hours on ICC and made some money by doing audio commentary for games broadcast on a Canadian Web site called the World Chess Network. He drank a lot, ate too much, and learned to cook. His days were not overscheduled with sports. "I was happy," he told me. "I was doing things most guys my age never did. Hey, I was living with a woman."

As it happened, the 2002 Canadian Chess Championship was being held in the Vancouver suburb of Richmond, a forty-minute bus ride away. "I never played in a Canadian Championship before," Pascal said, "so my expectations were not high."

His Vancouver buddy Jack Yoos, whom he knew from their days together as roommates and teammates at the 2000 Chess Olympiad in Turkey, helped him prepare his openings. "Pascal is a great natural talent," Yoos told me, "but his openings are truly atrocious. He can't bring himself to study. So I would take some of the openings I play and create elaborate computer files about them and incorporate the latest wrinkles from recent top-level games. Pascal would breeze through the files in an evening and then go out and play *my* openings. It was frustrating because he was immediately getting much better results than me."

In the eighth round of the eleven-round championship, Pascal faced twenty-six-year-old Alexandre Lesiege, his chief Quebecois rival, who was leading the tournament by a full point. Pascal needed to beat him to catch up, but that would not be easy: Lesiege had 200 rating points on him, which meant that Pascal had only a 24 percent chance of winning. Lesiege played the Caro-Kann Defense, a staple of his repertoire, and Pascal departed from his usual response, the Panov-Botvinnik Attack, and played the ultra-sharp Advance Variation, aiming to cramp Black from the start. By the eleventh move, Pascal had a big lead in development, but after inaccuracies on both sides, he failed to score a quick win. By the twenty-sixth move, Pascal was again much better; he was winning material, an advantage he converted into a victory thirteen moves later. It was the first time Pascal had defeated a Canadian grandmaster in a slow game.

"The timing was good," Pascal recalled. "I started feeling confident about my chances because I had already faced nearly all of the other top players in the field." Indeed, he cruised through the next three games and, having tied Kevin Spraggett for first, played him the two-game tiebreak match, in which he triumphed with a win and a draw.

The surprise victory surprised no one more than the eighteen-year-old winner. Yoos told me that "it took Pascal weeks before it fully dawned on him that he really was the champion of Canada."

By this time, Pascal had had all the adventure he needed and was ready to go home and enter college. His parents welcomed him back. "We get along well now," he said, "but we've never really discussed what happened. It would be too emotional for both sides." In May 2002, he visited the University of Maryland, Baltimore County, which was ready to give him a full academic scholarship if he joined the chess team. He played one-on-one basketball with David Brogan, the president of the chess club. Pascal described Brogan as "a cool guy with an earring" who was trying to change the image of chess by having the club organize a bikini contest among undergraduate girls (an idea that was vetoed by the UMBC administration). When Pascal had possession of the ball and was trying to fake out Brogan by abruptly switching direction, he heard his right knee grind. Somehow he twisted it, tore ligaments, and collapsed on the court. "I never had a sports injury before," he said, "but I was totally out of shape from my hedonistic life in British Columbia."

Six weeks later he injured his knee again, on a nude beach in Vancouver. He and Yoos had taken a chess-playing friend there as a kind of joke. "I was running in the water and suddenly I fell down and started screaming,"

Pascal said. He twisted his leg, and his friends, who thought at first that he was kidding, had to carry him out of the water and onto the beach. Fortunately, he'd kept his bathing suit on: as he lay there, in incredible pain, "a bunch of aging naked hippies with bad bodies and everything hanging out crowded around me to see if I was OK." Finally a hovercraft ambulance pulled up on the beach and transported him to the hospital.

In September 2002, Pascal began his freshman year at UMBC with a bad knee. (One downside of Canada's touted socialized medicine is the long waiting time for surgery.) UMBC was one of only two American colleges—the other was the University of Texas at Dallas—that gave full scholarships to chess players. UMBC had won the Pan American Intercollegiate Championship five years in a row, and the university's president, Freeman A. Hrabowski III, credited the chess team with "an enormous amount of publicity focused on the life of the mind," which helped to attract not just chess players but top students in general.

During Pascal's second semester, however, the chess team's exemplary reputation unraveled and the team was exposed as being a haven for Grobster grandmasters and opportunistic IMs who accepted the scholarship and housing stipend, but had no real commitment to the school. "One day," Pascal recalled, "the administration contacted all of us and told us not to take any calls from the press. We thought it was strange that they didn't want us to publicize chess, but one look at the Internet and it all became clear."

On May 9, 2003, fellow teammate Alex Sherzer, a grandmaster whose nickname was "The Surgeon" because he had a medical degree from Hungary, had been arrested outside a juvenile detention center in Mobile, Alabama, and charged with traveling across state lines to solicit sex from one of the center's underage residents, a fifteen-year-old bulimic with developmental problems. Sherzer had paid for a nearby hotel room with a hot tub; in the room, investigators had found a doctor's bag, a statuette of Hippocrates, chess manuals, two sex toys, three bottles of Viagra, two dozen condoms, a few bottles of liquor, two shot glasses, recipes for mixed drinks, a copy of *Lolita*, three self-help books (*Secrets of Seduction, How to Be the Best Lover a Girl Ever Had,* and *A Guide to Picking Up Girls*), and a handwritten to-do list with reminders to eat lightly, exercise, and "sex w/a 15-yr-old in a few days!!!!!!"

Sherzer had met the teenager on the Internet in December 2002—she had posted a picture of herself in her school uniform—and the two chatted online for four months before her mother discovered the relationship and reported it to the authorities. Two weeks before Sherzer drove to Mobile, he conversed online with a male investigator for the Alabama Bureau of Investigation who was now impersonating the girl. In Sherzer's trial in September 2003, his defense attorney called Judit Polgar, who had come all the way from Hungary, as a character witness. He also argued that it was the agent's flirtatiousness that led his client to reserve a hotel room for the girl: if the agent hadn't gotten involved and ratcheted up the sexual content of their interchange, Sherzer would have waited until the girl was of legal age. The attorney likened Sherzer to Sonny Bono, who apparently waited patiently for Cher to reach adulthood. The jury, which deliberated while Polgar played chess in the courtroom hall with a fellow grandmaster, accepted the entrapment defense and Sherzer was acquitted.

"I'm glad he wasn't locked up and his career ruined," Pascal said, "but the whole thing was pathetic, and had negative repercussions for our team. It was especially surprising because Sherzer is a buff-looking, smart man. He's thirty years old and a doctor. You'd think he could get a girl." Sherzer was attending UMBC as an undergraduate on a full chess scholarship (tuition and a $15,000 housing stipend) and was majoring in emergency health services. ("How hard can that be for a doctor?" Pascal said of his classmate's choice. "It's as if I majored in French.")

The press made fun of Sherzer's age. "Disturbing questions have arisen," *The Dallas Morning News* reported, "not the least of which: What's a 32-year-old man with a Hungarian medical degree doing in college chess? Answer: Making his 40-something teammates feel old, probably. Actually, despite the sex scandal, UMBC is . . . like the AARP." Sherzer's teammates included grandmaster Aleksander "The Polish Magician" Wojtkiewicz, forty, and Willie "The Exterminator" Morrison, forty-three, a chess hustler from New York City.

"On the college chess circuit," *The Baltimore Sun* weighed in, "there are certain maxims: Advance your pawns, protect your king—and don't be surprised if your opponent has gray hair." When the UMBC chess program was under siege, the administration asked Pascal, all of twenty, with a full head of brown hair and a near straight-A average, to speak to the media.

UMBC had awarded chess scholarships for more than a decade, but it was not until 2004 that the first player with the rank of international master or grandmaster, former U.S. junior champion Eugene Perelshteyn, actually graduated from UMBC. A parade of top players attended the school but never made it all the way through.[6] Some were shown the door when their grade-point average fell below a C. The organization that governed intercollegiate chess finally cracked down in the spring of 2004 by limiting a player's eligibility to six years and setting a maximum age of twenty-six for newly recruited grandmasters.

In the wake of the sex and age scandals, Pascal noticed a change in professors' attitudes toward the chess team. "They feared we were cheaters who couldn't care less about school," he said. When Pascal and teammate Pawel Blehm, twenty-two, took an accounting exam, the teacher asked them not to sit next to each other. "There was fifteen feet between us but that still wasn't good enough," Pascal said. "She made us move again and sit on opposite sides of the room. She kept staring at me and finally asked me how old I was. I guess she was afraid I was some perpetual undergraduate in my thirties milking my chess scholarship and she was relieved to learn I was only twenty."

UMBC chess players often jetted off to collegiate, national, and international championships, and they depended on the cooperation of their professors to let them make up missed assignments and tests. "I had one professor who wouldn't give us a break," Pascal said. "I think he felt burned because Wojtkiewicz took his class and never made up the work. When I missed a quiz because my grandfather died and I went to Montreal, he wouldn't believe me. The jerk penalized me."

ALEKSANDER WOJTKIEWICZ, KNOWN AS WOJT OR WOJO, WAS ONE OF THE busiest chess professionals in the United States, making a living driving and flying around the country to weekend tournaments and the Tuesday night all-masters competitions at the Marshall. Wojt resembled a burly Jack Nicholson, with his gravelly voice and insatiable passion for liquor, cigarettes, and women. He was born in Latvia in 1963 to a Russian mother and a Polish chess-master father, from whom he learned the game at the comparatively late age of ten or eleven. Wojt caught on fast, though, and at seventeen became the champion of Latvia. His mentor in those years was the fiery tactician and former world champion Mikhail Tal, with whom he played blitz for a couple of hours each morning. "Tal did not live in this world," Wojt recalled, when we met at a bar in Vermont, where he was recovering from an embarrassing thumping at a late-summer weekend tournament. "I once had to lend Tal three rubles to pay the postman," he said, "because his wife was out and Misha had no idea where she kept money."

As a teenager, Wojt was one of the Soviet Union's most promising young players and a fervent anti-Communist. The Russians, he told me, had killed his father and his grandfather. To evade the Soviet draft and the country's "unjust" war in Afghanistan, Wojt disappeared, at the age of nineteen, into the St. Petersburg underworld. Four years later, in 1985, he was arrested for avoiding conscription and imprisoned in a KGB facility near Leningrad. He was released in 1987, after Ronald Reagan pressed Mikhail Gorbachev to set him free. Wojt apparently had the raw talent to reach the stratosphere of chess, but his progress had been thwarted by six years on the lam and in confinement. Even so, he had made the best of his time in prison by studying the game and devising an important opening innovation, dubbed the Prison Novelty, in his favorite variation of the Sicilian, the Accelerated Dragon.

In a chess world full of oversize characters, Wojtkiewicz was still a standout. He was equal part hustler and naïf, and the stories about him were endless and amusing. Like the time he wandered unknowingly into a gay bar with a male friend and a woman. At some point the woman had a nosebleed and Wojt got the attention of the place when he anxiously and loudly asked the bartender for Vaseline, an old Polish remedy for her affliction. There was also the time that he was staying with friends, disappeared for a weekend without telling them, and returned with no explanation, as if he had just stepped out to buy a paper, except that he was now on crutches.

Most Tuesdays, when their classes at UMBC were over, Pascal would drive all the way from Baltimore to the New York Masters with Wojt and Jaan Ehlvest,[7] an Estonian grandmaster who was Wojt's roommate. They'd play four games of chess at the Marshall between 7 P.M. and midnight. "I always tried to take my own car," said Pascal, "so I knew I could get back after the tournament by 3:00 A.M. because I had class again at 9:30 A.M." Once the two GMs persuaded Pascal to drive Wojt's car instead. "I was doing seventy to eighty miles per hour on the highway so we'd get there and Wojt says, 'I have something you'll like' and pops a hard-core French porn film into a DVD player that he's placed on the dash. I couldn't drive and watch. Anyway, my idea of fun was not raunchy movies with two drunk middle-aged grandmasters."

The trip got worse. Wojt and Ehlvest disappeared at midnight, leaving Pascal with the car. "I didn't feel right driving his car back without them," he said. They wouldn't answer their cell phones, and Pascal missed a day of classes. "The next day I went from bar to bar in Manhattan until, after a tip from someone at a social club called Estonia House, I found them, arguing. Wojt can be a loud drunk, and he was accusing Ehlvest of being an Estonian Nazi."

Wojtkiewicz lived up to the stereotype of the scheming Russian. To maintain his chess scholarship at UMBC, he signed up for courses like Russian Choir, which he assumed he could pass without attending by just making an arrangement with the teacher, who was Russian. When Wojt was away from UMBC playing chess during the last week of classes, he realized that he had forgotten to speak to the teacher. He contacted Pascal and another student and asked them to forge a note from him and leave it along with a $100 bottle of cognac in the teacher's faculty mailbox. "We felt a bit strange doing this," Pascal admitted. "The mailboxes were open, and I had doubts about whether the cognac would ever make it to the teacher." When Wojt received an F, he sent a letter of appeal, claiming that he had missed choir because the Baltimore air, unlike the moist Baltic air he was used to, was bad for his vocal cords. He lost his scholarship.

On July 14, 2006, Wojtkiewicz, forty-three, died in Baltimore of complications of alcoholism. He won his last five tournaments, including the prestigious World Open, played just a few days earlier, over the Fourth of July weekend. At the memorial service in Baltimore, his chess students fondly recalled his tough-love approach to teaching. Kevin McPherson, a rated expert, described how he had proudly shown Wojt some games from the World Open. Wojt laughed as he played through them and asked after almost every move, "Why didn't you play here?"

Finally, at one particular juncture, he paused respectfully. "Kevin," he said, "I've been teaching you for four years, you've spent thousands on chess lessons and finally, you play a good move!"

PASCAL AT LAST HAD KNEE SURGERY, AFTER HIS FRESHMAN YEAR, BACK IN Montreal. That ended any dreams he had of a tennis career, but he claimed that the accident was one of the best things to happen to his chess. During the period of recuperation—he was the youngest person in a facility that catered to amputees—he diligently studied chess for the first time in his life. "I was fuzzy from painkillers," he said, "but some of what I studied must have sunk in." In August 2003, ten weeks after the operation, he achieved two grandmaster norms in a single month, at the Montreal International and at the prestigious Continental Championships for the Americas in Buenos Aires, where he tied for third through eighth place in a strong 151-person field that included thirty grandmasters. His performance in Buenos Aires qualified him for the second time for the 2004 World Championship in Tripoli.

LIBYA, WITH NO KNOWN CHESS TRADITION AND A QUARTER CENTURY OF isolation, was a peculiar place to stage an international chess championship, particularly because players from Israel, a powerhouse of ex-Soviet talent, did not seem to be welcome.[8] Not many Americans had been to Libya since 1969, when Muammar Gadhafi, a twenty-seven-year-old army officer, staged a coup against the ruling constitutional monarch. My view of Gadhafi was shaped in the 1980s, when the United States considered Libya to be more of a threat than the Soviet Union. Gadhafi, whom Ronald Reagan famously called "the mad dog of the Middle East," had all but invented global terrorism. By funding guerilla organizations around the world, Gadhafi hoped to undermine countries allied with Israel, which he pledged "to drive into the sea." In 1972, he reportedly financed the Palestinian massacre of Israeli athletes at the Olympic Games in Munich. In 1986, Libyan agents blew up a Berlin nightclub that was frequented by U.S. servicemen, and Reagan retaliated by bombing Gadhafi's compound in Tripoli. Gadhafi narrowly survived, but his fifteen-month-old adopted daughter and fifteen others died. The United States held him responsible for the era's deadliest terrorist attack, the 1988 bombing of Pan Am Flight 103 over Lockerbie, Scotland, that killed 270 people.

By the summer of 2004, when Gadhafi put up $1.5 million for the World Championship, the Libyan leader had apparently mellowed. He was suggesting that Jews and Palestinians live together harmoniously in a land called Israetine. While not admitting that he was involved in Lockerbie, he paid $2.7 billion to the families of the deceased. And most significant of all for the world community, he renounced his quest for weapons of mass destruction (even if he did not account for missing nuclear equipment) and permitted international inspectors to oversee the dismantling of his weapons laboratories.

Gadhafi's conversion to nuclear pacifism was a coup for the Bush administration. Washington claimed that Gadhafi disarmed because he didn't want to go the way of Saddam Hussein. In October 2003, the United Nations rewarded Gadhafi by lifting the sanctions that had left his country economically and culturally isolated. Four months later the Bush administration ended the ban on U.S. citizens traveling to Libya, but did not remove the country from the list of states that sponsored terrorism. In May 2004, when Pascal and I were planning our trip to Tripoli, the United States seemed on the verge of resuming diplomatic ties with Libya. The chess championship would be the benign new Libya's first international sporting event, a high-profile opportunity for Gadhafi to show the world that his country was now a peace-loving Mediterranean paradise with a lot of history, where hostilities would be confined strictly to the chessboard.[9] Not everyone bought the conversion: the United States Chess Federation declared Libya unsafe for American players and discouraged them from going.

Despite the USCF's warning, I was excited about the trip. However, there was the practical issue of money: Washington made it hard to spend any in Tripoli. The Web site of the U.S. State Department said that Americans were free to visit Libya, but could not use credit cards or write personal checks—and ATMs did not exist. I assumed traveler's checks were permitted, and I called the State Department to make sure. "Cash only," an expert on Libya told me. Even though UN sanctions had been lifted, the U.S. Treasury Department had not yet eased monetary restrictions. "But, don't worry," the expert added, "you probably won't have to spend money. Gadhafi will treat you like royalty and keep you safe."

The Libyan organizers had promised bodyguards to all the players. I was hoping they'd look like Gadhafi's own reputed security detail, gorgeous machine-gun-toting women in skintight outfits and stiletto high heels. As an added safety measure, the State Department advised me to register before my trip with the Belgian embassy in Tripoli, which, in the absence of a U.S. embassy, had some limited power to handle the needs of Americans who got in trouble. As a Canadian citizen, Pascal was fortunately not bound by U.S. Treasury Department regulations. We presumed that if we ran low on money he could use a credit card. We did not know that in Tripoli none of the restaurants, and only a single hotel, actually accepted credit cards.

I had read an article about the abysmal state of health care in Libya. Poor Libyans who needed medical care went across the border into neighboring countries and wealthier Libyans flew to Europe. More than four hundred children had been infected with HIV through improperly screened blood transfusions. Rather than acknowledging and addressing the awful mistake, the government framed five Bulgarian nurses. A mock court convicted them on trumped-up charges and sentenced them to execution by firing squad. The Bulgarians had been on death row for two months before the chess championship. The incident became an international scandal and an impediment to the normalization of trade between Libya and the European Union. A host of European prime ministers and scientific superstars, such as Luc Montagnier, the co-discoverer of the HIV virus, had pleaded to no avail with Muammar Gadhafi to reverse the death sentences.

When I registered by e-mail with the U.S. Interests Section of the Belgian embassy, I asked where I should go if I had a medical problem. I explained I had allergies that seemed under control but in the past had landed me in the emergency room. The Belgian attaché in Tripoli wrote back that Libya had fine English-speaking physicians and that, because my host was Gadhafi himself, he would undoubtedly make sure that I received the best care. But the attaché gave me his cell phone number just in case.

The next step was obtaining a visa. I could not get one in the United States because of the absence of diplomatic relations. I was in contact by e-mail with Nijar Al El Haj, the head of the North African Chess

Federation and chief organizer of the championship, who promised that a journalist's visa would be waiting for me when I arrived. I asked Nijar if he could arrange for me to meet Gadhafi and play a friendly game of chess with him as a symbol of the emerging relationship between his country and mine. To grease the way for an interview, I shamelessly noted that many great world figures—Napoleon, Franklin, Trotsky, Lenin—had been fine chess players. Nijar quickly responded that Mohammed Gadhafi, Muammar's son and presumed heir apparent, would certainly meet with me and that the two of them would try to set up an interview with Leader, as Gadhafi senior was called.

My friend Matt was ecstatic that I would be meeting Gadhafi junior. "Mohammed the son!" he e-mailed me. "The weed of the desert! That is cool. I like the term Leader with no name attached. A little Hitlerish. You and junior can discuss your respective father-son issues."

Nijar and I stayed in touch by e-mail, and I kept gently pressing him to arrange the meeting with Leader and offered new reasons why Leader might want to speak to the American people through me. My pandering disgusted some of my Jewish friends. Others thought I was crazy to go to Libya at a time when, in the wake of the abuses at Abu Ghraib, kidnappings and beheadings of Americans were on the rise. Matt joked that it was a good thing I was already a two-fingered typist and suggested that my chess book be called *Where's the Rest of Me?* An Iranian friend said that I might finally learn the identity of my dad's father after Libyan intelligence agents tracked him down to see if he was Jewish. Joel Lautier told me to remember to say *Salaam Aleikum* not *Shalom Alechem*—"These few different letters could save your life or spell your doom." My wife worried that it would be a mistake for me to try to crush Gadhafi at the chessboard.

For my part, I had a nightmare about Bush having a sudden change of heart toward Gadhafi and following Reagan's lead in blowing up his tent while I happened to be playing chess inside. I even called the State Department one last time to tell them which days I might be with Gadhafi and request that they keep the cruise missiles away. The woman who answered the phone laughed and promised to relay my itinerary to the commander in chief.

Everything pointed to a smooth trip. Our plan was for Pascal to pick me up in Woodstock on his drive from Irina's home in Sheepshead Bay,

Brooklyn, to Montreal, where we would say *au revoir* to his parents, take the red-eye to London, spend one night in an airport hotel, and catch a connecting British Airways flight to Tripoli on June 17, 2004, the day before the opening ceremony.

A week before we set out, Bush complicated my travel plans by changing his mind. On June 9, the White House accused Gadhafi of masterminding a plot to assassinate Crown Prince Abdullah of Saudi Arabia and hinted at the possibility of renewed sanctions. On June 13, the day before we left for Montreal, I received an unsigned e-mail from Tripoli addressed not to me personally, as Nijar's chatty e-mails were, but to "Dear Sir." It said my visa was ready at the Libyan embassy in the United States. The problem was that there was no such embassy. I thought maybe they meant the Libyan consulate to the United Nations, but a clerk there told me Tripoli hadn't authorized a visa.

The next morning I called Nijar, but the Libyan phone system was not reliable and it took me two hours to get through. Nijar apologized about the "silly new rules" that required all press to get visas in their country of origin, a seeming impossibility for an American. I told him I was on my way to Montreal and asked whether a visa could be issued at the Libyan embassy in London during my one-day stopover. Failing that, I proposed that I change my status from press to "accompanying person" and get my visa in Tripoli with Pascal. Nijar explained that it was too late to claim I wasn't a journalist because my request to interview Leader was now "at the highest level." He chuckled and said the government had read everything I'd ever written. He said that he would try to get a press visa issued in London and asked me to call him the next day before I boarded the plane in Montreal. I got up early, at 4:00 A.M., and started phoning Libya. It took four hours to get a clear connection. Nijar said he had arranged for me to attend the championship as Pascal's second, or coach, and obtain my visa in Tripoli.

I told Pascal about the new arrangement. "That's very cool," he said. "I've never had a second before. This will be great."

GADHAFI'S GAMBIT AND MR. PAUL

"The threat is mightier than the execution."
—ARON NIMZOWITSCH

"We did not and will not invite the Zionist enemies
to this [chess] championship."
—MOHAMMED GADHAFI

EARLY ON IN OUR TRIP, IT WAS CLEAR THAT PASCAL WOULD
do anything to avoid preparing for the World Championship. The first
flight of our journey to Libya—a British Airways red-eye from Montreal to London—put us down in Heathrow at about 8:00 A.M. Pascal's
original plan was to check in early to the airport hotel, spend most of the
day preparing for Etienne Bacrot, and then go downtown in the evening
because, for all his international chess travel, he had never been to London before. But then we couldn't get into our hotel room for a few hours,
and when we did, he wanted to nap. And when he got up in the late afternoon, he decided to help me with my own chess.

I was puzzled by a critical, razor-sharp line in the Dragon. He showed me an amazing continuation in which Black sacrificed his queen for a rook and a minor piece but effectively fought on because of the power of his two bishops raking the board.[1] This was the first time we had done chess together, and I liked that he took my questions seriously and evidently enjoyed the positions we examined. I was grateful for his help, but wondered if it was the best time. "Shouldn't you be working on your own chess?" I said. "If I remember correctly, you're playing for the World Championship in three days."

"I know," he said, laughing. "But I'm allergic to studying. I always put it off. If I weren't helping you, I'd find another diversion." Indeed, as soon as we were finished with the Dragon, he got on the Internet and smashed grandmasters at three-minute chess. Two hours and some twenty games later, it was time for dinner. We decided to eat nearby rather than go out on the town, in case the spirit finally moved him to prepare for Tripoli.

It was raining hard, and the concierge recommended an old pub called the White Horse. "It's five to ten minutes away, depending on how fast you walk, lads," he said. "Just go through the door into the parking lot. Take an immediate left. When you reach the street, take another left. Follow the road and it will be on your right." The directions could not have been simpler.

Pascal and I headed out the door, and he started walking straight across the parking lot. I reminded him that the man had said to go left, and Pascal backtracked and followed me. When we reached the road, he wanted to turn right. Then, after I steered him in the proper direction, he was impatient when we didn't immediately see the pub, and he persuaded me to abandon our search before ten minutes had passed. We went back to the hotel and asked the concierge to repeat the directions. This time when we reached the street where we were supposed to turn left, Pascal wanted to keep going straight. We needed to duck into a shop and confirm the directions before he was convinced we were heading the right way.

He was amused now by his failure to find the pub. "I can be really stupid," he said. I was delighted by his self-deprecating sense of humor, which set him apart in a chess world full of arrogant men who were too insecure ever to admit weakness. But I was also slightly taken aback: Pascal had neglected to tell me that one of my jobs as his second was to make sure he didn't get lost.[2] Here was someone who could beat me at chess blindfolded, ably navigate his way around a basketball or tennis court, but could not find his way to dinner.[3] His inadequate sense of direction was surprising because spatial-relations ability and chess skill seemed to be closely linked (and numerous clinical studies had shown a strong correlation between spatial ability and athleticism). Moreover, by his own admission, it was the geometry of the chessboard, and mathematical motifs involving the respective ways the pieces moved, that he found so beguiling about the game.

"I love the little geometries in chess," he explained, as we charged through the rain. "Now, don't laugh, Paul, but have you ever thought about the fact that if a rook is attacking a bishop, the bishop can't be attacking the rook?"

I couldn't say I had.

"OK," he continued, "it's obvious once I point it out. But a chess game is in some sense an accumulation of obvious ideas. Even the most complicated tactical sequences are built up from elementary things. I like thinking about the simplest things in chess. There are many of them. If a bishop is attacking a knight, the knight can't be attacking the bishop."

"If a lowly pawn is attacking a rook," I chimed in, "the rook can't take the pawn."

"There you go."

"If a knight is threatening a rook," I said, "the rook can't be threatening the knight." I was on a roll. "If a queen is attacking a knight, the knight can't be attacking the queen."

"Many strong chess players never consciously think about this stuff," Pascal said. "If I said to Irina, 'I think it's cool that if a pawn is attacking a knight, the knight is not attacking the pawn,' she'd look at me blankly. It would never occur to her. But that's how I look at chess."

So awash were we in the geometry of chessmen that we nearly passed the pub. After some hardy curry and a couple of beers, Pascal was finally ready to tackle the prospect of Bacrot. We brought Guinness back to the hotel room in order to make the preparation seem like fun. I knew then that another of my responsibilities as Pascal's second was to locate beer. He fired up his laptop and connected it to The Week in Chess Web site.

Pascal downloaded Bacrot's most recent games as well as his own and then combined them with older games from *MegaBase 2004*. He now had a database of 874 of Bacrot's games. He set up one file for the 441 games in which Bacrot had White and another for the 433 in which he was Black. He similarly split his own 486 games into a White file (231 games) and a Black file (255 games).

To my surprise he began by playing through his own most recent games. It wasn't vanity that led him to do this or an attempt to impress me. Rather, he was trying to look at his own games from Bacrot's perspective. "Obviously he's going to download my games," he said, "and examine them one by one to assess my strengths and weaknesses and predict how I'm going to play against him. I'm trying to imagine what he'll conclude."

Success in chess is dependent, of course, on anticipating the opponent's responses. Every newcomer learns the hard way that he cannot judge his own moves in isolation but must also consider his adversary's replies. A beginner often makes the psychological mistake of attributing weak moves to his opponent, effectively abetting his own plans. Even a premature attack will succeed if a player is allowed to make his opponent's moves for him. A better player is able to turn the chessboard around figuratively, freshly evaluate the position from the adversary's perspective, and poke holes in his own intended moves. Successful players can't be so in love with their own ideas that they are blind to strong moves that refute them.

The idea of approaching the game from the opponent's point of view also extends to figuring out the opening sequences of moves he's likely to play. That much I expected Pascal to do. But I didn't realize that he would pull a kind of Victor-Victoria and try to get inside the head of Bacrot trying to get inside the head of Pascal. This exercise took almost an hour.

When Pascal played over a few of his own games from the 2003 Continental Championship, he looked content. "Maybe Bacrot will think I'm dangerous," Pascal said. "I hope so. He's got to be worried. It's not like I'm an ordinary 2500. My rating is going up and I've had 2700 performances. On a good day I can give almost anyone in the world a hard time. I want one of those days!"

"Wouldn't you rather he think you're weak?" I asked. "Then he might let down his guard."

"I guess if he concentrated on the games where I fucked up, he might get overconfident, play sloppily, and screw up. Not likely, though! Besides, I don't want anyone thinking I'm a wimp."

Pascal focused next on the games in which he had White. "My first move will not be a secret," he said. The database showed that Pascal always began with the move e4, advancing his king pawn two squares. He told me that someday he'd like to open also with d4, advancing the queen pawn two squares. Then he'd be what Irina approvingly calls a two-headed monster. "That would be awesome," he said, "because my opponents wouldn't know what to expect." But for him to master d4 would require hundreds of hours of work. "And I haven't put in nearly enough effort on e4 yet."

Pascal turned to the file of games in which Bacrot had Black and ran through a dozen of them, move for move, at breakneck speed. "So, Paul," he said, "how will he respond to e4?"

I was glad that Pascal was involving me in his preparation, but was suspicious of his motives. Talking to me was yet another way to avoid studying.

"Who has White first?" I asked.

"I won't know until the day before."

I rifled through some of Bacrot's games and predicted he'd play one of the numerous lines in the Sicilian that promised an unbalanced, fight-to-the-death struggle.

"Why's that?" he said.

"Well it's the sharpest response in his repertoire, and in a two-game match, unless he's already ahead a game—and you're not going to let him be ahead—he'll want to play for a win and the Sicilian is perfect."

"Your logic is good," Pascal said, "but you don't take it far enough. You're not considering what I'll do. Have a look," and he opened the file of his own games as White and made a subfile of all of his Sicilian games. The ChessBase software has a command that sorts a collection of games into a tree so that you can see where one game branches off from the next. Well, the tree of Pascal's games as White in the Sicilian had very little trunk because the branching began as early as the second move. It was more of an unruly bush, a hedge that had never been trimmed, than a tree. A good number of the branches said 1–0, indicating that he had won. "I've played many different things against the Sicilian with good results," he said, "so Bacrot has to prepare for a lot of possibilities. It's not that all these things, the so-called Anti-Sicilians, are objectively great, but they have hidden poison if you don't know them well. I don't think he's had much time to prepare. He has other things on his mind now." Up until the championship, Bacrot was busy competing in an important team tournament, Russia v. the Rest of the World.

"I think he'll play . . . e5," he said, meaning that Bacrot would advance his own king pawn two squares, mimicking Pascal's first move, to bring about a double king-pawn opening. "I'm sure of it." Of the 224 games in which Bacrot faced e4, he responded . . . e5 just one third of them.

I was impressed by Pascal's confidence. If I were in his place, I'd be worried about all the defenses Bacrot had never played that he might debut for the first time. But you can't prepare for the unknown—there are just too many damn chess openings—and given that Bacrot was favored to win, he'd probably save any opening surprises for tougher opponents in later rounds.

Pascal's plan, if they reached a double king-pawn opening, was to develop his king knight on the second move, immediately attacking Bacrot's advanced pawn. This was the most forceful continuation, and the move commonly made in the position by players of all levels. The database showed that Pascal had faced . . . e5 eighty-five times. Besides developing the king knight, Pascal had assayed three rarer moves in this position, leading to the King's Gambit, the Bishop's Opening, and the Vienna. "I used to do anything to avoid mainline opening theory," Pascal said, "but there's a reason these old openings aren't played too often. Black can equalize if he's knows what he's doing. They're good on occasion for surprise value but they won't surprise Bacrot." He'd be ready for them after reviewing Pascal's previous games.

Pascal took comfort in knowing that Bacrot would have wasted some of his limited preparation time on the King's Gambit, the Bishop's Opening, and the Vienna, openings that he had no intention of repeating. But unfortunately Pascal would also do unnecessary preparation, starting in fact with Bacrot's second move. After the expected double king-pawn opening and White's development of his king knight, the database revealed that Bacrot responded in three different ways. Seventy-six percent of the time he defended the pawn with his queen knight—the commonest move in this position. Ten percent of the time he ignored the attack and instead used his king knight to attack Pascal's own king pawn—resulting in a trendy symmetrical position known as the Petroff or Russian Defense. Fourteen percent of the time he defended the king pawn with his queen pawn—a very unusual option called the Philidor Defense.

For the next hour Pascal concentrated on the Philidor, which he had rarely faced in tournament play. (He was not worried about the Petroff because he had studied the defense with Irina, who often played it.) At first glance, the Philidor looks suspect because it violates a basic tenet of opening theory: develop your pieces freely and quickly. Instead Black makes a quiet pawn move that hems in his own dark-squared bishop. But Bacrot's games demonstrated that the bishop has potential energy—it can spring to life later on. "The Philidor is very strange," said Pascal. "Nobody plays it these days except Bacrot. He's done OK with it. I doubt he'll play it against me, but I need to look at it in case."

IT WAS 10:30 P.M. AND PASCAL WAS READY TO GO TO SLEEP. ASIDE FROM OUR short dinner at the pub, we had spent the entire day in the hotel and yet he had managed to study chess for only two hours. The match with Bacrot was just three days away, and Pascal still hadn't looked at the openings that were most likely to arise.

At midnight he sprang up in his bed. He thought it was morning and was afraid we'd miss our flight. He was surprised when I told him that he had slept only an hour and a half. He asked why I was up.

"I've been playing through Dragons."

"That's not the way to get sleep," he said.

"I know," I said, "but I can't get them out of my mind. Why are you awake?"

"I'm not sure."

"Are you nervous?"

"No, I'm calm so far. I have a special motivation for trying to beat Bacrot."

"What's that?"

"Irina thinks he's cute."

"Get out!"

"It's true. And that's more motivating for me than hours of opening analysis," he continued. "Bacrot is playing now in Russia—the chess has probably tired him out and he won't get a break before Tripoli. Maybe he met a stunning Russian girl and is sad to leave. Maybe she kept him up late and distracted him from preparing for me.[4] Perhaps he's in love with her and won't be able to focus when we play. Maybe his mind will keep wandering back to those special nights while I quietly improve the position of my knights. I know there is hope for me." Chalk it up to sleep deprivation, or middle-of-the-night delirium, but the Canadian champion, normally a pillar of skepticism and reason, had revealed a sentimental side.

As we lay awake and talked, Pascal told me how difficult it was to be with one of the few women in a chess world full of male vultures. "The tournaments we play in together are often stressful in ways besides the chess," he said. Strong grandmasters, some with less than honorable intentions, offer to take Irina under their wing and turn her into the next women's world champion. Some don't even bother to conceal from Pascal their desire for her. At one tournament, a top GM pleaded with him to lend Irina out to him for the evening.

There were only fifteen people in the world who, like Bacrot, were rated higher than 2700. Many of Irina's closest male friends besides Pascal have come from this elite club. Her 2700-plus friends have included the Ukrainian world champion contender Vassily Ivanchuk, fourteen years her senior, and the American phenom Gata Kamsky.

When she was a teenager, she defied her parents by moving to Moscow for four months to live with Alexander Morozevich, six years her senior, one of the top ten players in the world. He was known for the startling originality of his openings, not to mention the originality of his personality. (Moro has a mystical outlook on the world and avoids making dates, Irina said, because he believes that people who are meant to be together will just show up at the same place at the same time.) He and Irina met after chatting online for months and playing hundreds of games on the Internet, none of which she won. Moro was being touted then as a future world champion, but their relationship was apparently deleterious to his chess. They broke up after his rating plunged a shocking seventy points, and she said that he blamed the decline on the fact that she was draining his energy. "Maybe I'm the sanest guy she's been with," Pascal joked. "But it sure sucks to be the lowest-rated boyfriend."[5]

Pascal was worried about what Irina really thought of his chess. He described to me the time she was watching him play a warm-up game on the Internet just before a New York Masters Tournament at the Marshall. She criticized the way he handled the White side of a Sicilian and told him his position was horrible. "I knew theory considered the line to be great," Pascal explained to me. "I told her the position would have been fine if I hadn't made an error. She still insisted the whole line was shitty." The discussion deteriorated into a colossal fight. "It was all about respect," he said. "I felt she didn't respect my chess, and she felt I discounted her opinions." With his confidence undermined, he blew two games at the Marshall against much weaker opponents and abandoned the tournament in the middle.

Pascal and Irina have been a conspicuous couple since the 2002 Olympiad in Bled. "Being a chess couple also has its pluses," Pascal told me. Each one understands what the other is going through at the chessboard and is tolerant of the crazy schedules and all the traveling that tournaments entail. "But it is very hard when we both play at the same time," Pascal said. "I don't think we've ever had a tournament where we both did well. If I'm playing great chess and she's not, I have to dampen my happiness and try to boost her spirits when I should be enjoying myself and concentrating on my own chess."

The two of them have completely different playing styles. He is a king-pawn player and wild attacker. She is a queen-pawn player and master of postional play. Their personalities are different too. He is sociable and extraordinarily polite and she is a recluse. When people meet her for the first time, they may judge her to be rude because she is prone to burying herself in a book or her favorite magazine, *The New Yorker*. "I hate initially talking to someone," she once told me. "I hate the hello part. Because I'm a chess player I'm used to doing stuff alone. So I like solitary activities—schoolwork, reading, studying, online poker."

Chess, of course, binds them together. It is such a rarefied art and sport that only a fellow international master of Pascal's strength can appreciate all the intricacies of his games, and the same is true for Irina. The two have spent hundreds if not thousands of hours analyzing each other's games and helping each other prepare for important tournaments. He has drawn the line at actually playing her. "I avoid it," he said, "because it bothers me that she can't turn her very competitive nature off when the player she's facing is me. I can't bring myself to be so competitive with her."

He told me that Irina thinks they should be able to play hard-fought blitz games and not let the result intrude on their relationship. "I don't think it's possible," Pascal said. "Our chess ratings are so close [only twenty-six points separated them] that if I started losing to her, I'd wonder what's wrong with me. But I wouldn't want to beat her, either, because I don't want to make her feel bad." Pascal was not looking forward to the possibility that someday they might have to play a crucial tournament game that neither of them could afford to lose or draw. "Maybe I have to win to get my GM title," he said, "and she has to win to clinch first place and a big cash prize." And he had a deeper worry: would their relationship survive if their ratings diverged and one of them advanced to the firmament of chess?

I WOULD LATER HAVE A CHANCE TO OBSERVE THEIR INTERACTION IN A seven-round blitz tournament at Susan Polgar's Chess Center in Rego Park, Queens. In the first two rounds, Pascal and Irina won easily. In the third game they found themselves scheduled to play each other. Tournament directors normally avoid pairing husband and wife or boyfriend and girlfriend. Although directors are not expected to know the details of every player's romantic life, this particular director, Paul Truong, the manager of the U.S. Women's Olympiad team, knew Irina and Pascal well. Either Truong was being mischievous or he was a stickler for adhering to the pairings served up by his computer program.

As the two of them waited for the round to start, Irina carefully adjusted her White pieces, looked down at the board so that she would avoid seeing him, and tried to focus and get herself into the zone. Her posture at the chessboard was very feline as she hunched over the pieces and curled a foot under herself on her chair. All and all, she was pretty relaxed. As for Pascal, he stared grimly into space with the look of someone who would rather be anywhere else. They limply shook hands, and then she predictably advanced her queen pawn two squares.

Pascal copied her move and soon they were playing a line of the Slav Defense that he had prepared extensively for a recent international tournament. Within the first minute, he had totally forgotten all of his preparation and made an inferior move. Her pawns now commanded the center, and soon she advanced one of them deep into his position, disrupting the communication of his pieces and tying his king to the middle of the back rank. Then she went straight for his king, throwing her army at him. To stave off immediate defeat, he had to jettison a rook for a less valuable knight. He used a lot of time trying to find a way out of the mess. When his clock had twenty seconds left and hers had forty seconds, she didn't try to finish him off or "flag" him—beat him on the clock—but slowly extended her hand to offer a draw. Of course, he accepted the act of mercy.

He was glum nonetheless. They had a brief, dispassionate discussion about where he went wrong. For him, the rest of the tournament was downhill. He overlooked simple attacks. He gave away pieces for no reason. His play was unrecognizable. He started coughing a lot during the penultimate round, and I handed him my Poland Spring. He told me after the game that he thought he was running a fever.

The next day he seemed tired but healthy, and I asked him why the game had made him ill. Was he mad at himself for forgetting his Slav analysis? Was he unhappy that Irina had completely dominated him? Nope, he said, it was because the game reminded him of something she wanted—to play chess with him at home—that he could not bring himself to do. "I was upset," he said, "because I know I can't satisfy her."

AT 10:00 A.M. ON JUNE 17, 2004, PASCAL AND I BOARDED A BRITISH AIRWAYS Airbus A320 for the three-hour, 1,470-mile flight from London to Tripoli. The boarding process was long. I recognized several chess stars among our fifty fellow passengers: thirty-three-year-old Michael Adams of England, the world's number seven player; Alexander Ivanov, a Russian

émigré from Massachusetts who has the curious habit, in the middle of a tense chess game, of cocking his head all the way back and staring at the ceiling for minutes at a time; and the American talent Hikaru Nakamura and his stepfather Sunil Weeramantry, the top player in Sri Lanka.

We had been buckled into our seats for half an hour when the pilot came on the loudspeaker and apologized for the delay. "We haven't left the gate," he announced, "because we must accommodate oversized cargo that is not easy to fit into the storage bay." I looked out the window and saw four men struggling with a huge wooden coffin. I wondered whether there was a corpse inside or whether it was being sent to Tripoli to retrieve the headless body of a hapless British citizen. Oversized cargo? I love pilot-speak. They talk of a *near-miss* when they really mean a *near-collision*, but collision is too scary a word to utter thirty thousand feet above the ground. The men finally got the oversized cargo into the storage bay, and the rest of the flight was uneventful.

Pascal and I were seated next to a Libyan national who introduced himself as an oil tanker captain. I realized how little we knew about his country. Back in the States I had failed to find a travel guide to Libya, and I wasn't any more successful in a bookstore at Heathrow, despite the direct flights to Tripoli. There was some information on the Internet, but it was geared more to people who planned to visit the desert. One Web page warned against swimming anywhere in Tripoli, including pools, because of African insects that carried disease.

The captain was friendly and told me about the capital city while Pascal slept. He wrote out a list of his favorite restaurants and the best traditional dishes to order. He did not live in the city, he said, but gave me the name and phone number of a fellow oilman in Tripoli and insisted we call him if we ever needed help. Help with what? the paranoid in me wondered. Why would we need help? He told me not to swim in the Mediterranean in Tripoli—it was polluted—but to go to the most beautiful beaches in the world thirty miles away. He warned me that alcohol was illegal in his country, but he thought that our hotel, because it catered to foreigners, might slip us some on the sly. I was amused by our mutual prejudices. I feared that all Libyans were closet terrorists and he thought that all Americans were lushes.

We arrived in Tripoli a little after 3:00 P.M., and the dozen of us on the plane who were heading to the tournament were greeted by Walid, a man in his mid-twenties who worked for the Libyan Olympic Committee. "Welcome, chess players!" he said.

"*Shookran*" ("Thank you" in Arabic), I replied.

"You are Libyan I see! Very good!"

Walid gathered our passports and gave them to a group of immigration officers huddled in a glassed-in office in the corner. Two other flights arrived, bearing another ten players and their companions, from China and India, and Walid took their passports, too. We were kept waiting in a stuffy receiving area whose muffled sound system played Celine Dion in French. On one wall near a prayer room was a giant portrait of Muammar Gadhafi, the first of many we would see in Tripoli. He looked like a dandy, in his turquoise jacket with a bright yellow lapel, oversize shades, and natty brown hat. His nose jutted upward in an arrogant, I'm-above-it-all pose. Next to the portrait were two trilingual signs, in Arabic, French, and English. One said: "Partners Not Wage Workers." The other read: "No Democracy Without Peoples Congresses and Committees Everywhere."

I took out my digital camera and started to snap a picture of Gadhafi's portrait. Pascal grabbed my arm. "I wouldn't do that," he said.

"But the Chinese players are taking pictures," I said.

"Still, I wouldn't."

Pascal was right. Later I asked one of the chess officials whether cameras were allowed and he said definitely not, because the airport was considered to be a military installation. He said he had seen officers confiscate cameras and smash them.

All the chess players were sweating, and a man named Hadi, Walid's young assistant, gave us bottled water and orange soda. After more than an hour, Walid returned the passports of all the London arrivals except me and told the group to proceed through customs. Pascal stayed behind. I asked Walid if there was a problem. He said everything was fine and that it just took time to write my visa in Arabic. He worked his cell phone as we talked and then he walked away.

I could see a compact man in the glassed-in office waving my passport and arguing with his colleagues. I knew it was mine because of the rainbow of airport security stickers on the back that I had never removed. For some twenty minutes I watched from afar as they flipped through the passport. I had had it for nine years, and in my last full-time job, as president of Encyclopaedia Britannica, I'd hopscotched often between our foreign offices, spending a day or two in Tokyo, a night in Poznan, Poland, a few days in Budapest. The Libyans studied the myriad of passport stamps and unfolded the attached visas from Brazil and Russia. Apparently they were not familiar with the concept of business travel, and I was too dowdily dressed to be a globe-trotting prince and too square to be a rock star. Besides, someone who traveled for pleasure would spend more than one night in Tokyo or Poland. I wondered if they didn't like my Jewish-sounding name.

I've never been good at waiting, particularly when I'm hot, so I took out my official letter of invitation from Mohammed Gadhafi and the Libyan Olympic Committee, walked into the immigration office— which was surprisingly cool, unlike the waiting area—and sat down on a couch between two uniformed men. The six officers were not pleased that I had entered their space. They glared at me and shook their heads. "Maybe this will help," I said, handing the invitation letter to a man whose name tag identified him as working for British Airways. He read the letter and calmed down. He started pleading in Arabic with the head honcho, who was holding my passport. But the man would not budge and motioned with annoyance for me to leave.

By this time, the Chinese and Indian chess players had all departed. Pascal and I were the only travelers left in the waiting area. We had long since finished our drinks, and no new ones were offered. The two of us were dripping and we tried to guess whether the temperature was 110 degrees or 120 or maybe even more. The man from British Airways approached. He said that the Libyan government had levied a hefty fine against the airline for letting me into the country without a visa. But the players didn't have visas when they arrived, I protested. Yes, he said, but their names and not mine were on a special list of 217 invitees. He said that he should have sent me right back to London, but it was now too late because the plane had already departed. He said that he needed to borrow my tickets and call London to see how the snafu had happened. I wanted to hold onto my tickets, but I didn't think I had a choice. After the man left, I was anxious and I slipped Pascal the name and phone number of my contact at the Belgian embassy.

Walid appeared, smiling. He raced with his cell phone into the immigration office and handed it to the top guy. Everyone was relieved. Walid had obviously reached someone who clarified my situation. Walid and the head guy came over. "Everything is OK, Mr. Paul," Walid said. "I ordered them to give you visa. It will take few minutes."

The head guy, who could not speak English, apologized to me through Walid: "I'm sorry for inconvenience."

"*Shookran,*" I said.

Walid urged Pascal to go ahead, explaining that the last bus to the hotel would be leaving soon with his luggage and that he would personally give me a ride as soon as they wrote up my visa. Walid left to take another phone call. I was feeling guilty that Pascal had stayed with me for three hours when he could have been preparing for the World Championship. He was a little hesitant to leave me but was concerned about his baggage. I believed that my problems were over, and I urged him to take the bus. I did ask him if he'd mind switching our hotel accommodations so that we shared a room. Ostensibly this was so I could watch him when the spirit finally moved him to prepare for Bacrot, but I was now nervous about staying alone. Pascal agreed, and Walid walked him to the bus.

Another half an hour passed before the man from British Airways returned. "I've arranged with another airline to fly you to Tunisia," he said. "You have no authority to be in Libya and must leave immediately." I told him that while he was gone my visa had been approved. He charged over to the immigration office. A flight arrived, presumably from Tunisia, and there was not one Western face among the crowd that disembarked. The British Airways man returned with three immigration officers. "Mr. Paul," one of them said, "you need to take this plane back to Tunisia." I told them I wasn't going and handed them the phone number of Nijar, the tournament organizer, and urged them to call him. They retreated to the office.

I started pacing, something I used to do as a child when I was terrified. I thought of Ann and Alex and was relieved that they were safe. I wished I was home with them. I recited in my mind Alex's favorite Dr. Seuss story, *If I Ran the Circus,* and when I thought about the Drum-Tummied Snumm, I noticed that I was surrounded by six uniformed men.

"Mr. Paul," the head officer said, "you arrived on this flight from Tunisia."

"No, I came from London."

"You arrived from Tunisia without a passport."

"I came from London, and *you* have my passport."

The men puffed out their chests and got as close to me as six men could without touching me. Walid returned at that moment. "Don't move, Mr. Paul," he implored. "Don't lift your arms." I stood still and the men did not back off. Walid stuck five fingers in the air, indicating, I thought, that he needed five more minutes to reach someone, and pleaded with my captors.

I was clammy and dizzy and told the man whose face was in mine that I had come to Libya to play chess with Mohammed Gadhafi. The men retreated, and Walid gave me a thumbs-up and told me again that everything would be OK. The officers had a loud, panicked discussion. The plane from Tunisia took off, and Walid, on his cell phone, walked away.

Twenty minutes later, the six men reappeared and made a half circle around me as I sat against the wall. "Since you refuse to go to Tunisia, Mr. Paul," one said, "you must go on a plane to . . . ," and he skipped a beat and intoned dramatically, "Moscow. Moscow with no passport."

I actually laughed. This must be their idea of an American's worst nightmare, but they were a couple of decades behind the times, and anyway I had friends in Moscow. I could always call Kasparov's office.

"Mr. Paul, you look faint," the man continued. "Please step into the Jetway, where it's cool." I stayed put, not wanting them to shove me onto the plane.

The men moved in closer. "I demand to speak to the Belgian embassy," I said, "the U.S. Interests Section of the Belgian embassy."

Now they laughed, but my request stalled them. I had this Monty Python image of Belgians armed with waffles and French fries rushing to my defense—funny thoughts are my way of distracting myself when I'm frightened. The men backed off again and huddled. Hadi returned and sat next to me. Of all the Libyans in the airport, he spoke the best English. "Will this turn out OK?" I asked him.

"I don't know," Hadi said. "I really don't know." While the words themselves were not encouraging, it was the first time anyone had been honest with me in Libya, and I wanted to hug him.

When Hadi left, I took comfort in Seuss.

Then he shakes himself loose!
He starts down in a dive
Such as no man on earth
Could come out alive!
But he smiles as he falls
And no fear does he feel.
His nerves are like iron,
His muscles like steel.

I overheard one of the men suggesting that if I refused to go to Moscow they should send me to Baghdad. He may have been joking, but Russia without a passport was starting to seem pretty good. The men moved in again, this time more menacingly. Walid reappeared and started yelling at them, punctuating his Arabic with words I understood: "*Time* yadda yadda yadda. *New York Times* yadda yadda yadda. *Wall Street Journal* yadda yadda yadda." I didn't think he was listing my writing credentials but was instead warning them that if they touched me it would become an international incident. His cell phone rang, and he looked relieved: he'd finally received the call he needed (I never learned from whom) to obtain me a visa—five or six hours after my arrival in Tripoli.

In a final Kafkaesque touch, the immigration agents called me into their office and explained that there was no blank page in my passport to which they could affix the visa. What do you mean, I said, the last four pages are empty. No they're not, they insisted, and they opened the passport to the back and displayed blank, completely blank, pages. I was parched and feverish, my contact lenses were too dry for me to see well, and in any event I didn't have the reading glasses I needed to wear over my contacts. But I knew there was nothing on those pages. There are country stamps here, they said, and it is illegal for us to cover them. This absurd discussion continued for five minutes, until Walid appeared, put his hand on my shoulder, and ordered them to attach the visa.

After they obliged, Walid whisked me out of the airport and into a van with Hadi and two other Libyans. "I told you everything would work out," he said. "I made it happen."

"Yes!" I high-fived him. "You're the man!" On the forty-five-minute ride to the hotel, they joked that they were driving me to Tunisia. I laughed but began to wonder where they were actually taking me. I was relieved when the van pulled up to the tournament site, the El Mahary Hotel, a fifteen-story building located off a major highway along a section of the Mediterranean filled with tankers and cargo ships.

Nijar Al El Haj, a large bear of a man, greeted me in the lobby. "Now that you're finally here," he said, "everything will be fine. You're among chess players now. You can relax."

When I found Pascal, he was ashen. "I'm sorry I left you," he said. "I'm happy you're here."

"It's OK," I said. "I suggested that you leave. Did you do any chess?"

"Nope," he said. "I just wandered around, thinking about what I should do if you didn't show up. I found the press room. I sent an e-mail to my mother telling her that you weren't here. I thought of sending you an e-mail, but that seemed silly because I couldn't imagine you had Internet access." We went to our room, and I told him everything that had happened. The State Department had warned me that the room would be bugged, but that didn't inhibit our discussion. I figured that any eavesdropper already knew about my detention in the airport.

As we talked, the room filled with an unfamiliar pungent burning smell. It took us a while to find the source. The lampshade on the nightstand concealed the corpse of a rotten pear that was stuck to the incandescent bulb and had ballooned, as it toasted, to larger than a softball. It was now close to midnight, and Pascal wanted to go to sleep. Yet another day had passed without his preparing his openings for Bacrot. Only one day, Friday, remained before the match.

THE EL MAHARY WAS ONE OF THE OLDER HOTELS IN THE CITY THAT CATERED to businessmen, and yet by Western standards it was scarcely adequate. The first time we plugged in Pascal's computer, which housed his all-important chess preparation, the outlet exploded and we lost electricity in that wall. Fortunately the computer was not harmed. The toilet ran loudly most of the time, and when it didn't, it was because we had no water at all. The shower water was brown. The air-conditioning didn't work, and so we needed to keep the sliding balcony door open at night, but the din of cars without mufflers interfered with our sleep.

Pascal rose early on Friday, having convinced himself that he was going to put in a full day of chess preparation. After breakfast we went to the press room and he checked his e-mail. A kid at an Atlanta chess camp was complaining that Pascal still hadn't answered his question about a game he had lost.

I had trouble checking my e-mail because I had forgotten my password. Pascal offered to find it.

"You can do that?" I said, wondering whether every twenty-something could pull off identity theft.

After a few minutes of tinkering with my computer and instant-messaging a friend for advice, Pascal had recovered my password. "You've seen the inner nerd in me," he said. "I usually try to hide it." Now I knew whom to suspect if my bank balance mysteriously plummeted.

Pascal then signed onto the Internet Chess Club under his nom de plume Charlatan and noticed that "Stanley Park," his buddy Jack Yoos, was online. "To the extent that I'm prepared at all for Tripoli," Pascal told me, "I owe it to Jack. I hate chess preparation. He does the heavy lifting. I'll tell him my feelings and intuition about opening ideas, and then he'll flesh them out or tell me why they don't work."

Pascal and Jack chatted briefly through ICC's instant-messaging software:

> STANLEY PARK: They posted your odds for the World Championship on ChessBase.
> CHARLATAN: Don't tell me☺
> STANLEY PARK: I thought about responding, "but what's Bacrot's blitz rating on ICC?" But then I thought better about giving away your hand.

Pascal excelled at speed chess. Although he was ranked 653rd in the world in leisurely over-the-board chess, at five-minute chess he had been ranked as high as third in the world on ICC. If Pascal and Bacrot tied their two slow games, they'd play two games at the rapid time control of twenty-five minutes each per game. If the rapid match was tied, they'd have a blitz playoff, in which Jack was convinced Pascal would prevail.

> CHARLATAN: Glad you didn't show my hand!
> STANLEY PARK: If you make it past Bacrot, I could try to send you some other openings to try to spice things up.

> CHARLATAN: Yes, but let's go one step at a time☺
> STANLEY PARK: Like some mainline Svesh material, for example.

Jack was referring to the Sveshnikov, one of the most popular and heavily analyzed openings of the year. (Jack had in fact prepared Pascal to play the Sveshnikov, but a sideline, not the mainline.) The 2004 ChessBase database had 20,850 games with the Sveshnikov.

> CHARLATAN: Ugh☹ Don't scare me!

Pascal signed off ICC and went to the ChessBase Web site to see what the bookmakers were saying about his chances. Pascal scanned the list of 128 players until he found his name near the bottom. As the 114th seed, he was given odds of 13 million to 1. (Irina's old flame Morozevich, who inexplicably withdrew at the last moment, had odds of 7 to 1.)

"Well we knew I wasn't the favorite," he said. "But look at Amon Simutowe's odds—one hundred million to one. I guess I can feel good." (International master Amon Simutowe, the top player from Zambia, was attending UMBC's arch collegiate chess rival, the University of Texas at Dallas.) Near the top of the list was number fifteen seed Etienne Bacrot, with odds of 62 to 1. Pascal told me that Bacrot had just had a string of great tournaments. "When those are rated," Pascal said, "Bacrot will actually be the number three seed. I'm OK with it. These top guys are not infallible. I've looked at Bacrot's games. He does make mistakes."

It was almost noon, and we decided to take our first and only walk outside the El Mahary. Friday and Saturday were the equivalent of the weekend, and so most Libyans were not at work and storefronts were boarded up. We stayed on the main road overlooking the Mediterranean. The street was pretty much deserted. We went by a small, makeshift amusement park in which the bumper cars were colliding and the teacups were spinning, but nobody was in them. The few people we passed stared at us or crossed the street toward us to get a better look. After we'd walked perhaps a mile, Pascal said he felt out of place being the only Westerners on the street and suggested we go back to the hotel.

He told me that he had also been uncomfortable on the bus ride from the airport because there was no security and anybody could tell that the bus was carrying foreigners because of a large banner that said "World

Chess Champions." The tight security FIDE had promised the Israelis was nowhere evident. We weren't provided with bodyguards, and although everyone who entered the El Mahary had to pass through a metal detector, no one was searched when it went off.

We returned to the hotel and got ready for the opening ceremony. It was a FIDE tradition that the ceremony include a traditional dance of the host country. I kept thinking of a dance my friend Matt had performed for me that he said we'd see in Libya. "Now we are airplanes," Matt said, with his arms stretched out like wings. "Gaboom!" he said, and he fell to the ground. "Now we dance disco," and Matt demonstrated. "Gaboom!" he said, and fell down again. The actual dance was much less exciting. It involved peasants and farmers fighting over an urn of scarce water.

Whoever choreographed the ceremony went out of their way to counter the image of the country as a militaristic police state based on a cult of personality surrounding Muammar Gadhafi. There were no armed guards or police officers. We all stood awkwardly for the Libyan national anthem and watched an interminable film on the history of the "peace-loving" Great Socialist People's Libyan Arab Jamahiriya. The film never mentioned Gadhafi by name, although we were treated to lots of footage of him in a bright red jacket inspecting construction sites and reclining regally inside a large concrete pipe. The film would have been more effective for a Western audience if it had not included the loaded word "jihad," even if it was in the context of Libyans' fighting their "Italian occupiers" in the early twentieth century.

Pascal noticed that Gadhafi himself—or if it was not him, a perfect body double—was sitting serenely in the audience next to Kirsan Ilyumzhinov and other FIDE dignitaries. Gadhafi had no conspicuous security detail and wore an understated gray jacket. The fact that he did not speak at the ceremony seemed to be a deliberate reinforcement of the message that the country no longer centered on him. I turned around in my seat and snapped a photo of Leader before Pascal, who had visions of undercover marksmen taking me down, could stop me.

Gadhafi's son Mohammed spoke at the ceremony. He, too, sported a tailored European suit to make the international guests more comfortable and gave a biblical-sounding speech that claimed chess was the human mind's highest calling and described chess champions as the finest

specimens of our species. The translator was amusingly bad. Her into-
nation was completely off ("wel-COME chess champ-EEE-ons"), and
Pascal giggled at inappropriate points during Gadhafi's solemn remarks.
Fifty-six women in paramilitary outfits, each carrying one of the fifty-six
flags of the participating countries, marched slowly to the stage. The flag
bearers did a catchy dance in which the all-green Libyan flag seemed to
pursue and ensnare its American counterpart and vice versa. This was
evidently the first time an American flag had flown in Libya under
Muammar Gadhafi's rule. After the stage was cleared, it was illuminated
by green strobes. Disco music blasted, smoke from dry ice filled the
stage, and a trapdoor opened in the middle. Out of the door rose a six-
foot-high phallic trophy for which the chess players thought they were
competing. Later the players learned that it was an oversize replica of the
actual, foot-high trophy.

Antoaneta Stefanova, the newly crowned women's world champion
from Bulgaria, came to the stage and drew lots to see which players
would have White in the next day's game. Pascal was pleased with the
drawing: he had Black in the first game. "That's good," he whispered,
"because if I win the first game, I'm in a great spot with White last. And
if I lose as Black, having White last will give me a chance to recover."

After the two-and-a-half-hour ceremony, we were ushered into a
crowded reception area for food and drink. Nijar told me that Mohammed
Gadhafi would see me shortly. I spied three bottles of Beck's on one of the
buffet tables and, in the interest of fulfilling my secondly duties, wound my
way through the thirsty players to snag a beer. Alas, it turned out to be nonalcoholic. Pascal was across the room talking to a woman from FIDE when
a young Libyan man approached me and introduced himself. He looked
around nervously and asked in a low voice in bad English whether I could
help him get a job in the United States. I told him I didn't know anything
about immigration or work permits. He whispered, in a tone of desperation, "I need to get out of here. You must help me." Then he headed off.

I downed the ersatz beer. A child waiter offered me a platter of dates.
I worked my way toward Pascal on the far side of the room but was
thwarted by two Libyan men my age who blocked my path. "Mr. Paul,
how are you enjoying the food of our peace-loving country?" one of
them asked.

"The dates are good," I said. "Very fresh."

"I'm glad, Mr. Paul," the man continued. "Why have you come to Libya, Mr. Paul?"

"For the chess tournament, of course. I'm a journalist and I write about chess."

"Please come with us a moment, Mr. Paul." And the two men guided me through the crowd into the corner of the room. "We are information officers, Mr. Paul, and we need you to complete some paperwork." He handed me a form and a pen. The form asked first for my name and home address. The Libyan authorities already had that information so I saw no harm in providing it again. The rest of the form asked for the names of any Libyans I had spoken to in Tripoli, and the date, time, and subject of the conversations. Clearly I was expected to report the exchange I just had, but I didn't want to get the man in trouble. I also wondered if he might have been a plant who wanted to goad me into saying something compromising that would get me tossed out of the country or worse. So I left that part of the form blank and just signed my name. The information officer who had been doing all of the talking shook his head and said in an incredulous tone, "No conversations, Mr. Paul. No conversations. Then you are free to go."

After the interrogation, I returned to the reception. Nijar told me an urgent matter prevented Gadhafi from seeing me that night but that the interview would happen in the morning. I found Pascal and vowed to myself that I'd stay by his side, so that it would be harder for the "information officers" to isolate me.

"That's Bacrot," Pascal said, pointing to a man in a black T-shirt and black pants.

"Did you guys speak?"

"Yeah, small talk. He said he was married and expecting a child."

"Was he civil?"

"Yes, but he looked arrogant. He wants to beat me."

"No surprise! You want to beat him."

"Yeah but I don't like it when it's so obvious. He also looked tired."

"Good."

Pascal had to attend a mandatory meeting of all the players. The meeting was not officially open to the press, but I tagged along anyway.

FIDE representatives explained the time control and the prize fund. They asked players to provide a bank account to which prize money could be wired. The international chess federation was generally inept and corrupt, but in this meeting I felt sorry for the FIDE representatives. The players acted like spoiled children and asked all sorts of questions that would have been better handled in private. One player said he didn't have a bank account and would have difficulty cashing a check as large as the prize he anticipated. Could FIDE give him the prize in cash? he wondered. Another semi-hysterical player was concerned that he might be penalized for violating the FIDE dress code. His luggage had been lost by the airline, he said, so he would be forced to wear the same rumpled clothes every day.

IT WAS 9:00 P.M. BY THE TIME WE GOT BACK TO OUR ROOM. OUR POSSESSIONS had been shifted around. The State Department had warned me that my hard drive would be copied, but it wasn't just my laptop that was in a different place. My tape recorder had been moved from my computer case to my garment bag. My contact lens case had been opened and moved from the sink in the bathroom to the top of the television.

Pascal was finally ready to look at a chessboard, and I didn't want to distract him by pointing out the dislocated items or describing my encounter with the officers. "Paul," he said, as he turned on his computer, "I'm running out of ways to avoid preparing. Now I know I have Black tomorrow, so I have no excuses."

Pascal explained that Bacrot generally opened with the queen pawn but recently had been starting with the king pawn. If he advanced the queen pawn on his first move, Pascal planned to push his own queen pawn and steer the game into what's called the . . . a6 Slav. "It is a good defense for me," he said, "because there's less theory than the King's Indian, the Queen's Indian, and the Nimzo-Indian." There was still plenty of theory to review because such heavy hitters as Kasparov and Morozevich had recently taken it up. But the beauty of the . . . a6 Slav was that it was a defense that Bacrot himself played as Black. "It can be a very good strategy to play what they play against them," Pascal said. "They may have no idea what to do because they've convinced themselves that Black is equal in all lines." Pascal opened the file of his own games and ran through the six in which he had played the . . . a6 Slav. "It's good," he added, "that there are not that many interesting games in ChessBase for him to see what I'm going to play." For the next hour Pascal looked at the most recent . . . a6 Slav games played at the highest levels, and he studied a published monograph about the opening that he had brought with him from the States.

"I know this stuff pretty well," he concluded, "so it's time to look at king-pawn stuff." He went through a dozen of Bacrot's e4 games. "Look here. He does badly against things that aren't standard. He prefers ordinary stuff." Because Bacrot was new to e4, he would understandably have focused his study on the most popular lines. "I'll vary quickly from the mainline," Pascal continued. "I'm not into working at home to unearth a novelty on the twenty-first move of the Sveshnikov. I don't spend hours in advance refuting things. That's what Kasparov has his team of *patzer* seconds to do—2600 *patzers*. I'll refute things at the board." So he told me he planned to vary on the eighth move of the Sveshnikov with a rare bishop move pioneered by Bent Larsen, my old simul foe. Pascal examined the file on the bishop move that Jack had put together. "I have a good short-term memory," Pascal said, "although I have been known occasionally to mess up move order. I can commit lots of lines to memory just by rapidly playing though them. Just don't quiz me a week from now."

Pascal quit studying around midnight when we were distracted by the smell of incense that seemed to be pumped into our room through the poorly functioning air conditioner. "Paul, maybe they're trying to poison you," he joked.

"That's Mr. Paul," I said, and I told him the story of my confrontation with the information officers.

He was concerned. "I will try to make all this crap worthwhile," he said, "by doing well tomorrow."

"Cool!"

"I'm in a pretty good mood, but this is a strange place."

ON GAME DAY, PASCAL GOT UP AT 8:00 A.M. AND REVIEWED HIS OPENINGS for a couple of hours. In the meantime I went to the press room and checked my e-mail. I had a message from British Airways that our return flight from Tripoli had been canceled because the airline was reducing its service to Libya from three flights a week to two. Because Pascal's and my reservations were not linked in the airline's computer system—I had simply matched his itinerary—there was no guarantee we would get the same flight home. Moreover, his flight could change again depending on how long he lasted in the knockout tournament. I did not want to return to the airport alone. I was determined to make sure our plane reservations were linked so that as Pascal's ticket changed, mine would automatically change, too. I returned to the room and tried to call Ann so that she could arrange this, but I couldn't get an outside line.

I decided to try the hotel's business center, and when I arrived, I was accosted by a Libyan who implored me to arrange for him to be admitted to an American university. After I brushed the man off, the smiling attendant in the business center, whom I had not met before, greeted me as if we knew each other: "Hello, Mr. Paul."

Everywhere I went in the hotel I had the eerie experience of strangers knowing my name. The business center attendant could not get me an outside line to the States, even though I noticed that he had no difficulty connecting two other people to their respective home countries. I was reduced to making an Internet phone call, which meant that I had to shout into a bad microphone attached to a PC. By the time I reached Ann, the two information officers who had questioned me the day before were sitting on a couch across the room. They heard my whole conversation. I asked Ann to call Pascal's mother and make sure his travel agent had my credit card number and instructions to match Pascal's flights however they changed. She expressed reluctance about giving out my credit card, and I struggled not to sound panicked as I impressed on her the importance of doing this. After the call ended, the officers interrogated me again.

"Mr. Paul, how is your stay?" the foreman asked.

"I'm looking forward to the chess," I said.

"A noncommittal answer, Mr. Paul," the man said. "Perhaps today you will be more committal in completing the paperwork." He handed me the same form he had given me the evening before. There were now two Libyans who had asked for my help in getting to the United States, but again I signed my name and left the rest blank.

"Still no conversations," the man said. "How very interesting! Enjoy the chess, Mr. Paul, if that's really why you're here."

I went to the tournament office to ask Nijar when my interview with Mohammed Gadhafi would take place. He said it had been canceled again. I wondered now whether there was a connection between the information officers' intercepting me twice just before scheduled interviews and their last-minute cancellation. If it was this hard to meet Gadhafi's son for a game of chess, I didn't think there was much chance of my getting together with his father. I put in a request through Nijar's office to meet Kalmykian and FIDE president Kirsan Ilyumzhinov and play chess with him. One way or another, I was determined to face a world leader at the board.

I reminded myself that I got into trouble whenever I was not with Pascal. I returned to our room and decided to spare him the details of my latest encounter until after his game. He had just finished his preparation—"I don't like to do much chess just before playing; I prefer to relax"—and so we went to the dining room for an early lunch. Bacrot arrived while we were eating dessert. He was dressed in all white, like Tom Wolfe. "He's gone from black to white," Pascal said. "Is that because he has the White pieces today or because he's in a peaceful mood?"

"Maybe we can tell by what he eats."

We watched him fill his plate with a pile of fruit and vegetables, in contrast to Pascal, who had been a real carnivore. "He's clearly not ready to fight," I said. "You chose the right food. Protein fuels the brain."

"There you go," he said. "Knowing science is useful. That's good. You boost my confidence."

Bacrot was hesitating at the soup pot. I reminded Pascal that the lamb and tomato stew was indigestibly spicy, and we joked about approaching Bacrot and recommending it. "My stomach is tough," he said, "but he looks like the delicate sort."

"He's a pushover," I said. "Look at him in the silly white outfit. He looks like a freshman sailor lost at sea."

We asked the waiter to charge our meal to the room. He asked us for the room number.

"510," Pascal said.

"610?" the waiter said.

"No, 510."

"610?" the waiter repeated.

"I said 510."

The waiter wrote down 610. As we left, Pascal said to me, "Well, I'm not going to be more Catholic than the pope. I don't plan to be very Christian this afternoon at the chessboard."

We returned to our room. There was an hour and a half before the game, and Pascal confided that he got nervous not when he was actually playing but when he was waiting for the game to begin. He said that he routinely used to get nauseated just seconds before the game and often vomited. The problem started in late elementary school, when he was ten or eleven. "I was going through puberty," he said. "My voice changed, I got tall overnight, and I became a bundle of nerves." He particularly disliked waiting around in the tournament hall before his game, and he tried to orchestrate his arrival so that he reached the board precisely as the game started.

When he was fifteen and played in the Canadian Junior Championship, the arbiter made them sit at the board for ten minutes before starting the clocks. "It was torture," Pascal said. "How do you pass the time? You can't warm up like in tennis. There's only so much time you can kill doodling on the score sheet or writing your opponent's name really slowly." Whenever he had a long wait, he got sick—and felt better once he did. "I hated the anticipation of getting sick," he said, "wondering when it was going to happen." Once the game started, he usually felt fine. Most of the time no one else knew he was ill because he would escape to the bathroom or go outside, but occasionally he didn't make it. He even managed to hide it from his parents. When his father eventually found out, he told Pascal that he, too, had gotten sick in his youth before exams and in other pressured situations.

Pascal got ill before tennis matches, too. His coaches would freak out— they couldn't believe he'd have the energy to play after he threw up—yet he didn't know any other way, and he managed not only to play but to excel, earning the commendation of Most Valuable Player at his school.

"Did you get sick on other occasions?" I asked.

"Yes."

"Around girls?"

"Yeah, it could happen."

"That could happen to anyone," I said. "I imagine you didn't have much experience at an all-boys school."

"It's fine to be clumsy or a little anxious around girls," Pascal said. "But for me it was very bad because I'd vomit. The charm of meeting a girl quickly goes away when you throw up." As the president of his high school, he once gave a group of girls a tour of the school. "I got sick in front of all of them," he said. "The first moment was awful but then the girls were very worried that I was ill—of course I didn't tell them it was because of nerves—and they fussed over me and were very solicitous. It turned out OK."

Pascal consulted two sports psychologists. "Maybe the techniques they suggested—about breathing and other things to get you in a good mood—work for less cerebral people," he said. "I found it too basic." He needed something more complicated than being told to inhale and exhale deeply and picture a quiet lake with a couple of whistling birds. There was one thing they said that he liked: if you're intimidated by an opponent, imagine him sitting on a toilet bowl. Realize everyone has to go to the bathroom, even the most formidable adversary. "So if you're playing Kasparov," he said, "just think of him in the position."

"Are you feeling OK now?" I said. "Just picture Bacrot taking a dump."

"No, no," he laughed. "I'm fine. I stopped getting sick a couple years ago, although I still don't like to arrive early."

"What changed?"

"Not sure."

"You just became more confident over time?"

"No, it wasn't confidence. I think I became super aware of getting ill, and somehow broke the cycle of anticipating getting sick and then actually getting sick. I also got involved with Irina. I think my priorities changed and I realized that it was not worth becoming ill over chess or tennis."

Even though his pregame anxiety was now under control, Pascal was not the kind of person who could sit down at the chessboard and put everything else that was going on in his life out of his head. "When Irina plays chess," he said, "she totally loses herself in the game and can escape from the annoyances of everyday life. It's not really an escape for me. I need to be in a good mood to play well. It doesn't happen all that often because real life is always intruding." When he won the Canadian Championship in Vancouver, it helped that he was with his friend Jack. "We were always having fun and cooking dinner together," Pascal said, "so I was in a great mood." When he played in the Montreal International last summer, where he made his first grandmaster norm, he was generally feeling good. Before each game he had this routine of speaking with Irina. "She'd wish me good luck," he said, "and then I'd play and try to focus. I did well for the entire tournament except for the one time when something was off in my conversation with her. Afterward I couldn't concentrate and I reached an endgame that should have been a draw but I started playing very quickly and very stupidly. I wanted to go home."

It was now forty-five minutes until his game with Bacrot, and he told me that it was time to put chess aside, stop our heavy conversation, and do "the most inane thing possible, something that requires no thinking whatsoever." We didn't have much to work with. The television in our room received only two English-language stations, and the first, CNN International, was hardly comforting. Paul Johnson Jr., an American engineer, had been kidnapped in Saudi Arabia, and CNN was replaying footage of his distraught wife pleading with his captors not to behead him.

Luckily, *Star Trek II: The Wrath of Khan* was on the other channel. We watched as Lieutenant Uhura told Kirk, "Captain, I'm getting something on the distress channel."

"Maybe," I said, "she's picking up Bacrot's cries of anguish as you crush him."

Pascal laughed.

A few minutes later Kirk was being philosophical: "Admiral, how we deal with death is just as important as how we deal with life."

"He's speaking to you, Pascal," I said. "He's telling you that if you reach a bad position, you must not cave in."

"I'll keep that in mind," he said, and he pantomimed a sizzling tennis serve.

"Strike!" I shouted.

Pascal looked deflated. "Shit! If you thought that was baseball, I'm in trouble."

"No, no. I meant to say, 'Ace.' I got the word wrong. Sports isn't my thing."

He served again.

"Ace!" I shouted.

"Better!" he said. "Now I'm going to beat the punk."

With fifteen minutes to go, he changed into dark trousers and a striped shirt, put aside the tie ("It's too constricting"), and made sure the long tails of the shirt were not tucked in.[6] Tails out was the fashion trend, and so there was little chance FIDE was going to fine him for dressing inappropriately. "Some chess players are superstitious about what they wear," Pascal said. "I couldn't care less. Irina always gives me this you're-too-rational speech. She's superstitious about her shirt, her jacket, the pen she uses." With ten minutes left, Pascal blasted Nirvana's "Smells Like Teen Spirit" on my computer, pretended to sink a basket, and aced another serve.

"What's Bacrot doing now?" I asked.

"Listening to the 'Marseillaise,'" he said, "and puffing on a Gauloise."

Pascal timed his exit from the hotel room so that he arrived at the chessboard just as the game was set to begin. He shook hands with Bacrot, who had swapped his all-white outfit for a dark jacket and blue dress shirt. The two men said nothing to each other. Pascal started the clock, and Bacrot quickly moved his king pawn forward two squares. Unlike our hotel room, the tournament hall was air-conditioned. For the first ten minutes, people were allowed to approach the players and take photographs. There were only three other journalists covering the first round, which I thought was not surprising, given my visa problems. There were no spectators at all. (Gadhafi, I learned later, is against spectating in many arenas, not just chess, and believes people should be participating in sports rather than watching them.) The other observers were FIDE officials, the players' seconds and family members, and four information officers, who did not watch the players but seemed to follow every move of mine, instead. After the photo opportunity, the tournament arbiters instructed us to retreat to a roped-off area where it was not possible for me to see the entire position on Pascal's board. Bacrot sat there impassively, while the Canadian champion's knees wobbled under the table.

I left the playing area and, shadowed by two information officers, went to the press room and connected my computer to the Internet, where I could follow Pascal's game. When my screensaver came on—it was a picture of my five-year-old—one of the officers said, smiling, "That must be your boy. He looks very happy." In any other situation I would have taken the comment as a friendly one, but here I couldn't tell if it masked something sinister. The State Department had warned me that all my e-mail would be read, and with the two officers standing behind me, they didn't have to resort to high-tech snooping. I wrote Ann an e-mail about how I missed her and added some platitudes for public consumption about how splendidly organized the tournament was.

Pascal had put a copy of his opening preparation on my computer. It was there so that he'd have a backup in case his laptop malfunctioned. While the game was in progress, I looked at the lines he had studied. That way I'd know when the game diverged from his home preparation and he was on his own. Pascal had warned me to guard my computer carefully in the press room. Players had been known to steal each other's analysis by slipping an external memory stick into a USB port.

I looked at the World Championship Web site and saw the position that Pascal and Bacrot had reached after Black's tenth move. It was the Sveshnikov sideline that he and Jack had prepared, and so far the position was one that they had investigated in depth. Now, Bacrot, on his eleventh move, could greedily grab Pascal's queen pawn, but in return Pascal would be able to chase the White queen and develop quickly. Bacrot shunned the indigestible pawn and sank a knight on the sixth rank, in the heart of Pascal's position, where it threatened a Black rook. All this Pascal had analyzed before, and he quietly shifted the rook one square so that it was safe. I did a search on the 2.2 million games in ChessBase and found that the position had previously been reached 136 times. Pascal now expected Bacrot, on his twelfth move, to stick a knight on the weak d5 square but instead he made a quiet bishop move, which Pascal and Jack had not considered. The move appeared toothless, though, and I saw in ChessBase that it had been played only once before, on December 14, 1978, in a forty-eight-move draw between Viktor Kupreichik and Evgeny Mochalov in the Sokolsky Memorial Tournament in Minsk. Pascal found an appropriate continuation and by the fourteenth move had achieved a dynamic position that was fully equal—a respectable accomplishment with the Black pieces against a player of Bacrot's strength.

I returned to the tournament hall. It was Bacrot's move, and Pascal had left his seat to walk around and examine other games—a sure sign that he was satisfied with his position.

I went back to the press room and looked again at his game on the Web. The position was equal, but eventually Pascal went astray, playing too passively before making an intemperate queen move. Bacrot, after pushing Pascal's queen around, was able to build up a kingside attack. The Frenchman gobbled two pawns in the process, and the Canadian had to swap queens to deflect the mating attack. But the endgame with two pawns down was hopeless.

I returned to the tournament hall for the finale. Pascal resigned on the fifty-first move, having played for a little more than three hours. He and Bacrot shook hands and placed the kings in a prescribed way in the center of the board to indicate that White had won the game. Pascal came over to me. He was fairly calm. "You know the king placement convention?" he said. "When the kings are placed on e4 and d5, White has won. And when they are placed on d4 and e5, Black has won."

I thought I knew the convention but was confused by his explanation. "You don't have to refer to the squares' algebraic coordinates," I said. "If White wins, the kings are placed on the two centermost white squares and after a Black victory, they are placed on the two centermost black squares."

Pascal was dumbfounded. "Stupid! I can't believe I never thought of that," he said. "That's why you went to Harvard and I go to UMBC."

I was surprised that Pascal, who approached chess in terms of geometric patterns, had overlooked the color coordination, but what was more telling was how he put himself down because he had just lost to Bacrot. It was mild self-deprecation, though, compared to his usual barrage of abuses. All things considered, he seemed OK, if a bit despondent.

He told me he needed to exorcize the game from his mind, so we returned to our room and set up a board. He went on a cathartic monologue as he replayed the moves for me.

"I didn't know how I'd feel in the World Championship," he said, "but I wasn't anxious. That was good. I was actually pretty confident after the opening. I knew Etienne hadn't played it quite right. He played solidly but got nothing special. I was happy that I was able to get this position as Black against someone like him. He started to play e4 again. I'm sure he knows a ton of theory in certain lines—because he has all these people helping him prepare and tons of files and everything. But chess players have to remember things and there's no way to put everything so quickly into one's mind. It takes a while to assimilate everything. He claimed after the game that he had never faced this particular sideline before. But I'm sure he's played similar stuff or faced it in blitz. Of course I hadn't really played it either, but I had thought about it a lot. It was a good decision. I mean, he didn't get anything with White. I can't complain. Maybe after the opening I showed him too much respect by playing somewhat passively. I got angry with myself because I knew I made some bad moves.

"My twenty-seventh move, the queen move, was obviously dumb. I was getting a bit low on time, but I had to go to the bathroom. I had maybe twenty-five minutes to make thirteen moves. I was not in time pressure yet, but it was getting there. Unfortunately the bathroom was not convenient—it was far. I just had to go. When I returned, I could tell from the clock that he had moved quickly and my clock was running the whole time I was away. It threw me off psychologically because I thought he was going to take a while, but he moved as soon as I left the board. Maybe it was a coincidence, maybe it wasn't, but it wasn't unethical. I was upset, and I reacted by playing too fast and that was my main error in the whole game . . . Qf4. I played it in only thirty seconds, and the move was no good. After that it was very hard for me to hold on. My position kept crumbling. I didn't feel like I was outclassed. But of course I was really disappointed that I had messed up a good position by making a couple of careless moves. So my advice is watch out for bathroom breaks." Pascal pushed the pieces off the board. "Someday, Paul, I want to get to Bacrot's level. On the next rating list, he'll probably be ranked twelfth in the world."

OUR ROOM WAS TOO HOT IN THE LATE AFTERNOON SUN, SO WE DECIDED TO seek relief in the hotel's outdoor pool, which was so heavily chlorinated that I assumed we could ignore the warning about insects. Swimming happens to be the only sport I'm good at—I used to do the crawl three miles a day in my teens and I'm a certified lifeguard—and swimming is the only athletic activity at which Pascal is not competent. At one point, while he was treading water, I flicked a nasty-looking beetle off his cheek. If he was going to get sick, it had better be after getting revenge on Bacrot.

That evening, after dinner, Pascal wanted to talk instead of preparing. "I thought about the scenario where I lost the first game," he said. "I can bounce back tomorrow. This guy is not invincible." I nodded encouragingly.[7]

The next morning Pascal seemed relaxed and confident. He spent a couple of hours reviewing the lines of the Scotch opening he hoped to play. An hour before the game, he turned off his laptop and we watched an Oprah special, "The Sexiest Man Alive," in which housewives indulged their fantasies of getting it on with hunky builders and repairmen. "This is about as inane as it gets," Pascal said contentedly. His air serves were stronger, and he was sinking imaginary three-point baskets. Today's pregame music was "Let's Get It Started" by Black Eyed Peas. Pascal changed into a dark blazer, like the one Bacrot had worn, and we timed our exit from the room so that we wouldn't arrive a nanosecond too early. When we exited the elevator, Pascal realized that he had left his identification badge in the room. I waited while he retrieved it. The moment the elevator door closed behind him, two information officers descended on me. "We need you to come with us, Mr. Paul," one of them said.

This time I protested. I told them the game was about to start, and that I was waiting for my friend, the Canadian champion, so that I could accompany him to his board, and that I planned to take pictures during the first ten minutes when photography was allowed. The officers were annoyed and insisted I follow them. I refused, and we had a testy exchange. Nijar happened to walk by and told the officers to wait ten minutes before interrogating me. They reluctantly retreated, like dogs being pulled back on a leash. Nijar promised that my interview with Mohammed Gadhafi would take place soon. The elevator door opened, and Pascal, wearing his picture ID, emerged.

"You're sweating, Paul," he said.

"I'm hot," I said. "I'll change into a T-shirt after your game starts." I walked with him to the board. I put my hand on his shoulder. "Play well," I said, "and try to have fun."

The reality of course was that I was worried. I took a lot of pictures during the next ten minutes but screwed up the camera settings. The information officers were hovering in the doorway, and they watched me as I walked around the expansive playing hall. I was pleased to see that Bacrot had not resorted to the Petroff or the Philidor, but had allowed Pascal to play the Scotch. I wanted to watch Pascal win and I hoped the officers would not detain me for much of the game.

When the photo session was over, the officers escorted me to a couch in a quiet corner of the hotel lobby. The chief officer got right to the point: "Mr. Paul, are you CIA?"

I laughed and said, "If I were CIA, I'd be making a lot more money."

"Clever, Mr. Paul, but your behavior is suspicious."

"What do you mean?"

"You look around a lot, you notice small things, and you write them in your notebook."

"I'm writing a book about chess. It will include Pascal Charbonneau, the champion of Canada. I want to describe this hotel where he is playing. That's why I write everything down." I opened the notebook randomly to a page with a lot of chess notation. "Look," I said. "It's all about chess. These are the moves of the game Pascal played yesterday." I started to wonder whether the Libyans might think the chess moves were some kind of code. I flipped to another page and showed them that I had recorded the slogans that appeared on signs around the tournament hall: "The House Belongs To Its Dweller," "Committees Are Everywhere," and "In Need Freedom Is Latent."

"Very, very interesting," the man said. "Writers and intelligence agents are so similar. We observe the smallest things that other people miss. Watch yourself, Mr. Paul. I still don't know why you're here."

"Can I go?" I asked.

"You're always free to go, Mr. Paul," he said, smiling. "Ours is a peace-loving country that respects the rights of individuals. I'm sure, Mr. Paul, you will get tired of the chess. Then we'd like to give you a private tour of the old city."

"Thank you," I said. "But I'm sure I won't get bored. I'm here to support my friend Pascal."

"Of course, Mr. Paul, that's why you're here," he said. "How could I forget?"

Did the Libyans really think I was there to find the missing nuclear equipment or pin down the Saudi assassination plot? Did they suspect that I meant Mohammed Gadhafi harm? That I might fire a poison dart at him from my pen? I had seen enough bad movies to know that espionage was a serious charge. The Libyan chess officials and Olympic committee members had always been kind to me, but they often gave me the same strange speech: "You know, Mr. Paul, that Libya and America are now friends. You believe that, Mr. Paul? You do share our view, Mr. Paul, that we are friends?" Whenever I reached into my money belt to pay for something, they'd ask me why I was wearing it. "Don't you trust us, Mr. Paul?" they'd say. "We are a friendly, peaceful country."

After the latest round of questioning, I returned to the hotel room to change my shirt. I turned on CNN. President Bush was reacting to the beheading of the American engineer in Saudi Arabia, and I was spooked to hear him say my name: "The murder of Paul shows the evil nature of the enemy we face. These are barbaric people. There's no justification whatsoever for his murder. And yet, they killed him in cold blood."

I was lonely and scared and missed Ann and Alex. At the same time I felt special being singled out by the Libyans and euphoric whenever I survived a round of questioning. I oscillated between fright, resigned acceptance of my fate, and total exhilaration. I had been sleeping less than I ever had. When Bush finished speaking, I retreated again into Seuss:

> Then he'll land in a fish bowl.
> He'll manage just fine.
> Don't ask *how* he'll manage.
> That's *his* job. Not mine.

I shut off the television and scanned *The Tripoli Post,* an English-language newspaper. The lead story said that Muammar Gadhafi regretted that Reagan had died before he could be brought to trial for crimes against Libyan children. Even as Gadhafi wanted the West to embrace him, he couldn't suppress his kooky contrariness. Nor could his daughter Aicha, a lawyer in her late twenties, who announced she was joining Saddam Hussein's legal defense team.

I thought about the Bulgarian health-care workers. They had come to Libya to cure disease but were framed and put on death row. I did not want to end up a casualty of the Libyan justice system. Why had I worked so hard to visit a country that clearly didn't want me? They had sealed their borders to American journalists, and I must have aroused suspicion when I switched the status of my visa from journalist to companion. I reminded myself that I had come to Tripoli for the chess, so I went downstairs to the press room to see how Pascal was faring.

He had just played his eleventh move, a bold knight foray, and I thought he must be pleased to have reached a complex position. On his twelfth move he tried to trade dark-squared bishops and naturally expected Bacrot to take back with the queen-bishop pawn, resulting in awkward doubled pawns. But instead Bacrot ignored the fact that he could recapture Pascal's dark-squared bishop and, short a piece, sent his own light-squared bishop on a kamikaze mission into Pascal's territory. The light-squared cleric offered itself for capture by its own kind. But it was a pseudo-sacrifice, a Greek gift, a deflection strategy. Pascal's light-squared bishop was busy defending a knight, and if the bishop moved to capture its counterpart, Bacrot's all-powerful queen would swoop down on the now-undefended cavalry and at the same time deliver a discomfiting check to Pascal's king and attack his rook.

The offer of the bishop was an exquisitely beautiful move, the geometry of which Pascal would fully appreciate. The only problem was that it was made by the wrong player. The Canadian champion found a way to avoid immediate disaster, but ten moves later, faced with the certain loss of a piece, he resigned on Bacrot's twenty-second move.

PASCAL WAS PUNCHY WHEN I GREETED HIM. HE JACKET WAS ASKEW, AND his hair was messed up because, out of nervousness, he had repeatedly scratched his head during the game. We went back to our room for a postmortem.

"I was happy that he played the Scotch," Pascal said, pacing. "He surprised me when he took my e-pawn. He played it fast, after thirty seconds or a minute. The move didn't worry me. I wasn't sure whether he had prepared it or found it over the board." Pascal adjusted his hair in the mirror. "I don't have so much experience playing guys like him," he added with characteristic understatement. Indeed, in North America, where Pascal played the majority of his tournaments, there was not a single player as good as Bacrot.

"It's hard to know the extent of his preparation," Pascal continued. "I guess as I play more games against super GMs I'll probably figure it out. He didn't move instantly because he wanted to keep me guessing about whether his moves were part of his preparation. But when he's spending no more than a minute per move and playing all this complicated stuff, you have to think they were prepared." Pascal set up the position on my board after his eleventh move. "When I played Nb5," he said, "I was happy but not completely happy. I thought it was my only real chance to do something interesting. But I also knew that my position was risky and might turn out badly because my kingside was a little weak." Live by the sword, die by the sword—Pascal had mixed things up to give himself winning chances.

"Then came the shocker," he continued. "Bacrot banged out . . . Bh3 and I froze. I thought, 'Oh my God, I'm lost immediately.' I sat there in a state of denial. The bishop move was so unusual, and he played it so quickly, that I suspected he had not found it at the board. I felt so dumb that I had fallen for some preparation trick. I couldn't think straight or calculate, so for a moment I just looked at him.[8] He was expressionless, but I sensed he was smugly satisfied because he knew he had me. After a minute or so I calmed down and saw a way to avoid immediate defeat. I gave up a knight with check. But the problem was his position was still very active. He had winning chances because it was easy for me to go wrong. His moves were kind of obvious— . . . Rd8, . . . Ne5, the other knight to c6, push the pawn to b5. His attack played itself, but I had to struggle on each move to find the right defense. So it was not ideal. The end was a complete disaster, which is typical when you know that a draw is unacceptable. There were these two forcing lines that I calculated earlier to be draws, and I'm looking desperately for a way to avoid them. So without calculating I played another move, and I expected him to try to repeat the position and then I'd have time to think again and look for something better. But unfortunately my move lost immediately to a very simple response."

He shook his head sadly. "When the game is published in databases and people play through it without knowing that I had to win, they're going to think my play was really dumb."

"I'm sorry," I said.

"That's OK. It's good the pain is over. We can go back to a better continent in two days. Not that I have anything against Africa—just this godforsaken place."

I told him about my latest run-in with the Libyan agents, and I said I felt badly that my troubles in Tripoli must have interfered with his concentration. "You played for the fucking World Championship," I said. "You shouldn't have to worry about agents kidnapping your roommate."

"I had a tough opponent," he said. "I knew it wasn't going to be easy. But I was ready. Although it looked like I was goofing off, I prepared for him more than for anybody ever. Our safety was more important to me than the championship. I would gladly have drunk scotch rather than have played the Scotch." He hesitated a moment and looked away. "I'm actually ashamed, Paul. In the airport I chose my bags over my friend. That was mean."

WE UNWOUND BY WATCHING *DUMB AND DUMBER* ON TELEVISION, WHICH Pascal renamed *Dumb and Dumber and Me* because of his loss to Bacrot. At 1:30 A.M. we went downstairs to the press room so that he could destroy grandmasters at blitz on ICC. He wasn't the only one trying to recover his chess rhythm. Simutowe had also been knocked out of the World Championship and was also playing on ICC in the press room. The Zambian international master was not having an easy time online. "They don't call them grand monsters for nothing," he said, as he went down to defeat for the third time in a row. "They know how to make life bad for you. I played terribly in the championship."

"Me too," Pascal said.

"If you play stupid in one game, it's difficult to bounce back," Simutowe said, after his fourth loss on ICC.

Even at this early hour, an information officer was still minding the press room. I had not noticed this particular agent before, and he apologized to me that yet another day had passed without my interviewing Mohammed Gadhafi. So there was a connection, I was now certain, between my interrogations and the canceled interviews. The agent promised that the interview would take place before I left Tripoli, but suggested I submit my questions in writing. I typed a list of softball questions, printed it out, and handed it to the agent.[9]

I looked at Pascal's computer screen to see how his games were going. I saw that he was doing much better than Simutowe. He had defeated a grandmaster four times at one-minute bullet chess. Pascal began the last game by shoving his rook pawn, a pointless first move favored by unschooled beginners like my son. "I get better positions," he said, "by playing this shit instead of my normal openings."

"That's because you're a creative genius," I said.

"That's because my openings suck."

Pascal stopped playing and looked in ChessBase to see where his Scotch game had departed from known theory. "Fuck it!" he said. "The 'brilliant' bishop move was not original!" Pascal discovered that it had already been played in Moscow in May 1989 by Yuri Balashov against Evgeny Sveshnikov, the leading Russian opening theoretician whose eponymous variation of the Sicilian was played by Pascal in his first game with Bacrot.

For a moment Pascal was literally pulling out his hair, and he instant-messaged Irina on ICC: "I walked into a trap. Bacrot was prepared to something like move 40! But he disguised it by taking a minute and a half on a move here or there. So he made it look like he's thinking on the spot and is a freaking genius."

As he finished his online conversation with Irina, he started chatting in French with a guest on ICC who said he was Bacrot. Top players who want to preserve their anonymity from the masses of chess fans, or practice openings without their fellow competitors observing, often sign on to ICC as guests rather than under their names or well-known pseudonyms.

GUEST: Hi, it's Etienne.

Pascal looked around the room to see if Bacrot was using one of the other computers.

> CHARLATAN: Hi. Where are you?
> GUEST: I'm nearby. Some of us are playing chess.
> CHARLATAN: I don't see you.
> GUEST: The players who are still up at this hour are either too serious or too reckless.
> CHARLATAN: You can't get on the Internet from your hotel room so you must be downstairs in one of the offices.
> GUEST: Good guess. So do you give blow jobs?
> CHARLATAN: I will come downstairs and break you into 32 pieces.

It was 2:30 A.M. and everything in the hotel—the dining room, the coffee shop, the business center, the pool, the gift shop—was closed and the hall lights were dimmed. Pascal was intent on peering into every office that wasn't locked to ferret out Bacrot or his impersonator. All we found were empty desks, powered-down computers, and a few information officers dozing in the shadowy corners of hallways.

PASCAL WAS STILL RESTLESS WHEN WE GOT BACK TO OUR ROOM. HE TOLD me he was bothered by the arrogance of many chess players. They all think they're the brightest people on the planet, he said, just because they have command of "a little world of sixty-four squares." He and Irina, he said, often disagreed about this. "She worships strong GMs—she thinks they're super smart—and wants to spend time with them at tournaments," he said. "I find them shallow and annoying. I want to play chess with them and get the hell out of there."

"What about Simutowe?" I said. "You seemed like you were buddies with him."

"No way," Pascal snorted. "I was just being polite back there. He's a jerk. He's not fun to play against because he'll do things like sit there and make this big production of eating a banana or peeling grapes and get the pieces all sticky. And once he cheated me, when UMBC played Texas."[10] Pascal had Black and reached a position in which he was only a tiny bit worse. Soon he was able to equalize and start outplaying Simutowe when the Zambian got into time pressure. They were playing with a digital clock with a fancy setting that displayed not only the time remaining but the number of moves played. The time control was two hours for the first forty moves and an extra hour for the rest of the game.

"I was almost winning," Pascal said, "when I noticed around move thirty-four that the counter on the digital clock was off and said move thirty-five." He summoned the arbiter and explained the situation. He told the arbiter that his opponent was in time pressure and expressed concern that Simutowe was going to be awarded the extra hour one move too early. The arbiter told Pascal and Simutowe to go by the move count on the score sheet, not on the clock. "We resumed play and his position gets worse," Pascal recalled. "He plays move thirty-nine and has about ten seconds for move forty. He ends up running out of time and I call his flag, but he refuses to acknowledge that his flag fell. There were a couple of cameras filming us for a PBS documentary. My teammates and their opponents were all watching our game. So were the two coaches as well as a USCF official. Even with all these witnesses, he won't concede. I said, Let's call the arbiter, and he objected. 'I didn't flag,' he said. 'I'm just going to continue to play.' His behavior was very improper. If a guy wants to call the arbiter, you can't stop him. As I turn around to call him, Simutowe quietly makes a move and presses the clock. People on his own team were like, oh my God, what is he trying to pull off here? The camera saw it, and the USCF guy saw it. Simutowe's own coach saw it and told him, Amon, come on, stop this. He didn't really listen. We had to replay the entire game for the arbiter and he confirmed that Simutowe had flagged. Still Simutowe didn't want to accept the loss, and he started telling my team that I was behaving badly, that I didn't have good sportsmanship. He thought I was too aggressive. I definitely was angry."

Of course it is against the rules to make an extra move on the board after your flag has fallen. That way it appears, when the arbiter arrives, that you made forty moves and did not in fact lose on time. But I'm struck by the very public and flagrant way in which Simutowe continued playing after he had already lost. His rational side could not expect to get away with this behavior, any more than my father, if he had been thinking clearly, could have expected me to believe that Baskin-Robbins didn't make milkshakes. Simutowe apparently found the loss to Pascal so painful that he could not accept that it had actually happened.

IT WAS 3:30 A.M. IN TRIPOLI AND PASCAL STILL WAS NOT READY TO GO TO bed. He reiterated his general disgust for chess players and told me about the time he and Irina were hanging around at a European tournament with a grandmaster friend of hers. For a couple of hours the GM was posing trivia questions—When did Bismarck do such and such?—and Irina was trying to answer them. "I thought the discussion was stupid and couldn't stand it," he said. "But she thought he was just brilliant. Later I told her I was sure he had memorized the questions and answers. She was offended and insisted he knew all this stuff because he was cultured. The next time we ran into him, I noticed a CD-ROM of trivia questions sticking out of his briefcase."

Pascal paused and then started berating himself. "Chess players suck. I suck. I totally suck. You were in the Ivy League. How can you possibly be around me? I'm a dumb idiot. I should just give up."

I really liked Pascal. His very existence—a national champion who struggled to reconcile his love of the game with his dislike of chess politics and chess players, a sensitive man who vomited when he swindled his opponent in the French League and ran a temperature when he played his girlfriend—disabused me of the notion that top players had to be coldhearted assassins who had Spock-like control of their emotions. I decided there was nothing wrong with me for not wanting to make a nine-year-old at the Marshall cry.

10

PRAYING FOR THE
PSEUDO TROMPOWSKY

"[The aliens] took me from my apartment and we went
aboard their ship. We flew to some kind of star. They
put a spacesuit on me, told me many things and showed
me around. They wanted to demonstrate that UFOs do
exist."
—KIRSAN ILYUMZHINOV, PRESIDENT OF FIDE,
the World Chess Federation

"I prefer to beat men."
—ANTOANETA STEFANOVA,
2004 Women's World Champion

THE NEXT DAY, OUR LAST FULL DAY IN TRIPOLI, I WOULD FI-
nally get the chance to play chess, too. At 11:00 A.M. we were awakened by
the phone: it was Berik Balgabaev, the assistant to His Excellency Kirsan
Ilyumzhinov. The FIDE president, he said, was ready to see me. I was
pleasantly surprised that the meeting was happening. I hurriedly dressed,
grabbed my chess set, and turned to Pascal for last-minute encouragement.

"No one knows if he's any good," he said, "so stick to your regular
game. Play your usual King's Gambit and you'll be OK. Downplay,
please, that you're a journalist."

"You mean tell him I'm your second?" I said. "Yeah, that's really kept
me safe."

"Well, maybe it'll work better with him."

"It doesn't alarm me that he may have ordered a reporter killed. I'm not trying to expose his finances. I just want to understand his wild chess philosophy."

Kirsan Ilyumzhinov, forty-two, was a mythic figure in Russia and the chess world, a head of state who claimed to communicate telepathically with his people and a globe-trotting evangelist who promoted chess as a universal antidote to war. Ilyumzhinov, a political prodigy, and a chess one, too—if you believe his account of his childhood play—had been the leader of Kalmykia since 1993 and FIDE since 1995.

The arid sheepherding region he rules, two hundred miles north of Chechnya, is one of the most impoverished areas of the world, with wages on state-run farms as low as $10 a month. Kalmykia is the size of Ireland, and many of its three hundred thousand inhabitants do not have electricity or running water, and fuel their stoves with sheep excrement. Ilyumzhinov himself lives well, tooling around Elista in one of seven Rolls-Royces or a Hummer and spending a fortune on chess. He is a multimillionaire by some accounts, a billionaire by others. In 1998, he built Chess City, a large glass-walled palace with accompanying cottages arranged like an Olympic village. Chess City is separated by a barbed-wire fence and armed guards from surrounding Elista, which is plastered with billboards of Ilyumzhinov pushing pawns, kissing babies, kicking a soccer ball, greeting the pope, and embracing the Dalai Lama. Kalmyk schoolchildren are encouraged to draw pictures of Ilyumzhinov in art class. At chess tournaments, he gives the players watches, ties, and tins of caviar all festooned with his likeness. Pascal has a kitschy T-shirt with Ilyumzhinov's portrait on the front along with the words "Kirsan is FIDE" and "FIDE is Kirsan." In creating a cult of personality, Ilyumzhinov has been as proficient as Muammar Gadhafi.

The chess world is full of dreamers—players who claim to be rated two hundred points higher than they are, players who believe that they could be world champion or break into the top ten if only they devoted more time to their obsession, players who get smashed in key games yet insist they were winning all along until their opponents got lucky. Many players persevere in their delusions even in the face of accumulating evidence that they are not as good as they think. Ilyumzhinov, although no longer a tournament competitor, is in many ways the consummate chess dreamer and schemer, someone who advances grandiose plans for the game while overlooking obvious problems with his ideas and ignoring his many detractors. But unlike other chess hustlers who live in a world of fantasy, Ilyumzhinov has the wherewithal—the money, the power, the connections—to turn his impractical dreams into reality.

Chess City, a $50 million cathedral to the game he loves, was one of those plans. Against the advice of his aides, he opened the city prematurely, in a flush of exuberance, for the 1998 Chess Olympiad. Some fifteen hundred competitors arrived from around the world to find that the tournament had to be delayed three days—and the number of rounds shortened from the traditional fourteen to thirteen—because the playing hall and living quarters were not completed. "When I showed up," Joel Lautier recalled, "the palace had no roof. There were gaping holes next to the stairs. It was very dangerous, particularly for a chess tournament where all these players were walking around thinking up chess variations and not paying attention to where they were stepping." The playing hall lacked ventilation and was unbearably stuffy. "Several players lost consciousness," Lautier said, "including FIDE Vice-President Zurab Azmaiparashvili. He just passed out in the middle of his game with Timman." Elista residents were forced to part with their refrigerators, televisions, and kitchenware so that the cottages were furnished when the players arrived. But the furnishings could not conceal construction problems. "The roof of one of the players' cottages became dislodged," Lautier said, "and flew off in the middle of the tournament."

Ilyumzhinov had wanted Bobby Fischer to live in Chess City, which he promised would be ruled by a king and a queen. He tracked Fischer down in Hungary and gave him $100,000 of his own money to compensate him for a pirated version of his classic *My 60 Most Memorable Games*, which had been a hot seller in Russia. "With relish Ilyumzhinov tells the story of Fischer stuffing the money into his coat pocket," wrote one grandmaster, "and the money then falling out of his pocket and onto the street, and both of them chasing the banknotes, which were being blown in every direction, down the windy streets of Budapest." Every week Ilyumzhinov would send Fischer a kilo of Kalmyk caviar but could not woo him to Chess City.

In the weeks before the 1998 Olympiad, one of Ilyumzhinov's few vocal critics, Larisa Yudina, the editor of the banned opposition newspaper *Sovietskaya Kalmykia Segodnya*, was preparing an exposé of his finances and Chess City. Ilyumzhinov had managed to establish Kalmykia as a corporate haven, like Delaware or Liechtenstein, for companies that registered there. But the price of registration was a steep contribution to a special presidential fund from which money was allegedly funneled to Chess City. While meeting an anonymous source who offered to expose the fund, Yudina was beaten, strangled, and fatally stabbed. Russian President Boris Yeltsin called the killing a "political assassination" and ordered the Moscow police to take over the investigation.

In response, Ilyumzhinov had the hubris to go on television and declare his candidacy for the Russian presidency, although in the end he did not run. Two of his former aides were charged with Yudina's murder, and Kremlin auditors found that tens of millions of rubles from Moscow that were intended for the "provision of drinking water for the population of Kalmykia" had been improperly diverted to Chess City. A prosecutor who was carrying a file on additional financial improprieties had a fiery car accident; he walked away, but the file was incinerated along with the car. Ilyumzhinov denied any involvement in Yudina's death. He was widely believed to have orchestrated the slaying. Even if Moscow had proof, Ilyumzhinov would escape indictment because presidents of Russian republics are immune from criminal prosecution.

Greater Russia and Kalmykia have been at odds for more than three hundred years. The people who settled the North Caspian steppe in the early seventeenth century were nomads from the Djungaria region of northwest Mongolia who practiced Tibetan Buddhism. Peter I enlisted them to protect the eastern frontier of the Russian Empire, but Catherine the Great did not want a Buddhist colony in her kingdom and expelled most of the settlers. Those who remained were called Kalmyks, from the Turkish word for "remnant." After the Russian Revolution, the Bolsheviks destroyed more than one hundred Buddhist temples in the region and forced Kalmyk schoolchildren to learn Russian. The Kalmyks defiantly constructed new places of worship and in World War II joined German forces in opposing Russia. In 1944, Stalin waged genocide on the Kalmyks by deporting the entire population of 150,000 to Siberia and torching their temples. It was not until 1957 that 70,000 survivors and descendants were allowed to return.

Two years after the dissolution of the Soviet Union, Ilyumzhinov was elected president of Kalmykia by promising a Buddhist revival and $100 to every citizen. (In a subsequent campaign he offered every shepherd in Kalmykia a free cell phone.) He also said he would legalize polygamy and chop off the hands of criminals. At the age of thirty-one, he became the world's youngest leader of a sovereign state. He rebuilt the temples, encouraged the teaching of Buddhist principles, and brought back the Kalmyk language so that it was on a par with Russian as one of the republic's two official languages. He got Moscow to reverse its years of refusal to grant the Dalai Lama a visa. In return, he persuaded his fellow Kalmyks to give up their ambitions to secede from the Russian federation. He tried unsuccessfully to get the Kremlin to shut down the KGB's Elista office with its staff of five hundred. Whenever his leadership was challenged, he rallied the citizens by reminding them of Stalin's horrific legacy, which he was working to undo.

A month before Tripoli, Pascal had gone to Chess City with Irina and Jennifer Shahade, where the two women represented the United States in the Women's World Championship that had been hastily moved to Elista from war-threatened Armenia. Outside the walls of Chess City, disenchanted Kalmyks furtively slipped leaflets to chess players claiming that children were starving because Ilyumzhinov had diverted money from food and medicine to the game. He was not known to tolerate political dissent, and a few prominent citizens opposed to Chess City were trying his patience by conducting a hunger strike. Pascal, Irina, and Jennifer witnessed for themselves Kalmykia's standard of living when they were driven an hour across the barren steppe to Yashkuly, a farming village, where they faced schoolchildren in a simultaneous exhibition. Even the mayor of Yashkuly, who entertained the trio in his home, had no electricity and only an outhouse for a bathroom.

By the time of Tripoli, the chess community had largely forgotten, if it ever knew, Ilyumzhinov's connection to murder, and the players were largely apathetic about his funding of chess at the expense of his people. The players were upset about things that affected their own pocketbooks, like the fact that the prize fund for the World Championship had been cut from $3 million in 2001–2002 to half that in 2004. Some top players had bowed out of Tripoli because of financial and other personal considerations. A few players, although not enough to organize an effective boycott, objected to Ilyumzhinov's failure to ensure that Libya admitted Israeli contestants. Some chess professionals were also unhappy with changes he had made to the top tournaments in the hope of popularizing the game. They felt the changes cheapened chess and had not in fact brought in more spectators. Ilyumzhinov had sped up the time control with the aim of getting chess on television without requiring a TV network to clear its programming schedule for a whole afternoon. But the only result, his critics saw, were games that were aesthetically marred because the players had insufficient time to find the best moves in the endgame. And he had "democratized" the World Championship (or "randomized" it, in the eyes of his detractors) by changing the format from long matches among a small elite to short knockout matches among a crowd of 128.

Ilyumzhinov's suite in the El Mahary was guarded by a plainclothed Libyan who announced my arrival. Presidential aide Berik Balgabaev showed me into the living room. The table, with its large spread of smoked salmon, was set for a sumptuous breakfast for eight that had never happened. Ilyumzhinov was casually dressed and greeted me with a toothy smile. "A fellow chess player!" he said, beaming, as he extended his hand. He was a thin man with Asian features, and his handshake was delicate. If we had been meeting back in New York at the Waldorf, I would probably have been struck by how little this man looked like a man who would order a murder—let alone the pugilist he claimed to have been in his youth. But here in Tripoli, where I had been detained and questioned repeatedly by shady characters, I was a bit spooked. I was saddened that the World Chess Championship, which was once an ennobling clash of minds, had become the plaything of a dictator who had no compunctions about holding the competition in a lawless, dangerous place with no chess tradition and virtually no fans. For me, the royal game had fallen into the sewer.

Berik asked to be excused and Ilyumzhinov replied, "Maybe you should stay for a moment in case Paul wants photos."

"I'd like a picture," I said. "How about he takes it while we play a friendly game of chess?"

"Very good," Ilyumzhinov said, "but I don't have a set."

Pascal, too, never had a chessboard with him, because he was able to play in his head or on the computer. But I found it odd that the world's leading ambassador of the game didn't routinely carry a set.

"I brought one," I said.

"Excellent. Let's play here on the sofa." He sat at one end and I sat at the other. I was so busy studying his face that I unrolled my vinyl chessboard without looking at it and placed it between the two of us on the couch. He grunted contemptuously when he saw that I had made the beginner's mistake of positioning the board incorrectly with a dark square in the right-hand corner instead of a light square.[1] Of course I never would have done that if I'd been watching what I was doing. He picked the board up with his bony hands and rotated it ninety degrees. "There," he said, "this will make a better photo. You want your readers to think you know how to play the game."

I found his comment funny. He was posturing for a psychological advantage by suggesting I didn't know how to play and at the same time offering me a recipe, no doubt integral to his political success, for deceiving the masses. I was also surprised by his command of English. I had seen him hold press conferences and he always spoke through an interpreter. This obviously gave him more time to compose his answers, and perhaps, if the discussion was being televised in Russia, he looked better to his people if he wasn't speaking English.

"You can have White," he said, continuing the posturing. He was giving me the advantage of moving first because he was convinced that he would beat me anyway.

"Thank you," I said.

I moved my king pawn forward two squares and he responded immediately in kind. I advanced my king-bishop pawn two squares—a King's Gambit it was.[2] He smiled broadly and snapped off the pawn. But I thought I sensed in his smile a bit of uncertainty. My giving up a pawn on the second move could be seen as confirming his suspicion that I was a rank beginner. But it also raised the possibility that I was actually a dangerous attacking player who knew something about this ancient opening.

"Berik, take some pictures," he said. I handed Berik my digital camera and he fired away. Then he left the two of us alone.

Ilyumzhinov's pregame posturing had stoked my competitive spirit, so I decided to move fast to keep him guessing about my playing strength. On the third move, I copied Fischer and slid my bishop to the fourth rank. Now there was no mistaking the signs of nervousness in his silly grin. My unusual move still did not betray whether I was a *patzer* violating general opening principles or a studious disciple of the eleventh world champion. Even experienced tournament players would now normally think before replying to my move—that's how rare it was—but Ilyumzhinov, attuned to the psychological dimensions of the situation, banged out his response. He moved his queen pawn two squares, offering to return the pawn in order to achieve free and simple development.

It was my turn to be taken aback. A weak woodpusher would try to hold onto his material advantage. Only a decent player would know that the modern treatment of this nineteenth-century opening was promptly to return the pawn. I had two ways to capture the proffered foot soldier, and I chose the way that was double-edged, taking it with a fellow pawn.

Now Ilyumzhinov slid his queen to the side of the board, checking my king along the weakened dark-squared diagonal. I had to waste time shifting my king out of check, but I knew I'd soon gain back the tempo by hitting his queen with my knight. After seven moves we reached a dynamic position, just the kind I enjoyed playing, but his body language suggested that he expected to play only a few moves for the camera and not an entire game. Now I was torn. As a player I wanted to beat him, particularly because of his annoying pregame behavior. As a writer and explorer of the chess world, I needed to make sure there was time in his busy schedule for us to talk. Also, I didn't want to offend him and risk his calling off the interview, if indeed he had expected to play just a few quick ceremonial moves for the photo op. And so I reluctantly offered him a draw.

"Very good," he said, bowing slightly. "It is a wonderful thing that you, a journalist from New York, and me, a Buddhist from Kalmykia, both speak the language of the chessboard. We have enriched ourselves as human beings by engaging in this thoughtful, nonviolent competition."

I nodded respectfully and wondered whether Larisa Yudina had lost her life because she did not value the language of the chessboard.

"Chess has helped my mentality," he continued. "It has helped my brain. It builds discipline in men. Most men act and then think. That's why we have wars. Chess teaches you to think first and then act. Half a billion people know how to play. My goal is to double that number. If a billion people played chess, I believe there would be no more conflicts or wars. If people think before they act, they won't turn to violence. The only wars people know will be the harmless ones fought on chessboards."

I asked him when he learned the game.

"My grandfather taught me when I was four," he said. "When I was five, the kids on my block organized an outdoor competition. The prize was ten bottles of beer. There were eleven kids, ages fifteen to seventeen. I was playing nearby and they needed a twelfth chess player, so I was drafted. I beat everybody. Then there was a big argument about whether they should give ten bottles of beer to a five-year-old. They decided to give me one can of Pepsi Cola. One can! They should have given me ten cans. It made me mad, but the experience launched my chess career. My whole life I've been chasing the other nine cans."

He rattled off his tournament successes: at seven, champion of his grade school; at ten, champion of all schoolboys in Kalmykia; at eleven, champion of all Russian schoolchildren; at fourteen, Kalmyk champion; at twenty, champion of the Soviet Army; at twenty-three, champion of all university students in Moscow. He gave up tournament chess, he said, to concentrate on his language studies at Moscow's Institute of International Relations (learning Japanese, Mongolian, English, and Chinese), make his first million (as the first importer of Japanese cars into Russia), and enter politics (as an elected member of the Russian parliament in 1990, when he was twenty-eight). He told me that he loved haiku and calligraphy, and he sketched in my notebook the Japanese signs for newspaperman, in appreciation, he said, of the chess articles I had written for *The New York Times* and *The Wall Street Journal*.

"When I became president of Kalmykia," he continued, "my first decree was about the development of chess. I asked teachers and the minister of education to start teaching chess. Now 100 percent of the kids in

Kalmykia play the game. Kids who play chess are able to study well and have excellent results in school. They don't do drugs. They're not hooligans. Parents are very happy. This is my dream—to export what we did in Kalmykia to the rest of the world."

"What do you think the future holds for chess in my country?"

"Maybe we'll hold the next World Championship in Vegas. One of my friends built a new hotel there. And you'll attend the championship as my honored guest."

"I'd be delighted. Which hotel do you mean?"

"Maybe it wasn't a new hotel but just an old one he repaired."

"What's the hotel?"

"I forget."

"Let's get back to your own chess for a moment. What was the highest rating you achieved?"

"I had a rating equivalent to 2300—a FIDE master. But it was twenty years ago so I don't really remember."

"As the president of FIDE," I said, "it must be hard to manage all these opinionated players."

"You are right. It is a little difficult. Chess players are very special sportsmen. They're not like football players, karate champions, or boxers. They think they're cleverer than everybody else. But they're also a little crazy. I say to them, 'Please, confine your cleverness to the chessboard. Do anything you want on the board. Your job is to produce good games and get paid for it. My job is to create tournaments and get you paid. Leave that to me.'"

"Are you disappointed that no Israeli players came to Tripoli?"

"Well, there are many reasons why someone might not come. Maybe he's upset because his neighbor's cat or dog died. Or he could be in bad health himself."

"Is that why the Israelis didn't come? Because their neighbors' pets died?" I did my best to sound more curious than incredulous.

"Gadhafi wrote official invitation letters to all of them. They probably each had a different reason. One player, I know, was concerned about security. But official inspectors from FIDE, security experts, came and examined the hotel and walked around Tripoli. They thought the security was fine."

"The Libyans must have very sophisticated security, because it's not visible at all."

"Yes, very sophisticated. Extremely sophisticated. But someone will always have concerns. If the tournament was in New York, one of the players would worry about security. When I visit New York, friends say, 'Kirsan, you must be careful when you walk around.'"

Berik returned and pointed to his watch. "It's OK, Berik," he said. "I am enjoying talking to our American friend. I think he understands me."

"I have one last question," I said. "Tell me why you have devoted yourself to the game."

"I do not think of chess as a game. Nor is it a sport. It is an activity that is inherent in our civilization. It is civilization. Chess is science and philosophy. Archaeologists have found chess pieces in India, South America, and Japan. There were chess pieces before there were aircraft, ships, and Communism. How could they exist at all these different places on Earth? No human could have distributed them. Maybe the pieces came from," and he paused, extended his palms toward the ceiling, and said blissfully, "outer space." (The extraterrestrial world is a place Ilyumzhinov knows well—he claims that aliens once put him on a yellow spaceship and transported him across the universe.) "Maybe chess is a gift from other planets. Or else chess sprung from the bones of mankind, from our very nature. It is somehow programmed into our genetic code. Tennis and golf are not played everywhere on Earth. But chess is. I am its guardian, its keeper. For me chess is religion. Join me please in spreading the faith."

Berik was now nervously pacing in the hallway because Ilyumzhinov was clearly late for another appointment. I thanked the two of them and headed toward the door.

"Tell me," Ilyumzhinov continued, "do you think George Bush plays chess?"

Berik laughed dismissively.

"I don't know," I said. "I know one of Bill Clinton's top aides, and he said that Clinton loved to play hearts."

"You must find out. I want to play chess with your president. You'll come with me to the White House and we'll have an evening of chess. It will be beautiful. Please see if that's possible."

The last thing Ilyumzhinov did was to show me photographs of the Buddhist temples he'd constructed. "Don't they look wonderful?" he said, savoring each picture. He was also proud that he had rebuilt the Christian Orthodox churches once leveled by Stalin. His republic, he said, respected religious minorities. Even with his checkered human rights record, history may give Ilyumzhinov credit for easing ethnic tensions in a pluralistic state where there were as many Orthodox Christians as there were Buddhists.

In 2006, top grandmasters would mount a concerted challenge to Ilyumzhinov's reelection bid at FIDE. "Either FIDE stays a cowboy organization mired in sleaze and shunned by corporate sponsors," said British GM Nigel Short, "or it becomes a modern, professional sporting body." Or, as Karpov put it, "Even a dickhead would do a better job than Ilyumzhinov." Despite the opposition, Ilyumzhinov was overwhelmingly reelected in June, in a one-vote-per-country system in which grandmaster powerhouses like Russia had no more weight at the ballot box than a Caribbean island whose Olympiad players were no stronger than me. In 2006, Ilyumzhinov also commandeered another term as Kalmyk high muckety-muck after criticizing the Kremlin for not properly attending to Lenin's embalmed body—the Soviet leader was one-eighth Kalmyk—and offering to purchase Lenin for a million dollars and grandly put him on display in Elista.

I RETURNED TO OUR HOTEL ROOM AND SHOWED PASCAL THE SEVEN-MOVE draw. "He played OK," he said, "better than I imagined." I agreed with Pascal's assessment of his play but was less certain about what to make of the man himself. I guess I had expected to meet a conspicuously bad guy—as a journalist I felt a nebulous affinity for the slain member of my profession. But instead I met a quixotic philosopher-king whose overblown ideas about the cultural importance of chess were certifiably nutty. He saw himself not as an ironfisted ruler, but as a poetic visionary who didn't need to get bogged down in details—like the absence of roofs in Chess City, the security in Tripoli, or the discrimination against Israeli players—as long as he was doing God's work by advancing the sacred goal of making chess universal. He believed he was quenching the spiritual thirst of his long-repressed people by restoring Buddhism and teaching them the uplifting game of chess, even if in fact he was also leaving them physically thirsty by not providing drinking water.

In the good times, when companies paid him a lot for the privilege of relocating on paper to his low-tax haven, and he also reportedly made money from trafficking in caviar, oil, and drugs, he rescued FIDE from insolvency. In the 1990s, he could afford to spend millions of dollars on international chess tournaments, and the chess community was the better for it. Now times were lean, and Ilyumzhinov had to rely on the likes of Muammar Gadhafi to fund his tournaments, and the funding was lower and sporadic and came with all kinds of conditions. Once the money started to dry up, the players were angry with Ilyumzhinov.

Chess City was certainly not Versailles—it was no more splendid than a clean California resort, although it was architecturally striking in the drably expansive steppe—but Ilyumzhinov undoubtedly saw his own overall contribution to chess as being as lasting and beautiful as Louis XIV's palace. He had personally spent more than $20 million staging chess matches—and "raised" $50 million for Chess City—and some of the resulting games are masterpieces that will be replayed and enjoyed by future generations of players. Versailles bankrupted a country and fomented a revolution. Ilyumzhinov may well do the same, in Kalmykia or FIDE. What will endure, he knows, are the exquisite chess games that he facilitated. They will survive as long as earthlings are still pushing pawns and moving knights. In his disturbingly elite royalist calculus, the creation of immortal beauty apparently outweighs any human suffering he may have caused.

PASCAL AND I CAUGHT THE END OF THE LUNCH BUFFET IN THE HOTEL. AFTER the prematurely aborted King's Gambit, I was eager to play some real chess, and luckily another opportunity soon presented itself. Outside the lunchroom, I ran into women's world champion Antoaneta Stefanova. The twenty-four-year-old Bulgarian was sitting by herself in a lounge chair, nursing two orange drinks (nonalcoholic of course—this was Libya after all) and playfully blowing smoke high into the air from a pungent cigarette. I noticed she was left-handed, which I found alluring because I didn't know any other female southpaws. She had prominent crescent eyebrows and thick, wavy blond hair that had bunched up on the shoulders of her trim black jacket. Her eyes sparkled but were also glazed and fatigued. She looked like a Hollywood movie star who was relaxing in her trailer after a taxing morning on the set.

I had never met Stefanova before, and my first impression was undoubtedly influenced by what Jennifer had told me. "I know it's strange for me to idolize someone who's just a year older than me," Jennifer had said, "but I love how she handles herself at tournaments. She doesn't hole herself up in her room between rounds but is out partying and drinking and exploring whatever strange city she's in long after most of her opponents have gone to bed. And yet she usually plays well the next day."

I introduced myself to Stefanova and told her I was a friend of Jennifer's. She nodded approvingly. I asked her about reports on the Web that she and her compatriot, Veselin Topalov, who was then the world's number three player, were giving a simultaneous exhibition in Tripoli to show support for the Bulgarian nurses on death row.[3] To me this seemed a very gutsy thing to do, and I didn't believe the Libyans would allow it. She shrugged and said she didn't know what was happening because she hadn't yet met with the Bulgarian ambassador. She did say that she was going to take on a group of local chess players early that evening. I asked if I could play, too. She perked up and inquired about my rating. I answered and she studied me for a minute before responding.

"I think I can handle that," she said, teasing.

"I'm sure you can," I said.

She told me I needed to get the permission of the organizers because the event was being televised and they might want to restrict the players to Libyans. I spoke to three of the organizers and they all seemed lukewarm, but a few hours later they said I could play. (Part of the problem was that for a while the entire event was in jeopardy because a government official thought it would be disgraceful for Libyan men to lose to a woman, especially a foreigner, on nationwide television.) I was excited—it would be my second game of the day against a chess celebrity.

There were two hours until game time, and Pascal was now my second. He realized that, apart from my incomplete effort against Ilyumzhinov, he didn't know how I played. I turned on my computer and opened a file of my tournament games. I was a bit self-conscious. The neurotic in me feared that he might think I was too weak to bother helping. But it was soon clear that he was having a good time. He played through half a dozen of my losses and observed that I had an advantage in the middle game in all of them. "Interesting," he said. "You're winning. Then you screw up. We'll work on that later. You should win won games."

For the time being, though, we focused on what Stefanova played as White, the color she would have on all the boards in the simul. Chess-Base contained 407 of her games as White, going back to 1989, when she was nine. We looked at the first few moves of the thirty-four games she played in 2003. Stefanova was one of the few women in the world to hold the rank of grandmaster, and a player of her strength would probably deviate from her normal repertoire against someone like me. She could play any opening well against amateurs, and would undoubtedly vary her moves from one board to the next. But Pascal and I needed to start somewhere, so we pretended I was someone she respected, against whom she'd employ her usual stuff.

Stefanova was generally a queen-pawn player. I told Pascal that I would respond by playing the Slav, not the modern . . . a6 variation that he tried against Bacrot, but the old-fashioned Slav that Vassily Smyslov, the seventh world champion, employed throughout his long career. If White enters the mainline of the Slav, he emerges with a bit more space in the center, but Black has counter-chances. When Stefanova faced the Slav in 2003, however, we saw that she shunned the mainline and played the unambitious Exchange Variation. She immediately resolved the tension in the center by swapping pawns, giving up her space advantage in return for a risk-free mirror-image position that gave her the chance to grind down her opponent by virtue of having one extra move to break the symmetry.

Pascal shook his head at some of the games. "I hate this stuff," he said. "It's slow. I'd lose from fucking boredom."

"You're really encouraging. If you think *you'd* lose . . ."

"It's not so bad. You just have to stay awake."

Pascal explained that even when Black adopts openings that are sharper and more rough-and-tumble than the Slav, a pacifistic White can usually find a way of avoiding all the complications and steer the game into a drawish position. "When White is a chicken," Pascal said, "it really sucks. I always want a fight."

"Of course if I draw her, it's good for me."

"OK. But if she plays the Exchange Variation, it's not because she wants a draw. She wants to wear you down without giving you winning chances."

For the next hour we reviewed specific lines in the Exchange Variation. Pascal showed me some ways to try to mix it up and inject life into an otherwise sterile position. If Stefanova and I were playing one-on-one, she'd presumably see through any complications I introduced, but in a simul where she couldn't spend much time on any given game, there was always a chance she'd go astray. In any event, to tread water against a grandmaster in this deceptively quiet position with identical pawn structures was a sure route to a slow and tortuous death. My positional understanding of the game was nowhere near as good as hers. She would just patiently and imperceptibly build up her position, accumulating microscopic advantages until they amounted to a win.

The last thing we did was look at another opening she might try. It had the wonderful name of the Pseudo Trompowsky, and it could arise on White's second move after we both advanced our queen pawns. Instead of now making a move that invited the Slav, she could develop her dark-squared bishop to the fourth rank on my side of the board. Nineteenth-century chess theoreticians would be apoplectic. Not only does the move violate cherished opening principles about developing knights first, it seems to accomplish little except "biting on granite," harmlessly attacking a defended pawn. Moreover, it invites Black to kick the bishop back to White's side of the board. But the move also has its advantages.

First of all, it avoids having to keep up with the latest wrinkles in opening theory in the commoner double queen-pawn openings. For players who don't have the time or temperament to play through hundreds of contemporary games, a little-analyzed opening like the Pseudo Trompowksy can be an important weapon. Second, the move anticipates that Black wants to develop his king knight, in which case White's bishop will be threatening the steed instead of granite. (In the real Trompowsky, White doesn't jump the gun, but waits until the knight is developed before attacking it.) Of course, Black need not cooperate and can hold back the knight, as I planned to do. I showed Pascal the line I wanted to play—punting her bishop immediately with my rook pawn—and he gave it his blessing.

I had to face Stefanova in five minutes, and there was no time to get pumped up with Nirvana. I put on a T-shirt that said "Village Chess Shop, New York City." With only eighteen hours left in Tripoli, I felt like flaunting that I was an American. We headed to the playing area, and I took my place alongside thirteen Libyan students, some in kaffiyeh, at tables arranged in a horseshoe. Now I understood why Stefanova had been eager for me to speak to the organizers—I stood out like a black sheep. A printed program released by the Libyan Olympic Committee said that Stefanova, who was inexplicably called "Siovanov," would square off against "13 male and female players from Libya under 20 years old and an American sportscaster named Huffman."

Pascal wished me success.

"It will be sexy playing a beautiful woman," I told him.

"It will be even sexier beating a beautiful woman," he said.

"You have experience?"

"Not exactly. Just follow my advice."

One of the male students approached me. "We count you," he said in broken English, "defend our manhood. We not good. You beat."

I laughed and told him I'd try. One of the information officers came over and sat on a sofa behind me. The simul was late getting started, and so to pass the time I thumbed through a copy of Muammar Gadhafi's slim *Green Book*—his manifesto for achieving a utopian society, the *Jamahiriyat* ("state of the masses")—that I had purchased in the lobby gift shop. The jacket copy set the tone for the quirky booklet, which was Leader's answer to Mao's *Little Red Book*:

> The thinker Muammar Al Qathafi does not present his thought for simple amusement or pleasure. Nor is it for those who regard ideas as puzzles for the entertainment of empty-minded people standing on the margin of life. Qathafi's ideas interpret life as it erupts from the heart of the tormented, the oppressed, the deprived and the grief-stricken. It flows from the ever-developing and conflicting reality in search of whatever is best and most beautiful.

I turned to a fourteen-page section called "Woman" on the off chance that it would have insights I could use to beat Stefanova—or at least an explanation of why Libyan men might find it unsettling to lose to her. "Woman is a female and man is a male," Gadhafi helpfully stated:

> According to a gynaecologist, woman menstruates or suffers feeble-
> ness every month, while man, being a male, does not menstruate or he
> is not subject to the monthly period which is a bleeding.... When a
> woman does not menstruate, she is pregnant. If she is pregnant she
> becomes, due to pregnancy, feeble for about a year, which means that
> all her natural activities are reduced until she delivers her baby.... As
> the man does not get pregnant, he is not liable to the feebleness which
> woman, being a female, suffers.

I wondered how ignorant the average Libyan was of human biology that
Leader felt compelled to give this simple lecture. His statement was a
prelude to his conclusion that men and women, although "equal as human
beings," do not have "absolute identity between them as regards their duties."

Before I could read further and learn the respective responsibilities of
each sex, Stefanova made a grand entrance into the playing area. She wore
a sheer embroidered black tunic over a dark pants suit. As a Libyan official
somberly read her long bio—"winner of Youth Chess Championship of
under 10 years old in Puerto Rico in 1989"—she surveyed her competitors one by one. When her eyes reached me, she arched her brows, smiled
winsomely, and winked. The official announced the beginning of play.

Stefanova elected to go clockwise around the tables, which meant that
I was her second opponent. She shook the first player's hand and advanced her queen pawn. She shook my hand, told me she was pleased I
could play, and made the same first move. So far so good: she was following my preparation. With only fourteen opponents, she was soon
back at our table. The Libyan on Board One mimicked her first move,
and she responded by whipping out her bishop—voilà, the Pseudo
Trompowsky. I also copied her first move, and for a moment she looked
at me instead of at the position. "Now what should I play?" she whispered, as she pushed her hair out of her eyes. "I could move my bishop,"
I thought I heard her say. She was speaking so softly—and I was so
groggy—I couldn't be sure. I tried to remain calm while thinking yes,
yes, move the bishop. I wanted a Pseudo Trompowsky on my board, too.

No luck. She picked up her king knight, flamboyantly lifted it high over
her pawns, and gently lowered it onto a square on the third row. Drat—it
was only her second move, and she had already taken me out of my preparation. I had seen this position before; I just didn't know how she handled

it. She was back in a couple minutes and I copied her knight move. She responded by caressing her dark-squared bishop and slowly sliding it until it was adjacent to my knight, which it was now attacking. I was on my own. I had reached the position several times at blitz on the Internet Chess Club but didn't know the recommended response. What to do? One disadvantage of developing her dark-squared bishop so early on the kingside, I thought, was that it left the dark squares on her queenside weak. Indeed, a flank pawn was no longer defended, and I decided, by pushing a pawn of my own one square, to open a diagonal path for my queen to go after her pawn. Afterward Pascal told me that my plan was good, but I should have been more aggressive and pushed my pawn *two* squares, thereby also challenging her domination of the center as well as creating the desired path for my queen. Still, I had a decent game until the fifteenth move, when I should have prevented her from trading a knight for my bishop. A knight and a bishop are generally regarded as equal in strength, but in the kind of unobstructed position we reached, the bishop was stronger because it can zip from one side of the board to the other in a single stroke.

For the next fifteen moves she slowly and efficiently choked me, increasing her space advantage with every move, just as I feared she would if she had played the Exchange Slav. My strangled position, though, was far from lost. She was always in a cheery mood when she came to my board, until, on the thirty-first move, she blundered badly, overlooking that I could win her king pawn. I captured it not because of my brilliance but because of her carelessness. Now, I thought, I might really experience the pleasure of beating a beautiful woman.

I had to suppress my newfound cockiness so that I could continue to focus on the game. She stood there silent, frowning, her body crouched low over the position. How, she must have asked herself, could she, the world champion, have overlooked such a cheap and obvious threat? She must have gazed at the board for five minutes—by far the longest she had taken on any move in any game—but she could not undo the past. Finally she picked up her king from the very corner of the board and banged it down on the adjacent square on the back rank—a move I didn't understand. But the audible thump of the king against the board—her previous thirty-one moves had all been quiet—signaled that she was mad.

By this time she had disposed of more than half of her opponents, and now she literally ran around the room, moving instantaneously on all of the other boards, trying to blitz me. She never left me more than half a minute to move. I wasn't sure how to exploit my pawn advantage, and I desperately needed time to think. When she arrived next, I said, "Pass."

"Move!" she commanded.

Simuls are usually conducted in one of two ways. Players are either required to move instantly when the grandmaster arrives or they are allowed to pass a maximum of three times. Often the rule is announced before the simul begins, but here it wasn't. I had noticed that she graciously let other players pass, so I had assumed of course that the rule also applied to me.

"Move now!" she repeated.

I reluctantly did as I was told, and when she angrily made a move in response, her unsteady hand knocked over a few of the pieces. Part of me wanted to beat her and punish her for her bad behavior. The other part wanted to run because I was unnerved by the sudden aggression of someone who moments before I had found so attractive. She reminded me of an old girlfriend who was sweet one moment and crazy the next. The intensity of my game with Stefanova had allowed me to forget about my problems with the Libyan authorities and the presence of the information officer who was still sitting two feet behind me.

Ten minutes earlier Pascal had gone to the dining room because the meal service was about to end. Now dinner seemed like a good idea. Because I didn't know how to win the game, certainly not in the time Stefanova was allowing me, I let the position repeat three times. She claimed a draw, calmed down, and was all smiles again. She shook my hand and signed my score sheet. Two of the men she defeated congratulated me. I had not exactly "defended our manhood," but I hadn't capitulated either. I was happy I hadn't lost, but was miffed at not having the germ of an idea of how to convert my pawn advantage. I felt better after dinner when Pascal looked at the game and didn't see an easy win either. He said I'd played well.

Stefanova, as I'd expected, never had the chance for a public expression of solidarity with the Bulgarian nurses. Instead she was shown on television visiting local hospitals to comfort children with AIDS. The children deserved comfort, of course, but in the upside-down world of Libya, a planned show of unity with the nurses on death row had morphed into a photo opportunity with the victims of the nurses' nonexistent crimes.

Later, when I was back in the States, I told Jennifer about my playing Stefanova. "That's funny," she said, "but, Paul, she's not really my idol. The idea of partying all night between tournament rounds is appealing as fantasy. But I can't do that. I'm generally wiped out after a game and want to relax and go to bed."

IT WAS OUR LAST NIGHT IN TRIPOLI, AND AT SOME POINT PASCAL AND I WERE awakened in the dark by enthusiastic shouting and gunfire. The disturbance was particularly loud because we had left the balcony door open to cool off the room. I slid the glass door shut and tried to stare out, but without my contacts I couldn't see what was happening. Both of us thought the hotel might be under attack, with crowds cheering the assailants on. But I was too tired to think of a constructive response, so I pulled the pillow over my head, hoped for the best, and went back to sleep. Pascal apparently did the same thing.

In the morning we learned that there had been a holiday celebration during the night. As we waited in the lobby for Walid to escort us to the airport, half a dozen information officers told me they had a special surprise. They led me to a couch and backed away smiling. I thought I was finally going to meet Leader or his son. But instead I was greeted by an aide to Mohammed Gadhafi, who ceremoniously presented me with four wrapped gifts from his boss.

I could tell that Pascal had the same thought: What if there were bombs inside? We made an excuse about wanting to double-check our room to make sure we hadn't left anything behind. We took the presents with us and carefully unwrapped them. Gadhafi had given me a handsome camel rug, an ornate saddle blanket, a colorful woven handbag, and a set of coffee table books on his country. We examined the gifts closely but weren't really sure what we were looking for; if a wire had been sticking out of a book, or a battery sewn into the rug, we'd have known we had a problem.

AN HOUR AFTER I RECEIVED MY PRESENTS IN THE EL MAHARY, WALID WAS fast-tracking Pascal and me through airport security. We bypassed long lines of crabby travelers, and our bags were never searched or X-rayed. A nice gesture to make our send-off more pleasant or a diabolical plan to get our explosive packages onto the plane? Maybe it was time to picture Muammar on the toilet.

Pascal and I relaxed once we reached cruising altitude and heard no rumblings in the cargo hold. I asked a British Airways stewardess if the crew ever stayed at the El Mahary. She laughed. "Are you kidding?" she said. "We never stay in Tripoli. The airline won't risk leaving the planes overnight. We always turn around and fly back to London."

There was one last oddity to our surreal trip. I took out a pen and my notebook—my infamous agent's notebook—so that I could jot down some reflections. The pen looked cheap; I think it came from one of the information officers. I must have inadvertently kept it when he had me sign one of the forms. When I started to take off the cap, the very top of the cap popped open—it seemed to have been cut—and a small projectile shot out, landed six feet away in the aisle, and rolled under the seats.

"I give up," I told Pascal, laughing. "I'm tired of trying to tell whether we're in danger or not. When we leave Libyan airspace, do you think they'll serve alcohol?"

I imagined the conversation we'd have with security when we switched planes in London and later when we drove across the Canadian border to the States.

"Where have you guys been?" they'd ask.

"To the World Chess Championship," we'd say.

"And where was that?"

"In Libya."

"Did anyone give you any gifts?"

"Oh yes, Gadhafi."

"I STUCK IT TO HIM REAL GOOD, WAY UP HIM"

"[In chess] the sense of overwhelming mastery on the one side matches that of inescapable helplessness on the other. It is this anal-sadistic feature that makes the game so well adapted to gratify at the same time both the homosexual and antagonistic aspects of the father-son contest."
——REUBEN FINE

"In the two things that comprise manhood, a serious career among men and the love of a woman, his chess past dogged and thwarted him."
——ERNEST JONES,
on Paul Morphy

"I DON'T KNOW WHETHER THERE'S A GOOD WAY TO DIE, BUT there are certainly bad ways...." I was in Nigel Short's apartment in Athens, reading aloud from his weekly chess column, which he was about to dispatch to *The Sunday Telegraph* in London, when his six-year-old son walked into the room. Short had been eager to share the column with me, one writer to another, but the particular topic—a gruesome patricide in the chess world—seemed inappropriate for young ears. So I stopped my recital and promised Short that I'd continue later.

"That's OK," Short said before addressing his son. "Nicholas, what's a bad way to die?"

"Shoot yourself! Cook yourself!" Nicholas said.

"How about being stabbed to death by your own son?"

Nicholas, normally a talkative child, did not respond.

"Now you promise," Short continued, "you aren't going to do that to me. You promise me you love me."

Nicholas thought about it and then broke into a wide grin. "I'll get a woodchopper and chop your head off." He hacked the air with an imaginary axe and danced around his father's office.

"All right, Nicholas, you should leave Paul and me alone now. He came all the way from New York to talk to me."

"But I want him to talk to *me*," Nicholas said.

"I have a little guy like you at home," I told him. "His name is Alexander, and he's five."

"Can I play with him?"

"He's across the Atlantic in the United States."

"OK, Nicholas," Short interjected. "Scoot along now."

IT WAS LATE MARCH 2005, AND I WAS IN GREECE FOR THREE DAYS TO INTERview Nigel Short about the peaks and valleys of his checkered chess career. In 1993, before I took up tournament chess again, I enthusiastically followed Short's games in the papers as he became the first Western grandmaster since Fischer to play a match for the world crown. Pascal had introduced me to Short, and he was the last grandmaster I'd interview in depth in my far-flung mission to understand the inner life of chess players.

Short's reputation preceded him: I was fascinated by the contradiction between the decorous maturity and control he displayed at the board and the crudeness so prevalent in his language and behavior away from it. To further complicate the picture, unlike many world-class players, Short has an unusually stable family life (with two children and a wife of many years, Rhea, who has her own career as a psychotherapist), and yet he can also regress in an instant into the locker-room swagger of a fourteen-year-old boy intent on letting his friends know that he has just lost his virginity.

Many middle-aged players, conscious of Capablanca's example, reinvent their early years, adding victories in the crib to their résumés. It is not in Short's nature to inflate his past—nor does he have to: he was one of that unusual breed, the true chess prodigy. He learned the rules in 1971, when he was six. In 1972, he contracted chicken pox and spent time in bed replaying Alekhine's greatest games from a book.

That same year, the newspapers were full of stories about the Fischer-Spassky match, and Short remembers being extremely put off by the American's behavior. "I must say I didn't like Fischer that much at the time," Short told me. "I thought he was behaving pretty badly. I saw this slightly older guy defaulting and complaining about money, the height of his chair, and other playing conditions, and giving a big fuss about the television cameras, so what was there to be impressed by? The whole Cold War thing passed me by."

Fischer's strong, crystalline play, however, was a different story— Short found his games intoxicating. "The family was on holiday in Sandown, in the Isle of Wight, during the championship," his father wrote in *Nigel Short*. "We traveled home by car and Nigel spent the entire nine-hour journey playing through games and trying out moves on his pocket chess set." From that point on, chess dominated the boy's life. "Nigel would pick up a chess book whenever he had a spare moment, and if we allowed it, he would read during meals. A chess book was the last thing he put down at night and the first thing he picked up in the morning." Short's mother called the local chess club to arrange for him to attend, but the manager turned her down, saying that a child that young should be in bed in the evenings. Other seven-year-olds in the coal-mining county of Lancashire, England, aspired to be footballers or cricketers, but Short announced that he was going to become a chess professional.

Five years later, he was the strongest twelve-year-old on the planet and the youngest participant in the World Under 17 Championship. A Russian magazine ran a story with the headline "Beware of Nigel Short," but some of his countrymen wondered if his approach to chess was too laissez-faire to make it to the top. Short was not as single-mindedly devoted to chess as Russian prodigies; he was known to wander off in the middle of a tournament game to play Space Invaders. He also spent time away from chess mastering the electric guitar; his punk-rock band The

Urge even appeared on British television. "He seemed far too happy a child to be a chess player," international master Bill Hartston said at the time. "He never cried when he lost. I thought this was the one *weakness* in Nigel."

His strengths as a player were also conspicuous. Writing in 1981, George Botterill, former British champion, identified three of them: "One is the highly concrete character of his thinking at the chessboard. Generalities do not feature in his approach unless they can be converted into variations. A second is that he always knows what he is doing. Planless play has always been most uncongenial and alien to Nigel. Thirdly and most important of all, he has a very cool head and never seems to get flustered." Temperament, Botterill argued, was the key to competitive chess. Downplaying the role of genius, Botterill suggested that chess is 30 percent talent, 50 percent temperament, and 20 percent preparation.

As for Short's temperament, the teenager displayed a blustery self-confidence, an obnoxious trait in everyday life but a useful prerequisite, it seems, to becoming a chess champion. "My friends think I'm boastful," Short told the *Daily Express*, "but what else can I say when I sincerely believe it? No one in the world has been able to match me at my age since I was eight." He was right: at fourteen, he became the youngest international master in the world, and at seventeen, the youngest grandmaster.

As a young teenager, he had a working-class patois, shoulder-length hair, and delicate features. "Nigel sported long hair and looked disconcertingly effeminate. He knew this and it didn't bother him in the least," recalled Frederic Friedel, founder of ChessBase software, in whose Hamburg home the fourteen-year-old Short stayed while playing in a German tournament. He used his looks as an improbable weapon at the chessboard. "He would sometimes go to the round wearing a silk blouse he borrowed from my wife," Friedel said. "It was priceless to see middle-aged GMs from Eastern Europe wondering whether they should be trying to look down his shirt or not."

The British press portrayed the young Short alternately as genius and brat. In *Nigel Short: Quest for the Crown*, his biographer Cathy Forbes quoted from a piece in the *Manchester Evening News*: "Nigel Short has been moaning about what a tough life he leads. He says: 'There have been television speeches, simultaneous challenges, matches, things to write . . . it's very deeply tiring. You probably need an absolute minimum of ten days to recuperate. . . .' Try factory work for a break, Nigel."

While Short was not reserved about describing his chess ability, he was also not sentimental or mystical. When his friend, journalist Dominic Lawson, called him a genius, Short demurred: "I was simply lucky that I came to chess at an early age and was totally absorbed in it. At the age of seven I would spend fifteen hours a day and do nothing but read about chess. That is not normal. . . . But as for genius: Chess at this level requires nothing more than a combination of above average intelligence, an early response to the game, and lots of practice."

Lawson did not accept Short's humdrum explanation and suggested, in the pages of *The Daily Telegraph*, that the teenager was effectively channeling the chess goddess Caissa:

> One could subject any number of . . . intelligent children, and from far more promising backgrounds, to an early diet of intense chess, without ever producing another Nigel Short.

Lawson approvingly quoted the British grandmaster Raymond Keene, who once argued that chess prodigies share something with mathematical and musical prodigies:

> "Chess, music and mathematics all have a kind of cosmic harmony: they just balance, because God, or whoever, built the universe in that way. I think that certain children are born with the ability to act as a conduit for this cosmic harmony, and if they are lucky, they retain it into adulthood. Nigel Short is one of those lucky people."

When Lawson told Short about Keene's theory, the British chess superstar dismissed it as "a load of bollocks," but Lawson found it persuasive, pointing out that whereas most people become more combative and anxious before a big competitive event, "Nigel's metabolism takes him in an opposite and less explored direction." In Lawson's eyes, Short was a yogi, who

> becomes glacially calm, his pulse rate seems to slow, his movements become sluggish and faint—in fact he appears to enter the trance to which Indian mystics might aspire. Most chess players of international standard make a great play of eyeballing each other and strutting

about, like heavyweight boxers or sumo wrestlers. Nigel, however, scarcely seems to notice his opponent."

AWAY FROM THE BOARD, SHORT HAS A DRY WIT, AN UNRESTRAINED, OFF-color sense of humor, and a remarkable ability to turn most any conversation to the subject of sex. He is a tall, gangly man with pronounced lips, a slow, deliberate speaking style, a cultivated upper-crust British accent, and a tendency to use unusual words (*crapulent, dipsomania, pulchritude, frugiferous*).[1]

Before I visited Short in Athens, we had met only once, at the 2004 World Championship in Tripoli. Pascal introduced us in the tournament lunchroom, and within five minutes the veteran British grandmaster, who can be so erudite and introspective in his writings about the sub-rosa dynamics of a chess match, had steered the conversation to a frat-boy discussion of girls and told us much more than we cared to know about what he wanted to do with them. At the championship in Libya there were few young women for him to ogle, and he said, in mock frustration, that a certain underage male chess prodigy was starting to look pretty good. I regarded his quip as harmless and tasteless, but was surprised that he'd joke about this with a journalist he had only just met.

It was easy to understand how his humor could get him in trouble. "Short learned the dangers of uninhibited flippancy," according to Cathy Forbes, at the World Under 20 Championship in Belfort, France, in 1983:

> He gave a mischievous interview, published in the tournament bulletin, in which his idea of a joke was to insult the host nation: "France represents everything I detest most in life. Your country's only useful products are porn films." The French were not amused; Nigel's comments resulted in innumerable rescinded invitations.

Short begged forgiveness two years later:

> "When you are 18, surrounded by your friends, you'll say almost anything. It was just kid's talk, and I regret that it was taken seriously," he groveled at Catherine Jaeg of [the chess magazine] *Europe Echecs*. "Would you believe me if I told you I love France and that I dream of being able to play there again?"

In truth, however, Short never outgrew his tendency to say whatever popped into his mind. In 2002, nearly two decades after he insulted the French, Short once again notoriously displayed his inability to censor himself in an obituary he wrote for *The Sunday Telegraph* of Tony Miles, a larger-than-life compatriot and rival who died, at the age of forty-six, from unattended diabetes. Miles was the only British player in history to become world junior champion, at Manila in 1974, and the following year he became the country's first grandmaster. He was the top British player for a decade, and, according to Short, "he spearheaded the explosion of talent in this country that took us from rank mediocrity to second strongest chess nation, behind the USSR, during the 1980s."

Once John Nunn, a grandmaster ten years Short's senior, Short, and other British players started to surpass Miles in the mid-1980s, however, he suffered episodes of mania and dementia. He would suddenly take off all his clothes in the tournament hall or on a city bus,[2] and he imagined that a fellow British GM was out to kill him not just on the chessboard but in real life. He was arrested and hospitalized after loitering outside Margaret Thatcher's residence at 10 Downing Street. And yet his games were crowd-pleasers; as Black against Anatoly Karpov in Skara 1980, Miles pushed a rook pawn on his very first move, a kind of shove-it-in-your-face response that announces, "I have such little regard for you that I can violate all known chess principles and still trounce you." The twelfth world champion was so insulted that he became discombobulated, launched a reckless attack, and lost the game.

Short's obituary captured Miles's seminal importance to British chess as well as his annoying behavior at the board:

> Tony was not above a bit of gamesmanship. Players complained of him burping at the board or blowing his nose loudly. He once won a major tournament lying on his back claiming that his back condition prevented him from sitting erect. Occasionally he would deliberately (and illegally) disturb his opponents by repeatedly offering them draws.

And Miles, observed Short, was also a disagreeable loser.

> At one Olympiad during an adjournment he sealed the move "Resigns"—which not only wasted a substantial amount of his opponent's

time but insulted him to boot. But to be fair it was his great ability, and not the odd dodgy practice, that accounted for his success.

Short, though, could never forgive Miles for exploiting his position as selector of the British team for the Dubai Olympiad in 1986. Miles put himself on a higher board than Short even though he had a lower rating. "I found myself occupying board three," Short wrote, "to the incredulity of most, including an astonished Kasparov. An American reporter who unwisely mentioned this irregularity in the tournament bulletin was punched to the ground by the robust Tony." Short concluded the Olympiad discussion with an unusual aside for a major-newspaper obituary: "I obtained a measure of revenge not only by eclipsing Tony in terms of chess performance but also by sleeping with his girlfriend, which was definitely satisfying but perhaps not entirely gentlemanly." Short was savaged on Internet messages boards for this malicious revelation.

Short is so upfront about his feelings that it would not occur to him to refrain from sharing them, even when others might regard them as nasty or disgusting. Personally, given my own family history, I found this forthrightness refreshing—and, as a journalist, I found it invaluable. If Short's descriptions of himself as a gleeful conqueror during a match were often brutal, his accounts of his defeats were equally raw. After all, losing is a critical aspect of any player's experience, no matter how great he is. Short's ability to articulate the complexities of the game, combined with the violence with which he described his encounters on the board, captured something essential about chess that no other player I interviewed was willing to discuss with such candor.

IN 1975, WHEN FISCHER RENOUNCED HIS WORLD TITLE WITHOUT SO MUCH as pushing a pawn, the Soviet Union again dominated the World Championship and chess fans in the West had none of their own to cheer for until the early 1990s, when Short defeated two top Russians, Boris Gelfand and Anatoly Karpov, to reach the finals of the World Championship Candidates cycle. His opponent was the Dutch champion Jan Timman, and when Short beat him in thirteen games by the score of

7½–5½, he earned the right to challenge world champion Garry Kasparov in 1993.

If there had been any residual doubts about Short's killer instinct, they were dispelled by his quarter-finals victory over Gelfand, the world number three from Belarus. In the eighth and final game of their match, Short needed just a draw to win. For a while it looked as if he might actually lose the game to an ingenious attack that Gelfand whipped up, but on the thirty-ninth move the Belarussian grandmaster blundered. Short could now force the draw—and guarantee his advancement to the semi-finals—simply by perpetually checking Gelfand's king. To the surprise and delight of his fans, the Englishman spurned the obvious draw, drove Gelfand's monarch into the open, and checkmated him.

After the game, Short himself admitted that his play had changed. "I'm getting much more pleasure out of humiliating a guy," Short said. "Maybe I'm just a mean bastard." But he also attributed his new ruthlessness to the kind of opponent he was facing. "You play these people over the years—the Soviets particularly—and they are warped, twisted and mean," Short said. "They won't spare you any pain. So when you get a chance to inflict suffering on them, I get a kick out of it. So now I like positions where I can torture the guy slowly. Slowly is important."

Short said he had nothing personally against Gelfand, but wanted to humiliate him all the same. Borrowing Fischer's words, he admitted that he liked "seeing 'em squirm." Later he came up with the acronym DTF to describe the sadistic thrill of overpowering his opponents. DTF—Dominate, Trap, Fuck.[3] "I like to stick it to 'em," he would say. The flip side of Short's new mind-set was that when he now lost, he was devastated. He likened the pain of one particular defeat to the feeling of putting his head in a cement mixer. He said that he thought about suicide.

I WAS FORTUNATE TO VISIT SHORT WHEN HE WAS IN AN UNUSUALLY REFLECTIVE mood, thanks to a confluence of three dramatic events that were surprising and unsettling even by the usual theatrical standards of the chess world. Simon Webb, the subject of Short's ruminations on patricide in the *Telegraph*, was an expatriate British international master who had returned home from a chess club at 1:00 A.M. and been stabbed twenty times by his drug-dealer son. Garry Kasparov, two years older than Short

and a few weeks shy of forty-two, had recently stunned his fellow players by announcing his retirement from professional chess. Finally, Bobby
Fischer had just been released from a Japanese detention center and, as
Short and I conversed, was on a plane to asylum in Iceland. We paused
periodically to turn on CNN for a glimpse of the disheveled genius dis-
embarking on the tarmac in Reykjavík.

"You take these things pretty seriously when you're about to turn
forty and review what your life has amounted to," Short told me. "I met
Simon Webb a few times at tournaments in the seventies—he seemed
kind and gentle. I'm a chess player because of Fischer. And I was not
world champion because of one man, Garry Kasparov."

Short had not expected Kasparov's retirement. "He was one of the
greats if not the greatest player of all time," he said. "Lasker may have
been world champion for twenty-seven years. Fischer's hottest streak may
have been a couple of degrees warmer than Kasparov's—he once won
nineteen games in a row. But in terms of sheer consistency and number
of tournaments, Kasparov can't be matched. He's done everything in
chess. He still plays very well, but it's a question of motivation. For a
player the guy is old. Just old. As a man he's nothing of the sort. He has
a huge amount of life left. If he spends ten or fifteen years faffing
around on the fringes of Russian politics, then he can make his move.
Good for him, although it saddens me."

Kasparov's retirement brought to a close a long, frustrating chapter in
Short's career. "I played him seventy-two match and tournament games
over a period of a quarter century," Short said. "Most were classical games.
That's a hell of a lot of games. I've spent months and months of my life
thinking solely about how to beat him, and I didn't have any real success."
Short won only seven of their encounters, lost thirty-two, and drew thirty-
three.

They first played each other in the World Junior Championship in
Dortmund in 1980, and the game was a draw. "Kasparov won the
championship by a mile," Short recalled. "He was already ridiculously
strong—there was this tremendous energy. Young players who have seen
Kasparov in recent years think that he is just an opening-theory machine. Maybe they're not aware of this tidal wave of energy that hits you
when you sit down opposite him and continues assaulting you for the

entire game.[4] I barely held a draw with White. The pressure went on and on until he missed something in time trouble. I had no idea what was happening on the board, and when he offered me a draw, I gladly accepted."

The two men have had a tumultuous relationship. It has not been easy for Short to put up with Kasparov's bravado and accept that he could not dethrone the Russian and become the top alpha male in the chess world. In *End Game*, a brilliantly detailed account of their title match, Lawson recalled Short's 1987 review for *The Spectator* of Kasparov's autobiography: after quoting Kasparov's self-description—"Many a player who has become World Champion and has scaled the Mount Olympus of chess, realizes that he can go no higher and begins to descend. . . . I see no danger of this for myself. I see only new peaks before me and no descent"—Nigel wrote,

> Unashamed conceit runs like a connecting thread throughout the book. We have repeated references to Kasparov's brilliant memory, which he imagines knows no limits. My own experience is different. I witnessed a game between Kasparov and ex-world champion Boris Spassky, where the younger man tried and failed miserably to recall his previous analysis. . . . Another facet of Kasparov's personality is his ability to manipulate a set of circumstances into a simplistic theory, to suit his emotional needs. Of course, this defense mechanism is present in us all, but in Kasparov it seems to be in permanent overdrive.

Short's dislike of Kasparov was reinforced by their encounters at the chessboard. "He'd simply laugh at my moves, literally laugh," Short told me. "It was disgusting. After I moved, he'd ridicule me with this sneering smile that said, 'What an idiot. Ha ha ha. Is that the best you can come up with?' I used to find his behavior extremely distracting. I'm not saying this always happened; over the years he's calmed down a bit in his body language. But he still can have incredible expressions which are calculated to disturb."

I reminded Short of Kasparov's assessment of him in *Child of Change*, the autobiography the thirteenth world champion published in 1987, when he was twenty-three and Short was twenty-one. In *Child of Change* Kasparov wrote, referring to himself imperially in the third person:

"Nigel Short, the British player, is destined, in my opinion, soon to be the leading grandmaster in the West. . . . All that now seems to stand between Nigel and the prospect of the world crown is the unfortunate fact that fate brought him into this world only two years after Kasparov." Short thought for a moment and then said in a soft, forlorn voice, of the man whom he once disparaged as the Grandmaster of Self-Delusion, "He was right. Unfortunately, he was right."

Short acknowledged how ironic it was that he and Kasparov had joined forces in 1993, just before their World Championship bout, to break away from FIDE and found the Professional Chess Association. "Before the match I was hardly on speaking terms with him because of stuff like the sneering," Short recalled. "I was also annoyed with his behavior in the GMA [the Grandmasters Association, a kind of players' union]. His idea of democracy in an organization is that you have to agree with him; if you don't agree with him, he quits. There is this immense egocentricity in him which sometimes shows its ugly side. All top people in whatever field are to some degree egocentric but Kasparov . . ."

Short stopped in mid-sentence and just shook his head for a while before continuing. "He has his faults. He has big faults. Nevertheless he is a great, great figure, and there is nobody even remotely close to him in the chess world. No other player has anywhere near his visibility. No other player writes a column for *The Wall Street Journal* and appears regularly on CNN. Take the two current world champions, Vladimir Kramnik and Rustam Kasimdzhanov—does the public know who they are? FIDE even removed Kramnik's name from the rating list in 2002 because he was inactive in tournaments. That's just grand—a world chess champion who doesn't want to play chess."

I was sitting across a desk from Short in his study, which contained a few thousand chess books and chess journals, when I noticed that he was distracted by something on his computer. He was admiring a cheesy, possibly Photoshopped image of a shirtless Russian sub-master, Yana Portnjegina, lying stomach-down on a bed, her hands covering the sides of her bare breasts. "Have you seen this?" he asked. "It's the World Chess Beauty Contest." The Web site contained pictures of dozens of female chess players. Many of the photos looked like they were for mail-order brides, and I suspected that some of these women were in the market for husbands to help them emigrate. The women came disproportionately from ex-Soviet republics and Eastern Europe, even more disproportionately than chess players did. Only one American, for instance, Anna Hahn—who defeated Jennifer Shahade and Irina Krush to become the 2003 U.S. women's champion—supplied a picture. Viewers were asked to rate the women on looks alone, on a scale from 1600 to 2700, mimicking the chess rating system. The pictures could be downloaded or sent as e-mail postcards, and there were message boards on which viewers posted ribald and raunchy comments. The site claimed that all the photos were submitted by the contestants themselves, but it included pictures of a sixteen-year-old American junior star, who never supplied any.

"I know that some people in your country like Jennifer Shahade think the site is degrading," Short said.[5] "She's right, of course, but what can I say—I like the girls." Short in fact was one of the official arbiters of the contest, and he took his work seriously, posting comments of his own below the photos that intrigued him.

Watching Short peruse the photos of the young women, I had a fanciful notion that the development of specialized skills and character traits in early childhood is like a country fair in which you are allotted a fixed number of tickets to spend on the various concessions. This particular fair is of short duration and happens only once in a lifetime. Nigel took the chess roller-coaster a dozen times, and rode the honesty ride twice, and so he had insufficient tickets left to take the Train Beyond Adolescence more than a stop or two. I myself missed the athletic concession, and I should have ridden—damn it—the chess coaster three or four times.

GIVEN THE ODD MIXTURE OF RESPECT AND CONTEMPT SHORT HAS ALWAYS felt for Kasparov, I was curious to know how he prepared himself mentally for their match. "I didn't do that much psychological preparation," Short said. "It may seem a strange thing to say, but I feel that psychology is overestimated. It only becomes important when players are equally matched. To use a ridiculous analogy, if I got into a boxing ring with

Lennox Lewis, I could be much better prepared mentally and have a healthier psychological approach, but at the end of the day . . . My main problem was Garry. The guy simply played stronger chess than me. The first thing to do was to try to bridge this gap. I needed ammunition."

For three months before the match, Short worked on his openings with his trainer and chief second Lubomir Kavalek, a former champion of both Czechoslovakia and the United States. Many of Kasparov's opponents, Short concluded, avoided taking him on in sharp, theoretical openings. "I realized I was totally outgunned as far as opening theory was concerned," Short said. "His preparation was light-years ahead of mine." Short decided he would play sharply, but at the same time sidestep theoretical lines that Kasparov and his coterie of high-powered seconds would have extensively studied. "I elected to play things I hadn't previously played," he said. "I made a conscious decision to avoid the French Defense, which was always one of my mainstays."

When you play a new opening, you obviously benefit from surprise value. But there is also something to be gained from adhering to a battle-proven weapon whose subtleties you've mastered from hundreds of hours of actual combat experience. Kasparov, for one, made a career of pretty much one king-pawn defense, the Najdorf Sicilian, and even though his adversaries expected it, his intimate familiarity with the resulting middle-game structures outweighed the occasional opening novelties unleashed by his opponents.

"After our match," Short recalled, "Kasparov told me he had discovered a forced win in a particular, highly theoretical main line in the French, one that I might easily have played. So it was good that I avoided his strength. My openings worked fine. Yes, I got hit in one sharp Nimzo-Indian, which he busted during the match. But one hit is almost inevitable in twenty games. I didn't lose the match because of the openings." Indeed, Short bravely came out swinging with forceful lines as White against Kasparov's expected Najdorf. "I lost because he created too many problems for me," Short explained. "He was in a lot of trouble in several Black games, but he put up tremendous resistance move after move. I was just too nervous. I was trying to play exactly. I was overthinking things and got into terrible time trouble in the first half of the match. I wasn't used to the enormous pressure. It was very easy for my seconds to say move faster—they weren't the ones sitting across from this volcanic force who kept creating one problem for me after another even in positions where I had the advantage. I simply got outwitted—not even outplayed."

Short was thumped in the first half, 7½–2½. The second half went much better, an even 5–5. "I played a lot faster," he said, "because I was finally finding my form. Still the winning margin, 12½–7½, was a very convincing victory for him, but I think it was harder than the final score indicated. He suffered to some degree, and he was more tired than I was at the end, but he was always going to come out on top—the difference was just too large."

I remember being impressed during the match by how Short kept returning, bruised and battered, to the chessboard and putting up a fight even when he was far behind. "You always have to find reasons for hope," Short told me. The searching for reasons actually started before the match began, and it centered on Short's perception that chess dominated too much of his opponent's life. Kasparov was generally accompanied to key events not by his wife of the time but by his mother, Klara, and Short derived strength before the match by imagining that Kasparov was envious of his relationship with Rhea and their two-year-old child, Kyveli. Three hours before the first game, Short told Lawson and his two seconds, "When I win this match, Kasparov will like me for it. Just mark my words. Something odd is going on here. Something very odd. He has a great burden, which he wants me to take on. But he doesn't quite realize it. He just envies me my normal, happy family life. I sense it. And it's something the world chess champion can never have."

At a ceremony in which the two players drew lots to see who would start with White, Short's wife studied Klara's appearance and concluded that Kasparov's team was worried. "Look at Mrs. Kasparov," Rhea told Lawson. "She has dyed her hair blonde. She is wearing clothes that are too young for her. I thought Mrs. Kasparov was a very strong woman. But if she is desperately trying to hold on to her youth, then that is a weakness. Maybe she is less strong than she was."

For Short, the nadir of the match was the ninth game. The British bookies had long stopped giving any odds on his winning the match. Short decided to repeat a Nimzo-Indian from the fifth game in which his home-cooked novelty on the tenth move earned him a quick draw as Black—he had used a mere twelve minutes for the entire game compared to the world champion's hour and a half. This time Kasparov was ready—his sous chefs had spent days and nights cooking up a good rejoinder to the innovation—and when Short repeated the same tenth move, the Russian shot him a crocodile grin and banged out an improbable-looking response that Short had not even considered, let alone analyzed.

Six moves later Kasparov could claim a decisive advantage, and by the fortieth move he had simplified the position into a winning two-pawns-up textbook rook ending, which Soviet chess trainers had surely drilled into him as a child. On the forty-sixth move, the world champion made an inexplicable error that permitted Short to escape with a draw, but then he, too, blundered and resigned six moves later. Short had now lost five games in the match and won zero.

"I was in tears," Short recalled. "I had been completely destroyed in front of the whole world. I was in a lot of pain, terrible pain. It was really awful. I wanted him to stop hitting me. I wanted to go home. I spoke to Rhea. She didn't quite say pull yourself together because she's a bit more sophisticated, but it came down to that. I realized that I needed to go out and bloody well fight. It was a real test of inner strength. If I had given up, as I was inclined to do, I can say now that I never would have forgiven myself. I chose to fight him."

What helped Short continue was the knowledge that Kasparov himself had been down five games in the first match against Karpov in 1984–1985 before finally getting on the scoreboard in the thirty-second game, after a nerve-wracking marathon of nineteen consecutive draws. In his own match with Kasparov, Short went on to draw the next five games before scoring his first win. He recalled his jubilation: "I won the sixteenth game. Since it took Kasparov until the thirty-second game to score against Karpov, I told myself I was twice as good as Kasparov. You have to seize on every angle to try to motivate yourself. OK, it wasn't good enough. But if you do your best, and your best isn't good enough, so be it. I lost to a better player, a really great player, so I don't regret it."

Short's eyes turned to his computer screen. He was checking out another Russian woman in the beauty contest. Twelve girls and twenty minutes later, he was ready to speak about chess again.

THE HIGH POINT OF SHORT'S CHESS CAREER WAS HIS 1992 VICTORY OVER Karpov in the semifinals match to choose Kasparov's challenger. Karpov had been the number two player in the world since 1985 and the number one for ten years before that. He had been Short's hero in the mid-1970s after Fischer retired prematurely. "I needed food as a player," Short said. "Fischer was no longer providing it. I was on a starvation diet. The last game in the Spassky match was this rook-against-bishop endgame. Was that supposed to suffice for the next twenty years? Were we expected to play it over again and again? A young player has to see something new. Then Karpov came along. I never understood people who thought his games were boring. I found his play very interesting if slightly cynical because he'd often be quite happy to make a draw with Black."

In 1976, when Short was eleven, he had the opportunity to meet Karpov in Amsterdam. The then-world champion invited the British prodigy to his hotel suite. "I went to meet the great Anatoly," Short recalled. "He was very polite and nice to me. These things are important—how people behave toward insignificant beings. It is one thing to be nice when you are standing next to Mr. Bush—the Kasparov approach. It's another thing how you behave with the nonentities. Little did Karpov know that he was going to have some trouble from me later."

When the media asked Short in 1992 what his chances were against Karpov, he said fifty-fifty. "Not a few people in British chess thought I had taken leave of my senses," Short told me. "They really thought I had completely lost it. How could I possibly think that I had a chance against this legendary player who had always been higher rated than me? But that was my honest assessment. I thought I had identified his weaknesses, and might succeed if I aimed solely at his weaknesses rather than playing to my strengths, which were to some degree his strengths, too. I made him uncomfortable, and it worked. I remember comments afterward by people like Susan Polgar—Karpov played very badly. Yes he played very badly, but I *made* him play badly. That's the point. That's what she didn't understand—OK, Susan was young at the time. If you give the guy enough problems, he's going to fuck up at some point. Maybe not fuck up all the time, but at some moment he's going to slip."

Short began his match preparation with a thorough analysis of Karpov's games. "I grew up on Karpov," Short said, "so it wasn't as though I was unfamiliar with his style. There wasn't a big difference between our ratings, but I understood well that there were certain types of technical positions—fairly quiet positions where it was a question of microscopically improving the placement of pieces—in which I couldn't hope to compete with him. It's not that I played these positions badly—I just knew he was better than me. I needed to take a page from our dear, late, multiply-stabbed friend, Simon Webb."

In 1978, Webb wrote a practical manual for players called *Chess for Tigers.* In one chapter, "How to Trap Heffalumps," he discussed how strong players (tigers) could defeat even stronger players (heffalumps):[6]

> On open territory a Tiger doesn't stand much chance against a Heffalump; he can't even dig a Very Deep Pit to trap it, because Tigers aren't much good at digging. What he *can* do, however, is to entice the Heffalump on to swampy ground and hope it falls into a bog and gets sucked underground by the quagmire. The only trouble is that Tigers are even more prone to getting stuck in bogs than Heffalumps are, and they're not much good at struggling out of them.

The poor tiger is in a quandary.

> He can put up a fight neither on open plains nor in the jungle; so his only chance is to head for a swamp and *hope* that the Heffalump gets stuck before he does. If the Heffalump has any sense he would keep well away from the swamp, but Heffalumps, in spite of their great strength, are not always sensible when it comes to staying away from swamp.

Short explained that his own strategy was to lead heffalump Karpov into the swamp. The Englishman had noticed that as Black, Karpov was not comfortable in slightly cramped positions in which White was able to advance his king pawn to the fifth rank, one row into Black's position, supported by the White queen pawn on the fourth rank. In response to White's king-pawn opening, history showed that Karpov either moved his queen-bishop pawn one square, initiating the so-called Caro-Kann

Defense, or responded in kind by moving his own king pawn. If Karpov played the Caro-Kann, Short would play the Advanced Variation and achieve the desired cramping that had frustrated the Russian in the past. And if Karpov instead copied Short's first move, bringing about a double-king-pawn opening, the Englishman planned to play an obscure variation of the Ruy Lopez called the Worrall Attack. "Does the Worrall win?" Short rhetorically asked. "No. It's probably weaker than the normal stuff. But Karpov had very little experience with it in his entire career. Someone used to play it at my local club in Bolton so I was familiar with it."

As Black, Short prepared only for the queen pawn. Earlier in Karpov's career the Russian had been a very successful king-pawn player—a leading slayer of the Dragon Sicilian—but Short thought that Karpov was so ossified in his current ways that he wouldn't turn back to it. "You have to reinvent yourself as a player just to force your brain to go in a different direction," Short said. "You can have your broad base of knowledge, but you always have to add to it—and I didn't see Karpov doing that." In his many weeks of preparation, Short followed his hunch and spent only ten minutes on a king-pawn defense.

"I would have looked like an idiot if he had played e4," he admitted. "I knew that Karpov was a fantastic natural talent—very competitive, very resilient, very determined, and most of all very practical. I remember a famous game against Korchnoi from Baguio 1978 when Karpov had a dead lost position but didn't give up. He was able to take advantage of Korchnoi's time trouble to make some tricky knight moves and get a mating attack. Karpov had this ability to create difficulties for his opponent at all times, even when he had the rare lost position. I have a lot of admiration for him. He was right up there in the pantheon. But I sensed that in the 1990s he was just coasting and would not put in the work necessary to play e4 again."

Fortunately for Short, the gamble paid off. Karpov stuck to the expected queen-pawn opening. As his chief defense Short chose the Queen's Gambit Accepted. "It's a respectable opening," he said. "It's not junk, and Karpov had never faced it in a World Championship match. He had loads of experience with King's Indians, Grünfelds, the Queen's Gambit Declined. Then you are down to real junk. So QGA was my main defense."

Short began the match as Black, though, by playing a much maligned gambit known as the Budapest—some called it "real junk"—in which he jettisoned his king pawn on the second move. "I don't think he had ever faced it—at least I couldn't find a game," Short said. "I did it just to get the guy thinking." If White knows his way, he can get an easy game and the advantage of the two bishops by returning the pawn at an early stage, but if he is too materialistic and tries to hold onto the pawn, Black gets active piece play as compensation. Unsound openings are only unsound if your opponent remembers the refutation—or figures it out when the clock is ticking. If you play the same flawed line more than once, you can count on your opponent looking up the correct response.

Short lost the game and was lambasted in the chess press for employing the Budapest and gambiting away his king pawn. "A painful move for me to see," four-time U.S. champion Yasser Seirawan wrote in his monthly magazine *Inside Chess*. "I had expected Nigel to try a few opening surprises, since his normal stodgy Queen's Gambit Declined is Karpov's bread and butter. But the Budapest Gambit? In Volume 1, Issue 20, we published a bust to the Budapest that still nets me points!"

Short explained to me that the Budapest wasn't responsible for his defeat. "I was a little bit worse out of the opening but the middle game was OK," Short explained. "I went down to defeat in time pressure. I had no intention of playing the Budapest again—win, lose, or draw. It was like a condom, to be thrown away after use and not used again in any circumstances. It was meant to get him off his stride, to constantly pose problems, to show him that I can try anything. To make him worry that I might play any odd opening, not just the mainstream ones his trainers had spoon-fed him."

WHEN I REJOINED THE CHESS WORLD AS AN ADULT, I DECIDED TO TAKE UP the Budapest, inspired in part by Short's bold example in 1992. If it had been good enough for the third highest-rated player in the world, it was certainly good enough for me. The main attraction was that my opponents wouldn't be booked up on it, and if they tried to hold the pawn, I'd get the kind of tactical position I liked. At the time I was unaware of

Seirawan's commentary on Short's game or his published refutation of the opening.

I ventured to Las Vegas in 2001 to play in the National Open, one of the few annual U.S. tournaments with a respectable prize fund. The tournament was really a chess festival, with grandmasters giving simultaneous exhibitions and lectures before and after the games. I signed up for a game with Yasser Seirawan, in the first simul I'd play in as an adult. (This was the first time I had met Seirawan, the simul having occurred before we did our commentary together on ESPN.) I was hoping to do better than I had against Larsen thirty-five years earlier. There were twenty-five opponents, and Seirawan, dressed in a double-breasted brown suit, exuded charm and confidence as he dashed around the boards that were positioned on long cafeteria tables arranged in a large square. A group of female admirers watched him—as befitted the only chess player to be named "Bachelor of the Year" by *Cosmopolitan* magazine. On my board he opened with the queen pawn, and on my second move I offered my king pawn à la the Budapest. He gave me a patronizing smile— which now I know meant, "You sucker! You should have read my article!"—and immediately grabbed the pawn.

Soon he moved his queen to an exposed position in order to protect the extra pawn. I gained tempi with my knights by chasing the grand dame back to Seirawan's side of the board, and I fractured his queenside pawns by exchanging my dark-squared bishop for one of his knights. I reached the kind of position that I often obtained in my local club when I played the Budapest successfully against fellow amateurs. After an hour Seirawan had disposed of the other twenty-three participants. I was the only player left, and I tried not to appear indecorously gleeful as I enjoyed the moment. Alas, it was only a moment, because it occurred to me that the defeat of all of my compatriots meant that he and I were now playing mano a mano. I downed a cup of water and told myself to stay calm. I remembered my childhood drama coach teaching us how to be still and tranquil by "acting" like a wall or a Japanese rock garden. I don't know whether I was a convincing wall as a kid, but in the simul I tried to project wallness and certainly failed—I was much too excited. "Don't fuck up, Paul," I told myself. "Don't fuck up."

Seirawan pulled up a chair, turned it around backward, and straddled it with the swagger of a cowboy mounting a horse. "And then there was one!" he said in a voice that was at once cheerful and ominous, echoing the words of the Agatha Christie story in which ten strangers are summoned to a mansion on a remote island and slaughtered, one after another.

"Very good," I replied, "but in Agatha Christie, the host never makes it off the island, either."

"Really? Is that so?" He studied me carefully, surprised, I think, by my chutzpah. "*I* intend to make it off the island."

"Then I'm joining you."

"Is that a draw offer?"

I examined the board. I thought I had the better position, but I wasn't sure. And if I did have the better game, it wasn't against some yokel at my club but against an American chess legend—and I was his only opponent. The prudent thing for me to do was to offer a draw, but prudence, I thought, was for wimps. Don't be an idiot, another part of me advised. Take the draw while you can.

An unwritten rule of chess prohibits the player who stands worse from proposing a cessation of hostilities, so Seirawan, who had the worst of the position, was not about to propose a draw directly but instead was clearly feeling me out. (Even if the position had been equal, as the stronger player he might have been too prideful to offer a draw directly.) "I want to play on," I heard myself blurt out. Paul, you're crazy, I thought.

"Very well," he said. He took off his jacket and rolled up his sleeves. He checked his watch and said, "If you want to play, you should move."

My courage abruptly evaporated. I was afraid of moving too fast and blundering but was uncertain about the etiquette of how much time I could take. Normally in a simul you're supposed to move the instant the grandmaster arrives at the board, but that assumes he is playing multiple games. Here he was already at the board, camped out in the chair. I hoped he did not expect me to respond instantaneously whenever he moved. So I asked him, in a shakier voice than I intended, "Am I allowed to think at all?"

He could have pounced on my uncertainty, but instead this heffalump showed a soft side. "It's an interesting position," he said. "You can think a bit if you want."

"Thank you," I said, but I still moved fairly rapidly, not wanting to take advantage of his reasonableness and keep him late for his next engagement. We reached an ending with even material—two rooks, a bishop, and four pawns each—but I had an outside passed pawn that had designs on reaching Seirawan's home rank and becoming a queen. He eventually needed to give up his bishop to stop the coronation, and he netted two pawns in the process. So now I had a rook, a bishop, and two pawns against his rook and four pawns. But all of our pawns were on the same side of the board, so there was not too much play in the position and we agreed to a draw on the forty-seventh move.

"Nice game," he said graciously and shook my hand. I asked him to autograph the chessboard, and he signed the e4 square. "So much for my refutation of the Budapest," he said. He looked around at the now near-empty room. "It's good that no GMs are watching," he joked, "or they'll know to play this stuff against me." He was the perfect gentleman grandmaster, a man who played hard yet remained civil. He spent ten minutes with me going over the game. If there was a chess heaven, this was it. Not only had I achieved every amateur's dream of making a grandmaster sweat, I had made him reassess an opening—albeit an obscure and ultimately dubious opening. Of course, it would have been even sweeter if I had won. Still, our encounter sustained me for days. Whenever I found my mood turning sour for reasons that had nothing to do with chess, I'd remind myself that I had been the last man standing and never in danger of going down.

SHORT HAD LOST WITH THE BUDAPEST OWING TO NERVOUS PLAY IN TIME trouble. Yet he emerged from that first game as the psychological victor because of the chance discovery of an impostor in the ranks of Karpov's otherwise illustrious team of opening theoreticians, end-game experts, doctors, masseuses, and fitness gurus. The Russian's entourage included a parapsychologist named Rudolf Zagainov.

Parapsychologists—specialized hypnotists who supposedly use mental telepathy to influence other people's minds—were a peculiarly Soviet phenomenon. In a state that monitored your private activities through a network of secret informers, it was easy to believe in the existence of so-called experts who could read and control your mind. Short was not a believer but was troubled nonetheless "by this creepy man who sat in the front row, stared at me, and took copious notes. Before the match a friend of mine said she'd sit next to him and counteract his voodoo."

When Zaiganov got up from his seat at the end of the first game, he dropped one of his pages of notes. Short had a look, expecting it to be in Russian. "Amazingly he had written in English, 'I love you' and 'I have no money,'" Short recalled. "It was obvious he was a fraud. He was sitting there getting paid by Karpov and was practicing his English which he hoped to try on some girl, like my young cousin Jayne who had come with us to baby-sit Kyveli. After reading the sheet, I thought, He can do whatever he wants. He's just a joke. Karpov probably took him on because he thought it didn't do any harm and might rattle me. Strangely it had the reverse effect. I got strength from this, from realizing that of everything Karpov had at his disposal, he chose a total bozo as a crutch." Short's hotel suite was adjacent to Karpov's, and at night, to mock Rudolph Zagainov, Short blasted "Rudolph the Red-Nosed Reindeer" on his electric guitar. He wondered whether Zagainov had learned sufficient English to understand the joke.

The loss of the first game with Black did not set Short back much. As White, he was unstoppable, scoring 4½ points out of 5. "I stuck it to him real good, way up him," Short said. "The guy was getting raped. I should have won some with Black. My QGA turned out to be an inspired choice. He had become so calcified in his approach to chess that he wanted to be on autopilot for the opening." Short forced Karpov to think for himself early in the game and threw his tempo off. The former world champion did not manage the clock well—on four occasions he came within five seconds of his flag falling.

In the Queen's Gambit Accepted played in the fifth game, Short was particularly proud of the sixth move that he sprang on an unsuspecting Karpov. Short called it the Beck's Beer Variation, and it was the result of the preparation he'd done with Kavalek in Reston, Virginia.[7] One evening Short and Kavalek were drinking Beck's after they finished their official chess work for the day. They were sitting by a board on which there was a QGA position that they had looked at earlier. "I just reached out suddenly, beer in hand," Short recalled, "and made the pawn move . . . c5. We both started laughing because it looked like such a stupid move. Then Lubosh responded as White, we each made a few moves, and I got a perfectly decent position. So now we had a big laugh about this. We set it up again, and we tried something else. Again I got a decent position." Even though the move was Short's idea, in the haze of beer he was still not sure that it was sound, but later he couldn't find anything wrong with it, either.

When he tried the Beck's Beer Variation against Karpov, the grandmaster commentators in the press room said Short had an atrocious position and claimed that something had gone terribly wrong with his preparation. For a few moves Karpov responded logically and reasonably quickly. On the fifth or sixth move into the variation, he went into a forty-five-minute think. "It dawned on him," Short said, "that the position was not as good for him as he had initially judged. I could tell that he still thought he was slightly better. But he was looking and looking and couldn't find a way to keep his imagined advantage. Then I could tell from his body language that he was now concerned about maintaining equality, but didn't see that, either. He finally moved and I got an advantage, then a clear advantage, and then a decisive advantage. Then I screwed up and we drew. It was very annoying. I was clearly winning."

In the seventh game, when Short was ahead by one point, he deviated from his opening strategy and played the Queen's Gambit Declined. He was an expert in the QGD, but so was Karpov, and it was an opening that the Russian expected him to play. "It was a huge mistake," said Short. "I turned to it because I was very comfortable with it. But it played into his strength, and he pressed and tortured me in a typical Karpovian way. It was like the tiger against the heffalump in the open field. The tiger was strong but the heffalump was stronger. So in the next game it was back to the swamp," where the heffalump got stuck in the quagmire. When the tenth game was completed, the tiger emerged victorious by a two-point margin, 6–4.

"I was very high afterward," Short told me. "Many people described the match as the end of an era for Karpov, and in a sense it was. Not that he didn't have good results later. Perhaps he had the best year of his life in 1994, when he won Linares with some ridiculous number of points [nine wins, four draws, and zero losses]. But it was Indian summer for him. I had exposed the flaws in his chess."

WHEN I LOOKED AT NIGEL SHORT'S GAMES IN CHESSBASE, I WAS PLEASED TO see that in several key encounters in the twenty-first century he assayed the Evans Gambit, a romantic throwback like the King's Gambit to the heady attacking days of the nineteenth century. I had often employed the Evans Gambit in my youth because it was a favorite of Paul Morphy, the pre–Civil War prodigy from New Orleans. When I first became a student of chess, I was eager to emulate Morphy's approach—the moves he made on the chessboard were flashy and powerful, while his overall decorum, at the board and away from it, was quiet and respectful. The Evans Gambit is a double-king-pawn opening in which White offers a pawn on the fourth move in order to deflect Black's bishop. In return for the pawn, White obtains control of the center and a lead in development. In the Evans Gambit, the pyrotechnics begin early because White presses hard to convert these transient advantages into a kingside attack before Black is able to catch up in development and exploit his extra pawn.

There was a clarity to Morphy's thrilling chessboard aggression that I found particularly instructive. His games illustrated the virtues of free and quick development. "Help your pieces so they can help you" was how he put it. Players before him favored cheap tactical tricks, launching early speculative sorties with only a couple of pieces. Games were won because the aggressor set a trap into which the opponent obligingly stepped. Morphy was the first to recognize that if the intended prey kept a cool head and simply sidestepped the snare, the potential trapper would be left with an inferior, if not a losing, position because his pieces were overextended.

Morphy's approach was every bit as exciting and bellicose as his predecessors' (and against amateurs he often went directly for the jugular), but he pioneered the purer strategy of amassing all his forces before launching a full-scale assault. In other words, he built up the ground troops before commencing air strikes. His well-prepared king-hunt would then unfold with atomic-clock precision and his helpless adversary would be outgunned.[8] Morphy also had better defensive skills than his contemporaries, and so he could rebuff any premature, rash thrusts of theirs. For me, Morphy had seemed to solve the dilemma of how to play chess with gusto and force and also do it with integrity and honor. He was an assassin on the chessboard and a mensch away from it.

As a child, I was also drawn to Morphy because of the way he came across in old engravings and photographs that I studied. He was a slender, well-dressed young man who always wore a bow tie. One of his friends described the five-foot, four-inch champion as having "a face like a young girl in her teens" and kid-size shoes "into which not one woman in a hundred thousand could have squeezed her feet." The pictures showed him surrounded by older men who towered over him or were twice his girth, and yet he emasculated them on the chessboard and made it look so easy. I was not short or frail like Morphy, but at various times in elementary school I was terrorized by bullies, and chess appealed to me because it didn't reward physical aggression.

Morphy's career was meteoric. In the fall of 1857, the twenty-year-old phenomenon, who had already earned a law degree from the University of Louisiana but was not of legal age to be an attorney, traveled to New York City and won the First American Chess Congress, a knockout event among the country's best players. Although his demeanor at the chessboard was completely proper—he sat motionless and avoided eye contact whenever it was his opponent's turn—his stony composure unnerved his adversaries. They didn't understand how he could sit for hours without food or drink. "When one plays with Morphy," one of his adversaries wrote, "the sensation is as queer as the first electric shock, or first love, or chloroform, or any entirely novel experience. As you sit down at the board opposite him, a certain sheepishness steals over you."

On his twenty-first birthday, June 22, 1858, Morphy arrived in Europe to slay the top players in the salons of London and Paris. He brought honor to the United States by becoming one of the first Americans in any field to shine on the international stage. The whole nation, even those who could not tell a knight from a bishop, was proud of his accomplishments. Cigars, packaged foods, and sports teams were named after him. His games were reported move for move on the front page of *The New York Times* and praised in poems and orations by Henry

Wadsworth Longfellow, James Russell Lowell, Oliver Wendell Holmes, and Louis Agassiz. Artists competed to sculpt his bust.

In Europe, Morphy was also lionized and feted by aristocrats. The Duke of Brunswick invited him to join the Count Isouard de Vauvenargue in their box at the Paris Opera. During *The Barber of Seville*, the duke set up chess pieces and implored the American to take on the two of them.[9] Although the noblemen consulted each other before every move, they succumbed to a dramatic queen sacrifice that led inescapably to checkmate a move later. At seventeen moves, the game was cruelly short. I remember the sacrifice making a strong impression on me when I looked at it as a child.

My father shared my interest in Morphy and other great players of yesteryear. He seemed to know every used bookstore in New York City, and we searched together for old books about Morphy. But my dad also went out of his way to make sure I knew that my childhood chess hero's life had ended badly.

When Morphy was abroad in 1858, he tried to arrange a match with Howard Staunton, an irascible Englishman and self-taught scholar of Elizabethan drama who had been the best player in the world in the 1840s. Staunton seemed interested and encouraged the American to extend his stay in Europe while they arranged the details. After keeping Morphy waiting for three months, Staunton finally backed out, claiming that he could not take time away from his important work as a Shakespearean scholar for "a mere game." The reality was that Staunton was apparently scared off when Morphy demolished the talented Johann Löwenthal for a £100 wager in Manchester. Of the American's seamless play against Löwenthal, one observer wrote:

> He seldom—in fact, in my presence never—expended more than a minute or two over his best and deepest combinations. I fancy he always discerned the right move at a glance, and only paused before making it partly out of respect for his antagonist and partly to certify himself of its correctness, to make assurance doubly sure; and to accustom himself to sobriety of demeanor in all circumstances.

Morphy also handily won a match against Adolf Anderssen, a German mathematician who had won London 1851, the world's first international tournament. Anderssen was the greatest practitioner of the romantic, go-for-mate-from-the-first-move school, and Morphy's victory was a repudiation of that style of play and a convincing demonstration that he was now the best player in the world.[10] Anderssen was undoubtedly stronger than Staunton in 1858, and yet Morphy, who was already conflicted about postponing his career as a lawyer to play chess, was profoundly unsettled by the Englishman's diminishment of chess as a "mere game."

In fact, Morphy never got over Staunton's refusal to play him. He returned to the United States and withdrew from chess in 1859, at the age of twenty-two, his career at the board ending just eighteen months after it started. He spiraled slowly into paranoid mania. His life had flipped: when he played chess, the only aggression he experienced was safely confined to the chessboard; now he saw violence everywhere. He thought strangers and friends were plotting to kill him, and he made a preemptive attack, with a walking stick, on an innocent brother-in-law. Morphy refused to eat food that was prepared by anyone besides his mother or younger sister for fear it was poisoned. He would live another quarter century, but never managed to practice law. He spent his last days walking the streets of New Orleans, staring at pretty faces. He would also pace on his veranda, muttering in French, "He will plant the banner of Castile on the walls of Madrid, with the cry 'The city is taken,' and the little king will go away utterly shamefaced."[11]

Morphy could take some solace, in 1874, when Staunton's home-court publication, *City of London Chess Magazine*, ran an obituary—of which Short would certainly approve—that condemned the Englishman for dodging the match:

> And now what was Staunton as a man? An old maxim has it that we must speak nothing but good of the dead. That may be all very well for epigraph writers, whose trade it is to engrave lies on marble, but, for ourselves, we repudiate any such doctrine, considering it to be ethically unsound.... We have, therefore, very little hesitation in saying that, in our opinion, the deceased often acted, not only with a signal lack of generosity, but also with gross unfairness toward those whom he had suffered defeat, or whom he imagined likely to stand between him and the sun.

On July 10, 1884, a hot and oppressive day in New Orleans, the forty-seven-year-old Morphy returned from his customary midday stroll through the French Quarter and settled into his usual one o'clock bath. When the punctilious Morphy did not emerge at the routine time, his widowed mother, Thelcide, banged on the locked bathroom door and, receiving no response, summoned a neighbor, who forced it open. They found Morphy dead, his hands clutching the rim of the tub. The physician who examined him attributed the death to apoplexy, or congestion of the brain, brought on by the shock of cold water to his overheated body.

When news of his death reached the Manhattan Chess Club, in New York, a memorial meeting was hastily called and a resolution was unanimously passed that "the portrait of Paul Morphy in the rooms of the club be draped in mourning for a period of three months." The officers of the Manhattan Chess Club found it sadly ironic that the man known for his virility on the chessboard was so fragile that he died from a cold bath.

Newspaper obituaries, however, disputed the cause of death. They attributed his demise to mental overexertion from blindfold chess years earlier. In his prime, Morphy liked to demonstrate his chess skill by playing as many as a dozen blindfold games simultaneously against "sighted" opponents. Such a feat demanded extraordinary concentration, and, according to *The New York Sun*, "The strain in his brain produced a brain fever from which he never recovered."[12]

FROM THE TIME I FIRST ENTERED TOURNAMENTS, I WONDERED WHETHER MY own interest in chess was too obsessive and stressful. My father, however, never seemed particularly worried about me in this regard. He no longer played chess with me, because the games were too one-sided. Instead, he encouraged casual games with Mike, his closest friend, a dyspeptic and dominating widower whom—let me be blunt—I found completely repulsive.

Mike had the strange, distinctive physique of a pregnant Indian squaw with big biceps. I remember him spending his days hobbling around the Village on a clubfoot while pumping hand-held weights. He had a lot of free time: his wife was a Maytag, so he inherited a fortune from the washing machine manufacturer and didn't have to work. My father told me that he had no children and I stood to inherit millions if I was nice to him and "played my cards right." I knew that, for my father, this would ideally include throwing some of our chess games, but I couldn't bring myself to do it. Even so, I experienced them as a terrible ordeal. Mike rarely showered—which was unnoticed by my father, who had no sense of smell (owing, he claimed, to a boxing injury)—and I had to keep from gagging whenever Mike leaned in toward me across the chessboard.

No doubt I disliked Mike even more than I would have otherwise because, when my parents separated, my father moved into an apartment with him. I never understood the nature of their relationship. Was he in love with Mike? Was it an unconsummated and unrequited love? Were they simply good friends? Or was my dad just cravenly looking after my financial well-being? All of these possibilities seemed distressing.

(Much later, after my father's death, I opened the envelope on which he had provocatively written "IF YOU DARE OPEN THIS ENVELOPE, MY HAND WILL GROW OUT OF THE GRAVE AND CHOKE YOU!" and found copies of a dozen letters he had sent to Mike. I pored over them for clues to their relationship, but the letters were bland and uninformative and certainly didn't need to be destroyed. I couldn't help feeling that the envelope was an elaborate practical joke: after all, my dad knew that I was curious about him and Mike. He also knew, of course, that I would open the envelope and study the letters as if they were cryptic texts. By leaving behind only innocent letters and calling attention to them—perhaps they were never even dispatched and were created specifically for me—he had indeed succeeded in needling me from beyond the grave.)

One thing was clear: my father was inordinately dependent on Mike. Perhaps it was simply because Mike lent him significant sums of money, bankrolling him for the year he was supposed to be writing his novel. Whatever the reason, my dad was very nervous about how I behaved around his friend. He'd discourage me from talking about things I liked that he thought might irritate Mike. For example, he didn't want me to mention that I played tournament bridge, because he feared Mike would dismiss the game as an activity for idle country club ladies. (There was no real money in chess for me. But bridge was a partnership game, and when I was a senior in high school, geriatric women who needed "master points"—the bridge world's equivalent of chess ratings—occasionally paid me to join them in a club tournament.) I don't know whether Mike actually disliked bridge—or whether my dad was communicating his own disapproval—but I hated being censored.

As for chess, I was allowed to talk about the game—Mike seemed to enjoy these discussions—until I started consistently beating him. He was a worse loser than Karpov and grumpily dismissed chess as the domain of idiot savants. After one game, Mike announced that he didn't want to play me again and insisted that I give up chess because a kid my age should not be sitting on his butt for hours but doing active things like weightlifting. When my father did not come to my defense, I felt betrayed. It was clear that he fervently hoped I would never mention the game again in Mike's presence.

It wasn't until later that I realized my father, too, wanted me to give up chess altogether. Yes, I sensed that he was jealous of my accomplishments in the game and envious of my ability to buckle down and focus on improving my play, but historically chess had been a big part of our bond. Besides, he knew how angry and contrarian I'd be if he asked me to abandon the one thing in life that I found so mesmerizing. Instead, he resorted to his signature indirect strategy—the artful positioning of a disturbing manuscript in a place where I'd "stumble" on it—to make me reconsider the wisdom of playing chess.

I returned to my father's apartment one afternoon in high school and found on the dining table a copy of a 1931 scientific paper called "The Problem of Paul Morphy: A Contribution to the Psycho-Analysis of Chess," by Ernest Jones, a heavy hitter in the world of psychology who was a colleague of Freud's. The paper was casually open to a page in which Jones wrote that in chess "the unconscious motives actuating the players is not the mere love of pugnacity characteristic of all competitive games, but the grimmer one of father-murder." My father had highlighted *father-murder*. Chess, Jones noted, was the sublimation of the Oedipal struggle. The goal was to render the king, the father figure, helpless through checkmate—that is, "to sterilize him in immobility" or, in other words, to castrate him. Naturally, Jones said, the most potent assistance was provided by the queen, the mother figure.[13] In Morphy's case, Jones observed, the Oedipal drive was clearly reflected in the skill he showed "in separating the opposing King and Queen," evident in the twelve-year-old's first recorded game, against his uncle.

But Morphy's unconscious motives were even more scurrilous. The object of chess, Jones continued, was to mate the king in two senses of the word *mate*: the sense of checkmate (from the Persian *mat*, meaning "death"), on the one hand, and the sexual sense, on the other. Jones concluded that Morphy suffered from "latent homosexual[14] and anal-sadistic aggression directed at his own father."[15] The evidence was the skill Morphy reportedly exhibited in "attacking the king from behind"—a phrase my father also underscored.

In case my adolescent mind was too naive, or shocked, to understand the full import of Jones's words, my dad left out and marked up another essay on the psychopathology of chess that decoded why Morphy exhibited this particular skill. This quiet young man, who could sit longer at the chessboard than any other top player of his day, secretly desired to penetrate his father until he rectally bled to death. Morphy's own father died just before he ascended to the world stage. Staunton became the substitute father figure, Jones concluded, and when Morphy didn't get a chance to sublimate his homo-patricidal impulses by buggering Staunton on the chessboard, his psyche collapsed.

Dominate, trap, fuck—it didn't get any more squalid than that. And to think that I, in the bloom of grade school innocence, had thought that chess was a battle royal of wits and stamina and that the refined and dapper Morphy, known as "the pride and sorrow of American chess," had been the game's most noble and tragic practitioner! Never mind that the king doesn't have a behind and that, try as I did, I couldn't find a single game of Morphy's in which one of his pieces sneaked around and attacked the king from the opposing side of the board—I was horrified that my dad left out this crap for me to read.

Of course, my father, like Staunton, never confronted me directly, and never acknowledged the hostility of bullying me into playing with Mike, or the aggression inherent in diminishing the importance of the game I loved. He was fucking with me. He intended to gross me out by suggesting that I wanted to fuck and kill him. And, given the master of misdirection he was, he may also have wanted me to be sickeningly alarmed by the reverse possibility—that he wanted to fuck and kill me. Or perhaps, in his darkest moments, he even felt that way. He did succeed in getting me to withdraw further from the game. Whatever faint hopes I still had that I could play chess unencumbered by psychological stress were now completely scuttled. The game had become a fairly joyless pastime.

SHORT IS ONE OF THE TOP PLAYERS WHOSE BEHAVIOR AT THE BOARD IS ALways entirely respectful. He doesn't glare at his adversary, slam down the rooks, twist the knights into the board, rock back and forth, tap his feet, or pace the tournament hall snorting like a feral animal. He doesn't laugh out loud at his opponent's moves or stab himself with a bishop if he loses. And the psychological warfare he wages on his opponents is largely confined to the board, like his choice of the Budapest against Karpov.

Like boxers who disparage prospective opponents in the press, the quick-witted Short can hold his own when provoked in prematch verbal fisticuffs. During Short's match with Timman, Kasparov was asked whom he expected to be his challenger and whether that person would put up a long fight. "It will be Short, and it will be short," Kasparov responded. Short got back at Kasparov at an awkward meal the two shared at a Chinese restaurant in London after they had hammered out the details of their upcoming world title bout. "At the end of the dinner," Lawson wrote,

> when the Russian was paying the bill, the waiter suddenly seemed to recognize Nigel. "Excuse me," the Chinese asked Short, "but aren't you the world chess champion?" "Kasparov looked amazed," Nigel told me, giggling with the memory of it. "So I said to the waiter, 'No, I am not the world chess champion. I am the next one.'"[16]

But Short has faced psychological pressure well beyond, and much creepier than, any he has ever exerted on his opponents. His worst experience was his 1994 Candidates Match against Gata Kamsky, the American star who was born in Siberia and trumpeted in the press as the new Bobby Fischer. Short had played Kamsky four times before, in Tilburg in 1990 and 1991, and emerged with the enviable record of three wins and one draw. Kamsky's father, Rustam, was notorious in the chess world for invoking vast conspiracy theories about how the chess establishment was holding back his immigrant son. At the Super Tournament in Linares in 1991, Rustam accused Kasparov of trying to poison seventeen-year-old Gata's orange juice. The press loved the story, and the other participants in the tournament reacted by ridiculing the Kamskys. Before playing Gata at Tilburg 1991, Short wrote "BEWARE POISON!" on a napkin and left it on the refreshment table. A humorless arbiter removed the sign before Gata saw it. Later, when Gata was set to face Kasparov, Short delivered a glass of orange juice to the youngster's side of the board.

"Gata's behavior at the board was always fine," Short said, "but away from the board it was completely disgusting. In 1994, he and Rustam waged total war on me even before the match began." Another Candidates Match, between Englishman Michael Adams and the Indian prodigy Vishy Anand, was scheduled for the same time in the same playing hall, enabling chess fans to enjoy both encounters. (The winners would later play a match among themselves for the right to challenge Kasparov.) "Gata demanded that a wall be erected on the stage to separate the two matches. Why? Because there was another Englishman there, and they said he might signal me. I don't know of any time in chess history when a wall was built to separate games, and of course it wasn't done here."

Short lost the first game, but the charges of unfair play continued. "Gata filed written accusations that I was cheating," Short said. "At no other point in my long career have I been accused of cheating, and he was claiming that I was looking at Anand a lot, which obviously meant we were communicating by telepathy, and that I was going to the toilet too much, where God knows what he thought I was doing. It was constant bombardment, all these spurious charges. So I lost the first three games. I must be the most incompetent cheater the world has ever seen. I'm losing game after game and being accused day after day of cheating."

In the fourth game, Short was playing the White side of the Ruy

Lopez and Gata was coughing uncontrollably. "It was my move and I remember counting the number of times he coughed. I don't think he was doing it deliberately—it was a nervous reaction. And I asked him, while my clock was running, if he would mind stopping coughing or maybe getting some water. That was it—he stopped coughing—and I went on to win the game. The match arbiter told me that after the game, Rustam rushed up to Gata and said, 'You must protest. You must protest. He disturbed your concentration by speaking to you during the game.' Gata said there was nothing to protest, that I didn't disturb him. Well, an hour later Gata submitted another written protest." Even as Gata Kamsky and his father were pretending to be victimized, they seemed to be doing everything they could think of to intimidate and destabilize Short.

"And it got worse," Short told me. "Much worse. Rustam threatened to kill me. I will never forget. He came up to me in the restaurant and said I had disturbed his son. He was all but foaming at the mouth. He started out being angry and got progressively angrier and stuck his face in mine. He was a former pugilist. Now, did I think he was going to kill me or just punch me and leave me with a broken nose? I think the latter was more likely. But either way it didn't sound particularly good. I was very shaken and lodged a complaint with the police. He was taken in and warned. With such a guy, you never know what he's going to do. Maybe you're out walking that evening on the *paseo* and the guy comes and whacks you."

Short thought that he had recovered his composure by the fifth game, in which he played the Black side of a Nimzo-Indian, but in the middle of the game he suddenly felt "this wave of complete exhaustion. It was obvious that this thing had stressed me beyond belief. The game continued. I was completely crushed and mated like an idiot. Rustam Kamsky succeeded. He won the game just as surely as if he had made the mating move himself. At the very minimum, after this death threat Gata should have forfeited a game. Other sports have rules about such things. In cricket, if the fans of one side go on a riot, it's just declared lost for them. The fans can set fire to the stands. They can throw bottles. But tough: checkmate. In chess we don't have a framework for dealing with this. So I lost the match badly. It was easy for Gata to be gentlemanly at the board when there was someone standing behind him with a baseball bat."

Before the match, Kasparov had given Short some unsolicited advice. "If you ever doubted that Garry Kasparov is a genius," Short told me, "listen to this. He offered to set me up with two bodyguards. He said that they should visit Rustam and tell him that if he ever stepped within ten meters of me, he was dead. I seriously considered the advice because of all of the nasty things I had heard about the Kamskys, but I turned him down because it seemed too extreme. I could have afforded the bodyguards. It was an investment I clearly should have made."

(Gata Kamsky would not let me interview him. I approached him directly and through Pascal. "I have absolutely no desire to have anything to do in the book that even mentions the name of Nigel Short," Kamsky e-mailed me. In 1996, Kamsky had pretty much mysteriously dropped out of chess for the next eight years and attended college and law school. In June 2004, he reentered the chess world by showing up at the Marshall to play in the New York Masters. His initial tournament results were mixed, but much of his old form returned and, in April 2007, he was ranked number nineteen in the world and had qualified to represent the United States in the 2007 World Championship cycle. In the first match of the cycle, he trounced Pascal's nemesis, Etienne Bacrot. Kamsky's father—who used to berate him in public when he lost—no longer accompanies him to tournaments. Kamsky's behavior now, in this, his second chess life, is unimpeachable.)

SHORT HAD LOST TO KAMSKY BECAUSE HE FELT EMASCULATED BY KAMSKY'S behavior off the board. I wondered if Short had ever lost a game for the reverse reason: that he was too cocksure and discounted his opponent prematurely. (One of Bobby Fischer's seconds, grandmaster Larry Evans, said that the American champion's one flaw was overconfidence, which "sometimes causes him to forget his opponents are also capable of finding good moves.") Short denied that he was ever guilty of this, but told me that one of his most important and hardest lessons was losing in the 1988 Candidates to Jonathan Speelman, his friend and neighbor.

Short was ranked third in the world then, and Speelman was fifth, and so West Hampstead, their neighborhood in London, had 40 percent of the world's top five players. "What I learned from the match is that I had underestimated the psychological aspect of chess," Short said. "I told you earlier that people tend to overestimate the psychological dimensions—and I still maintain that. But here we were of similar strength—I was better but the difference was not immense. I found his play very confusing. I was not ready for the rough and tumble."

At the time Short was training with British GM John Nunn, who had been a triple gold medalist in the Thessaloníki Chess Olympiad in 1984. "He was a very good second for me in many respects," Short said. "I had a high opinion of him as a player. He had an invincible record in the Olympiad, he was a killer on the White side of the Sicilian, he was very well prepared in the openings, and he was a great tactician. But he has an algorithmic personality, and algorithmic personalities aren't good at psychology. His approach to chess was here is this opening system, and you look for a novelty within the system. It was sort of a technical approach. He was very, very good about analyzing positions on the board. Yet he was pretty useless when it came to thinking about who Speelman was, how the match might turn out, what to do if it should twist in a different way. I was too naive then in my approach to matches. We spent too much time patching holes in my opening repertoire as opposed to thinking about Speelman and figuring out how he would approach the match and how we should counter his approach."

In the early 1980s, Speelman, a tall vegetarian whose nickname was the "Gentle Giant," was not among the chess world's elite. He suffered from an eye disease that was causing him to go blind.

> Staring at the board for hours at a time gave him terrible headaches. His doctors forbade him from reading books or engaging in activities that would excessively strain his eyes. Jonathan languished in limbo, trapped in an ever-deepening darkness. Unable to study at length and handicapped by his eye disorders, his play was strictly hit or miss. Success in a given tournament depended on how well his eyes felt.

Once ophthalmologists were able to arrest his condition through surgery, the headaches disappeared, his rating shot up above 2600, and he decimated Yasser Seirawan 4–1 in a 1986 match.

Speelman was in peak form when he faced Short in 1988. "Jonathan had these two switches," Short recalled. "There's his vegetarian switch which was usually on—he played quiet moves, safe but a little bit dull. I remembered a magazine mocked him for not playing full-bloodied carnivore openings; it called one of his innocuous openings the Anemic Parsnip. Then he had a manic switch, where he created complete chaos. He had almost nothing in between dull and chaos. The intelligence on his part was deciding when to flip which switch. I didn't cope with the changeups. I simply didn't cope. I would expect a slow positional encounter and then he'd suddenly go manic on me." Short lost, 3½–1½.

In the 1991 Candidates cycle, Short faced Speelman again for eight games en route to Karpov and Kasparov, and this time he had studied his opponent. "I exposed certain weaknesses in Jon's preparation," said Short. "I aimed at his weaknesses where in the first match I had worked on my systems. But Jon still gave me problems." Short won the first game on the Black side of the Grünfeld, but after five games was a full point behind. He was in danger of being eliminated in the next game, and even if he won two games in a row, the best he could do was tie the match and send it into rapid playoff games.

"This was the same dismal situation I had faced in our first match," Short recalled. "I was very, very depressed. There was a free day before the sixth game and I got up incredibly late. I didn't want to get dressed. I thought, here we go again three years later—history is repeating itself. Rhea said, Come on let's go out and watch a film, and I said I can't be bothered. I was moping, just wallowing in self-pity. She told me to pull myself together and stop feeling sorry for myself. She had a *Time Out* and started reading the titles of the films in London and asked me to choose. And I said no, no, no to title after title. Then she came to one— *Reversal of Fortune*. Yes, that's the one we're going to see. It made a total difference to my mood. I'm not really a superstitious person, but sometimes you start to think: maybe there is a God.

"The next day I played a very good game. I employed the Four Knights. It was an interesting choice because people think of this old opening as very drawish. Grandmasters often used it as a means of agreeing to a quick draw, but of course I was looking for more. In the previous match in this situation, I played sharply—he chose the Pirc Defense and I responded with the Austrian Attack—and the crisis in the game came early. This time I wanted to delay the crisis because I thought slow tension would be difficult for Jon, and the Four Knights fit the bill.

"When you feel you're under pressure—it could be real pressure on the board or self-imposed pressure, as Jon's was, because he was eager to put me away and win the match—it's very good when the crisis comes quickly. Either you solve the crisis or you don't. The most unpleasant thing is a sort of steady building of the tension. You start off the game feeling tense and it just gets worse and worse and worse. And when the crisis finally comes, you'll often be in no condition to meet it. I think I played well, psychologically well. I didn't try to force anything out of the opening. Just got a reasonable position and kept playing from there. I won the game—it was the comeback moment—and the momentum in the match changed dramatically." The next game was a draw, and then Short won in overtime, at the rapid time control of forty-five minutes a game.

Six years later, in 1997, another movie helped Short at a defining moment. He was playing for the World Championship in Groningen. The format was a series of two-game knockout matches. After disposing of Korchnoi and Andrei Sokolov, he faced Alexander Beliavsky. "We played a wild, fascinating game with tremendous tension," Short said. "First I sacrificed a piece and got a lot of play. But rather than trying to hold the material, he started attacking me and in the end I succumbed to the onslaught. I lost the game and was facing imminent elimination if I couldn't win the next day. [Russian GM and fellow cricket fan] Peter Svidler said, 'Come on Nige, let's see a film.' I wasn't in a great mood, but I went with him anyway into town. We saw the Bond movie *Tomorrow Never Dies*. And I thought, yes. Tomorrow never dies. This is it. I'm not going down tomorrow. Sure enough, I beat him in a great game and then I crushed him in overtime.

"So I might be right to be a little superstitious. The logical part of my brain says this is complete bollocks. But actually, so what? It doesn't matter as long as it helps you at that time. Karpov was famous for not washing his hair when he was on a winning streak. Unfortunately, he had long tournaments where he never lost a game—the guy got greasy. The most opportunistic thing I ever did was to get religion. I'm basically an atheist—I like to tell Christians I'm a Satanist—but in the middle of important matches I go to church."

And what exactly does he pray for? At the time of the Karpov match, Short told a journalist: "At first I said, 'Please, God, let me win this game,' but I realized this was asking too much. So instead I asked, 'God, please give me the strength to beat this shithead!'" Since the conversation with the Almighty didn't hurt his cause, Short told me that at his next match, in El Escorial, Spain, against Timman, he visited the beautiful Cathedral of the Monastery of Philip II every day and prayed for victory.

I'M NOT A SUPERSTITIOUS PERSON, BUT I DO FIND MYSELF SEIZING ON ANY-thing that could conceivably boost my confidence at chess. On an unsea-sonably cold spring day, David Blaine was standing on top of a ten-story pillar in Manhattan's Bryant Park, behind the New York Public Library. After thirty-five hours on the twenty-two-inch-diameter column, and no sleep or food, he planned to jump and land on a pile of cardboard boxes below. He had been training for this stunt for more than a year, starting from a ten-foot pillar and gradually working his way up to eighty feet. Twenty-eight hours into the feat, I joined a crowd of people in the park who were cheering him on. David was wired with an earpiece and micro-phone, and I spoke to him for a few minutes via his assistant's phone. He sounded mellow and he asked me how my chess was going. I told him I was playing in a tournament in a few hours, and he said he wished he was doing that. He told me that the hardest part about his stunt was keeping his legs from cramping. He needed his legs to work so that when thirty-five hours was up, he could jump out from the pole and not hit it as he fell. He was confident, he said, that he could do it.

I wished him luck and drove an hour and a half to a chess club in Middletown, New York. That night I was scheduled to play Sergio, the toughest player in the club, against whom I did not have a good record. He usually moved pretty fast and I'd get nervous as I fell behind on the clock. This time, after a few moves, I could feel myself getting anxious again, and I told myself that my response was ridiculous given that my friend had been standing now for thirty-two hours atop a freaking pole and was calmer than I was. David was putting his life at risk, I reminded myself, and I'm just playing a game. I settled down and played one of my better efforts, in which I dominated Sergio from the opening all the way through to the endgame. I won the game just fifteen minutes before David successfully leaped off the pole and was taken away, dazed, to a hospital and pronounced in good health.

SHORT HAS A PENCHANT FOR POSTMORTEM ANALYSIS OF MORE THAN JUST the moves he makes at the board. As he looks back over his career, he is disturbed by the madness in chess. "Have you concluded, Paul," he said, laughing, "that we are all megalomaniacal psychopaths?"

"My wife doesn't like it when I use the word *all*," I responded.

"OK, Dr. Hoffman. Are 90 percent of us psychopaths?"

"My pocket Fritz is crunching the data right now. But that sounds about right."

Short showed me a review of *The Defense* that he wrote for *The Spectator* in 2000 in which he confessed that "the subject matter is, for one who has spent his life immersed in studying the intricacies of chess sometimes to the detriment of normal existence, deeply unsettling." Short believed that Nabokov was "uncannily prescient" and told the story of dining with Lembit Oll, "an Estonian grandmaster of an age and a psychiatric history not dissimilar to Luzhin's." Oll claimed that the strong Ukrainian grandmaster Vassily Ivanchuk, known as Chucky, a man of nervous disposition who rarely looked people in the eye or held a linear conversation, would never become world champion because he knew little about life. "We burst out laughing," Short wrote,

> a little cruelly perhaps—not that we disagreed with the view, but at the irony of the remark coming from one so deeply disturbed himself. Lembit looked bewildered.

While we were discussing this anecdote, Short's son burst into the room once more and asked, "When a bomb goes off, how do you die? Does it crush you or does your body burst from the inside?"

"Nicholas, where do you get this stuff?" Short said.

"On TV. Military stuff. I have no school tomorrow."

"Why's that?"

"It's Greek Independence Day."

"I didn't know that." Nigel Short has lived in Athens since 1994, but six-year-old Nicholas, who attends an English school, already speaks more Greek than he does. I returned to his piece on the oddity of chess players:

> Within the year, Oll would fling himself to death from his fourth-floor apartment. Luzhin did it from the third. By 1929, when Nabokov began writing the book, there were already ample examples of mentally ill chess players from whom to draw inspiration. Today one could produce encyclopedias of case-histories. It is all too real for this particular reviewer and, in my advanced age, pleasure and not enlightenment is what I seek.

As I sat there reading the review, Short was being true to the words he had written. He was engrossed once again in the World Chess Beauty Contest, searching for any new photos that had been posted since the last time he looked—fifteen minutes before.

ENDGAME: YOUR FINGER
BEATS KASPAROV!

"The King immediately fell flat on his back and lay
perfectly still!"
—LEWIS CARROLL,
Through the Looking Glass

ONE SATURDAY MORNING DURING THE SUMMER OF 2005, I
met Pascal in Williamsburg, Brooklyn, for lunch. I was glad that we had
been thrown together in the cauldron of Tripoli—the scary craziness had
accelerated our friendship, and in the year since, he had become very important to my own chess playing. Whenever I didn't understand a position, I could turn to him to get an answer. It was immensely satisfying to
know, while I was enmeshed in bewildering complications at the chessboard, that there would be clarity and wisdom later that day. I could also
talk to him unguardedly about my chess neuroses because he had shared
his own mental demons. It was comforting to have a good friend in the
lonely and often hostile world of chess: someone who understood first-

hand that even at the amateur level the game was as stressful as it was singularly rewarding; someone who appreciated those occasions when I did something beautiful or crafty at the chessboard.

It was also fun having a friendship that crossed generations. Once I got a panicked call from him at 3:00 A.M. when he needed help writing his first résumé, for a possible job on Wall Street. I liked that he had most of his life in front of him, but also found it comforting that he was so absentminded—leaving shirts, for instance, in his refrigerator—which made me more tolerant of my frequent misplacing of my keys and wallet.[1]

I was still sometimes tempted to challenge Pascal to a blitz game, but I knew he'd refuse. Some time ago I'd called him in a jitter just before an important tournament game. I was afraid my adversary was going to play a certain tedious variation of the French Defense, and I wanted to confirm that I knew how White could keep the position interesting. We both logged onto the Internet Chess Club—he signed on as Charlatan and I as Smothered-Mate—and we set up the starting French position on a board that we could both manipulate.[2] We continued our conversation online, and I asked him to take Black so that I could test my understanding of White's strategy. He made a move, then I made a move. He made another move and I responded. He said I was playing just fine. We each made another move, and then he instant-messaged me:

> CHARLATAN: Are you trying to trick me? ☺
> SMOTHERED-MATE: What?
> CHARLATAN: You want me to play a game!
> SMOTHERED-MATE: Huh?
> CHARLATAN: You're trying to trick me into playing you ☺

"Everyone in the chess world thinks I'm their friend," Pascal had told me in Tripoli, when I first broached the idea of playing him. "I have many superficial relationships with people in the chess world. But it's hard to be friends because I compete with them. They want to kill me on the chessboard. I don't have many close friends. I don't want to risk what we have by introducing competition between us."

On this particular day in New York, I was Pascal's chess therapist, and we reviewed his tournament record since Libya. I had accompanied him and Irina to Toronto, where he successfully defended his title as Canadian champion in the face of the organizers' unfairly giving him too many Blacks in a row. He had also weathered a petty political coup to oust him from the Canadian Olympiad team. As for the quality of his chess, he had purposely played more solidly, not striving for chaos in every game. He had forced himself to spend more time preparing openings and had seen the investment pay off.

He had faced a parade of Bacrots, members of the elite 2700-plus club. "These guys showed me respect," Pascal said. "It was nice." On Board One at the Olympiad in Calvia, Pascal managed to equalize as Black against world number two, Vishy Anand, who hadn't lost a game with White in a year and a half. He got a good position, too, against world number eighteen, Teimour Radjabov, the Azerbaijani prodigy who had survived Kasparov's tantrum in Linares. And Pascal achieved a decent game against Irina's friend, the world number five, Ivanchuk.

But in all three games Pascal had self-destructed by the end. He overlooked a combination and lost a piece to Anand. He let Radjabov escape with a draw when he should have murdered him. He collapsed in time pressure against Ivanchuk. For the past two years he'd needed only one strong result to achieve his grandmaster title, but that result continued to elude him. "As soon as one gets close to that wretched title," British GM Tony Miles once said, "nerves begin to creep in and strange things happen." Pascal played in tournaments in Italy, Spain, Iceland, Montreal, Philadelphia, and Edmonton and always came up disappointingly short.

"Somehow I lose interest and my mind wanders," he said.

"Did you put in so much work equalizing against these monsters that you ran out of steam?"

"No, it's not a question of energy."

"OK. Were you so happy when you got good positions that you let down your guard?"

"I don't think so. I don't know why."

"There has to be an explanation. It's now happened five or six times. It can't just be coincidence."

"Yeah, but I don't know."

"Did you get cocky? Overconfident once your position was good?"

"No, I think I was bored. These tournaments are long. It's hard for me to maintain my interest in chess for a couple of weeks."

"I know they're long. And it's good you're not a chess automaton and value others things in life. But, Pascal, I don't believe that in these particular games you were bored. How can you be bored playing super GMs? It's not like you do it that often. What did you do today? 'It was just an ordinary day, Paul. I got up, went to class, called Irina, played the world number two.' You love winning. I've watched you smash GMs on the Internet. These guys decide you're cheating and using a computer because their egos can't handle how many times you've beaten them. You're a great competitor. So why can't you put these guys away? It would be boring to beat Radjabov?—No!"

"I don't know, Paul."

"I'm running out of possibilities. Maybe it's because you're afraid."

"You think that," he said, softly.

"I wonder. Maybe you're holding back because you're afraid that if you put yourself on the line, you could fail. And you don't know how you'd deal with that."

"Maybe you're right."

"I don't think you'll fail. In fact, I'm sure you won't. But worst of all would be for you to get to my age, look back, and wonder why you never tried. I don't mean to sound harsh. But think about whether I'm onto something."

I WAS NOW FIVE YEARS INTO MY ADULT IMMERSION IN CHESS AND HAD curtailed my own playing—and my exploration of the latest wrinkles in the Dragon and the Slav—in order to write this book in earnest. I had just separated from Ann and was splitting my time between Woodstock and Brooklyn. In many ways, it was a melancholy and discouraging time, and the parallels between my own childhood and my son's were impossible to ignore: Alex was visiting me on alternative weekends, just as I had split my time between my own father and mother—and I had taught Alex to play chess, at the same age that my dad had introduced me to the game. My book had prompted a great deal of reflection on my own difficult childhood, and I hated to see anything that resembled it in my son's.

In brighter moments, though, I could see that Ann and I had done many things differently from my parents—both before and after the end of our marriage. We were not in overt competition with our child, and we took care not to use him as a weapon against each other, as my parents had. In addition, we had welcomed my mother into our lives, so that even as the nuclear family fell apart, all three of us gained a loving parent.

When Alex was one, and we moved full-time to Woodstock, in 2000, Ann and I made the decision to encourage my mother to join us there. I was nervous about how we'd get along—and so was she—given all the bad chemistry between us. But I wanted to give it a try because it still bothered me that my dad had died when things between us were at their worst. I didn't want to lose my remaining parent under similar circumstances, even though I wasn't sure how we were going to mend forty-five years of hard feelings.

Before I was born, my parents had rented a summer cottage in Woodstock, where I was apparently conceived. I knew my mother had liked the physical beauty of the Catskills—she was a bird-watcher and a gardener—and the artistic temperament of the town's inhabitants. And yet when I first invited her to visit my own place in Woodstock, she demurred. What if I run out of gas? she said. Fill the tank before you set out, I suggested. What if the car breaks down? she persisted. You have triple A, I said, and there's only fifteen thousand miles on your car. Will there be a place to park when I get there? she wondered. No, Mom, I sarcastically replied, there'll be no place to park—you'll have to hike in, through the dense, bear-ridden woods, from ten miles away. I ordered my mom to come visit, and when she arrived, after a thoroughly uneventful ride, she had a thoroughly great time. In 2002, she bought a house of her own in the town next to Woodstock. And the next four years, before she died suddenly of a massive stroke, proved to be a tremendous gift.

Once my mother and I started seeing each other more frequently, I came to realize that the negativity that had so bothered me as a child reflected not her disapproval of me but instead an incapacitating anxiety about engaging the world. In the three and a half decades since my parents had separated, I knew her to have gone on only one date, with a geriatric man who hobbled up to her Westport home on a walker. Even sadder and more bewildering was the fact that she had never had a single friend with whom she shared meals or went to the movies. She was smart and engaging, even if she didn't have a high school diploma—a fact that had always made her self-conscious about her intelligence around my speed-reader father. She and Ann genuinely liked each other, and thanks to Ann's gentle prodding, I'd join the two of them for tea, farm-stand outings, and country fairs.

Alexander, of course, was the great connecting force in the lives of my mom, Ann, and me. He often stayed at her home overnight, and she would spend hours drawing pictures with him, playing hide-and-seek, and mending his teddy bears. My mother adored Alex, and she was able to be loving toward him in a way that she been unable to be with me.

My mother and I were simultaneously developing our own satisfying closeness as I realized that, at this point in our lives, our roles were reversed: my job was to go out in the world and bring her along with me. When I suggested that she try anything new, like a Mexican restaurant, she would have her typical knee-jerk response: "No way! I might hate the food." Instead of taking her reaction as a rejection of me, however, as I would have done in my youth, I would reply, "Yes, you might hate it!" and drag her there anyway. Soon she was cooking regularly with cilantro and making her own tacos from scratch.

My writing of this book also drew us closer because it engendered many thoughtful conversations about our family history. As I struggled to come to terms with what couldn't be undone in my past with my father, my relationship with my mother continued to grow and change. Her crippling worries, she said, had started early: when she was four and emigrated by ship from Poland to Ellis Island, she had dropped her favorite doll into the ocean. It had been a devastating experience; ever since, she had been afraid of water and she never really learned how to swim. She also revealed that during her childhood her own mother had been periodically institutionalized for paranoid schizophrenia.

My friends couldn't believe that my mother had ever been a recluse, because she was always so warm and animated when they saw her: it was as if she could relax and be herself because they had, in effect, been pre-screened for her. When Pascal and I returned from Libya, my mother embraced him and called him "an angel" for getting me safely home. At moments like this, I realized how far my mom and I had come.

CERTAINLY ALEX'S INTRODUCTION TO GAMES WAS RADICALLY DIFFERENT from mine. For one thing, he had world-class chess opponents from the start. For another, these adversaries had no investment in beating him. Pascal and Alex played their first chess game when Alex was five, and Pascal had come to visit us in Woodstock. Pascal opened by pushing his king pawn two squares, and Alex said, "I wouldn't do that."

"Why not?" Pascal said.

"Someone could get him," Alex replied, as he picked up Pascal's king pawn and put it back on its original square.

"I'll think I'll play it," he said, and repeated the move.

"I really wouldn't. I don't want anything to happen to him."

"It's OK," Pascal said, laughing. "I've done fine with this move before."

As it happened, Pascal had to work hard to "lose" the game. Alex kept all of his pieces close to himself, out of fear that Pascal would capture them if they ventured too far from their home squares. Even when Pascal purposely left his queen *en prise*, Alex failed to take it for a few moves: at first my son didn't see that he could capture the queen, and then he still hesitated because he thought Pascal was trying to trick him.

When Alex finally won, though, he was beside himself. The next day, when the two of us went into the hamlet of Woodstock to get hot chocolate, he corralled strangers on the street and proudly told them that he had beaten the Canadian champion. Alex decided then that he and I were great players. "You can beat Garry Kasparov," he said. "Right, Dad?" His chess games as a five-year-old also included fumbling efforts against two U.S. women's champions, Jennifer and Irina, with the French champion, Joel Lautier, looking on and kibitzing. But Alex was not starstruck by his celebrated opponents—chess held much less interest for him than soccer, drawing, and Jedi Knights. For him, the game's chief appeal was that I liked it. For my birthday he drew me a picture of a dragon and a cow playing chess.

Pascal's caution about competing with those close to him is certainly borne out by my son's behavior, though. Alex may be casual about chess, but he doesn't like it when he loses at it—or at any other game. Whenever Pascal or I was about to win, he would change the rules on us. One afternoon, he and Pascal were kicking around a soccer ball on the deck of my Woodstock house, using commandeered Adirondack chairs as makeshift goalposts. When Pascal scored a goal, Alex discounted it, saying that the object of the game was to get the ball around the *outside* of the goalposts, not through them.

Alex liked to race from the door of the house to our car. "First one to touch the car wins," he'd say. If I didn't try, he wasn't happy. But if I ran ahead and reached the car first, he'd be upset and say, "Actually, Dad, the second person to touch it wins." Nor did I find the pablum "It's not whether you win or lose, but how you play the game . . ." particularly effective. Finally, my solution was to tell him that the two of us were a team racing against imaginary heffalump-like creatures called the Oodles and that he and I were both winners if we arrived at the car before the Oodles did. Now he was calmer no matter which of us got there first, but he still always had to know if we had indeed defeated the Oodles.

It makes me uncomfortable to compete with Alex, or any child, because it reminds me of my tense relationship with my own father. Once, improbably, I agreed to fill in for one of the assistant coaches at Alex's soccer scrimmage. Roberto, the chief coach and an Italian Air Force pilot, divided the five-year-olds into two groups, so that they could shoot practice goals past us. Our styles of play drastically differed: Roberto blocked every shot his group took, as if he were playing for the World Cup, whereas I dove theatrically at every shot, pretending that I was trying to block it, but letting each ball slip through for a goal. Alex, who was in Roberto's group, was visibly frustrated after repeatedly failing to score on Roberto. He also kept looking over his shoulder to see how I was faring. After the drill, he came over and whispered, so as not to embarrass me in front of the other five-year-olds, "Dad, you're not very good at soccer."

Some months later it occurred to him that perhaps I had let the kids score, and he started wondering whether I was letting him win at chess, too—like the time he checkmated me in just two moves (in the very way that had impressed the owner of Britannica in my job interview). Alex didn't like that I was being easy on him at chess and asked me to go all out. But he also wasn't happy when I beat him quickly.

"Why do I always have to lose to you?" he asked.

"Because I've spent way too much time playing chess to get as good as I am."

"Can you beat Pascal?"

"No."

"I think you can."

"Not a chance. But I'm glad you believe in me, Alex."

"When will I beat you?"

"It takes a while to master the game."

"I don't want to wait a while. You're beating me too much. But I don't want you to lose to me on purpose."

Our solution, arrived at after much discussion, was to play chess games that we aborted long before I came close to mating him. The games were more of a lesson than a competition because we discussed the positions we reached and he was free to retract his moves. "This is fun," Alex said. "Teach me more tricks! I want to fork all of my friends."

Alex is a quick learner, and his curiosity and mastery provide a nice counterbalance to the frustrations of game playing. I remember when Alex returned from a medical appointment at the age of three, and I asked him how it went.

"She used the otoscope," he said.

"The what-a-scope?"

"The otoscope." Later Ann explained to me that the doctor had looked in his ears through an instrument and Alex had asked what it was called.

I was delighted that he had used a word I didn't know. I proudly told everyone—just as Alex had done when he had "defeated" Pascal at chess. Later it sadly occurred to me that if I had employed a word at the age of three—or thirteen or twenty-three—with which my father was unfamiliar, he would have felt upstaged and told no one.

Thankfully, my relationship with Alex is different: I find that I love it when he does well. I'm happy that he has talent in areas, like soccer, where I don't. And I'm pleased that he has his mother's gift for chatting up strangers and feeling comfortable in any social situation; certainly it is preferable to my loner behavior at parties of hovering awkwardly near the chips and salsa.

CHESS HAS BEEN MORE REWARDING THE SECOND TIME AROUND. I FINALLY made real friends in the chess world in a way that I never had in my youth. Pascal and Jennifer are kind. They're honest. And they're a lot of fun. However bizarre and untrustworthy other inhabitants of this world may be, I know I can count on them. And yet, not coincidentally, their commitment to this world is conditional: they have important things besides chess going on in their lives. Sometimes, however, our common love of the game brings the three of us together at chess events.

One summer day in 2005, we all got to work together, providing live commentary in the ABC Studios in Times Square for a sixty-minute game between the twenty-six-year-old FIDE world champion Rustam Kasimdzhanov from Uzbekistan and the Accoona chess-playing computer program. Kasimdzhanov had never been to New York before, and Pascal and I went to meet him at his midtown hotel the night before the game. "Where's Jennifer?" he asked. "Isn't she coming to dinner, too?"

"Yes," I said, "but remember, I was going to interview you first." Joel Lautier had told me that Kasimdzhanov's nickname was Fucking Genius, because of the range of his knowledge of literature, poetry, and other non-chess subjects. I asked Kasimdzhanov various questions about his chess playing, and, although he answered me, he seemed more interested in talking about women. Maybe this was his idea of what American men spoke about whenever they got together. He wanted to know what the age of consent was in the United States and whether his hotel was in the right neighborhood for meeting women.

We took F.G. to a fancy Korean restaurant in SoHo, where Jennifer joined us. Her presence did not stop him from continuing to talk incessantly about women. If I had been alone with him, I would have felt a bit alienated, but since Kasimdzhanov was effectively outnumbered, the situation was instead quite humorous. The three of us listened, exchanged pointed glances, and started on a bottle of wine.

"I don't need to drink," Kasimdzhanov said. "My friends say that I normally act the way other people do when they're drunk."

One of our appetizers was a pancake stuffed with seafood that came with a bowl of wickedly hot sauce. Kasimdzhanov dabbed cautiously at the sauce. "Do you think it's really spicy?" he asked.

"It is," I replied. "But it's good."

"I'm not so sure I should try it. What if I don't like it?"

Jennifer, who was put off by Kasimdzhanov's preoccupation with sex, saw an opening to rib him. "Who do you think makes a better lover?" she asked. "Someone who likes spicy food or someone who prefers bland?" Kasimdzhanov looked confused, while I proceeded to smother my portion of pancake with hot sauce.

"The person who prefers spicy, of course," she said.

"Do you eat bishops?" he asked, a sly reference to the title of a wacky newspaper interview with Maria Manakova, a thirty-year-old Russian master and self-proclaimed "sex specialist" who poses nude for the media and believes that the way to make chess as popular as poker is for women to exhibit their sexuality at the board.

"It depends on the position, of course," Jennifer cleverly responded. Her rejoinder played on the fact that on the chessboard bishops are preferable in open positions and knights in closed, bottled-up pawn structures.

When the meal was over, we showed Kasimdzhanov around the East Village. Around 11 P.M., Pascal and I got into a cab. "Where are you going?" Kasimdzhanov asked.

"To our hotel," I said.

"And where are you going, Jennifer?" he asked.

"I'm going home."

"Then I should come with you and make the situation symmetric." I was amused by this pickup line, uttered by one world-class player to another. Symmetry—when to follow it and when to break it—is a fundamental concept in chess. For someone who taught himself English from audiotapes, F.G. was pretty witty. But of course I was also pleased that Jennifer gently rebuffed him. She knew how to handle herself after years of experience in a sport overrun by sexually immature men.

IF KASIMDZHANOV HAD READ THE SPRING 2004 ISSUE OF *BUST* MAGAZINE, whose tagline was "For Women with Something to Get Off Their Chest," he would have known that he didn't have a chance with Jennifer.

"For the last couple of years," the magazine stated, "Jennifer has only dated men who have nothing to do with chess." It also quoted Jennifer as saying—in a bizarre stroke of coincidence, given Kasimdzhanov's country of origin: "Chess guys are likely to be really competitive and obsessive. Plus, so much chess is played overseas. Do I really want to have a long-distance relationship with someone from Uzbekistan?"

The piece then went on to use Jennifer's description of the game to slyly suggest that perhaps chess made sex less necessary:

> "Sometimes when you reach the end of a variation, there's a certain *je ne sais quoi* that feels so good," she croons. "It's hard to describe. It's like trying to describe an orgasm—how do you do that?"

This explanation of chess's appeal has been made by many other writers, as well. George Steiner, in the pages of *The New Yorker,* compared sex unfavorably to the royal game: "The poets lie about orgasm. It is a small, chancy business, its particularities immediately effaced even from the most roseate memories, compared to the crescendo of triumph in chess, to the tide of light and release that races over mind and knotted body as the opponent's king, inert in the fatal web one has spun, falls on the board."

Other writers have compared the pace of blitz chess to the rhythm of sexual excitement. "There is in, say, five-minute games, a pattern of moves progressing, faster and faster, building up toward a climax, marked by a time-scramble or a checkmate, signaling a sudden release of tension," wrote David Spanier, a chess enthusiast and foreign correspondent for the London *Times*:

> The king is mated, the flag falls, the pieces are set up again and the process repeated. This is not sexual excitement per se; but the activity does have an edge of excitement to it which is emotionally very satisfying (if you win); and I suppose even if you lose, there is always the next game coming up, to get back into it, so to speak. Yes . . . it's not sex, but more of a substitute for sex, in that having experienced the intensity of excitement again and again, a player's emotions are spent, he (or she) must feel to an extent exhausted, and certainly far less motivated to pursue what one might call normal social relations. I mean, after such a chess session who needs a routine evening of talk or drinks or TV?

For me the most powerful similarity between sex and chess is that I can totally immerse myself in both of them, to the exclusion of the world around me. Time stops. For the few hours at the chessboard, the mundane and profound concerns of life thankfully fade away—they'll be there when I'm done. I forget the misunderstanding I had with a friend. I forget how disturbed I am by the situation in Iraq. I forget that it has rained for five days straight.

For some players chess also offers a break from disturbing events in their personal lives.[3] For better or for worse, it's not that extreme for me. When I had a scary result from a medical test before the National Open in Las Vegas in 2003, I could not concentrate on the chessboard and dropped out after losing three games. The only other time I withdrew in the middle of a tournament was the National Chess Congress in Philadelphia on the three days after Thanksgiving in 2004. My wife was dismayed that I was spending the long post-holiday weekend playing chess, and I was preoccupied during the games with wondering why she and I were growing apart.

Yet I am amazed by the power that chess has to divert me from less serious matters. Few other activities offer me this degree of respite from everyday life.[4] When my writing is going well, I can do it for eight- or ten-hour stretches without getting up to eat or visit the bathroom, and I have no idea how long I've been at the keyboard. The same is true of a good chess game. Of course, I've also had bad chess games, in which I was too self-conscious, too focused on the end result, on whether my rating would go up or down, and never relaxed enough to get completely into the game. Alas, there is bad sex, too. But when this intense focus is accompanied by inspired play and a win, it's an extraordinary, addictive feeling.

"When I'm absorbed in a chess game," Jennifer told me, "I'm living completely in the present. I lose my sense of the past and the future, and I love that. Chess was the first thing I was really passionate about." Playing a great game, sacrificing a piece for a wild attack, living on the edge between victory and defeat, setting a neat trap, seeing a beautiful combination—these send shivers through her, she said. "It's very physical and primal," she said. "After I found passion in chess, it was easier to find passion elsewhere, in relationships, in art, in good writing, in simply being alive."

ON THE SAME DAY I ACTED AS PASCAL'S CHESS THERAPIST, I SPENT THE AFternoon watching my friend Matt doing personalized performance art at a children's street fair and block party in Chelsea. He sat holding a pad of paper and a rubber stamp that said "THE ADVENTURES OF YOUR FINGER!" A kid would sit down next to him, and Matt would instruct the kid to stamp a sheet of paper, and then he'd ask the kid what he liked to do. Some of the children were shy and tongue-tied, while others answered immediately. "I like ballet," an eight-year-old said. So Matt wrote "YOUR FINGER STARS IN SWAN LAKE" in big letters at the top of the sheet. Next he drew a studly prince for the girl and next to the prince, a tutu without a body. He poked a small hole where the body should be and asked the girl to put her finger through the hole from the back of the sheet. With a thin Magic Marker, he drew a face on the tip of her finger. "I see," she said, beaming. "The finger is me! I'm dancing!" I watched Matt draw "YOUR FINGER SCORES THE WINNING GOAL AT THE WORLD CUP" for a boy who had on a soccer uniform. One kid wanted his finger to commit suicide but his embarrassed father quickly nixed the idea and shepherded the boy away.

Finally it was my turn. "You don't need to share your fantasies," Matt said. "I already know them." He had me stamp the sheet, and he proceeded to draw a hairy Russian with very thick eyebrows who was huddled over a chessboard, his head in his hands, the Black king in front of him lying prone in resignation. "Dratski!" Matt wrote in a comic-strip thought bubble next to the Russian's head. He then drew a White bishop and wrote "Triumph!" in the accompanying bubble. He poked a hole in the paper so that my finger was making the winning move with the bishop. He titled the drawing "YOUR FINGER BEATS KASPAROV!"

THE MOST EXCITING CHESS GAME I EVER PLAYED AFTER BECOMING PASCAL'S unofficial student took place at a rapid tournament at the Marshall. By then Pascal had dissected many of my previous games and helped me understand how I disassembled after emerging from the opening with an advantage. Either I was too aggressive, prematurely launching an attack before putting all of my artillery in place, or I was too passive, scrambling to suppress the seeds of real and imagined counterplay by my opponent and not proceeding with a constructive plan of my own. There is an old saying in chess, "A bad plan is better than no plan at all," and I was often guilty of the latter.

I had hoped to do well at the Marshall and demonstrate that my chess had improved because of what Pascal had shown me. Then I slept fitfully the night before the tournament because I was putting too much pressure on myself to justify my adulthood absorption in the game. I was worried that if I didn't do well Pascal would lose interest in helping me. On the day of the tournament, I was so tired and nervous that I decided at the last minute not to play. I called to tell Pascal because he was planning to come to the Marshall and watch. He assured me that he wouldn't abandon me even if I lost all four games, and he told me, in so many words, to get my butt over there and play even if I was exhausted. I needed the push.

My first-round opponent was Asa Hoffmann, a fixture on the New York chess scene. Hoffmann, a gaunt man with the physique of Abraham Lincoln, made his living by playing chess for money on street corners throughout the city and peddling antiquarian books he purchased at flea markets. He doesn't like to be called a hustler, because he says he doesn't do anything shady or underhanded to win. He doesn't try to conceal his playing strength and pretend that he just learned the rules—he simply gives his marks time odds that appear too favorable to turn down. Hoffmann was a contemporary of Fischer's—they were both born in 1943—and he loves to tell the story of beating Bobby at blitz, although he is quick to concede that the future world champion usually got the better of him.

Hoffmann was rated close to 2400, two full rating classes higher than mine, and he had the advantage of playing White. He was known for employing offbeat openings, and in our game he chose the Pseudo Trompowsky, the double-queen pawn opening in which White immediately develops his dark-squared bishop.

The game was an emotional roller-coaster for me. Delight!—Pascal and I had looked at the Pseudo Trompowsky when we were preparing for my encounter with Antoaneta Stefanova in Tripoli. Confidence!—I play my first three moves quickly. I boot his bishop with my rook pawn, I bolster my queen pawn with a fellow foot soldier, and I slide my queen so that it attacks a wing pawn that he left undefended when he developed the bishop early.

Pascal and I had considered two ways for White to respond to my attack on his pawn. White can advance the pawn or defend it with his own queen. Disappointment!—Asa chooses a third way we hadn't examined: he blocks my attack by placing a defended knight between my queen and his pawn. So much for the preparation—it is only the fourth move and I am already entirely on my own. I am disoriented for a moment and tell myself to remain calm and try to look objectively at the merits of his move. Self-deception!—I psych myself up by convincing myself that it would be robotic and boring for me if Asa followed my preparation. Instead I can now exercise my full creativity by charging into the unknown. Insight!—the knight move looks artificial to me, the steed relegated to the sidelines. Foresight!—I envisage at some point resuming my attack on his flank pawn by using one of my own pawns to kick his knight away. Over the next few moves I follow through with this plan and land the first blow by fracturing his queenside pawns. Then I invade his weakened queenside with heavy weapons, my two rooks and my queen. Joy!— he gives up material to try to ease the pressure.

Fear!—I notice I have less time than he does on the clock. Soon I will have only five minutes to complete the game. I'm a pathetic blitz player and in time trouble I've been known to drop pieces and discard winning positions. Resignation!—I'm going to collapse yet again in time pressure. He starts blitzing out moves and frenetically hopping his knight around, hoping that I'll overlook a devastating fork. Composure!—I tell myself that I'm not fated to screw up, that I don't have to repeat the past, that I can do better this time. I tell myself to focus and make sure he has no tricky forks or bothersome checks. I tell myself not to be intimidated by the speed of his play. I tell myself that I am a champion and will beat this hustler. I tell myself to pick up the pace and not lose on time.

Mischievous!—I set a sly little trap of my own. My bishop has been defending my king pawn. I move the bishop away so that the pawn is undefended. He looks at the delicious, helpless pawn, hesitates a few seconds, and then gobbles it with his own bishop. Panic!—I have only forty seconds left for the rest of the game. My hand is trembling. My throat is parched. I feel queasy. Stay focused, Paul. Sip some water. Take in air. Second thoughts!—Does my combination really work or did I have a hallucination and recklessly jettison a key pawn? Collect yourself. Don't let this slip. Courage!—I enact my plan. My play is muscular now, my mind and hand working in tandem. My fingers are no longer jittery; they dart deftly across the board and purposefully move the pieces. I check his king. It can only move to one particular square. Domination!—I pick up my knight. It feels good in my hand. I like the ragged mane and the asymmetry of the overall shape. I lower the knight to the board and it makes a wonderful thump as it forks his king and bishop. He flinches as if I had poked him with a needle. He wearily moves his monarch away and—Zap!—I chomp his bishop.

Elation! He tips his king over in resignation and shakes my hand. I've won the game with only twenty seconds to spare. I did not fall apart. I more than held my own. He's the highest rated player I've beaten over the board. I am a fucking genius. Asa defeated Fischer and I crunched Asa, so does that make me better than Fischer? For one manic moment I wonder if I should give up writing and play chess full-time. I feel young inside. My joints may creak, but my brain whirls. Maybe I can set a world record as the oldest person to become a grandmaster. I am so exhilarated and distracted that I aimlessly play my three remaining games. I'm inattentive to the outcome. It doesn't matter anymore. I've succeeded in playing a great game.

The tournament ends after midnight. I am staying near the Marshall, at David Blaine's. Pascal and Irina accompany me there so that we can analyze my victory. David is entertaining a few leggy dancers and supermodels, and they all stop what they're doing and crowd around us for an hour as we replay the moves of my game. How sublime is this? A group of gorgeous women are watching me reenact my greatest chess triumph. Pascal praises my play, and he and Irina have a lively argument about whether I conducted the early middle game correctly. He approves of my take-no-prisoners, tactical approach, and she thinks I should have played more quietly.

Later I find an ice cream shop that's still open at 2:30 A.M. and order a chocolate milkshake. I go on the Internet and buy half a dozen chess books, including *The Survival Guide to Rook Endings, Mastering the Najdorf,* and *Grandmaster Preparation.* I already have five hundred unread chess books on my shelves, but these, I'm convinced, will finally reveal the secrets I need to understand the game. Of course that's what I thought when I purchased the previous six, and the six before that, and the six before that.

I feel incredibly competent tonight. It is rare for me to feel this strong. Nothing beats the feeling, though—not even Dexedrine—and I'm staying up a couple more hours to enjoy it while it lasts. I wish that feeling for everyone I love. I wish it especially for my son, Alex.

DURING THE JANUARY 2006 BREAK AT UMBC, PASCAL ENTERED A NINE-ROUND international tournament in Chicago. At the end of eight rounds, he had five points (two wins, six draws, and zero losses). If, in the last and ninth round, Pascal defeated Rusudan Goletiani, the 2005 U.S. women's champion (and the person who almost displaced Jennifer on the Olympiad team), he would finally earn the grandmaster title. Alex had given him a good-luck charm, a little alien Buddha figurine, to keep in his pocket in Chicago.

Pascal spent a late night preparing for the game, concentrating on an offbeat line of the Sicilian that Goletiani had played twice before in earlier rounds. In his midnight preparation he had not discovered a way to wipe her off the board, but he did come up with a peculiar-looking queen shift that would give him a solid position and leave her with weak squares on the queenside.

The next morning she repeated the line against him and he unveiled the queen move. As he subsequently probed her queenside during the middle game, her weaknesses multiplied, and by the nineteenth move he had a dominating position. But then gremlins interfered with his concentration, and he squandered much of his advantage with aimless wood-shifting.

Goletiani then broke out of his chokehold and started recklessly lashing out at his king. Pascal renewed his focus and rebuffed her attack. After her thirty-eighth move, he told himself to stay calm. He tried to forget that the GM title was at stake and pretended that the position in front of him was not his own game but was from a book with the instructions "White to play and win." His geometrical skills helped him. With a simple bishop move, he started to weave a mating net. She tried to distract him by queening a pawn, but his concentration was not jolted. He saw that by shifting his rook just one square—sometimes the simplest move is the best—he could force a sequence that would lead to checkmate.

Pascal hesitated for a minute before moving the rook. Not to recheck his calculations—he knew that they were right—but to savor the moment. After two frustrating years of near-misses, the grandmaster title was only one move away.

Irina was also playing in the tournament. Although she was short of time in her own game, she abandoned her board and went to watch the end of Pascal's game. She witnessed him pick up the rook and make the decisive, title-winning move. "I was very happy Irina came over," Pascal told me. He now knew that the woman he loved respected his play.[5]

IN MY RECENT YEARS EMBEDDED IN THE WORLD OF CHESS, I'VE HAD MANY disturbing nights after tournament games that didn't go as smoothly as my encounter with Asa Hoffmann. I've seen players cheat, and I've seen them cry and hurl clocks across the room. I've watched Pascal beat himself up after losing. I've played chess with the crazy dictator who is the commissar of the game. I've visited the emergency room after the greatest player in chess history was too competitive with me at dinner. And yet, despite my misadventures in the chess world, I still sometimes fantasize—just as I did when I was a kid—about being a world-class player instead of a competent amateur.

In another life, I want to be a grandmaster. Not for the financial rewards, because they are few unless you're a Karpov or a Kasparov. But for the unadulterated pleasure of peering further into the abyss of chess and glimpsing the game's deeper beauty. I want to work magic with the chess pieces the way Morphy and Fischer did. I want to launch daring, unexpected attacks the way Jennifer and Pascal do. I want to achieve a small degree of immortality by the ingenious manner in which I coordinate my knights.

 ANNOTATIONS

CHAPTER 1: The Insanity Defense

1: I now prefer the definition in *The Great Soviet Encyclopedia*: "a sport masquerading as an art."

2: Perhaps the young retiree had been influenced by the familiar story of how world champion Alexander Alekhine (1892–1946) allegedly destroyed his hotel room furniture after a devastating loss. *Allegedly* is the operative word because chess players thrive on gossipy lore about the giants of the game, and this particular anecdote cannot be substantiated.

In the main text of *King's Gambit*, I tell my share of droll, irreverent, even prurient stories. With few exceptions, which are duly telegraphed by adjectives like *fictional, apocryphal,* and *reported,* the stories were witnessed by me or by those whom I interviewed. The historical anecdotes that I repeat in the main text were gleaned mostly from contemporary chess periodicals and newspaper columns, not secondary sources. In these footnotes, however, I allow myself the guilty liberty of sharing legendary yarns—flagging them as such, of course.

3: In another mounting-the-table story, which is too amusing to ignore even if its truth is questionable, the great Aron Nimzowitsch (1886–1935) climbed on the chessboard, dropped to his knees, and shouted to the heavens, "Oh Lord, why did I have to lose to this idiot?"

4: The illness alibi is old. In 1842, *The Chess Player's Chronicle* advised, "Do not be alarmed about the state of your adversary's health, when, after losing two or three games, he complains of having a bad headache, or of feeling very unwell. If he should win the next game, you will probably hear no more of this" [as quoted in Edward Winter, *A Chess Omnibus*, 2003: Russell Enterprises, p. 412].

In 1848, a sponsor offered to fund a twenty-five-game match on the condition that "whatever may be the result, we hear nothing of indigestion, headache, indisposition, want of preparation, rest, or any other excuse, however ingenious, as palliative of defeat" [*Morning Post*, Thomas Beeby's letter to Captain Kennedy, September 30, 1848, as reprinted in T. Beeby, *An Account of the Late Chess Match Between Mr. Howard Staunton and Mr. Lowe*, 1848, and quoted in *A Chess Omnibus*, p. 383].

5: Religious leaders have had other reasons, too, for censoring chess. They feared it was associated with gambling. Islamic authorities banned figurine chess pieces because of Mohammed's prohibition on humanlike images.

6: The artistic element of chess, as opposed to the sporting aspect, is emphasized in the composition of chess problems (constructed positions in which, say, White is asked to force a mate in two moves), a pursuit that attracts only a small subset of chess players. Vladimir Nabokov's most obscure chess book, *Poems and Problems,* was published in 1970. The book begins with fifty-three poems and concludes with eighteen chess problems, such as a mate-in-two—"a self-interference freak not for the conservative solver"—composed in Montreux in 1968. After discussing the poems in the introduction, Nabokov wrote, "Finally, there is the chess. I refuse to apologize for its inclusion. Chess problems demand from the composer the same virtues that characterize all worthwhile art: originality, invention, conciseness, harmony, complexity, and splendid insincerity. The composing of these ivory-and-ebony riddles is a comparatively rare gift and an extravagantly sterile occupation; but then all art is inutile, and divinely so, if compared to a number of more popular human endeavors. Problems are the poetry of chess, and its poetry, as all poetry, is subject to changing trends with various conflicts between old and new schools" [Vladimir Nabokov, *Poems and Problems,* 1970: McGraw-Hill, p. 15].

7: Until recently there were questions about the identity of Fischer's father. Because Fischer's mother had studied medicine in Russia and was a political radical, the FBI had her under observation. Through the Freedom of Information Act, *The Philadelphia Inquirer* reviewed the government's file on Fischer's mother and discovered that his biological father was Jewish, too. Fischer's mother, Regina Wender, was born in Switzerland in 1913 and raised in the United States. In the 1930s, she lived in Germany and then Moscow. She was married to Hans Gerhardt Fischer, a German biophysicist, and they had a daughter, Joan. When they tried to move to the United States in 1939, immigration officials would not let Hans Gerhardt into the country because he was an alleged Communist sympathizer. He went instead to Chile. In 1942, Regina had an affair with Paul Nemenyi, a Hungarian mathematician who worked on the Manhattan Project. Bobby Fischer was their child. Fischer never met Nemenyi, who died in 1952, when Fischer was nine.

"In 1959 when Tal won the [World Championship] Candidates Tournament and treated the other participants, among them the 16-year-old Bobby Fischer, to a celebration dinner, his trainer Koblenz pronounced a toast. Thinking of how happy Tal's deceased father would have been, he shouted: 'To our fathers!' The remark was innocent enough, 'but,' writes Koblenz, 'you should have seen Fischer's reaction! His eyes filled with tears, and he left at once.' 'Children who miss a parent become wolves,' Fischer said later" [Tim Krabbe's March 2003 column for *AD-magazine* as quoted in Hans Böhm and Kees Jongkind, *Bobby Fischer: The Wandering King,* 2003: BT Batsford, p. 24].

8: In February 1942, the Vienna-born Zweig and his wife committed suicide in Brazil, to which they had emigrated, by way of England. (They had left Austria in 1935, in anticipation of the Nazi takeover.) Zweig, an admirer and a correspondent of Freud's, was influenced by the psychoanalytic thinking of his times. When he killed himself, he left behind an autobiography, an incomplete essay on Balzac, and a novella called *Schachnovelle,* which was subsequently published in English as *The Royal Game* or, in the more faithful translation, *Chess Story.* The novella, which has undergone at least fifty-two printings, told the story of a heated chess match, casually arranged on a cruise ship, between world champion Mirko Czentovic and Dr. B, an Austrian attorney with Royalist sympathies who had taught himself to play mental chess in order to alleviate the isolation of solitary confinement by the Nazis.

9: "The Russian title of this novel is *Zashchita Luzhina,* which means 'the Luzhin Defense' and refers to a chess defense supposedly invented by my creature, Grandmaster Luzhin: the name rhymes with 'illusion' if pronounced thickly enough to deepen the 'u' into 'oo,'" Nabokov wrote in the foreword to the English edition of his novel about a World Championship challenger who descends into madness when he comes to regard his whole life as one big chess game. "I began writing it in the spring of 1929, at Le Boulou—a small spa in the Pyrenees Orientales where I was hunting butterflies—and finished it the same year in Berlin. I remember with special limpidity a sloping slab of rock, in the ulex- and ilex-clad hills, where the main thematic idea of the book first came to me. Some curious additional information might be given if I took myself more seriously" [Vladimir Nabokov, *The Defense,* 1970: Capricorn Books, p. 7]. Under Nabokov's pen name, V. Sirin, *Zashchita Luzhina* was first published in Paris by the émigré Russian quarterly *Sovremennye Zapiski* and then in Berlin in 1930 by the émigré publishing house Slovo. It did not appear in English until 1964, as *The Defense.*

10: Luzhin's death can be seen as the death of "classical" chess. In the 1920s, a fierce debate raged in chess circles between the classicists who insisted that the only way to control the middle of the board was the time-honored approach of occupying it with pawns bolstered by pieces and the hypermodernists led by the Hungarian theorist Richard Réti who believed the center could also be controlled from afar by training distant pieces on the central squares. Luzhin was a classicist, and his chief opponent, the Italian star Turati (whose very name incorporates Réti's), was "a representative of the latest fashions in chess, [who] opened the game by moving up on the flanks, leaving the middle of the board unoccupied by Pawns but exercising a most dangerous influence on the center from the sides. Scorning the cozy safety of castling he strove to create the most unexpected and whimsical interrelations between his men." Although Réti himself died young, at the age of forty in 1929, hypermodernism triumphed [*The Defense,* p. 96].

11: Bill Wall's Web site, http://us.share.geocities.com/wallw_99/trivia5.htm, includes an alphabetical list of chess player deaths. Omitting the suicidal jumpers, as well as Paul Morphy, Vera Menchik, Efim Bogoljubow, and Nicholas Rossolimo, whose deaths I discuss in the main text, the list reads: "Georgy Agzamov (1954–1986) died after falling down between two rocks at a beach. Alexander Alekhine (1892–1946) choked to death on a piece of meat. . . . Paolo Boi (1528–1598) was poisoned. José Capablanca (1888–1942) died of a stroke after watching a skittles game at the Manhattan Chess Club. Edgar Colle (1897–1932) died after an operation for a gastric ulcer. Ed Edmondson (1920–1982) had a heart attack while playing chess on the beach. Janos Flesch died in a car wreck in 1983. Nikolai Grigoriev (1895–1938) died after an operation for appendicitis. Alexander Ilyin-Genevsky (1894–1941) got hit by an artillery shell on a barge in Leningrad. Klaus Jung died at the front line in Germany.

Salo Landau (1903–1944) died in a German concentration camp. Paul Leonhardt had a heart attack while playing chess at a chess club in 1934. George Mackenzie (1837–1891) died after an overdose of morphine. Frank Marshall (1877–1944) died of a heart attack after leaving a friend's house in Jersey City. . . . Johannes Minckwitz (1843–1901) committed suicide by throwing himself in front of a train. . . . Julius Perlis died in a mountain climb in the Alps in 1913. Vladimir Petrov died in a Russian prison camp in 1945. Harry Pillsbury (1872–1906) died of syphilis. David Przepiorka died in a mass execution outside Warsaw in 1940. . . . Pierre Saint-Amant (1800–1872) died after falling from a horse and carriage. Carl Schlechter (1874–1918) died from pneumonia and starvation. Gideon Stahlberg died during the 1967 Leningrad International tournament. Howard Staunton (1810–1874) died of a heart attack while writing a chess book. Vladimir Simagin (1919–1968) died of a heart attack while playing in a chess tournament. Herman Steiner (1905–1955) died of a heart attack after a game in the California State Championship. Alexei Troitzky (1866–1942) died of starvation during the siege of Leningrad. Abe Turner (1924–1962) was stabbed nine times in the back by a fellow employee. Frederick Yates (1884–1932) died in his sleep from a leak in a faulty gas pipe connection. Alexander Zaitsev died of thrombosis after a minor operation to remedy a limp by having one leg lengthened. Johann Zukertort (1842–1888) died of a stroke while playing chess at a London coffee house."

12: Dutch grandmaster Jan Timman (1951–), after losing in the semifinals of the World Championship in 1985, was immediately ready to return to the board: "Even if I had to negotiate a roaring waterfall in a wooden tub with natives armed to the teeth below me, I will continue fighting" [Genna Sosonko, *The Reliable Past,* 2003: New in Chess, p. 148].

13: Here are the USCF rating classes and the percentage of tournament players someone at the top of each class is better than: Master (2200 plus—99.22 percent), Expert (2000–2200—96.99 percent), Class A (1800–2000—92 percent), Class B (1600–1800—83.55 percent), Class C (1400–1600—73.25 percent), Class D (1200–1400—63.34 percent), Class E (1000–1200—54.11 percent), Class F (800–1000—44.1 percent), Class G (600–800—31.61 percent), Class H (400–600—19.04 percent), Class I (200–400—8.9 percent), Class J (0–200—5.33 percent).

14: In the Fool's Mate, White first advances his king-bishop pawn two squares. Black nudges his king pawn forward one square. White moves his king-knight pawn forward two squares (as only a duffer or someone with a death wish would do). And Black delivers checkmate by triumphantly sliding his queen to the side of the board.

CHAPTER 2: **Fathers and Sons**

1: I guess my father was never too keen with numbers. This headline from a 1966 *Pageant* falls apart if we are so unsporting as to dissect it. The U.S. population then was 197 million. If we eliminate the percentage of the population that was under nineteen and over sixty-five (on the assumption that few in those age brackets were sexually active daily), we are left with 120 million adults. Are we really to believe that half of them were having oral sex every night? If this was true, we should be even more nostalgic about the sixties.

2: It is characteristic of the knight that it alternates colors as it moves. So if it is on a dark square, its next move must be to a light square. And if it is on a light square, it can only move to a dark square.

3: Castling is the only time a player is allowed to move two pieces at once. It is a way of giving the king some protection by shifting it toward the corner of the board and of activating a rook. A player can castle if there are no pieces between his king and rook and neither the king nor rook has moved. Castling consists of moving the king two squares toward the rook and then moving the rook to the other side of the king. Castling can only happen if the king is not in check and the square it moves to and the square it moves across are not under enemy fire. *En passant* is a curious move that happens when a pawn initially advances two squares. If that puts the pawn next to an opposing pawn, the other side has the option of immediately capturing the pawn by acting as if it had moved only one square, not two. In other words, the *en passant* rule prevents one pawn from slipping unmolested past another.

4: Many other champions could be added to the list of players who absorbed chess without being formally taught the rules. To wit, Arnold Sheldon Denker (1914–2005), the 1944 U.S. champion, who "learned the moves of chess by remote control. At the age of eight he had observed his older brothers playing, day in and day out. Although shunted aside by his elders, Denker had seen enough to know the rudiments" [*Chess Life*, August–September 1944]. Denker became the U.S. champion in 1944 with a winning percentage of 91 percent (fourteen wins, three draws, and zero losses), a record that stood for twenty years, until Bobby Fischer scored 100 percent in eleven games in the 1963–1964 championship.

The great Frank Marshall (1877–1944), U.S. champion for twenty-seven years, also learned by observation: "In our home in Montreal, my father played chess in the evenings with his friends. One night, he asked me if I would like to play him a game. I suppose he had noticed that I had been watching and decided to try me out" [Frank Marshall, *My Fifty Years of Chess*, 1942: *Chess Review*, p. 3].

5: Chess pieces come in all shapes and sizes, and can be made of wood, stone, metal, glass, or plastic. Serious players prefer the classic Staunton set. In 1944, Marcel Duchamp (1887–1968), the legendary surrealist who played on the French national chess team, organized a show in New York for which Max Ernst, Alexander Calder, and other leading artists designed chess sets. As works of art, many of these sets were spectacular, but even Duchamp himself favored playing actual games with the familiar Stauntons.

6: Grandmasters need to brace themselves for revisionist thinking about their own most cherished games. Russian grandmaster Mark Taimanov (1926–) published a collection of his own games in which he included a favorite victory in 1969 over Anatoly

Lutikov (1933–1989). "Over the years, Taimanov had often publicized this game. In his notes, he always took care to reveal that Lutikov could have chosen a better defense and forced him to draw the game by perpetual check [repeated checking of the king without mate]. This barely took away from the beauty of the game. Then, one day, Taimanov got a letter from his [English] translator . . . [who] wanted to know how the perpetual check in that game was actually supposed to work; he hadn't been able to find it. It turned out there was no perpetual check. Lutikov could not only have obtained a draw, he could simply have won the game. That really did put a blemish on what was otherwise a beautiful game" [Hans Ree, *The Human Comedy of Chess*, 1999: Russell Enterprises, p. 307].

7: Anyone can enter an open tournament. Chess tournaments can also be *closed*, meaning that they are by invitation only. Tournaments, whether open or closed, can be *round-robin* (everyone plays one game against everyone else), *double round-robin* (each entrant has both White and Black against every other player), *knockout* (one contestant plays a match of a predetermined number of games against another contestant, the winner moving on to the next round and the loser going home), or the *Swiss system* (a player is paired whenever possible in each round with someone who has the identical score). So in the Swiss system, if a player has two wins after two rounds, he will be paired in the third round with somebody else who is 2–0.

8: Sometimes it is a child who gives the exhibition. Samuel Reshevsky (1911–1992), the Polish-born prodigy who emigrated to the United States and became one of the top three players in the world, learned chess at the age of four. Wearing a little sailor suit, he toured Poland at the age of six, giving simuls against twenty or more people, and then did the same elsewhere in Europe and the United States. As a boy, Reshevsky was somewhat of an idiot savant; he did not learn to read or write until after the age of eleven. As an adult, he supported his chess and his family by working as an accountant.

9: "There is one story—perhaps apocryphal—of an extended bit of thinking that tops even Paulsen's alleged 11 hours," Andy Soltis wrote. It involves an adjournment (the suspension of the game until the next day) with one of the players not making his move on the board but rather sealing his move in an envelope until the resumption of play, at which time the move is unsealed and made. (The reason the move is sealed is so that neither player, during his long night of analysis, has the advantage of knowing what move he'll next face when play resumes.) "At a European tournament before World War I Akiba Rubinstein was trying to decide which of two king moves he should seal in an adjournment envelope. The wrong one might throw away the win, perhaps even lose. Rubenstein could not make up his mind so he hit upon the ingenious solution. He sealed an illegal move.

When the envelope was opened the tournament officials found themselves in a quandary. The rule in force then required the offender to replace his illegal move with a legal one—of his king. This meant Rubinstein had all night and much of the next day to analyze with a board and pieces which king move to make" [Andy Soltis, *Chess Lists*, Second Edition, 2002: McFarland & Company, pp. 49, 50].

Postal chess games, of course, can drag on for years. In 1975, "Glaswegian Lawrence B. Grant and Dr. J. Munro MacLennan from Ottawa ... had been playing a correspondence game for forty-nine years at the rate of about one move a year. As Mr. Grant said, 'Ye cannae hurry these things' " [Mike Fox and Richard James, *The Even More Complete Chess Addict*, 1993: Faber and Faber, p. 258].

10: When I attribute a number to a world champion, describing Kasparov as the thirteenth or Tal as the eighth, I am talking about the century-old classical lineage beginning with the first champion, Wilhelm Steinitz, in 1886.

11: In the June 1857 issue of *The Chess Monthly*, "a Pennsylvanian ... vouches for the truth of the following: You and I have both read, in fanciful chess stories, incredible accounts of men who have won wives, or of women who have caught husbands, by means of our glorious game. But I believe that I am the first person who can narrate an authentic incident of this kind. In a little village situated in the shadow of our iron-bearing Alleghenies my friend R—— has lived and labored for half-a-dozen years. He is a bold Chess Player but as bashful a man as you can find in our whole State. At length he fell, as men will fall, into the entangling meshes of love; but for nearly a twelve-month his unfortunate diffidence kept his tongue hopelessly tied. The lady saw, with the rare perception of her sex, the real state of the case and determined to bring matters to a crisis. Having heard that R—— was accustomed jestingly to remark that whoever decided to wed him must first be able to conquer him at chess, she sent for a Staunton from Philadelphia and devoted her womanly wit to mastering the arcane of the game. After two months unwearied study she dispatched a note to R—— stating that she had been learning chess and requesting him to come and play with her. My unsuspecting friend went at the appointed time and after a regular Sebastopol struggle found himself obliged to capitulate at the fifty-second move. When he read an invitation in her eyes or heard it softly whispered from her lips I know not, but at the end of the game the bashful R—— summoned up his courage and put the fatal question to his victorious mistress. They were married in March" [*The Chess Monthly*, June 1857, pp. 191, 192].

12: And patients leave their sickbeds. Mikhail Tal (1936–1992), the eighth world champion, suffered from a kidney disorder, and during convalescence from surgery in 1969, "he would sneak out of the hospital to play at the local chess club." During the operation itself, he "reportedly talked chess until the anesthesia-mask was strapped on!" [Lev Alburt and Al Lawrence, *Three Days with Bobby Fischer & Other Chess Essays*, 2003: Chess Information and Research Center, pp. 26, 27].

The media had mistakenly reported that Tal had died during surgery. "A month later ... he made a beautiful queen sacrifice and was highly amused at the comment of one of the spectators, who said: 'Not bad at all for a dead man' " [*The Human Comedy of Chess*, p. 114].

13: The subject of the inherent incompatibility of chess and marriage was raised in 1862 by *The Chess Player's Chronicle*, which quoted an item from the *Belfast Northern Whig*: "Let it be understood that I call marriage an evil only as regards chess; for your new-made wife is a sad drag on your ardent chess player, and we have even known ladies, married for years, who still cry out loudly, as their lord's weekly club-night comes around; for that night they make every possible kind of engagement—that night is the only one of the week on which they can entertain their friends, and for that night, of all others, they must gladly accept an invitation. Then the great female failing is antagonistic to the silent game, and the players are obliged to dispense with ladies' society at their meetings. This leads to bachelor parties, another great cause of conjugal offence. I entertain all possible love and reverence for the sex; but still, with this my experience, I cannot refrain from advising the bachelor chess player, contemplating matrimony, to pause before he takes the fatal leap. He must choose for himself; but let him do it deliberately between his board and his wife—between his chess-box and her band-box. Except through many a matrimonial row, there is no middle way" [as quoted in *A Chess Omnibus*, p. 406].

I have heard more than one chess player joke that the demands of marriage have cost him one hundred rating points.

In *Shakhmatnaya Goryachka* ("Chess Fever"), a silent film made by Vsevolod Pudovkin during the Moscow International Tournament of 1925, a player's fiancée wants him to quit chess and focus more attention on her. She complains to world champion José Capablanca, who makes a cameo appearance in the film, that she cannot even stand the thought of chess. Capablanca, in keeping with his reputation as a Don Juan, responds: "I understand how you feel. I cannot stand the thought of chess when I am with a lovely lady."

Contrast this with the views of Luzhin's fiancée: "An artist, a great artist, she frequently thought, contemplating his heavy profile, his corpulent hunched body, the dark lock of hair clinging to his always moist forehead. And perhaps it was precisely because she knew nothing at all about chess that chess for her was not simply a parlor game or a pleasant pastime, but a mysterious art equal to all the recognized arts" [*The Defense*, p. 88].

The artist Marcel Duchamp was a tournament competitor. He was married in 1927, and according to his friend Man Ray, for most of the first week that the newlyweds lived together, Duchamp studied "chess problems, and his bride, in desperate retaliation, got up one night when he was asleep and glued the chess pieces to the board. They were divorced three months later" [David Hooper and Kenneth Whyld, *The Oxford Companion to Chess*, 1991: Oxford University Press, p. 116].

And Fischer's views on marriage? "I would not marry an American girl," he said in 1961. "With a foreigner would be much better. First you get her without customs, second, if you don't like her you can send her back" [Michael Fox and Richard James, *The Complete Chess Addict*, 1987: Faber and Faber, p. 188].

By the 1992 rematch with Spassky, Fischer had ruled out marriage altogether. "Fischer says that he will never marry," said the girlfriend of one of his bodyguards. "He needs all of his time for chess" [Tim Hanke, "Finding Bobby Fischer," *American Chess Journal*, 1992, No. 1, p. 63].

CHAPTER 3: **The Pandolfini Variation**

1: There are tournaments in which all the players, despite beginning the game with more than two hours for forty moves, end up in time trouble. In AVRO 1938, the world's top eight players came together in the Netherlands for a double round-robin. "The outstanding feature of [the first] round, one which was to prove characteristic of the entire tournament, was the time pressure felt by all the players," *Chess Life* reported. "As usual, Reshevsky is in time trouble. He has to make 20 moves in 8 minutes... 16 moves in 6 minutes. His opponent, Alekhine, becomes very nervous, gets up and paces restlessly back and forth. Reshevsky, on the contrary, is quiet. He even takes one minute of precious time to tell Alekhine to calm himself! 12 moves to make in 2 minutes! Everyone, players as well as spectators, is jittery, except Reshevsky, who, with lightning rapidity, completes his fortieth move on the last second of the allotted time.

"Time pressure seems contagious: Keres, 11 moves in 9 minutes; Capablanca, 16 moves in ten minutes; Botvinnik, 12 moves in 9 minutes; Euwe, ditto, overlooking a win because of it and having to be satisfied with a draw" [*Chess Life*, December 1938].

2: There are four ways to draw, or tie, a game. First, the players can agree to a draw, presumably because they judge the position to be equal. Second, a player can claim a draw if the position on the board repeats three times. Third, a draw can be claimed if fifty moves pass without a pawn moving or a piece or pawn being captured. When there is a draw by perpetual check, the players are agreeing to draw because they both realize that one of them could keep checking the other's king forever without mating it. If they played out the position, after enough checks the threefold-repetition rule or the fifty-move rule would take effect. Finally, it is a draw if the player who is supposed to move is not in check but has no legal move. It is against the rules to move into check, and the player who cannot move is said to be stalemated.

3: I can't say that I had any real friends at the tournaments I entered in New York as a teenager. But there was a boy named Peter Winston, two years my junior, with whom I sometimes got a bite to eat between games. Or we relaxed between rounds by playing "giveaway chess," a topsy-turvy variant of the game in which the object is to give away all of your pieces. (As in checkers, if you can capture a piece, you have to take it.) Once, after a spirited session of giveaway, Peter blew an important regular tournament game by giving away one of his pieces on the fourth or fifth move. He was much better than me at normal chess—he was co-winner of the U.S. Junior Championship in 1974. He was smart and kind. I lost track of him after I cut back on tournaments and went off to college in the fall of 1974. While working on this book, I learned what became of him. In 1977, he played in an internationally rated tournament at Hunter College High School in New York. After losing an unprecedented nine games in a row, he left the tournament hall and never made it home. He hasn't been seen since. Nor has his body ever been recovered. He is presumed to have committed suicide.

4: In an interview on French television, Nabokov agreed that Fischer was "a strange person." He explained that "there is nothing abnormal about a chess player being abnormal, this is normal. Take the case of [Akiba] Rubinstein, a well-known [Russian] player of the early part of the century, who each day was taken by ambulance from the lunatic asylum, where he stayed constantly, to a café where he played, and then was taken back to his gloomy little room. He did not like to look at his opponent, but an empty chair at the chess board irritated him even more. Therefore in front of him they placed a mirror, where he saw his reflection, and perhaps, also the real Rubinstein" [Genna Sosonko, "The Jump," *New in Chess,* 2000, No. 3, p. 63].

5: Garry Kasparov, who was the reigning world champion at the time of Fischer's 1992 match, dismissed the American's comeback: "Here sits this poor fellow with whom one cannot talk normally, and what's more he plays bad chess." Fischer had taken a twenty-year-long hiatus from chess. His understanding of the game, Kasparov told *New in Chess,* was antiquated, "like Borg playing tennis with a wooden racket. . . . Now he's someone from the past. He doesn't belong to our world. He's an alien."

Botvinnik, too, saw little of the 1972 Fischer in the 1992 match: "This is not the Fischer we used to know, the Fischer who used to fascinate us with his play. He was a virtuoso of calculation. That Fischer is no more, nor can he be."

Although Fischer won the 1992 match, he was unable to shine despite the fact that Spassky was oddly complicit in his victory, behaving more like a friendly sparring partner than a real opponent. "I'm ready to fight and I want to fight," Spassky said at a press conference during the match, "but on the other hand I would like Bobby to win because I believe that Bobby must come back to chess and show his best. So I'm trying to give him excellent training." After Fischer uncorked an opening innovation in the eleventh game, Spassky said: "I was a little surprised, and at the same time I became very happy. I realized that Bobby was playing like a young man, and it was my principal goal to make him stronger and stronger in every game" [all quotations in this endnote from "Finding Bobby Fischer," pp. 74 and 66].

6: Fischer's hate speech can be found on his Web site, http://home.att.ne.jp/moon/fischer/. His fellow grandmasters have trouble explaining his descent into anti-Semitism. "I do not want to speak as a psychiatrist," the Dutch grandmaster Hans Ree told a filmmaker. "But one is inclined to do so. It is in my opinion an ailment, a paranoid mental derangement that expresses itself in this manner. I do not wish to say that all anti-Semites are insane, but he is that to a certain extent. He said, for instance, that the Jews want to eradicate the African elephant because their trunks make them think of uncircumcised penises. That is so bizarre that the average anti-Semite would not easily think of that" [*Bobby Fischer: The Wandering King,* p. 45].

7: Dutch filmmakers who made a 2003 television documentary on Fischer tried hard, through intermediaries, to track him down and arrange an interview. The only response they had was an e-mail he dispatched just before the United States invaded Iraq. It said nothing about their interview request: "The cat is out of the bag! U.S. Secretary of Defense Donald Rumsfeld is a f**king Jew. Thanks and have a good day" [*Bobby Fischer: The Wandering King,* p. 20].

Through a Japanese intermediary I, too, engaged in months of fruitless negotiations for an interview with Fischer in 2004 and 2005, and one of the first questions his handler asked me was whether I was Jewish. Fischer requested copies of my biographies, *The*

Man Who Loved Only Numbers and *Wings of Madness,* and he studied videos of me that were posted on the Web. *Gentlemen's Quarterly* had asked me to profile him, and he was afraid that I might clean up his remarks so that they were less offensive and vituperative. The magazine and I tried to accommodate him by proposing that the *GQ* Web site include an unedited transcript of our interview and any response Fischer cared to make to my published article. Still, no go.

8: Illness is not the only excuse that adults make for losing. In 1908, Siegbert Tarrasch (1862–1934) could not wrest the world title from Emanuel Lasker in a match in Düsseldorf and Munich. Tarrasch blamed his inadequate play on his sensitivity to the sea. This excuse, *The British Chess Magazine* opined at the time, "does not leave altogether a pleasant taste in the mouth. Düsseldorf is some 170 miles from the coast. A gift so sensitive to sea influence is not robust enough to carry the world's championship" [Harold Schonberg, *Grandmasters of Chess,* 1973: J. B. Lippincott, p. 124].

Alibis or not, Tarrasch deserves his due as a great player not least for his sage practical advice: "When you don't know what to do, wait for your opponent to get an idea—it's sure to be wrong!" [Bobby Fischer, *My 60 Most Memorable Games,* 1969: Simon & Schuster, p. 368].

When Fischer thrashed Larsen 6–0 in their 1971 semifinals Candidates Match, the Danish grandmaster blamed high blood pressure as well as the inhospitable Denver climate.

William Golding, author of *Lord of the Flies,* had one of the most novel excuses ever for losing. While pondering the seventeenth move of a postal game in 1983, he received the news from Stockholm that he had received the Nobel Prize for Literature. Delirious with joy, he mailed off a howler of a move [*The Even More Complete Chess Addict,* pp. 38, 39].

9: In this respect, I was like Luzhin: "The nights were somehow bumpy. He just could not manage to force himself not to think of chess, and although he felt drowsy, sleep could find no way into his brain; it searched for a loophole, but every entrance was guarded by a chess sentry and he had the agonizing feeling that sleep was just there, close by, but on the outside of his brain: the Luzhin who was wearily scattered around the room slumbered, but the Luzhin who visualized a chessboard stayed awake and was unable to merge with his happy double" [*The Defense,* p, 126].

Many top players have difficulty sleeping. "The main problem during important tournaments was how to fall asleep," wrote the Estonian grandmaster Jaan Ehlvest (1962–). "It was a real pain if you could not do it quickly" [Jaan Ehlvest, *The Story of a Chess Player,* 2004: Arbiter Publishing, p. 116].

Marshall managed to do useful chess work in his sleep. According to the December 1944 *Chess Life,* "he even took a pocket set to bed with him at night so that he might record the inspirations of his dreams."

Vladimir Bagirov (1936–), the leading proponent of Alekhine's Defense, a dodgy response to the king-pawn opening in which Black encourages White to advance his pawns and kick around Black's king knight, took up the defense after Alexander Alekhine appeared in a dream and urged Bagirov to rehabilitate his eponymous defense.

Timman has learned from his dreams to persevere at the board. In one dream, he and Kasparov were in a castle surrounded by water. "We are talking about a position in which I am two pawns down but I have the two bishops," Timman recalled. "We argue, and in the end Kasparov agrees with me that I have sufficient compensation for the material" [*The Reliable Past*, p. 153].

10: Pandolfini was echoing the words of Russian-born Saviely Tartakower, who became a French citizen in the 1920s and was said to be more interested in playing a beautiful move than a winning one. Tartakower was known to make wry observations about the game. Harold Schonberg compiled many "Tartakowerisms":

> *The blunders are all there, waiting to be made.*
>
> *Sacrifices only prove that somebody has blundered.*
>
> *It is always better to sacrifice your opponent's men.*
>
> *Moral victories do not count.*
>
> *An isolated Pawn spreads gloom all over the chessboard.*
>
> *Tactics is knowing what to do when there is something to do; strategy is knowing what to do when there is nothing to do.* [Grandmasters of Chess, p. 160]

CHAPTER 4: **Russian Domination**

1: *Pravda's* description was double-speak. If Marx believed that chess was a good way to build character, it was apparently not effective in his own case. "When Marx got into a difficult position he would get angry," a contemporary recalled, "and losing a game would cause him to fly into a rage!" [D. J. Richards, *Soviet Chess,* 1965: Clarendon Press, p. 39]. It is difficult to believe that Lenin didn't care if he lost. He was reportedly a Class A tournament player like me. If he was genuinely apathetic about losing, he would not have been that good.

2: The field at Nottingham 1936 included the reigning world champion (Max Euwe), three former world champions (Emanuel Lasker, José Capablanca, Alexander Alekhine), and three renowned rising stars (Reuben Fine, Salomon Flohr, Samuel Reshevsky).

3: If the Russians are allowed to include Alexander Alekhine as one of their own—he was born in Moscow but lived abroad after the Bolshevik Revolution and during his reign as world champion—the Russian hegemony goes back to 1927 and was broken only briefly by Fischer and the Dutchman Max Euwe. The classical champions since 1927 are Alekhine (1927–1935, 1937–1946), Euwe (1935–1937), Mikhail Botvinnik (1948–1957, 1958–1960, 1961–1963), Vasily Smyslov (1957–1958), Mikhail Tal (1960–1961), Tigran Petrosian (1963–1969), Boris Spassky (1969–1972), Robert James Fischer (1972–1975), Anatoly Karpov (1975–1985), Garry Kasparov (1985–2000), and Vladimir Kramnik (2000–).

4: The Kremlin could also be ruthless in punishing players who let Russia down. After Mark Taimanov, the pianist and grandmaster, was shut out by Fischer 6–0 in the quarter finals of the World Championship Candidates Matches in 1971, his wife and musical partner denounced him and left him, and Moscow cut his salary, banished him from the national team, and prohibited him from playing chess abroad.

5: When asked why increasing numbers of Russians were learning chess in his mother country, Alekhine had an explanation as simple as Karpov's: "What else is there for them to do?" [*The Reliable Past*, p. 140].

6: Adjourned games often featured masterfully played endgames. Russian GM Lev Polugaevsky (1934–1995) sometimes spent fifteen hours "to get to the bottom of an adjourned position," wrote Hans Ree. "By banning the adjournment of games, we have lightened our burden as chess players, but we have also lost a glorious piece of our chess culture." Ree described the time he was one of Korchnoi's seconds and helped him analyze an adjourned game until 3:00 A.M. "At that point, being simply too tired to think of anything meaningful, I went to bed. Korchnoi didn't, although his day had been much more tiring than mine, since, in addition to all the analyzing, he had played the actual game. He simply continued his analysis. The next morning he showed me something important he had discovered at about six . . . something we had completely missed the day before. Korchnoi was never too tired to look at a chess position" [*The Human Comedy of Chess*, pp. 300, 301].

In the early 1990s, the practice of adjournment was eliminated, because of the availability of chess software that could aid in the analysis of adjourned positions; now all tournament games are completed in a single session without interruption. Adjournments were always unfair in a sense because they were popularity tests. Each player would employ the strongest seconds he could cajole into helping him analyze the game—or to let him sleep while they did the all-night analysis.

7: Botvinnik did not have an easy time in the match. He fell behind and had to win the twenty-third and penultimate game in order to survive. His second, Salo Flohr, (1908–1983), was pleased when the game "was adjourned in a position where Botvinnik's two bishops were clearly stronger than Bronstein's knights. After lengthy thought Botvinnik sealed a move and together with Flohr left the Tchaikovsky Concert Hall. The move sealed by Botvinnik was fairly obvious, and a contented Flohr, analyzing in his mind the variations that promised victory, accompanied Botvinnik to his place. After supper they once more looked at the position, and Salo set off home for a final polishing of the variations. The following day Flohr was again at Botvinnik's place. 'Salo, could you show the variations to [my wife], I should like to have one more look at the position,' said the world champion. Flohr was somewhat dumbfounded, but nevertheless, after setting up the position on the board, he began demonstrating something to Botvinnik's wife, although she barely knew the moves of the pieces.

"Some time later the champion himself came back, the friends had lunch, and set off to the playing venue. Before climbing up onto the stage, Botvinnik quietly, so that no one could hear, admitted to his helper: 'You know, Salo. I sealed a different move.'" Tears welled up in Flohr's eyes, and for a long time he was unable to forgive the resentment that he felt towards his suspicious and mistrustful old friend Misha" [*The Reliable Past*, pp. 166, 167].

8:   Mikhail Tal, the eighth world champion, was known as the Wizard of Riga (or, in Smyslov's words, the Gangster of the Chessboard). In the late 1950s he revived the flashy sacrificial play that had receded in the late nineteenth century when defensive skills improved. Many of Tal's fellow grandmasters could not accept that they were losing to him because they were bamboozled by his chessboard fireworks. Instead they blamed their defeat on his hypnotic stare. At Curaçao 1962, the Hungarian-born grandmaster Pal Benko wore dark glasses to avoid being mesmerized, but still expired in only thirty moves. Tal had a sense of humor, and he donned a pair of oversized novelty spectacles when he faced Benko later.

    Three-time U.S. champion Lev Alburt, who defected to the West from Ukraine, disagrees with Kasparov's assessment that Tal was purposely trying to intimidate his opponents. In *Three Days with Bobby Fischer & Other Chess Essays,* Alburt and coauthor Al Lawrence wrote about Alburt's own encounters with Tal: "Alburt had a run-in with the Dreaded Stare. At the start of their first game together, Lev couldn't help but glance up at Misha, whose wide-open brown eyes, topped by their prominent dark brows, were riveted on Alburt. Lev, from a younger, less superstitious generation that had already incorporated Tal's imaginative approach into their own games, reacted as if the stare were some kind of joke, smiling. Tal immediately roused himself from his trance. Never one to distract his opponent on purpose, he remembered Lev's reaction. Alburt was never again the recipient of the Stare. Our conclusion: the much-touted stare was probably only an absent-minded habit" [p. 36].

    In all fairness, it should be noted that some of the game's first theoreticians, aside from offering their views on advantageous ways of developing the bishops and knights, proposed ingenious schemes for distracting the opposing player. In the 1400s, Luis Ramirez de Lucena recommended placing the board so that light shined in the opponent's eyes. "Also," Lucena advised, "try to play your adversary when he has just eaten and drunk freely." To rattle their opponents, chess players have done everything from banging the pieces and glaring menacingly to chewing with their mouths open and rocking maniacally in their chairs. Lisa Lane (1938–), who won her first U.S. Women's Championship in 1959 and is one of the few chess players to grace the cover of *Sports Illustrated* (August 7, 1961), remembered how "one Russian woman performed noisy breathing exercises whenever it was her opponent's turn to move" [James Hoffman, "Chess: Once the Game of Kings, Now the King of Games," *Lithopinion,* Winter 1970, p. 77].

    Benjamin Franklin objected to such tactics. "If your adversary is long in playing you ought not to hurry him or express any uneasiness at his delay," he wrote in a widely published essay on the morality of chess. "You should not sing, nor whistle, nor look at your watch, nor take up a book to read, nor make a tapping with your feet on the floor, or with your fingers on the table, nor do anything else that may disturb his attention." Chess players are happy to claim such an illustrious personage as Franklin as one of their own, but they have universally ignored his plea for gentle-manly behavior [Benjamin Franklin, *The Morals of Chess,* 1779, as quoted in Jerome Saltzmann, *The Chess Reader,* 1949: Greenberg, p. 115]. At an international tournament in New York in 1927, Nimzowitsch complained to the referee that his opponent, the Yugoslavian master Milan Vidmar (1885–1962), was destroying his concentration by puffing on a smelly cigar. The official asked Vidmar to stop smoking, and he readily obliged. A few minutes later, though, Nimzowitsch protested again. This time the referee was puzzled. "Your opponent isn't smoking," he said. "Yes, yes, I know," Nimzowitsch replied, "but he looks as if he wants to." (This story is probably apocryphal, because another, more colorful version has Nimzowitsch responding, by borrowing an aphorism apparently coined by Tartakower: "Yes, but you know that in chess the threat is always mightier than the execution." And in some versions Nimzowitsch's opponent is Emanuel Lasker [1868–1941] not Milan Vidmar.)

In 1972, the Argentine star Henrique Mecking (1952–) faced former world champion Tigran Petrosian at a tournament in San Antonio. Mecking complained that the Russian player "was only quiet when it was his own turn to move. All the time I was thinking he was kicking the table and elbowing the board to make it shake. If this was not enough to upset me, Petrosian kept making noises, stirring his cup of coffee, all the time varying the rhythm. And rolling a coin across the table." Mecking retaliated by making some noise of his own, but Petrosian calmly turned off his hearing aid and proceeded to crush him [*Grandmasters of Chess*, pp. 21, 22].

The fourteenth world champion, Vladimir Kramnik, even succumbed to the very distraction—bright light—that Lucena proposed half a millennium ago. On the day before the first game of his 2002 match against the computer Deep Fritz, Kramnik examined the pieces. To the surprise of the match organizers, he pronounced the chessmen unacceptable because they were apparently too shiny and reflected the stage lights. "First we got some sandpaper," recalled match director Malcolm Pein, "but this ruined the pieces." Then they bought some dark varnish and hastily painted the pieces to try to reduce the glare. But on the morning of the first game, the chessmen were too sticky to handle. "We faced the prospect of Kramnik picking up his king's pawn and being unable to let go," said Pein. "Frankly I was panicking and I was not alone." Just before the game, someone had the clever idea of hastening the drying by placing the pieces in the refrigerator in Kramnik's dressing room. (His private stash of chocolate bars had to be removed to make room for the chessmen.) To everyone's relief, the Russian champion approved of the freshly dried pieces. Deep Fritz, of course, was oblivious to the fuss [Paul Hoffman, "Report from the 'Brains in Bahrain,'" time.com/time/sampler/article/0,8599,3643100,00.html].

9:   This magnanimous gesture says a lot about Pascal's character. Commentators on chess have long believed that a person's behavior at the board mirrors his true character. To wit, Henry Chadwick wrote, in 1895: "If ever there was a game calculated to bring into prominent view the idiosyncrasies of individuals, it is chess. It shows up a man's prevailing characteristics at times so plainly that he who runs may read. The faults of human nature, as shown in conceit, selfishness, obstinacy, ill-temper and meanness, are brought out into prominence in playing the game, as strikingly as are the virtues of humility, generosity, good temper, and a charitable consideration of your adversary's weak points. The amenities of social life, of course, have their influence in suppressing, to a certain extent, any conspicuous exhibition of one's faults; but they do not altogether repress the tendency to show a man up in his true colors. In fact, in the eager desire for victory in a contest in which one's mental power is brought into play, and in a game in which the element of chance is entirely eliminated, a man is apt to exhibit his prominent traits of character very plainly at times" [Henry Chadwick, *The Game of Chess*, 1895, as quoted in *A Chess Omnibus*, p. 386].

10: Kasparov's claim was an echo of an allegation that Napoleon had made two centuries before. In 1809, Napoleon played chess at Schonbrunn Castle, in Vienna, against the Turk, a turbaned mannequin that was heralded as the world's first chess-playing automaton. Napoleon suspected that a human chess master was somehow hidden inside, and he reportedly tried to interfere with the master's view of the board by wrapping a shawl around the Turk's head and torso. But the blindfolded Turk still moved the chessmen quickly, in a jerky, mechanical fashion. Napoleon lost the game and angrily knocked the pieces to the floor. He was apparently so rattled that it took him several months to regain his concentration at the chessboard. He continued to insist that the automaton was a fraud, and indeed it turned out to conceal a human being.

CHAPTER 5: An American in Moscow

1: In rapid chess, however, Kasparov walloped Lautier 3–0.

2: Murey was Victor Korchnoi's second in 1978 when he challenged Karpov for the World Championship.

3: Lautier didn't need to witness Kasparov's cursing to know that he was beating the Russian. But body language can tip off an opponent to a threat on the board that he might not have noticed otherwise. Fischer wrote about his victory on the White side of a Ruy Lopez over the Yugoslavian grandmaster Petar Trifunovich (1910–1980) at Bled 1961. A dubious opening experiment of Trifunovich's backfired, and after the sixteenth move, Fischer was happy with his position: "White has a strategically won game," he wrote, "but the technical problems are considerable. Moreover a tempting trap now stared me in the face. . . . I was considering the blunder 17 B-N5? . . . but Trifunovich seemed too quiet all of a sudden, and I suspected he had tuned in on my brain waves." At the last minute Fischer saw that Trifunovich could win his queen at the end of a four-move sequence [*My Sixty Most Memorable Games*, p. 203].

   The opponents of Max Euwe (1901–1981), the world champion from 1935 to 1937, always knew when he thought he was in a tight spot: his ears were red.

4: Some players have the annoying, unethical habit of trying to retract a move in progress by saying *J'adoube* after they've already touched a piece and suddenly realized that moving it would be costly. "GM Milan Matulović has more than once been caught trying to get away with stuff that would get him thrown off any primary school chess team. Against Bilek at Sousse in 1967 he, not liking his position, *took a move back,* saying as he did so, *'J'adoube.'* Bilek's jaw dropped, but the arbiter hadn't seen the outrage and Matulović went on to win . . . which is why, for a while, Matulović was known on the tournament circuit as J'adoubovich. A more eminent practitioner of this tactic may have been a former world champion. Alekhine was accused of having touched a rook *before* saying *'J'adoube,'* against Schmidt in 1941" [*The Even More Complete Chess Addict*, pp. 225, 226].

5: "Look at me, I'm laughing, I'm making pleasantries, and I'm not going to be able to sleep tonight," proclaimed Argentinean grandmaster Miguel Najdorf (1910–1997) after losing a game [Anthony Saidy and Norman Lessing, *The World of Chess*, 1974: Random House, p. 216].

6: "Mikhail Tal . . . on being told that the Soviet state was launching a campaign against alcoholism, commented, 'The state against vodka. I'll be on the side of vodka'" [*The Even More Complete Chess Addict*, p. 268]. Alekhine had a lifelong problem with alcoholism, and some commentators believed that he lost the 1935 World Championship to Max Euwe because he was inebriated during the games. Euwe knew that Alekhine had been drinking, but doubted that he was drunk. "I think it helps to drink a little, but not in the long run," Euwe said years later. "I regretted not having drunk at all during the second match with Alekhine [which Euwe lost]. Actually Alekhine's walk was not steady because he did not see well but did not like to wear glasses. So many people thought he was drunk because of the way he walked" [*Chess Life & Review*, August 1978].

At Gijón 1945, Alekhine consulted a doctor who found that his "liver was so swollen that it was almost touching his right nipple." The doctor insisted he stop drinking. "'You are not the first one telling me that,' said Alekhine. 'If you don't stop, you will die in a short time,' said the doctor. 'And if I do stop?' 'You'll live maybe a couple of years.' Alekhine said that in that case it made no sense to stop drinking, and thanked the doctor for his straightforwardness." He died the next year, at fifty-three. "According to some it was a heart attack, while other sources reported he had suffocated after choking on a piece of meat. A plate of food and a chessboard were found on the table in front of him" [*The Human Comedy of Chess*, pp. 186, 187].

7: It may have been the Web sites themselves, rather than anything Vaganian said, that were responsible for the notion that he had calculated everything in advance. Chess commentators often downplay the role of intuition and promote the erroneous image of top players as superhuman, all-seeing calculating machines. In his autobiography, Tal described a complicated game in which he sacrificed a knight against Evgeny Vasiukov (1933–) in the 1965 Soviet Championship: "The sacrifice was not altogether obvious, and there was a large number of possible variations, but when I conscientiously began to work through them, I found, to my horror, that nothing would come of it. Ideas piled up one after another. I would transport a subtle reply, which worked in one case, to another situation where it would prove to be quite useless. As a result my head became filled with a completely chaotic pile of all sorts of moves, and the famous 'tree of the variations,' from which the trainers recommend that you cut off the small branches, in this case spread with unbelievable rapidity.

"And then suddenly, for some reason, I remembered the classic couplet by Korney Ivanovich Chukovsky: Oh, what a difficult job it was/ To drag out of the marsh the hippopotamus.

"I don't know from what associations the hippopotamus got onto the chessboard, but although the spectators were convinced that I was continuing to study the position, I, despite my humanitarian education, was trying at this time to work out: just how would you drag a hippopotamus out of the marsh? I remember how jacks figured in my thoughts, as well as levers, helicopters, and even a rope ladder. After a lengthy conversation I admitted defeat as an engineer, and thought spitefully: 'Well, let it drown!' And suddenly the hippopotamus disappeared, going off the chessboard just as he had come on—of his own accord! And straightaway the position did not appear to be so complicated.

"Now I somehow realized that it was not possible to calculate all the variations, and that the knight sacrifice was, by its very nature, purely intuitive. And since it promised an interesting game, I could not refrain from making it.

"And the following day, it was with pleasure that I read in the paper how Mikhail Tal, after carefully thinking over the position for 40 minutes, made an accurately calculated piece sacrifice" [*Three Days with Bobby Fischer & Other Chess Essays*, pp. 31, 32].

CHAPTER 6: **Anatomy of a Hustler**

1: My honors thesis was called *W. V. O. Quine's Philosophy of Science: An Empiricism Without the Analytic-Synthetic Distinction.*

2: An inflated rating is also possible because a newcomer to a closed pool of high-rated players may be issued a rating that is artificially high. When a player obtains his first provisional rating from the USCF, it is computed by adding 400 points to the rating of anyone he beats, subtracting 400 points from the rating of anyone who defeats him, and averaging those numbers. So if his opponents all have very high ratings and he loses all his games, he will get a rating that is 400 points less than his opponents' average rating—which may overstate his actual strength. In a larger pool of players, this could not happen because as he lost game after game he would be paired with lower-rated players who were also faring poorly.

3: The Grob played in reverse is known as the Borg, which, of course, is Grob spelled backward.

4: The "Heroes of Chernobyl" tournament was by no means unique. On March 9, 2006, the FIDE Web site (fide.com) had this report: "The Ethics Commission received a complaint from the German Chess Federation against IM Miroslav Shvarts concerning a GM norm he said he received in the Kali Cup GM tournament held in Mindzentkalla Hungary in February 2004. According to the Hungarian Chess Federation investigation, the Kali Cup never took place. Therefore the Ethics Commission has decided to apply sanctions against all the participants in the tournament, not just Mr. Shvarts."

5: Azmaiparashvili was once Kasparov's chief second and a participant in a 1992 tournament that Kasparov himself organized in Moscow. In one game, according to Nigel Short, Azmaiparashvili wanted a draw as Black against American GM Nicholas de Firmian and offered him $2,000. "Nick declined," Short said. "Kasparov went up to Nick and was very angry with him. He said that $2,000 was a very generous offer for a draw and that he should accept. Of course he's a friend of Azmaiparashvili and wanted to help him. But he was also the tournament organizer, and this was something really shady" [Dominic Lawson, *End Game*, 1994: Harmony Books, p. 6].

Kasparov and Azmaiparashvili eventually had a falling out. At Novgorod 1997, Nigel Short was set to play Kasparov in the final round. In his chess column in the *Telegraph*, Short told the story of how the evening before the game he "was set upon by a large dog while walking. I received a nasty bite in my arm and was admitted to hospital. Bandaged and bleeding, I was in no condition to play chess. Thus, for the only time in my life, I proposed a pre-arranged draw to the great man, which he duly accepted (in fact a draw with Black guaranteed him at least a shared first place). We then decided to concoct [a] game for public benefit." They decided to "play" the first twenty moves of a game that they believed Azmaiparashvili had faked for the suspect tournament in Macedonia [Nigel Short, London *Sunday Telegraph*, May 22, 2005, chessbase.com/newsdetail.asp?newsid=2406].

6:   The USCF has been rocked by cheating scandals, too, but has done a better job than FIDE in ferreting out hustlers among its own leadership. In July 2006, Sam Sloan (the USCF board member who played the Grob opening) filed a complaint with the USCF ethics committee against fellow board member Robert Tanner. Sloan accused Tanner of artificially obtaining the master title by repeatedly playing rated games against the same small pool of low-ranked players—gaining one point at a time, as Bloodgood had. Tanner was a certified tournament director, and Sloan suggested that some of the games Tanner had asked the USCF to rate were never actually played. The ethics committee, while declaring that it "saw no evidence that any fictional games were submitted for rating," concluded that Tanner had in fact manipulated his own rating by methods that were "inconsistent with the principles of fair play, good sportsmanship, honesty and respect for the rights of others." Robert Tanner resigned from the USCF's board of directors on December 5, 2006.

7:   There are also cases of players double-crossing each other and not following through on agreements to throw games. The most famous case occurred at the Fifth American Chess Congress in New York in 1880. The winner, James Grundy, was suspected of reneging on an arrangement with Preston Ware, a master from Boston. The tournament was a ten-person double round-robin. With one round to go, Grundy was tied with Captain Mackenzie. Grundy had lost the previous round to Ware, who had had the audacity to shove his rook pawn two squares on his very first move in response to Grundy's king-pawn opening. Ware later told the tournament committee that on a walk along the Bowery with Grundy after the game, "he remarked to me that he was poor, and really needed the second prize [$300]; I had in beating him, knocked him out of the first prize [$500] . . . and it would not make any difference to me if I played easily in our next game, so as to give him the second prize; . . . he would be willing to give a consideration for it. 'I suppose you mean for us to play for a draw.' He said: 'Yes,' and I agreed to do it, and $20 was agreed upon as the consideration.

"We agreed to play on very slowly until the other games were terminated, and to move back and forth . . . and after I had done so, perhaps three or four times, I observed he was making desperate efforts to win, and finally did so, perpetuating an infamous fraud upon me."

Grundy of course denied everything. It was his word against Ware's, and so the tournament committee let Grundy's victory stand, even though the moves of the game corroborated Ware's story [Andy Soltis and Gene H. McCormick, *The United States Chess Championship, 1845–1996*, Second Edition, 1997: McFarland & Company, pp. 24, 25].

8: Korchnoi is one of the larger-than-life figures in modern chess. Many players have been on the receiving end of his unrestrained rudeness. Players are prohibited from speaking to each other over the board except to offer draws. Korchnoi was playing a master from an Arab country and in the middle of the game leaned forward and asked, "Do you speak English?" The opponent replied in the affirmative. "Then why don't you just resign?" Korchnoi said.

Like many Russians, Korchnoi is superstitious but tries to disguise this from his skeptical Western friends. The Dutch GM Hans Ree joined Korchnoi for his 1977 match in Italy against Petrosian. On their way to the match, Ree wrote, "Victor showed me a letter he'd recently received from a Russian emigrant. . . . It outlined the science fiction–like scenario of a military laboratory in Moscow where they had the modern technology to project the positions in the games played by Korchnoi and Petrosian in Italy live onto their screen. A crucial position would immediately be spotted by one of the many grandmasters the laboratory had at its disposal, and a paralyzing ray would then be beamed from Moscow 'straight into the chess centers of the brain' leading Korchnoi to make the decisive mistake. Viktor and I thought it was hilarious. Chess centers of the brain!

"They played in a hotel on the top of a mountain. There was also a radio transmitter up there. When the match was over I heard that Victor had arranged for the transmitter to be used as a jamming device during the hours of play to prevent radio waves from Moscow from getting through. Just to make sure" [*The Human Comedy of Chess*, p. 37].

Korchnoi apparently believed in mental telepathy. In 1985, Korchnoi "transcended the real world when he won a prolonged game, a French Defense, against one of the strongest players from the early twentieth century—Géza Maróczy (1870–1951). As the Hungarian grandmaster had been dead for many years, Korchnoi had to resort to the help of a medium, who received Maróczy's moves from the other world. Stated the winner: 'Of course, one cannot be absolutely sure that the game was indeed played by Maróczy's spirit, but the entire course of it, with its not altogether certain handling of the opening, but good play in the endgame, is certainly evidence of this'" [*The Reliable Past*, p. 36].

Maybe Korchnoi was just trying to top the legendary story of Steinitz and his wireless hotline on which he played chess with God after generously offering Him the handicap of a pawn.

9: In 1960, Korchnoi entered the Soviet Championship in Leningrad. Going into the last round, he had a half-point lead over soon-to-be world champion Tigran Petrosian and Yefim Geller. But Korchnoi found himself in an inferior position and offered his opponent a draw. His adversary turned him down and "then, before my very eyes, went and consulted with Geller and Petrosian. . . . In the subsequent course of the game, in a time scramble which was the more severe for me, fortune smiled on me." Korchnoi won a pawn and then the game, keeping his half-point lead over Geller and Petrosian, who had both won their individual encounters. He was crowned Soviet champion.

Fourteen years later, Geller's opponent in 1960, David Bronstein, confided in Korchnoi that he had purposely lost the game. Bronstein explained that he detested Petrosian and "during the game . . . saw how unscrupulously and crudely" Petrosian's opponent was capitulating. He told Korchnoi that he could not bear to give the guileful Petrosian the satisfaction of being sole winner of the championship. "In an excellent position," Bronstein recalled, "I made an incorrect piece sacrifice and soon resigned."

"But what about me?" Korchnoi asked. "In that way you were betraying me as well!"

"You were in a bad way. I thought you were losing, and I couldn't leave Petrosian as the sole winner," Bronstein repeated.

Korchnoi concluded that "to become Chess Champion of the USSR 'honestly' means to accomplish a great feat. However there is nothing surprising about this. In the professional chess world inside the Soviet Union, the top places lead to colossal privileges, and the battle for these places is bound to involve means not associated purely with chess. . . . Soon after the championship, on the initiative of the Sports Committee, I was granted a two-room flat. Up to then I had 20 square metres in a flat where there were several families, who shared a communal kitchen, toilet and bathroom, whereas now I had 27 sq. m. in a self-contained flat" [Victor Korchnoi, *Chess Is My Life*, 1978: Arco Publishing Co., pp. 38, 39].

10: Fischer used Lasker's words to start *My 60 Most Memorable Games*. Fischer was one of the most honest players when it came to annotating his own games. He freely admitted mistakes and gave credit to his opponents. Of a King's Indian Defense he played against Tigran Petrosian at Portoroz 1958, Fischer wrote: "I was amazed during the game. Each time Petrosian achieved a good position, he managed to maneuver into a better one" and "Panicking and giving him the opportunity he's been waiting for to sneak P-QN4 in. . . . Petrosian likes to play cat-and-mouse, hoping that his opponents will go wrong in the absence of a direct threat. The amazing thing is—they usually do! Witness a case in point, I should have just ignored his 'threat' with, say, 36 . . . R-R1." Of a Caro-Kahn with Euwe at the Leipzig Olympiad 1960, he wrote: "After the game Euwe showed me a cute trap he might have played for—and almost fainted when I fell into it! The line arises after. . . . It's these tidbits that you remember best" [pp. 27, 136].

11: "Alekhine's relations to women were markedly disturbed," wrote Reuben Fine. "He was married five times. His last two wives were much older; one was thirty years his senior, the other twenty. It was said that he became impotent early in life. Towards his last wife he was openly sadistic" [Reuben Fine, *The Psychology of the Chess Player*, 1967: Dover, p. 54].

"Unlike Capablanca, Alekhine was much more interested in chess than women. During the London Tournament in 1922, he and Capa were taken to a show. It was reported that Alekhine never took his eyes off his pocket chess-set, while Capa never took his eyes off the chorus line" [*The Complete Chess Addict*, p. 189].

12: Of Karpov and Kasparov's first marriages, during the years that they contested the world title, Hans Ree wrote: "Initially, their wives may have thought there would be room for something else besides chess in the heart of a world champion. However, they must have realized very quickly that that was not the case. At times some of their laments reached the outside world. Kasparov's marriage was dissolved very quickly, and his wife told a newspaper that she was going into hiding because she was afraid of her husband. Karpov's wife, Natasha, was asked on television: 'Do you like chess players?' 'No,' she replied, 'Not at all, they are very tiresome people' " [*The Human Comedy of Chess*, p. 9].

CHAPTER 7: **Female Counterplay**

1: Here's the record of youngest grandmasters, as compiled by chessbase.com.

NO.	PLAYER	NAT.	YEARS	MONTHS	DAYS	YEAR
1	Sergey Karjakin	UKR	12	7	0	2002
2	Parimarjan Negi	IND	13	3	22	2006
3	Magnus Carlsen	NOR	13	3	27	2004
4	Bu Xiangzhi	CHN	13	10	13	1999
5	Teimour Radjabov	AZE	14	0	14	2001
6	Ruslan Ponomaryov	UKR	14	0	17	1997
7	Etienne Bacrot	FRA	14	2	0	1997
8	Maxime Vachier-Lagrave	FRA	14	4	0	2005
9	Peter Leko	HUN	14	4	22	1994
10	Yuri Kuzubov	UKR	14	7	12	2004
11	Nguyen Ngoc Truong Son	VIE	14	10	0	2004
12	Hikaru Nakamura	USA	15	2	19	2003
13	Pentala Harikrishna	IND	15	3	5	2001
14	Koneru Humpy	IND	15	1	27	2002
15	Judit Polgar	HUN	15	4	28	1991
16	Alejandro Ramirez	CRI	15	5	14	2003
17	Bobby Fischer	USA	15	6	1	1958

2: In *Breaking Through*, Judit's oldest sister, Susan, explained that the "blunder" Kasparov was trying to avoid wasn't as bad as it first seemed. Although Judit could fork him and win the exchange (a rook for a bishop), Kasparov could have forced a draw by perpetual check [Susan Polgar with Paul Truong, *Breaking Through*, 2005: Everyman Chess, p. 34.]

3: "Time trouble is an addiction, perhaps even a physical addiction to the opium-like substances secreted by a chess player's brain during the time trouble phase" [*The Human*

Comedy of Chess, p. 110]. Among top Americans, Samuel Reshevsky (1911–1992) was the strongest player who was addicted to time trouble. He justified his approach by claiming that the time he took allowed him to work out deeply all good continuations in the positions—and he blamed his occasional flagging on his adversary's "bad moves" that he had not considered in his long think. After Reshevsky beat Isaac Kashdan in a playoff match to win the U.S. Championship for the fifth time, in 1942, Kenneth Harkness asked the thirty-one-year-old grandmaster the question that was on every chess fan's mind:

"Why do you sit for an hour or more over one move and invariably get into time trouble?"

"Well," Reshevsky answered, "I've heard people say I do it deliberately, just to rattle my opponent and make him blunder—but that's silly! Why should I make it difficult for myself? All you have to do is look at the two games I lost to Kashdan. Both were lost on blunders I made when I was in time trouble."

"Why do you do it, then?" I asked him.

"To exhaust all the possibilities in the position."

"What do you mean by that?"

"Well, I consider all the best lines for my opponent and myself and work out all the possible variations. I want to be quite sure of what I am doing."

"How far ahead do you analyze?"

"Oh, I can see 20 moves ahead quite easily."

"You mean with all variations?"

"All variations of the best lines, yes. That's how I am able to play the final moves quickly. I know exactly what I'm doing. The only trouble is that my opponent doesn't always play one of the best defenses and I've done all that work for nothing."

"Is that why you are likely to blunder yourself?" I asked him.

"Sometimes . . ." [*Chess Life*, February 1943].

4:   "The Soviet Chess Federation was used to seeing its players dominate the chess world and the world rankings," Polgar wrote. "However, by late 1986 it was clear that in the January 1987 list my rating was going to be 2495, 65 points ahead of the Soviet [Women's] World Champion, Maia Chiburdanidze. During the Chess Olympiad in Dubai, they held the FIDE Congress where an unthinkable decision was made. All women players in the world would receive 100 bonus points except for me!!!! So when the official world rating list came out, I had 2495 and Maia had 2530 with the added 100 point gift! It was amusing, that even with this colossal injustice, I still remained the third-ranked [female] player in the world and only 35 points behind Maia. According to the rumors, this was part of some political favor owed by FIDE to the Soviets. There was no proper logic to this and there was definitely no justification for it. But when you deal with chess politicians, they can turn a chicken into a turkey without blinking an eye" [*Breaking Through*, p. 15].

5:   FIDE had previously granted the title to two women's world champions—one of them was Chiburdanidze—even though they did not meet the rating and performance requirements.

6: "Chess players have a very retentive memory with regard to the games which they win," warned Richard Penn in 1842 in *The Chess Player's Chronicle*: "Never (if you can avoid it) lose a game to a person who rarely wins when he plays with you. If you do so, you may afterwards find that this one game has been talked of to all his friends, although he may have forgotten to mention 99 others which had a different result" [Richard Penn, *The Chess Player's Chronicle*, 1842, as quoted in *A Chess Omnibus*, p. 412].

7: Michael Khodarkovsky, the chief trainer of the U.S. Women's Team, was not immune to scandal, either. He apparently inflated his playing strength, claiming that he was an international master. On January 21, 2007, he was the subject of an article in *The New York Times* called "Prominent Chess Trainer Retreats From Claim He Held Title."

CHAPTER 8: "I'm Not the World's Biggest Geek"

1: I should have taken solace in John Mortimer's contrarian view about chess and intelligence: "It will be cheering to know that many people are skillful chess-players, though in many instances their brains, in a general way, compare unfavourably with the cognitive faculties of a rabbit." There are those, like Raymond Chandler, who think chess playing takes brains but is "as elaborate waste of intelligence as you could find anywhere outside an advertising agency" [*The Complete Chess Addict*, pp. 1, 38].

2: Pascal's kindheartedness was well known on the chess circuit. One (true) story has him changing the bedsheets of a debilitated old grandmaster at chess camp, only to learn that the man had a urinary infection.

3: It should be noted that Fischer claimed to refute only the commonest version of the King's Gambit, in which White develops his king knight after giving up the pawn. Fischer himself occasionally played a much rarer form of the King's Gambit, practiced by the first world champion, Wilhelm Steinitz, in which White violates a general opening principle—"Knights before bishops!"—by holding back the king knight and immediately posting his light-squared bishop.

4: Tarrasch once said that the object of playing a gambit was "to acquire a reputation of being a dashing player at the cost of losing a game" [*Chess Life*, July 1935]. For every top player like Spassky who enjoys a particular gambit, there is one like Lautier who looks down on it. For instance, in 1928, Frank Marshall said of his favorite Wing Gambit: "It may not be absolutely sound, but it always leads to an interesting game, affording plenty of opportunities to attack." Of the same gambit, William Napier (1881–1952) said: "It is easily defined as capital offense against common sense in chess. It is comparable with pitching one's young to the crocodiles, so the devil may not get them. Black justifiably puts the pawn in his pocket. If out of the troubled waters that ensue he fishes nothing, it is because he fishes ill in the shallows" [*A Chess Omnibus*, p. 168].

5:

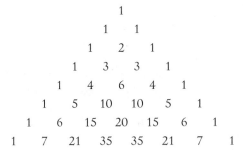

```
                        1
                    1       1
                1       2       1
            1       3       3       1
        1       4       6       4       1
    1       5       10      10      5       1
1       6       15      20      15      6       1
1   7       21      35      35      21      7       1
```

Each row in Pascal's triangle begins and ends in 1, but each of the other numbers is the sum of the two numbers that are a bishop's move above it—in other words, that are diagonally above it. These numbers are tied into probability theory, which Blaise Pascal pioneered. Let's say you have five different socks in a drawer and you want to know how many different ways you can pick two of them. Go to the fifth row down in the triangle—OK, mathematicians are a bit strange and start counting with zero—so the fifth row is 1, 5, 10, 10, 5, 1. Now count in two places, remembering again to start with zero, and you'll hit 10. So there are ten ways to choose two socks from five. Two socks from four? Well, find the fourth row—1, 4, 6, 4, 1—and go in two spaces to the 6. Voilà, there are six ways. Those who are intrigued by simple mathematical ideas should consult my book *The Man Who Loved Only Numbers*, the story of a nomadic Hungarian who combed the world in search of the most beautiful mathematical problems [Paul Hoffman, 1998: Hyperion].

6: The chess players who never matriculated from UMBC include former World Junior Champion Tal Shaked, Israeli star Ilya Smirnin, 2003 U.S. champion Alexander Shabalov, U.S. Grand Prix winner Aleksander Wojtkiewicz, and Samford chess fellowship winner Greg Shahade.

7: Ehlvest, who was once ranked number five in the world, invited me to his six-game match against Zappa, the world amateur computer champion, on April 29 and 30, 2005. The match was being held in an auditorium in Estonian House, an old ornate building in Manhattan that had been a speakeasy during Prohibition. The promotional flier billed Alexander Shabalov, the 2003 U.S. champion, as doing the play-by-play commentary for the audience. Ehlvest set the admission price for the first evening at a whopping $59. I showed up at the scheduled hour as his nonpaying guest. The event was a disaster. The auditorium was empty. There was not a single paying customer, Shabalov stayed home because he forgot that it was his wife's birthday, and the computer itself never arrived. We ended up drinking vodka for the evening after Ehlvest was unable to reach the machine's programmer and handler on his cell phone.

8: Libya had a long-standing policy of denying entry to Israelis and other nationals who had Israeli stamps on their passports. If Libya did not grant visas to the Israelis, FIDE planned to split the games between Tripoli and nearby Malta, although many players objected to the idea of ghettoizing the Jewish participants. The problem seemed defused when FIDE announced that Tripoli had decided to admit all 128 qualifying players regardless of nationality. The Israeli Chess Federation praised the decision and sought an exception to its own government's ban on travel to Libya.

The peace did not last long. Gadhafi's son Mohammed was reported by the Associated Press as saying, "We did not and will not invite the Zionist enemies to this championship." The Israeli players protested, and FIDE said not to believe everything in the media. FIDE continued to claim the Israelis were welcome, although the Libyans themselves waffled, suggesting that if the Israelis were permitted to come, they would have to travel alone, without the coaches, trainers, family members, or friends who were allowed to accompany other players. The Israelis also wanted to bring a security detail, which FIDE said was unnecessary. Three Israelis and seven Americans withdrew in protest.

9: Tripoli and the surrounding area were once part of the Roman Empire, and they boasted the best preserved Roman ruins in the world. Gadhafi had outlawed outdoor advertising and signage in the old part of the city so that it retained its original look. After the collapse of the Roman Empire, the Vandals moved into Libya in the fifth century and the Byzantines followed in the sixth century. The Arabs invaded the country in the seventh century and ruled it for nine hundred years, until the Turks conquered it in the mid-1500s. Italy took over Libya in 1911, but was forced, in the wake of losing World War II, to turn the country over to the British and the French. Libya got its independence in 1951 and was ruled by a constitutional monarch until Gadhafi's coup in 1969. Each of the many occupiers left its stamp on Libyan culture. For example, on one Internet message board I visited, French travelers marveled at the authenticity of the French country cuisine, noting with amazement that the country had finer bistros than Paris.

CHAPTER 9: Gadhafi's Gambit and Mr. Paul

1: The Dragon has not been slain yet, even though generations of grandmasters have doubted the opening's soundness. In 1969, when Fischer annotated a crushing 1958 victory over Bent Larsen's pet Dragon, he dismissed the opening as too dangerous for Black: "White's attack almost plays itself. . . . Weak players even beat Grandmasters with it. I once thumbed through several issues of *Shakhmatny Bulletin*, when the Yugoslav Attack was making its debut, and found the ratio was something like nine wins out of ten in White's favor. Will Black succeed in reinforcing the variation? Time will tell" [*My 60 Most Memorable Games*, p. 18].

2: This was a more reasonable task than the assignment Bobby Fischer had given Bent Larsen at the 1959 Candidates Tournament: read Tarzan stories aloud to him.

3: When playing an over-the-board game sans blindfold, the 550-point difference in our ratings means that Pascal should score on me 98 percent of the time.

4: This invariably raises the question of whether sex before chess is a help or a hindrance. At Buenos Aires 1960, the Hungarian player Laszlo Szabo had a hotel room adjoining

Fischer's. "One night, a grandmaster took a lady up to him," Szabo recalled. "I do not know how long she stayed there. The next morning, though, when we stepped out of our rooms at the exact same moment, Fischer said: 'Chess is better.' " Buenos Aires 1960 is the only international tournament in which Fischer lost more games than he won ["Finding Bobby Fischer," p. 62].

Valentinov, Luzhin's trainer in *The Defense*, "encouraged Luzhin a great deal in his passion for sweets. Finally he had a peculiar theory that the development of Luzhin's gift for chess was connected with the development of the sexual urge, that with him chess represented a special deflection of this urge, and fearing lest Luzhin should squander his precious power in releasing by natural means the beneficial inner tension, he kept him at a distance from women and rejoiced over his chaste moroseness" [*The Defense*, p. 94].

So much for fictional trainers, but the reality is stranger. Botvinnik, schooled as a scientist, believed that men should refrain from pregame sex because ejaculation depletes the body of phosphorous, a brain fuel. "Botvinnik did believe in vigorous exercise of other kinds before a game, however, such as walking briskly for a half-hour. When [GM Lev] Alburt, a young and popular bachelor, explained to his great mentor that it was difficult to resist women and that walking so far before a game made him sleepy, the Soviet Superman looked at Lev with the pity of the mighty for the weak, the prophet for the proselyte. 'Well,' he said ruefully, 'then try to refrain as much as you can from losing your phosphorus right before a game. And try to walk at least a few blocks' " [*Three Days with Bobby Fischer & Other Chess Essays*, pp. 47, 48].

Grandmaster Alexsander Wojtkiewicz disagreed with the patriarch of Soviet chess. "It depends on what kind of sex," he told me. "If it is good sex, it can make you much more creative at the board." When I pressed Pascal on whether Botvinnik or Wojtkiewicz was right, he gave a characteristically unsentimental answer: "I haven't noticed that it makes any difference."

Male players seem to agree, though, that a prolonged dry spell is not conducive to strong chess because then they are more likely to be distracted by erotic thoughts at the board. Alexander Shabalov, the 2003 U.S. champion, told Jennifer Shahade that "in most games, I am thinking about girls for about fifty to seventy-five percent of the time, another fifteen percent goes to time management, and with what's left over I am calculating." When Jennifer told him that twenty-five percentage points is a big range, he responded: "You can tell if it's closer to fifty or seventy-five percent by the quality of the game. Fifty percent is great chess, seventy-five percent I can play okay, but where it is really dangerous is when it slips up to ninety percent" [*Chess Bitch*, 2005: Siles Press, p. 6].

5: In *Chess Bitch*, Jennifer Shahade noted that "many women chess players find the prospect of dating a player weaker than they unpalatable. 'I would just as soon date someone outside the chess world than a weaker player than I,' said [2004 U.S. women's champion] Anna Hahn.... Elizabeth Vicary, a chess expert and coach from Brooklyn, has always been attracted to strong chess players and is unapologetic about it. 'There must be some reason to be initially attracted to someone, and I admire people who are good at what they do. Liking someone for their chess strength is not as superficial as liking them for their appearance or money.' " The German chess whiz Elisabeth Paehtz also admitted liking strong players, although she said she'd be reluctant to date super GMs because "a player over 2700 is likely to be crazy!" [pp. 65, 66].

Some strong male players avoid serious relationships within the chess world. "The idea of having a 'chess family' is not so good," wrote GM Jaan Ehlvest. "Competitive chess, like any other competitive sport, is not for women because it is very stressful and harmful to your health. I do not believe that any caring man should want that his sweetheart gets hurt" [*The Story of a Chess Player*, p. 115].

6: In Alekhine's 1937 rematch for the World Championship with Max Euwe (1901–1981), he wore a favored white pullover, knitted by his wife, for five consecutive games in which he scored four wins and a draw. Emblazoned on the front was a large black cat to remind Alekhine of his lucky Siamese named Chess that often accompanied him to tournaments.

7: The second's role is to remain upbeat even in the face of adversity. Lev Alburt and Al Lawrence wrote about one second who failed miserably in this regard. When Alexey Suetin (1926–) was playing in one of his first Soviet invitational tournaments, he was provided with an old Belorussian master, a noted opening theoretician, as a second. Suetin told him that he had Black against Semyen Furman (1920–1978), and the second responded that no opening preparation was required because the game would take a predictable course: Furman would open with the queen pawn, gain an advantage, and keep pressuring Suetin. Suetin was disappointed by his trainer's lack of help and confidence, and was even more distressed when the game proceeded as the second had forecast. Suetin then informed him that he had White against Rashid Nezhmetdinov, the first person to hold the Soviet rank of master in both chess and checkers. The second responded: " 'Well, color won't matter. Nezhmetdinov can play any opening. Somewhere he will sacrifice a pawn for the initiative. Then he will sacrifice another. Then he will sacrifice a piece for an attack. Then he'll probably sacrifice another piece to drive your king into the center. Then he will checkmate you.'

"Suetin was upset. What kind of help was this? Alexey went to the game, and the old trainer's prediction again came true. (We should note . . . if one knows Nezhmetdinov's games, such a prognostication is hardly difficult. Nezhmetdinov polished off many strong opponents in this same way.)

"Now Suetin was very upset. He called the Belorussian sports ministry, telling him that they must recall this fatalistic fellow immediately. The shocked trainer was sent back to Minsk, where he walked around the chess club complaining of his unfair treatment.

" 'I don't understand why this young Alexey is so upset with me,' the trainer would say. 'Everything I told him turned out to be exactly right!' " [*Three Days with Bobby Fischer & Other Chess Essays*, pp. 155, 156].

8: All players have had the experience of not being able to think when confronted by a surprising move. Samuel Reshevsky shared with *Sports Illustrated* (November 3, 1958) a journal entry on his loss to German grandmaster Wolfgang Unzicker (1925–) at the 1958 Olympiad in Munich: "Suddenly he made an inobvious move I had completely overlooked. I began to perspire; my face turned red. My mind became a complete blank. I sat there a few moments gazing at the board. There was no way out. I finally reconciled myself to the fact that I was lost. I made a few more moves, then I resigned" [*A Chess Omnibus*, pp. 18, 19].

9: The printout read:

> I understand it may not be possible for Engineer Mohammed Gadhafi to sit down with me for a quick chess game. (I thought that a photograph of our playing chess would have great symbolic value in showing how two people of different cultures can play this peaceful game.) So here are some questions:
>
> 1. Do you play chess much?
> 2. How popular is chess among Libyans?
> 3. What's the most popular board game in Libya?
> 4. Fifty-six countries are represented in this world championship?
> 5. Does this set a record for the number of countries participating in an event in Libya?
> 6. Was there much security needed in the hotel for the championship? Or was that unnecessary?
> 7. In the film at the opening ceremony, your father was seen standing in front of large pipes. I was curious to learn what they're used for. Are they oil pipelines?
> 8. I found it very moving to see the Libyan flag next to the American flag at the opening ceremony. Has the American flag ever flown before in Libya? Or is this a first that marks the new friendship between our two peoples?
>
> Your team did a wonderful job of organizing the championship.
> —Paul Hoffman

10: The old fruit distraction: Lisa Lane, the U.S. women's champion in 1959 and 1960, said she faced a Russian player who pared an apple whenever it was Lane's turn to move ["Chess: Once the Game of Kings, Now the King of Games" p. 77].

CHAPTER 10: Praying for the Pseudo Trompowsky

1: When stone chess tables were cemented into the ground outside Au Bon Pain in Harvard Square, the concrete had already hardened by the time that passing chess players noticed that the white square was in the wrong corner. The tables had to be ripped out of the ground and rotated ninety degrees.

2: I would probably be stronger if I broadened my opening repertoire so that I was familiar with a wider variety of positions. But like so many players, I am monogamous when it comes to my first moves. When a colleague urged British champion and heartthrob David Norwood to try some new openings, he responded, "I only ever play the Modern Benoni and the Pirc Defense. I may not be faithful with my women, but I'm always faithful with my openings."

3: Topalov was not yet FIDE world champion. In the autumn of 2005, he earned that title in an incredible performance in San Luis, Argentina. His games, like Tal's, are full of surprising sacrifices.

CHAPTER 11: "I Stuck It to Him Real Good, Way Up Him"

1: According to *Webster's Third New International Dictionary, Unabridged*, the word *crapulent* means "suffering from excessive eating or drinking." *Dipsomania* is defined as "an uncontrollable often periodic craving for alcoholic liquors" and *pulchritude* as "physical comeliness." *Frugiferous*, which is not even listed in Webster's, means "fruitful."

2: Miles's nakedness at high-level chess events was not unique. "A continental tournament shortly after the Second World War was interrupted when one of the spectators, overcome by the excitement of the moment, started to remove all his clothes. The clocks were stopped while he was hustled out into the next room. But shortly afterwards he was back again doing the same thing. Again play was halted, and this time he was forcibly dragged back to his hotel room, while the local constabulary was called. A few minutes later he could be seen again, performing in his hotel window. At this point, Dr. Tartakower, the wittiest of grandmasters, claimed a draw by three-fold repetition" [Fox and James, *The Complete Chess Addict*, pp. 182, 183].

In *The Psychology of the Chess Player*, Reuben Fine told a story of unconfirmed authenticity about the great Mexican player Carlos Torre (1905–1978). He suffered a breakdown in New York and took off all his clothes on a Fifth Avenue bus [1967: Dover, p. 65].

3: Some journalists have gotten this wrong as TDF. In a special issue devoted to losers, the magazine *Granta* ran a profile of Short called "Trap, Dominate, Fuck." Short assured me that *Granta* had transposed the words, as had his friend Dominic Lawson in *End Game*.

4: In this respect, Kasparov was similar to Alekhine, whose "play emanates a surging, restless spirit—an emotional tension which seeks fulfillment in the mastery over obstacles. He is a fighter. His style is a combination of psychological belligerence and egoistic assurance. In this he is spiritually akin to Dr. Lasker, who believed that the urge to struggle, to fight, was the true *ethos* of chess. And this nervous tension reveals itself in the mannerisms of the man, in the tremendous concentration reflected in his face as he studies the board and his opponent, in the sharp, excitable movements of his body; in his habits of twisting a wisp of hair between his fingers, of smoking almost ferociously, of pacing like a caged tiger. If music could express the *psyche* of Alekhine, it would be the music of Tschaikovsky." [Paul Hugo Little, *Chess Life*, October 1938].

5: On the popular Web site ChessNinja, Jennifer Shahade started a long thread on the "Daily Dirt" discussion board: "A few weeks ago I received an e-mail from GM Robert Fontaine asking if I'd like to participate in the 'World Chess Beauty Contest.' When I went to the site [www.1wcbc.com/main.htm], I was subjected to an image showing a group of cartoon-like forms of women lined up against a rating chart.... To the creators, this 'grandiose' idea was designed in order to promote women's chess. Rather than promote chess, it promotes that women's looks are all-important. Feelings are liable to be hurt by low ratings and unkind comments. And why do they keep calling the participants girls when most of the women are over 18? There is one nine year old participant—if that's a joke, I'm not laughing.... There is nothing wrong with making chess sexier by highlighting the hip, interesting players who participate. But I find the World Chess Beauty Contest project misguided and juvenile and would be embarrassed to be a part of it. Sure, many other sports have similar contests—one of the disturbing aspects of this one is that the arbiters and creators are not anonymous fans, but prominent members of the chess community who are very proud of their idea. Would you ever see Tiger Woods bragging about how he started a golf-babe contest?" GM Arthur Kogan, one of the originators of the beauty contest, posted a response in broken English: "Jen's main points are very strange and seems to show a self-complex . . . come on, u look good enough, don't be afraid to get a rating for it!☺"

6: The word *heffalump* was coined by A. A. Milne in *Winnie the Pooh* (1926). Pooh never actually saw the creatures, but imagined them when he tried to fall asleep. Milne did not describe what heffalumps looked like but his illustrator, E. H. Shepard, depicted them as elephants.

7: There is no universal nomenclature convention for chess openings. They can be named for a piece or the side of the board that figures prominently in them: Bishop's Opening, Two Knights Defense, King's Gambit. They can be named for the masters who pioneered, promoted, or rehabilitated them—Bird's Opening, Richter-Rauzer Attack, Nimzowitsch-Larsen Attack, Falkbeer Counter Gambit, Benko Gambit. They can be named for the nationalities of the players who first favored them—English Defense, Slav Defense, Spanish Game—or for the tournament—Cambridge Springs, Grand Prix Attack—in which the openings made their mark. As for subvariations—a line within a line like the Beck's Beer Variation—there is more room for the originators of new sequences to be humorous. There is now a Toilet Variation, named for where its inventor thought it up. Short told me about an insipid sequence of moves called the Monkey's Bum, so named, he thought, because someone reacted to the moves by saying, "If that's any good, I'm a monkey's bum."

8: Morphy developed this approach over time. In his youth, he played rashly, but his opponents were too weak to take advantage of it. "One peculiarity of Paul's play, during the infantile stage of his chess life, while his father and his brother were his chief adversaries, used to create considerable merriment among the circle of chess lovers with which he was brought into contact. His Pawns seemed to him a hindrance and his first work, upon commencing a game, was to exchange or sacrifice them all, giving free range to his pieces, after which with his unimpeded Queen, Rook, Knights, and Bishops he began a fierce attack upon his opponent's forces which was often valorously maintained until it resulted in mate" [*The Chess Monthly*, December 1857, pp. 381, 382].

9: Or *Norma, La Cenerentol*, or *The Marriage of Figaro*—the historical record is not clear [Edward Winter, *Chess Facts and Fables*, 2006: McFarland, pp. 34, 35].

10: Fischer said in 1964: "A popularly held theory about Paul Morphy is that if he returned to the chess world today and played our best contemporary players, he would come out the loser. Nothing is further from the truth. In a set match, Morphy could beat anyone alive today. . . . Morphy was perhaps the most accurate chess player who ever lived. He had a complete sight of the board and never blundered, in spite of the fact that he played quite rapidly, rarely taking more than five minutes to decide a move" [Bobby Fischer, "The Ten Greatest Masters in History," *Chessworld,* January-February 1964, p. 58].

11: The curious, literary remark about Castile and the shamefaced king sounds like a quotation, although I've never seen the source identified. Among the Morphy legends that are fodder for Freudians is the fabrication that he slept surrounded by a protective ring of women's shoes. In truth, he was a fashion plate who fancied *men's* shoes, which he would arrange in a half crescent in his bedroom so that he could survey them all before picking out a pair.

12: The film director Miloš Forman, who often visited top-level chess events, questioned various grandmasters about Morphy's life and wrote a script about him. When Forman shopped the script, Hollywood expressed interest provided he turned the chess player into a musician. Thus was born *Amadeus.* Nabokov did not give up on chess as easily as Forman did. "Poor Luzhin had to wait thirty-five years for an English-language edition," he wrote. "True, there was a promising flurry in the late thirties when an American publisher showed interest in it, but he turned out to belong to the type of publisher who dreams of becoming a male muse to his author, and our brief conjunction ended abruptly upon his suggesting I replace chess by music and make Luzhin a demented violinist" [*The Defense,* pp. 7, 8].

13: Irrepressible Freudians do not stop here. The fact that a player cannot touch a piece unless he is going to move it decodes in the unconscious to a prohibition against masturbation. And since he can't touch the other guy's pieces either, against mutual masturbation. The inherent weakness of the king represents a prepubescent penis or a flaccid, impotent one.

14: In Frances Parkinson Keyes's classic American novel, *The Chess Players,* Morphy's sweetheart Charmian Sheppard rejects him because he never consummates their relationship. "Perhaps, you *could* have married me, if you'd really tried, if you'd 'forgotten yourself,' as you said once long ago you were afraid you might, and swept me off my feet," Sheppard tells him. "But you didn't—either then or later. You went on playing chess. Afraid! You needn't have been afraid! All you had to do in Paris was to go a little further—so far I couldn't have stopped you if I'd tried and I wouldn't have tried very hard. . . . And I may as well tell you, now as any other time, that I'll never marry a mere chess player!" [1960: Farrar, Straus and Cudahy, p. 290].

15: It is astonishing to me that Ernest Jones and Reuben Fine, the men who popularized the plug-pop interpretation of chess in the widely cited book *The Psychology of the Chess Player,* were themselves both chess players. Fine in fact was one of the very top players in the world and would have had a shot at becoming world champion if, for want of money, he had not foregone tournaments in order to earn a living as a psychoanalyst. Only men who loathed their own fascination with the game could invent such an outrageous, sordid interpretation.

16: Alekhine, too, had a gift for verbally putting his opponents in their place. The great chess writer I. A. Horowitz told this story about the world champion: in an impromptu speech, Alekhine aired his grievances about Bogoljubow, an arrogant rival. "Last night," he began. "I dreamed that I had died. Naturally, I headed for heaven. As I neared the portals, I was hailed by St. Peter, asking who I was. 'I am Alekhine,' I hastened to explain, but the statement made no impression. 'I am Alekhine, chess champion of the world,' I reiterated. 'Sorry,' said St. Peter, shaking his head. 'There is no room in heaven for chess players.' My spirit was dejected. Before leaving the pearly gates, I took one last look around. Eureka! Whom did I spy? Why, none other than my good friend Bogoljubow. Quickly I drew St. Peter's attention to my rotund crony: 'There's Bogoljubow. He's a chess player.' St. Peter smiled sadly: 'He only *thinks* he's a chess player'" [I. A. Horowitz, *Chess Life,* September 1948, pp. 366, 367].

CHAPTER 12: Endgame: Your Finger Beats Kasparov!

1: Pascal's memory for names and dates is also conspicuously bad. It is part of the game's mystique that chess masters are thought to have great memories. This view was put to the test in the 1890s, when two professors in London presented Harry Nelson Pillsbury, Morphy's successor as the strongest U.S. player, with an odd list of words and phrases: antiphlogistine, periosteum, takadiastase, plasmon, threlkeld, streptococcus, staphylococcus, micrococcus, plasmodium, Mississippi, Freiheit, Philadelphia, Cincinnati, athletics, no war, Etchenerg, American, Russian, philosophy, Piet Potgleter's Rost, Salamagundi, Oomisillecootsi, Bangmamvate, Schlecter's Neck, Manzinyama, theosophy, catechism, Madjesoomalops. Pillsbury glanced at the list, handed it back to the professors, and then recalled the words perfectly, in order. As an added flourish, without being asked, he repeated the list in reverse. Nevertheless, subsequent investigations found that Pillsbury's talent was anomalous. Skilled chess players turn out to be able to recall chess positions from actual games (although not "positions" where the pieces are randomly scattered) but don't otherwise have better memories than the rest of us.

2: *Smothered mate* is a term that refers to a particularly beautiful and rare form of checkmate: the king on the back rank is hemmed in by its own pieces, and an opposing knight, "reaching" over these pieces, delivers the coup de grace.

3: Lest you think I exaggerate, let me share a story from Susan Polgar's *Breaking Through* about one player's ability to concentrate in the face of death. The player was Ildiko Madl, who along with the Polgar sisters was a member of the four-person Hungarian team at the Women's Olympiad in Thessalonika in 1988. "The Olympiad started smoothly," Polgar wrote, "but then a tragedy happened. The fiancée of our teammate Ildiko, IM Bela Perenyi, was on his way from Hungary to support us and to participate in one of the side events in the Olympiad. Unfortunately, he never made it to Greece, as on the way he was killed in a car accident. It was quite admirable that, after such shocking and sad news, Ildiko was still able to play well and even score a win against our big rivals, the Soviet Union" [p. 16].

4: Victor Korchnoi was notorious for losing track of his surroundings when he was playing. A sewage pipe burst at the 1970 USSR Championship in Riga. "First this was sensed by the spectators, who gradually began leaving the tournament hall, and soon the chief arbiter was forced to announce a temporary break. The players, exchanging jokes, began moving off the stage. The lone figure of Korchnoi remained at the chess board. 'What's the matter?' he asked, raising his head, of the arbiter who had stopped his clock. 'Has something happened?' " [*The Reliable Past*, p. 32].

5: In April 2007, Pascal and Irina were married, in a judge's chambers in Manhattan. The ceremony took less time than a game of bullet chess, and Alex and I were the witnesses. When the bored judge, who never looked up at them and presumably married dozens of couples that day, told Pascal that he could kiss the bride, Alex blurted out, "My least favorite part!" I shushed him and whispered that he wasn't being very nice. "I'm kind of joking, Dad," he said. "It's about time they got married!"

♖ ♖　SOURCE NOTES

I want to thank *The New Yorker* ["The Pandolfini Defense," June 4, 2001] and *Smithsonian* ["A Chess Player Realizes the Game Controls His Life," July 1987, and "Chess Queen," August 2003] for giving me permission to incorporate these articles of mine into this book. When I've quoted printed sources, I've taken the liberty of adjusting the spelling of Russian names so that they are consistent throughout *King's Gambit.*

CHAPTER 1: **The Insanity Defense**

5　"a nice and abstruse game...": Samuel Johnson, *A Dictionary of the English Language,* 1755, as quoted in Jerome Salzmann, *The Chess Reader,* 1949: Greenberg, p. 107.

7　"Your body has to be in top condition...": Frank Brady, *Profile of a Prodigy: The Life and Games of Bobby Fischer,* 1973 revised: David McKay, p. 216.

14　"Chess-players once again...": "The Luzhin Defense," *British Chess Magazine,* August 2000, p. 437.

15　"In no other type of sport...": Genna Sosonko, "The Jump," *New in Chess,* No. 3, 2000, p. 63.

16　"The intermittently institutionalized Mexican...": Nigel Short, "Chess Can Seriously Damage Your Health," *The Spectator,* September 2, 2000, p. 35.

17　"I have always a slight feeling...": Tarrasch as quoted, in many places, including Cathy Forbes, *Nigel Short: Quest for the Crown,* 1993: Cadogan, p. 2.

17　"The most important thing for anyone...": ibid., p. 15.

CHAPTER 2: **Fathers and Sons**

32　"DOCTORS PHOTOGRAPH...": *Pageant,* January 1966.

32　"OPEN LETTER TO NEGROES...": ibid.

33　"CHASTE...MISUNDERSTOOD...RESTLESS...": ibid.

33　"HOW FEMALE TEACHERS WARP OUR": *Pageant,* October 1966.

33　"THE MEN WHO STEAL CHILDREN'S...": *Pageant,* February 1966.

33　"THE 'QUEER' ONES...": *Pageant,* March 1966.

33　"A MINISTER'S OWN STORY...": *Pageant,* August 1966.

38　"Without disturbing the silence that prevailed...": Capablanca, quoted in E. G. Winter, *World Chess Champions,* 1981: Pergaman Press, p. 53.

39　"My parents used to like solving the chess problems...": Garry Kasparov, *Unlimited Challenge,* 1990: Grove Weidenfeld (originally published as *Child of Change,* 1987), p. 7.

39　"I felt the harmony of the game...": Anatoly Karpov, *Karpov on Karpov,* 1990: Atheneum, p. 12.

40   "Nigel's first exposure to chess . . .": David Short, *Nigel Short: Chess Prodigy*, 1981: Faber and Faber, p. 25.

40   "It became difficult . . .": *Unlimited Challenge*, p. 7.

44   "after 15 moves . . .": Andrew Soltis, *Soviet Chess 1917–1991*, 2000: McFarland, p. 23.

45   "that with a Knight's move of this lime tree . . .": Vladimir Nabokov, *The Defense*, 1990: Vintage International, p. 99.

45   "best architect . . .": Ralph Ginzburg, "Portrait of a Genius as a Chess Master," *Harper's Magazine*, January 1962, as quoted in I. A. Horowitz and P. L. Rothenberg, *The Personality of Chess*, 1963: Macmillan, p. 146.

46   "Eye witnesses present at the closing stage . . .": Siegen Olympiad tournament book, quoted in Dominic Lawson, *End Game*, 1994: Harmony Books, p. 164.

47   "I am like the chess King of Charles XII . . .": Anthony Saidy and Norman Lessing, *The World of Chess*, 1974: Random House, p. 19.

49   "When a player, upon system, consumes hours over moves . . .": Howard Staunton, *The Chess Player's Chronicle*, 1851.

49   "each player have a three hours' sand-glass . . .": *The Chess Player's Chronicle*, February 1852, p. 62.

52   "In my country there is only one man . . .": Hans Ree, *The Human Comedy of Chess*, 1999, *Russell Enterprises*, No. 1, p. 83.

55   "Wherever chess nuts gather . . .": James Hoffman, "Chess: Once the Game of Kings, Now the King of Games," *Lithopinion*, Winter 1970, p. 75.

56   "The game lasted a long time . . .": ibid., p. 78.

57   "In the cab . . .": ibid.

CHAPTER 3: The Pandolfini Variation

69   "While Fischer has always been . . .": Timothy Hanke, "Finding Bobby Fischer," *American Chess Journal*, 1992, No. 1, p. 72.

69   "We were in the fifth hour . . .": Brad Darrach, *Bobby Fischer vs. the Rest of the World*, 1974: Stein and Day, p. 167.

70   "I like to see 'em squirm": Harold Schonberg, *Grandmasters of Chess*, 1973: J. B. Lippincott, p. 264.

77   "The only goal . . .": Rudolph Chelminski, "In the Game of Chess 'Your Opponent Must Be Destroyed,'" *Smithsonian*, January 1998.

CHAPTER 4: Russian Domination

92   "Thank you, darling . . .": Pushkin, in many places, including Garry Kasparov, *Child of Change*, 1987: Hutchinson, p. 49.

93   "Our great teachers . . .": *Pravda*, August 29, 1936, as translated in D. J. Richards, *Soviet Chess*, 1965: Oxford University Press, p. 63.

93   "I am infinitely happy to report . . .": ibid., p. 64.

93   "Sitting at the chess table in Nottingham . . .": ibid.

94   "such a lot of people playing chess": *Soviet Chess 1917–1991*, p. 2.

95   "Pure paranoia is a rare mental illness . . .": London *Sunday Times*, as quoted in *Soviet Chess*, p. 43.

95 "This may sound strange . . .": *New in Chess,* as quoted in *Soviet Chess 1917–1991,* p. 2.

96 "The Soviet chess world was aghast . . .": *Grandmasters of Chess,* p. 231.

96 "Almost all of the top players . . .": Howard Goldowsky, "A Conversation with Hikaru Nakamura," ChessCafe.com.

97 "Those who were brought up under the Soviet system . . .": *End Game,* p. 17.

98 "When Karpov is being mentioned . . .": *The Human Comedy of Chess,* p. 7.

99 "had been waiting long enough . . .": ibid., p. 3.

99 "knew that should he lose the next game . . .": ibid., pp. 3, 4.

100 "whoever gets such a chance . . .": ibid., p. 4.

100 "Each time before I sit down . . .": *Karpov on Karpov,* pp. 179, 180.

101 "Some people seeing my intense concentration . . .": *Child of Change,* p. 46.

101 "Steinitz, the first world champion . . .": ibid., p. 33.

108 "How could you give . . .": chessbase.com/eventarticle.asp?newsid=851.

108 "Kasparov launched one of the most violent . . .": Ian Rogers, *Sun-Herald,* March 16, 2003.

108 "It saddens me . . .": chesscenter.com/twic/event/linares2003/rdprize.html.

116 "Calculation most often comes . . .": Paul Hoffman, *Archimedes' Revenge,* 1988: W. W. Norton, p. 182.

123 "I was lying . . .": chessbase.com/newsdetail.asp?newsid=3505.

124 "Once again . . .": chessbase.com/eventarticle.asp?newsid=3382.

125 "I cannot really . . .": chessbase.com/newsdetail.asp?newsid=3512.

CHAPTER 5: An American in Moscow

140 "that Vaganian played . . .": Genna Sosonko, *The Reliable Past,* 2003: New in Chess, p. 75.

140 "[He] lacked the obsessive desire . . .": ibid., p. 73.

141 "The only way to go was all out . . .": Evgeny Atarov, "Russian Roulette in Hotel Rossyia," *New in Chess,* No. 3, 2004, p. 42.

CHAPTER 6: Anatomy of a Hustler

160 "can be created by giving . . .": Bertrand Russell, *The Autobiography of Bertrand Russell 1872–1914,* 1967: Atlantic Monthly Press, pp. 115, 116.

165 "The game of chess is the second most entertaining diversion . . .": Claude Bloodgood, *Nimzovich Attack: The Norfolk Gambits,* 1997: Chess Digest. p. 9.

181 "highly irregular": London *Daily Telegraph,* May 22, 2005, chessbase.com/newsdetail.asp?newsid=2406.

182 "a dead drawn position . . .": Viktor Korchnoi, *Chess Is My Life,* 1978: Arco, p. 17.

183 "he went into raptures . . .": ibid., p. 30.

184 "All of a sudden . . .": Susan Polgar's column, August 17, 2003, www.chesscafe.com/text/polgar14.pdf.

189 "On the chessboard . . .": Lasker, as quoted, in many places, including *Nigel Short: Quest for the Crown,* p. 2.

CHAPTER 7: Female Counterplay

191 "the female is much less deadly . . .": *Child of Change,* pp. 49, 50.

193 "We learnt what we needed . . .": London *Daily Telegraph,* January 16, 2002.

194 "Come on, what do you think...": Dirk Jan ten Geuzendam, *Linares! Linares!,* 2001: New in Chess, p. 75.

194 "He's only got to say...": ibid.

195 "You bring down shame...": ibid., p. 74.

195 "How could you...": ibid., p. 79.

196 "Now I wonder if I could be so prudent to give a pawn...": Kasparov in *The New York Times,* Sept. 22, 2002.

199 "a regular Tuesday-morning...": *Vogue,* November 2000.

206 "She is still a little miffed...": Walter Isaacson, *Benjamin Franklin,* 2003: Simon & Schuster, pp. 357, 358.

206 "Never again...": ibid., p. 362.

206 "I get so much pleasure...": ibid.

206 "This is as it should be...": Paul Hoffman, "Chess Queen," *Smithsonian,* August 2003, p. 75.

207 "would come under great strain...": ibid.

207 "Miss Muller Hasting's...": Ben Karpman, "The Psychology of Chess," *Psychoanalytic Review,* July, 1937, p. 69.

208 "I didn't expect her to see so much...": *The World of Chess,* p. 180.

209 "No one could ever...": Jennifer Shahade, *Chess Bitch,* 2005: Siles Press, p. 8.

222 "Michael began...": ibid., p. 15.

226 "I wandered around the streets...": ibid., p. 284.

229 "I just don't understand...": chessbase.com/newsdetail.asp?newsid=2632.

229 "There is one fact I would like to clarify...": ibid.

CHAPTER 8: **"I'm Not the World's Biggest Geek"**

240 "I thought I was...": indochess.com/news_maint_public.php?news_id=1236.

240 "lifted two clenched fists...": Yvonne Zacharias, "Good Nerves Move 'the Kid' to Victory," *Vancouver Sun,* April 2, 2002.

247 "an enormous amount of publicity...": Alec MacGillis, "Chess Teams Checkered by Recruiting Practice," *Baltimore Sun,* May 18, 2003.

247 "sex w/a 15-yr-old in a few days!!!!!!": Joe Danborn, *Mobile Register,* September 18, 2003.

248 "Disturbing questions have arisen...": Kevin Sherrington, "Masters of Chess-Thumping," *Dallas Morning News,* May 25, 2003.

248 "On the college chess circuit...": "Chess Teams Checkered by Recruiting Practice," *Baltimore Sun.*

251 "Why didn't you play here...": "GM Aleksander Wojtkiewicz Dies: Memories, Life and Games," beta.uschess.org/frontend/news_7_67.php.

CHAPTER 10: **Praying for the Pseudo Trompowsky**

303 "With relish Ilyumzhinov tells the story...": *The Human Comedy of Chess,* p. 88.

312 "Either FIDE stays a cowboy...": Tom Parfit, "King of Kalymkia," *The Guardian,* September 21, 2006, http://sport.guardian.co.uk/chess/story/0,,1877426,00.html.

312 "Even a dickhead...": "Anatoly Karpov Speaks His Mind," chessbase.com/news detail.asp?newsid=2495

317 "The thinker Muammar...": Muammar Al Qathafi, *The Green Book,* 1984: World Center for the Study and Research of the Green Book.

317 "Woman is a female...": ibid., pp 93, 94.

CHAPTER 11: "I Stuck It to Him Real Good, Way Up Him"

323 "I don't know whether...": London *Sunday Telegraph,* March 27, 2005.

325 "The family was on holiday...": *Nigel Short: Chess Prodigy,* p. 26.

325 "Nigel would pick up...": ibid., p. 27.

326 "He seemed far too happy...": *Nigel Short: Quest for the Crown,* p. 9.

326 "One is the highly concrete...": *Nigel Short: Chess Prodigy,* p. 23.

326 "My friends think I'm boastful...": *Daily Express,* quoted in *Nigel Short: Quest for the Crown,* p. 10.

326 "Nigel sported long hair...": chessbase.com/newsdetail.asp?newsid=2426.

326 "Nigel Short has been moaning...": *Manchester Evening News,* quoted in Forbes, p. 15.

327 "I was simply lucky...": Raymond Keene, *Nigel Short: World Chess Challenger,* 1992: Henry Holt, pp. 6, 7.

327 "One could subject...": ibid.

328 "Short learned the dangers...": *Nigel Short: Quest for the Crown,* p. 15.

329 "he spearheaded the...": London *Sunday Telegraph,* November, 2002.

329 "Tony was not above...": ibid.

330 "I found myself...": ibid.

331 "I'm getting much more pleasure...": *Nigel Short: World Chess Challenger,* pp. 8, 9.

333 "Many a player who...": *End Game,* p. 4.

334 "Nigel Short, the British player...": *Child of Change,* p. 15.

337 "When I win this match Kasparov...": *End Game,* p. 101.

337 "Look at Mrs. Kasparov...": ibid., p. 96.

340 "On open territory a Tiger...": Simon Webb, *Chess for Tigers,* 1990: Pergamon Chess, p. 38.

342 "A painful move for me to see...": *Inside Chess,* May 25, 1992, p. 6.

348 "Help your pieces...": *Grandmasters of Chess,* p. 71.

349 "A face like...": ibid., p. 79.

349 "When one plays with Morphy...": ibid., p. 80.

350 "He seldom—in fact...": ibid., p. 83.

351 "He will plant the banner of Castile...": Phillip Sergeant, *The Unknown Morphy,* 1971 Dover reprint, p. 30.

351 "And now what was Staunton...": *City of London Chess Magazine,* as quoted in *Grandmasters of Chess,* p. 54.

352 "the portrait of Paul Morphy...": David Lawson, *Paul Morphy: The Pride and Sorrow of Chess,* 1976: David McKay, pp. 310, 311.

352 "The strain in his brain...": *New York Sun,* as quoted in *Grandmasters of Chess,* p. 95.

354 "the unconscious motives actuating...:" Ernest Jones, "The Problem of Paul Morphy: A Contribution to the Psycho-Analysis of Chess," as quoted in *The Chess Reader,* p. 240.

356 "It will be Short, and it will be short": *Nigel Short: Quest for the Crown,* p. 114.

356 "At the end of the dinner...": *End Game*, p. 74.

359 "sometimes causes him to forget...": Andy Soltis and Gene McCormick, *The United States Chess Championship, 1845–1996*, Second Edition 1997: McFarland, p. 112.

360 "Staring at the board for hours...": Yasser Seirawan, "The Secret of Speelman's Success," *Inside Chess*, Sept. 23, 1998, p. 4.

363 "At first I said, 'Please, God...'": *Nigel Short: Quest for the Crown*, p. 48.

364 "the subject matter is, for one...": "Chess Can Seriously Damage Your Health," *The Spectator*, September 2, 2000, p. 35.

CHAPTER 12: Endgame: Your Finger Beats Kasparov!

368 "As soon as one gets close...": Miles told *New Statesman*, as quoted in *Nigel Short: Quest for the Crown*, p. 15.

377 "For the last couple of years...": Carly Jacobs, "Knight Moves," *Bust*, Spring 2004, p. 68.

377 "The poets lie about orgasm...": George Steiner, "Fields of Force," *The New Yorker*, October 28, 1972.

377 "There is in, say, five-minute games...": David Spanier, *Total Chess*, 1984, Secker & Warburg, pp. 98, 99.

INDEX